T0347309

Indexing

for

Maximum Investment Results

Albert S. Neubert
Editor

Routledge
Taylor & Francis Group

LONDON AND NEW YORK

© 1998 Robert A. Klein

First published 1998 by Fitzroy Dearborn Publishers

This edition published 2013 by Routledge
2 Park Square, Milton Park, Abingdon, Oxon, OX14 4RN
711 Third Avenue, New York, NY 10017

Routledge is an imprint of the Taylor & Francis Group, an informa business

ISBN: 1-888998-11-3

Library edition: Fitzroy Dearborn Publishers, Chicago and London
ISBN: 1-884-964-50-8

Contents

Preface

Indexing for Maximum Investment Results is a compendium of works about one of the more hotly debated investment methodologies. The controversy arises within the active management community, where indexing tends to be viewed only from the perspective of the S&P 500—by far the most popular index used by passive managers.

The active manager's perception of S&P 500 index funds is one which is often distorted because of a lack of understanding of the concept behind indexing. Most active managers are aware of the fact that indexing involves lower turnover and, hence, lower transactions costs, and that management fees are virtually zero, a clear blow to their pride. However, the most obvious of realities escapes the typical active manager. That is, the fact that the performance of all active managers combined with passive managers and individual investors must equal the return of the market as a whole.

Some managers will exceed the performance of the market for certain periods of time and fall short in others. But the track record of performance, especially when factoring in the transactions costs and management fees incurred by active managers, and the subsequent negative tax effects suffered as a result of their management styles, ensures that indexing is a most favorable investment methodology.

Perhaps what needs more clarification is a better understanding of what is meant by the term "the market." Are we talking about the stock market? In the U.S. or globally? What about fixed income securities? Certainly the S&P 500 is not the U.S. domestic equity market. There are many other indexes that cover U.S. stocks in general, and on a capital-ization-weighted basis.

Indexing is also far from a no-brainer strategy. Indexing involves low management fees because the target investment portfolio—the index—is set by the index provider but, it is the execution of the strategy that requires some of the most sophisticated investment management techniques ever devised.

In Chapter 1, Burton Malkiel discusses the academic evidence in favor of randomness of returns for stocks. He promotes the notion that any perceived patterns of behavior cannot be effectively exploited for several reasons including the turnover costs associated with executing an investment strategy. Also, any predicted behavior would attract enough investors over time, which ultimately would arbitrage away any potential profits. As a result, Malkiel supports the role of an indexed approached whereby the investment decision is made based on the relative attractive-ness of the asset class and, not on the individual assets that comprise the class. Thus, he believes there remains a role for the financial analyst.

In Chapter 2, I go over the importance of understanding the method-ologies used in creating benchmarks to measure asset and sub-asset class-es. I discuss the importance of the compilation, calculation and dissemi-nation processes in producing indexes as well as the critical role played in defining an asset class. By way of example, I extend my analysis by using the U.S. domestic equity market as the asset class that is being mea-sured by various benchmarks.

Chapter 3, by John Bogle could best be described as the ultimate his-torical perspective on the evolution of indexing. Bogle spends consider-able time in providing the rather simplistic and yet eloquent logic behind the rationale for indexing. That is, the sum of returns to all investors in the market must equal the returns of the market with some important dif-ferences. The differences are in that investors must pay for the transac-tions that they incur in buying and selling securities and they also must pay, either in time or money, for the process of selecting which securities to include within their investments. Therefore, Bogle postulates, the process of buying an efficient portfolio of securities that closely, if not exactly, mimics the returns of the market, will always provide the investor with the greatest return opportunities over the long run. The theory is described in practice, through his experiences over 23 years as the founder and Chairman of the Vanguard Group, the pioneering indexed mutual fund provider.

In Chapter 4, Shucheng Liu, Aamir Sheikh and Dan Stefak examine the mechanics of indexing. They point out that what may seem obvious in using a full-replication technique for matching the returns of an index, the implementation and maintenance costs of doing so may cause an unacceptable tracking error. By optimizing the number of holdings in an index an acceptable tracking error can be achieved. This can be done using simple methods based on weighting factors or a stratified sampling approach that keys on industry and sector exposures. Finally, a quantitative approach that takes into account a number of risk factors can be employed to select the optimal basket for replication.

The relative merits of enhanced indexing are the topics of discussion in Chapter 5. Jim McKee explains the two major approaches to enhancing the returns of a benchmark index, which include stock selection and derivatives based cash management strategies. McKee examines the record for the various approaches by comparing their performance after accounting for residual risk, the value added after adjusting for market risk and the information ratio, or more simply, the alpha divided by residual risk.

In Chapter 6, Judy Bednar discusses the issues surrounding the selection of an index for replication purposes. She focuses on the coverage of the targeted asset class and the methodology for compiling and calculating indexes. Certain methodologies are more conducive to better tracking by the index fund manager but, are not necessarily the best measures of performance. Also, she explains how the rebalancing and weighting schemes used by the index compiler can have significant impact on he transactions costs and, hence, the tracking error for the index manager.

A well documented impact of indexing is the effect it can have on the securities that comprise the index that is being tracked. This is the subject of Chapter 7 in which, Claudia Mott and Eddie Cheung examine the price effect on securities that are added to and deleted from the S&P 500, S&P MidCap 400 and S&P SmallCap 600 Indexes. The addition of the 400 and 600 indexes means that S&P now managers a SuperComposite 1500 portfolio where low turnover is a primary objective. Mott and Cheung point out that the substantial amounts indexed to the 500 tends to exert a negative impact on stocks when they are removed from the index but, the impact is not as severe if the stocks are added to MidCap 400. They have found, however, that there are some interesting anomalies in the performance of certain additions to and deletions from the S&P index family.

In Chapter 8, Tom McManus provides insight into the changes over time in one of the most followed market indexes—the S&P 500. McManus carefully dissects the makeup of the index over the last 35 years and shows how the forces of economic change have rightfully been captures in the composition of the S&P 500. In fact, he stresses that the perceived lofty valuations in the recent market may be quite justifiable in view of the new demographics of the S&P 500, and more significantly, its top 50 companies. The trend-setting performance of the new nifty fifty may indeed be what is keeping the 500 as "so hard a bogey to beat."

The performance track record of indexing versus active management is often a subject for debate. In Chapter 9, Rod Baldwin opens with an anthology of news clips over the past 30 years covering a variety of stories dealing with indexing. Then, Baldwin looks at the return data for pension funds as provided by SEI and for mutual funds, which comes from the Morningstar database, to determine the performance of indexing. Baldwin makes sure to compare apples to apples in his analysis of managers, being careful to explain the various management styles and the mix of asset classes in actively managed portfolios versus the singular approach of the index fund manager.

Todd Johnson provides an overview of the most popular indexes used for creating index funds in Chapter 10. He mentions that although the S&P 500 still has the dominant share of the index fund marketplace, there has been increasing demand for additional index fund products to give investors a more diversified approach to their indexing strategy. Johnson also discusses the mutual fund providers who offer index fund products and how they are growing in number although the range of product offerings still tends to be limited.

In Chapter 11, Andrew Olma covers implementation issues in managing an index fund. He compares full replication, sampling and optimization methodologies on their own and in consideration of the type of index that is being targeted for tracking. Olma also emphasizes the many factors that can cause tracking error simply being the result of the manner in which an index is managed. He discusses the importance of trading to the index fund management process as well as the use of derivatives. Olma describes a number of methods in which derivatives can be used, including equitizing cash flows and by gaining direct exposure without holding the underlying securities.

The significance of style exposure to a portfolio's return is the theme of Chapter 12. Bruce Westervelt gives insight into the need for managers to be cognizant of the impact that managing style allocation can have on their portfolios. He argues that rather than using a strict index fund approach to manage a fund, actively managing style exposure of the portfolio is the best way to add value. He also discusses the issues associated with using current style benchmarks to evaluate performance, citing the capitalization methodology as a potential drawback.

The use of style analysis is again the topic in Chapter 13. However, here Steve Hardy talks about its usage in the context of determining true diversification within a portfolio. Hardy uses a sample fund to walk through the process of evaluating where there might be style over or under exposure and how to compensate for style drift through the use of a completeness fund. He also assesses the role that growth and value derivatives can have in managing the process.

In Chapter 14, Gary Gastineau and Cliff Webber give an overview of exchange-traded index shares, one of the more innovative and successful financial products launched in recent years. Gastineau and Webber explain the differences between Unit Investment Trusts, open-end mutual funds, closed-end funds and the new index shares. They describe the process by which the index shares are created and redeemed and the positive effect on liquidity and pricing in the secondary market. Finally, they mention that the new index share structure has been so successful that an entire new array of equity indexes, and even actively managed portfolios, will eventually be available to investors.

Rolland Lochoff extends the indexing concept to the fixed income universe in Chapter 15. Lochoff talks about the many similarities to the equity indexing market with some notable differences. In particular, the bond indexes that are used to track tend to be very broad and include many issues that either do not trade or are very illiquid. Full replication is impractical, meaning that optimization and sampling techniques must be used to create the typical fixed income index fund. Lochoff also discusses the difficulties of obtaining accurate pricing for the underlying fixed income securities within the index fund and he states how this adds to the potential for tracking error.

One of the hidden benefits to an indexing strategy is the performance advantage gained from savings in taxes. In Chapter 16, Bill Zink explores the tax consequences that arise from portfolio turnover and dividend distributions in actively managed funds and passively managed funds. He also takes a look at a number of the more popular indexes used for passive investments and explains how construction and maintenance of the indexes cause the index fund manager to incur directly related taxable transactions that, ultimately have a bearing on fund performance.

In Chapter 17, Wai Chiang presents a practitioner's viewpoint on managing an index fund. Chiang explains that despite what appears to be a relatively straightforward process of mimicking an index, there are many variables which can cause tracking error. Unfortunately for the index fund manager, most of the tracking error tends to be negative. However, knowledge of the target index construction, maintenance and management by the fund manager can be used to his or her advantage through active trading and implementation strategies designed to pick up positive tracking events. Also, Chiang mentions the use of securities lending and derivatives-based strategies to positively impact the returns to the index fund.

The widespread usage of indexes as the basis for passively managed funds, exchange-traded derivatives and a host of other index-linked products gives rise to the legal aspects of the index business. That is, index providers offer other parties the right to license their indexes for the pu: poses of creating and marketing products based on those indexes. This is the subject of discussion in Chapter 18, in which Jim Overdahl provides insight into the intellectual property theory behind the licensing of index-es. He discusses the many types of index-linked products that are now under license as well as terms for the licenses.

I hope readers of *Indexing for Maximum Investment Results* will benefit from the combined knowledge and experience of the contributing authors in the index business. From the historical perspective on indexing to the hands-on application of index fund management techniques, *Indexing for Maximum Investment Results* is a must-read for anyone involved in the investment management process.

Albert S. Neubert

Contributors

Roderick G. Baldwin

Roderick. G. Baldwin, Director of Index Investment Management, Bank of America Capital Management, Inc., has overall responsibility for index investments at the Bank of America in San Francisco. Mr. Baldwin joined the Bank in 1976. Prior to that he worked at Paine Webber, Jackson and Curtis, and Marine Midland Bank in New York. He earned his MBA at The Wharton School of the University of Pennsylvania and his BA at Hamilton College. He was a member of the Board of Directors of the Institute for Quantitative Research from 1976 to 1984 and belongs to the Quantitative Analysts group of the San Francisco Analysts Society.

Judy M. Bednar

Judy M. Bednar is a Director of Passive Investments at Northern Trust Quantitative Advisors. She manages domestic and international equity index portfolios, and develops and implements hedging strategies for Northern Trust clients. Before assuming her current role, she was an International Economist at the Northern Trust Company. Prior to joining Northern Trust, Ms. Bednar was an analyst in Harris Bank's Economic

Research Office Service. Ms. Bednar has a BA from Wheaton College with a and an MBA from the University of Chicago. She is a Chartered Financial Analyst, and a member of the Association for Investment Management and Research. She is also registered with the National Futures Association.

John C. Bogle

John C. Bogle, 68, is Chairman of the Board of The Vanguard Group, Inc., and of each of the Vanguard mutual funds. Mr. Bogle founded The Vanguard Group in 1974. He had been associated with a predecessor company since 1951, immediately following his graduation from Princeton University, *magna cum laude in Economics*. He is a graduate of Blair Academy, Class of 1947.

The Vanguard Group is one of the two largest mutual fund organizations in the world. Headquartered in Malvern, Pennsylvania, Vanguard comprises more than 90 mutual fund portfolios with current assets totaling more than $300 billion.

In 1996, Mr. Bogle was named "Fund Leader of the Year" by Fund Auction magazine, received the Humanitarian Award from Magee Rehabilitation Institute , and was presented with the Alexis de Tocqueville Award by the United Way of Southeastern Pennsylvania. In 1997, he was named one of the "financial leaders of the 20th century" by Leadership in Financial Services (Macmillan Press Ltd. 1997).

Mr. Bogle served as Chairman of the Board of Governors of the Investment Company Institute in 1969 and 1970, and as a member of the Board from 1969 to 1974. He has also served as Chairman of the Investment Companies Committee of the National Association of Securities Dealers, Inc.

In 1991, he was named by Chairman Richard C. Breeden to the Market Oversight and Financial Services Advisory Committee of the U.S. Securities and Exchange Commission. In 1997, he was appointed by SEC Chairman Arthur Levitt to serve on the Independence Standards Board.

Mr. Bogle is the author of Bogle on Mutual Funds: New Perspectives for the Intelligent Investor, published by Irwin Professional Publishing in October 1993. This book received widespread critical acclaim, and has been a best-selling investment book since its publication. Irwin is also the publisher of John Bogle and the Vanguard Experiment: One Man's Quest to Transform the Mutual Fund Industry, by Robert Slater, released in November 1996.

Mr. Bogle is the author of numerous articles on investing. His most recent articles have appeared in The Journal of Portfolio Management, and include "Investing in the 1990's (Spring 1991); "Occam's Razor Revisited" (Fall 1991); "Selecting Equity Mutual Funds" (Winter 1992); and "The 1990's at the Halfway Mark" (Summer 1995). In 1993, he received the lifetime "Award of Distinction" from the Financial Analysts of Philadelphia.

He is a Director and Chairman of the Finance Committee of The Mead Corporation, a Director of Chris-Craft Industries, a Director of the General Accident Group of Insurance Companies, and a Director of the Princeton University Investment Company. In addition, he serves as Chairman of the Board of Trustees of Blair Academy and as Trustee of the American Indian College Fund. In 1997, he received an honorary degree (Doctor of Humane Letters) from Widener University.

Mr. Bogle was born in Montclair, New Jersey, on May 8, 1929. He now resides in Bryn Mawr, Pennsylvania, with his wife, Eve. They are the parents of six children.

Eddie Cheung

Eddie Cheung is an Associate Quantitative Analyst at Prudential Securities Inc. He joined the Small-Cap Quantitative Research group at PSI in 1996, focusing his efforts on maintaining the existing small-cap quantitative model and providing support for a variety of research assignments. Prior to joining Prudential Securities, he was a quantitative analyst at Abel/Noser Corporation and a system programmer / analyst for AT&T Corp. Mr. Cheung received his Bachelor of Science degree in MIS and Economics from the State University of New York at Albany in 1992. He lives with his wife in New York City and is an amateur photographer.

Wai C. Chiang

Wai C. Chiang is a Managing Director of Portfolio Management for Prudential Investments, a division of The Prudential Insurance Company of America. Since joining Prudential in 1986, Mr. Chiang has been involved with the start-up of more than fifteen new funds. He currently manages and trades eighteen domestic portfolios, including index funds, quantitative core equity funds, and futures tactical asset allocation accounts, on behalf of institutional and retail clients. These funds are benchmarked against the S&P 400, 500, and 600 Indexes, as well as the Wilshire 5000 and various Russell indexes.

Earlier in his career, Mr. Chiang was a stock research analyst for Salomon Brothers and a research and development engineer for Westinghouse Electric Corporation. He has developed proprietary computer-based models and authored a number of Salomon and Westinghouse publications. Mr. Chiang holds a B.S. in Mechanical Engineering from Syracuse University and an M.B.A in Finance from the Wharton School at the University of Pennsylvania.

Gary L. Gastineau

Gary L. Gastineau is Senior Vice President, New Products Development at the American Stock Exchange and an independent risk management consultant. Mr. Gastineau has prepared and published risk management research for S.G. Warburg, Swiss Bank, Salomon Brothers and Kidder Peabody. He is the author of The Options Manual (Third Edition, McGraw-Hill, 1988), the Dictionary of Financial Risk Management (Probus, 1992) and numerous journal articles. In addition, he has served as a Practitioner Director for the Financial Management Association and as a Director of the National Options and Futures Society. He is on the editorial boards of the Financial Analysts Journal, The Journal of Derivatives, the Journal of Portfolio Management, the Journal of Financial Engineering, Derivatives Quarterly, and Financial Practice and Education. He is also a member of the Advisory Board of the Research Foundation of the Institute of Chartered Financial Analysts. He is an Adjunct Professor at The Center for Technology and Financial Services at the Polytechnic Institute and is a frequent speaker on risk management policies and techniques, execution costs and regulatory issues. Gary holds an A.B. degree from Harvard College and an M.B.A. from Harvard Business School.

Steve Hardy

Steve Hardy is the President and Founder of Zephyr Associates, Inc. which licenses the StyleAdvisor software program to over 200 major institutional investor clients. StyleAdvisor was the first commercially available software program designed to utilize Bill Sharpe's unique returns based style analysis. This program measures manager style and creates customized style benchmarks (normal portfolios) using only manager and index returns. This software is licensed to pension plan sponsors, money managers and consultants. Prior to forming Zephyr Associates, Steve Hardy was a principal of the firm Balch, Hardy, Scheinman & Winston, Inc., a money management firm. During its twenty one year history, the firm perfected the use of options and developed a number of quantitative stock and options strategies for large tax exempt funds. Prior to the founding of BHSW, Mr. Hardy was the Vice President of Dean & Witter Company. He received his degree in Business administration from Whitter College in 1968.

Todd B. Johnson

Todd B. Johnson is an investment professional with twelve years experience in the area of indexed and quantitative investments. He currently resides as President and Chief Investment Officer for World Asset Management. He started his career in 1986 with Manufacturers Bank, Trust Investments. In 1992, with the formation of Woodbridge Capital Management, Mr. Johnson was appointed Portfolio Manager in the Quantitative Investment Group. In 1994, with the creation of World Asset Management, he was appointed Director, Equity Investments and Vice President of Comerica Bank.

Mr. Johnson was a featured speaker at the Superbowl of Indexing, Palm Springs, CA, December 1996, and at the Public Fund Boards Summit, Phoenix, AZ, March 1997. He is also co-author of "Equitizing the Cash in Your Portfolio," The Journal of Investing, Fall 1996.

Shucheng (Scott) Liu

Shucheng Liu is a Senior Consultant in the Research Optimization Group. He joined BARRA in February 1992 and was involved in developing the Portfolio Optimization Model. He previously worked as a visiting scholar at the Graduate School of Management, University of California, Irvine. Shucheng has a Ph.D. in Operations Research from Columbia University and an M.S. in Operations Research from the Institute of Applied Mathematics (Beijing). His B.S. degree was in Mathematics from Nanjing University (Nanjing, China).

Roland W. Lochoff

Mr. Lochoff leads the U.S. Fixed Income team for PanAgora Asset Management. He is responsible for domestic and global fixed-income, encompassing active, passive, and structured strategies. Prior to joining PanAgora, Mr. Lochoff was the Director of Fixed Income Services at BARRA. He also worked at Chase Econometrics. He is the author of numerous articles in investment journals. Mr. Lochoff holds a B.Sc. in Computer Science and Psychology and a B.Sc. (Honors) degree in Computer Science from the University of Witwatersrand in South Africa, and an MBA in Economics and Finance from the University of California at Berkeley. Mr. Lochoff is on the Board of Directors of the Boston Bond Analyst Society. He also is a member of PanAgora's Investment Committee.

Burton G. Malkiel

Burton G. Malkiel is a specialist in the field of finance and is currently serving as Chemical Bank Chairman's Professor of Economics at Princeton University. His many writings cover the entire field of financial instruments, institutions, and markets and include the popular book, A Random Walk Down Wall Street, now in its sixth edition. He is a former chairman of the Economics Department and Director of the Financial Research Center at Princeton University and has held the position of Dean of the Yale School of Management during the 1980s. He has also served as a member of the President's Council of Economic Advisors during the Ford Administration. He holds a Ph.D. from Princeton University (January 1964); an M.B.A. from Harvard Graduate School of Business Administration (June 1955); and a B.A. from Harvard College (June 1953).

He is currently serving on the Board of Directors of The Vanguard Group of Investment Companies, Prudential Insurance Company of America, Amdahl Corporation, Baker, Fentress and Company, Southern New England Telecommunications Co., and The Jeffrey Company.

James C. McKee

Jim joined Callan's Quantitative Consulting Group in 1989, where he currently produces asset allocation and manager structure studies for institutional investor clients. He also specializes in U.S. equity research and analysis, covering related trends in futures, options, convertibles, active vs. passive issues, and market neutral strategies. Jim is also the editor of Callan's Capital Market Review, covering recent quarterly performance of all major asset classes. Prior to his career at Callan Associates, he worked at the Pacific Stock Exchange (PSE) from 1982 to 1989. Until 1985, Jim served as a trading clerk on the PSE's options floor. Thereafter, as manager of the PSE's Listings Department, he was responsible for researching and developing new stock, bond, and option listings. He holds a B.A. in Economics/Environmental Studies from Dartmouth College (1982) and a M.B.A. in Finance from Golden Gate University (1987).

Thomas McManus

Thomas McManus is a well-known investment strategist who focuses on opportunities available in the United States equity market. He writes for various publications, including his investment newsletter, *The Strategy Connection.* Until recently, Tom was Chief U.S. Investment Strategist at NatWest Markets, a division of the National Westminster Bank in London. Previously, he was a senior U.S. equity strategist at Morgan Stanley. Tom holds a Bachelor of Science degree in Industrial Engineering and Operations Research from the Columbia School of Engineering and Applied Science. Besides being highly regarded by financial institutions around the world, Tom's opinions and forecasts are widely featured in financial and news media, including CNN, CNBC, *The Wall Street Journal, Barron's, The New York Times,* and *The Financial Times.*

Claudia E. Mott

Claudia E. Mott is a First Vice President of Prudential Securities Inc. and Director of Small-Cap Research. She provides quantitative research to small-cap and mid-cap investors in the form of stock valuation and earnings surprise models, topical studies, and screens and is well known for her work on the various benchmarks used to measure small-cap performance. A frequent source on the small-cap market for *The Wall Street Journal, Money Magazine,* and CNBC, Ms. Mott's research has also been published in the *Journal of Portfolio Management* and the *Journal of Investing*. In addition, she was a contributor to the Probus Publishing title, *Small-Cap Stocks*, and the Irwin publication, *Equity Style Management*. Ms. Mott joined Prudential Securities in 1986 as a quantitative analyst supporting the existing large-cap quantitative model and related screening software. She was voted to *Institutional Investor* magazine's annual research all-star team in 1991, 1992, 1993, 1994, 1995, and 1996, ranking first in the Small-Company category for the past four years. Prior to joining Prudential Securities, she was a senior consultant for Interactive Data Corporation in Boston and a financial analyst for Bostongas Company. Ms. Mott has a B.B.A. degree, cum laude, from the University of Massachusetts at Amherst, and an M.B.A. from Boston University. She lives in New Jersey with her husband and two sons and is an avid gardener.

Albert S. Neubert

Albert S. Neubert is an independent consultant in the index business. Mr. Neubert was the Director of the Domestic Indexes Unit within the Retail Services Group of Standard & Poor's. He was a member of the S&P Index Committee for 15 years, where he contributed to the strategy and policy formation for the S&P 500 and other S&P Indexes. Mr. Neubert led S&P's efforts in new product research, development, and implementation. Under Mr. Neubert's guidance, S&P launched the S&P MidCap 400, SmallCap 600, SuperComposite 1500, and REIT Composite Indexes. He is also a frequent speaker at index and related industry conferences. Mr. Neubert holds a B.S. in finance from Pace Univertiy and a M.B.A. from New York University.

Andrew Olma

Andrew Olma, CFA, is an investment strategist for U.S. and international (developed markets) equity index strategies. After joining Barclays Global Investors in 1992 (it was known as Wells Fargo Nikko then), he served as a portfolio manager for domestic non-S&P 500 funds. Prior to joining BGI, Andrew was an investment consultant in the Chicago office of Wyatt Asset Services for four years. He has an SB in electrical engineering from the Massachusetts Institute of Technology and an MBA in finance from Boston University. Andrew is a member of the FT/S&P-Actuaries World Index Policy Committee and the Security Analysts of San Francisco.

James A. Overdahl

James A. Overdahl is a senior financial economist in the Risk Analysis Division at the Office of the Comptroller of the Currency in Washington, D.C. He serves as a staff consultant on issues involving trading risk at federally chartered multinational banks. He has also worked as a staff economist at the Commodity Futures Trading Commission and the Securities and Exchange Commission in Washington, D.C. He has taught MBA finance courses at the University of Texas at Dallas, Virginia Tech, Gorge Mason University, and Georgetown University. He has also served as a risk management consultant to several leading financial firms. He holds a Ph.D. in economics from Iowa State University and a B.A. degree from St. Olaf College.

Aamir Sheikh

Aamir Sheikh is Manager, Derivatives Research, at BARRA. He joined BARRA in June 1994 and has worked on BARRA's equity and derivatives risk models. He is currently working on incorporating derivative securities in BARRA's equity models. Prior to joining BARRA, Aamir taught at Indiana University and at Washington University in St. Louis. His work on options has been published in the academic finance literature. Aamir has a Ph.D. in Finance from the University of California, Berkeley. He received his A.B., summa cum laude, from Columbia University in New York City, where he was elected to Phi Beta Kappa.

Dan Stefek

Dan Stefek is Manager, Analytics Research, at BARRA. When Dan joined BARRA in 1987 he focused on international risk models, leading the development of BARRA's two international equity models: the Global Equity and Emerging Markets risk models. Dan then developed the new optimizer featured in BARRA's Aegis system. Today, he is responsible for expanding and enhancing BARRA's analytics. His current set of projects includes macroeconomic risk modeling, valuation models, performance systems, portfolio construction, and downside risk.

Clifford J. Weber

Clifford J.Weber was appointed Vice President of New Products Development at the American Stock Exchange in April 1997. He is responsible for the creation and development of new derivative products, and has responsibility for admini-stration of the Exchange's Index Program. Prior to joining the AMEX in 1990, Mr. Weber worked as an actuarial consultant at Kwasha Lipton, a New Jersey based employee benefits consulting firm. Mr. Weber holds a B.A. degree in biochemistry from Dartmouth College and an M.S.E. degree in systems, with a concentration in operations research, from the University of Pennsylvania. He is a member of the International Association of Financial Engineers.

Bruce D. Westervelt

Bruce D. Westervelt, CFA, is Executive Director, Chief Financial Officer, and Director of Research at First Madison Advisors. He is responsible for the firm's research, creation, and development of First Madison's Dynamic Style Allocation investment process and model, portfolio implementation, and investment strategy. Prior to his work on DSA, Mr. Westervelt was engaged in style analysis research and software development for First Madison. His work on equity style management and allocation has been published by; *Institutional Investor, Pension and Investments*, McGraw-Hill Publishing, and Glenlake Publishing. A founder of First Madison Advisors in 1990, he has worked for Smith Barney Inc. since 1981. Mr. Westervelt holds a BBA in Finance from the University of Wisconsin. He is a chartered financial analyst and a member of the AIMR, ISFA, and the Madison Investment Analysts Society.

William G. Zink

William Zink is a Vice President in the Global Structured Products Group at State Street Global Advisors. Prior to joining State Street he was a senior investment manager in the U.S. equity area at PanAgora Asset Management. He holds both S.B. and S.M. degrees from MIT.

Why the Case for Indexing Remains Strong

Burton G. Malkiel
Chemical Bank Chairman's
Professor of Economics
Princeton University

I have been a believer in indexing for 25 years. I began advocating an indexing strategy in the first edition of my book, *A Random Walk Down Wall Street*, published in 1973—before index funds were publicly available. This paper will first review the intellectual justification for indexing, as well as the critique of that justification. Then I will present the evidence that has accumulated during the past quarter century that supports the original indexing thesis. Finally, I will review the practical arguments used against too narrow a definition of indexing and show the applicability of the strategy to markets other than large-capitalization United States stocks. The chapter concludes with a discussion of the role of financial analysis in determining the overall portfolio mix.

The Intellectual Case for Indexing

The intellectual case for indexing rests in large part on the efficient-market theory. The basic idea behind the theory is that securities markets are extremely efficient in digesting information about individual stocks or about the stock market in general. When information arises about a stock (or the market as a whole), the news spreads very quickly and gets incorporated into the prices of securities without delay. Thus, neither technical analysis (utilizing past price patterns in an attempt to predict the future) nor fundamental analysis (studying individual company's earnings, dividends, future prospects, and so on to determine a stock's proper value) will help an investor to achieve returns greater than would be obtained by buying and holding a well-diversified portfolio of equivalent risk.

The efficient-market theory is associated with the idea of the "random walk" theory, which is a term loosely used in the finance literature to characterize a price series where all subsequent price changes represent random departures from previous prices. The logic of the random walk theory is not that pricing is capricious, but rather that if the flow of information is unimpeded and information is immediately reflected in stock prices, then tomorrow's price change will reflect only tomorrow's news and will be independent of the price changes today. But news is by definition unpredictable and, thus, resulting price changes must be unpredictable and random. As a result, prices fully reflect all known information and even uninformed investors buying a diversified portfolio at the tableau of prices given by the market will obtain a rate of return as high as that achieved by the experts. The way I put it in my 1973 book, a blindfolded chimpanzee throwing darts at *The Wall Street Journal* could select a portfolio that would do as well as the experts. Of course, the practical strategy for investors is not to throw darts, but rather to simply buy and hold a diversified portfolio such as that contained in one of the broad stock-market indexes.

In a world where markets are reasonably efficient, switching among securities in an attempt to achieve superior performance will be useless at best. In fact, such portfolio turnover will be worse than useless because it will entail two important detractions from performance: transactions costs and taxes. At present turnover levels for mutual funds, transactions costs may be expected to subtract between 0.5 and 1.0 percent annually from gross portfolio returns. Trading involves brokerage costs on both the buying and selling side of the transaction of perhaps a few pennies a share. Much more important, there is typically a spread between the bid price for a share (the price at which it can be sold) and the asked price (the price at which it can be purchased). Moreover, when investment managers attempt to move large blocks of stocks, they tend to move equity prices away from their desired purchase and sales levels. Most active portfolio managers turn their portfolios over every one or two years. Such high activity is invariably costly.

In addition to turnover costs, actively managed funds incur substantial management fees. For example, the average general-equity mutual fund has an expense ratio of about 1 1/3 percentage points per annum. Passively managed index funds are available to individuals with an annual expense ratio of only 1/5 of one percentage point per annum. (Of course, institutions can obtain such indexed portfolios at far lower fees.)

Over time such expense differentials compound to substantial differences in net returns.

Indexing has another substantial advantage over active management: It tends to minimize taxes. Because the stock market has a long-run uptrend, portfolio turnover involves the realization of capital gains. For taxable investors, this can make an enormous difference in net returns. Dickson and Shoven (1993) took a sample of 62 mutual funds with long-term records and found that pre-tax, one dollar invested in 1962 would have grown to $21.89 in 1992. After paying taxes on dividends and capital gains distributions, however, that same dollar invested in mutual funds would have grown to only $9.87. By not trading from security to security, index funds tend to avoid the realization of capital gains and thus help solve the tax problem.

The Critique of Indexing

The general thrust of much of the academic empirical work over the 1980s and 1990s has been that, at least to some extent, stock prices and returns are predictable. For example, there appears to be a predictable relationship between the returns realized from stocks over several quarters or years and the initial dividend yields at which they were purchased. Several researchers have found that when stocks could be purchased at relatively high (low) initial yields, subsequent returns tended to be above (below) average.[1] Similarly, Shiller (1996) found that the high initial price-earnings (P/E) multiples for the market as a whole are associated with low future returns and vice versa. These findings have been confirmed cross-sectionally by Basu (1983) and Fama and French (1992). There has been a tendency for stocks with low P/Es to outperform those with high P/Es. Fluck, Malkiel, and Quandt (1997), as well as Fama and French, confirmed that stocks that sell at low multiples of their book values also tend to produce higher subsequent returns.

There is even some evidence that past price patterns have some predictive power for future price behavior. Lo and MacKinlay (1990) found that broad portfolio stock returns for weekly and monthly holding periods displayed positive serial correlation, i.e., a positive return in one week is more likely than not to be followed by a positive return in the next week. On the other hand, Poterba and Summers (1988) found that when stock returns were measured over longer periods, such as years or decades,

---

[1]See, for example. Fama and French (1988).

there was likely to be negative serial correlation, i.e., relatively high returns in one period were more likely than not to be followed by relatively low returns in a subsequent period. Similarly, there have been findings of seasonal effects and day-of-the-week effects. Haugen and Lakonishok (1988) have documented a "January effect" where stock returns, especially for smaller firms, have been abnormally high during the first few days of January. French (1980) has documented a "weekend effect" where average stock returns tend to be negative on Mondays.

Exhibit 1   Basic Series: Summary Statistics of
Annual Total Returns from 1926 to 1996

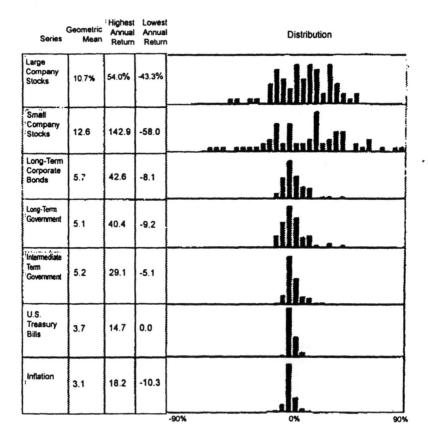

Series	Geometric Mean	Highest Annual Return	Lowest Annual Return	Distribution
Large Company Stocks	10.7%	54.0%	-43.3%	
Small Company Stocks	12.6	142.9	-58.0	
Long-Term Corporate Bonds	5.7	42.6	-8.1	
Long-Term Government	5.1	40.4	-9.2	
Intermediate Term Government	5.2	29.1	-5.1	
U.S. Treasury Bills	3.7	14.7	0.0	
Inflation	3.1	18.2	-10.3	

-90%   0%   90%

* The 1933 Small Company Stock Total Return was 142.9 percent.
Source: Ibbotson Associates.

Perhaps the strongest predictable pattern concerns the relationship between firm size and subsequent return. Exhibit 1, with return data since 1926, shows that stocks of smaller companies have returned about two percentage points more than the stocks of larger companies. Fama and French (1992) separated a sample of exchange-traded stocks into deciles according to their market capitalization and found a clear relationship showing that smaller stocks have produced larger rates of return than larger stocks over time. Exhibit 2 presents the results updated through the mid-1990s. Finally, a number of researchers, such as Shiller (1981, 1984) and DeBondt and Thaler (1985) have argued that stock prices clearly overreact and suggest that fads and psychological contagion influences markets as much as hard news.

Exhibit 2   The Relationship of Return and Size: 1963-1994

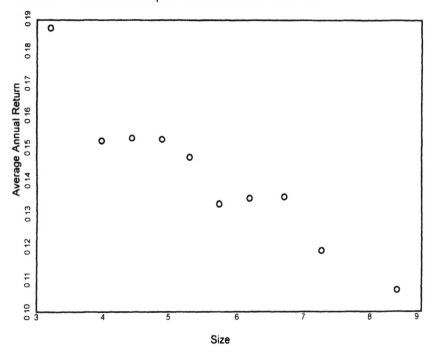

Source: Burton G. Malkiel and Yexiao Xu, "Risk and Return Revisited," *The Journal of Portfolio Management*, Vol.23, No. 3, Spring 1997.

The general conclusion from this work is that stock prices do not conform perfectly to the random walk/efficient market model. Moreover, the existence of several predictable patterns in the stock market, as well as the likelihood that there are periods when mass psychology overtakes fundamentals, suggests that it should be possible for an astute professional money manager to outperform the market as a whole.[2] Before we examine the evidence, some general comments should be made concerning the body of empirical work on predictable patterns.

The Indexing Counter-Attack

Indexers admit that the stock market may be somewhat predictable. But they deny that the predictable patterns that exist are large enough or dependable enough to overcome the substantial costs involved in trying to exploit them. Moreover, they argue that some of the apparent predictable patterns may be the result of spurious statistical techniques or, even if valid, may be perfectly consistent with the efficient functioning of markets. Finally, they suggest that any exploitable opportunities to earn excess returns will self-destruct in the future as they are arbitraged away.

Many of the patterns of stock price behavior that have been uncovered by researchers may be statistically significant but economically insignificant. For example, the short-run serial correlations documented by researchers (as well as the January effect and the day-of-the-week effect) are small relative to the transactions costs required to exploit them. Any investor who pays transactions costs cannot outperform a buy-and-hold strategy by employing a trading strategy designed to exploit the pattern. Moreover, some statistical regularities are not dependable in every period. For example, the mean reversion phenomenon discussed above, which appears to support a contrarian strategy, is far stronger in some decades than it is for other periods. Moreover, it may not be possible to profit from the tendency for individual stocks to exhibit patterns of return reversals. For example, my colleagues and I at Princeton tried to simulate a strategy of buying stocks that had particularly poor returns over the past three to five years.[3] We found very strong *statistical* evidence of return reversals, but it was truly a reversion to the mean, *not* an opportunity to make extraordinary returns. We found that stocks with very low returns over the past three to five years had higher returns in the next period.

---

[1] See, for example, Lakonishok. et. al. (1994) and DeBondt and Thaler (1985).

[2] See Zsuzsanna Fluck, Burton G. Malkiel, and Richard E. Quandt (1997).

Stocks with very high returns over the past three to five years had lower returns in the next period, but the returns in the next period were similar for both groups. While we found strong evidence of mean reversion, we could not confirm that a contrarian approach would yield higher than average returns. Statistically there was a strong pattern of return reversal, but not one you could make money on.

It is also the case that some predictable patterns may be perfectly consistent with the efficient functioning of markets. One pattern with strong statistical support is that between 25 and 40% of the variance of stock market returns can be "explained" by the initial dividend yield at which the stocks were purchased. When stocks could be bought at higher initial dividend yields, subsequent returns have been high. But dividend yields on stocks tend to be high when interest rates are high and low when interest rates are low. Consequently, this finding may simply reflect the adjustment of the stock market to general economic conditions. Also, many people argue today that companies are more likely to institute a share repurchase program rather than increase their dividends.

It is also important to point out that this phenomenon does *not* work with individual stocks. At Princeton, we tried simulating strategies whereby investors would form portfolios of stocks with high and low dividend yields. If investors simply purchased a portfolio of individual stocks with the highest dividend yields in the market, they would not have earned a particularly high rate of return.[4] Moreover, some of the patterns that have been discovered may simply represent the adjustment of market prices to perceived risk. For example, the long-run higher returns from the stocks of smaller companies (documented in Exhibits 1 and 2) may be a reward for the increased riskiness of smaller firms. And even if an extra reward for investing in small companies continues in the future, the relationship is not likely to be a dependable one in all periods. Certainly there has been little if any extra reward for holding small companies during the 1990s. Similarly, the "dividend effect" and the "long-run mean reversion effect" did not serve investors well in the 1990s. If investors sold stocks during 1994 because dividend yields were unusually low or because returns in the prior decade were so high, they would have lost out on extraordinary stock market returns in 1995 and 1996.

Some of the apparent predictable patterns in the market may also be the result of researchers' failure to adequately account for "survivorship bias," or the biases associated with "data mining." Survivorship bias may have a strong influence on research claims that valuation relationships

---

4 See Fluck, Malkiel, and Quandt, *op. cit.*

such as P/E, P/Book-Value, and size have predicative power to explain differences in the pattern of stock returns. Data tapes available today contain information about companies and securities that *presently* exist. They do not contain information on companies that may have declared bankruptcy or whose existence ended in some other way. Consequently, the sample of companies chosen includes only survivors. To the extent that some small companies or low P/E stocks were earlier available for purchase that subsequently did not survive, the researcher working with presently available data tapes will tend to overestimate the returns from these securities and may thus be misled into accepting a spurious hypothesis that low P/E and small-company stocks offer unusually large returns.

I would like to demonstrate the potential magnitude of the problem by using an illustration from my own work contained in Fluck, Malkiel, and Quandt (1997). We tried to estimate the extent to which the higher returns available from low P/E stocks (as well as from stocks with low P/Book-Value ratios) may be an artifact of survivorship bias. The strategy tested is to own a portfolio of stocks which at every quarterly time period represents the one-tenth of the universe of stocks with the lowest P/E or P/Book-Value ratios over the decade 1979 through 1988. In one portfolio simulation, we did the study based on a sample of companies in existence in 1988, i.e., a sample conditioned by survival. To test for survivorship bias, we repeated the experiment on a special computer tape containing all companies that had existed in 1979, the start of the sample period. The results are shown in Exhibit 3. In performing the portfolio simulations, we charged ourselves appropriate transactions costs when the portfolios were rebalanced.

Exhibit 3   Estimates of Quarterly Returns Available to Investors Employing a Strategy of Buying the 10% of All Stocks with the Lowest P/E and P/Book-Value Ratios

	End of Period Sample Conditioned by Survivorship	Beginning of Period Sample Free of Survivorship Bias
Low P/E Strategy	6.9%	5.9%
Low P/Book-Value Strategy	6.0%	5.0%

The exhibit shows that the simulated returns from these strategies were approximately one percentage point lower when derived from the sample free of survivorship bias.

Data mining is a second problem with much financial research. The ease of experimenting with financial data tapes of almost every conceivable dimension makes it quite likely that investigators will find some seemingly significant but wholly spurious correlation between financial variables or among financial and nonfinancial data sets. Given enough time and massaging of data series, it is possible to tease almost any pattern out of every data set. Moreover, the published literature is likely to be biased in favor of reporting such results. Significant effects are likely to be published in professional journals, while negative results, or boring confirmations of previous findings, are discarded or relegated to the file drawer. Data-mining problems are unique to nonexperimental sciences, such as financial economics, which rely on statistical analysis for their insights and cannot test hypotheses by running repeated controlled experiments.

In summary, there are indeed many predictable patterns in the stock market. The market is not totally random, but these patterns are not dependable in each and every period, and some of them, like the size effect, may simply reflect a better way of measuring risk than can be found from traditional measures. Moreover, many of these patterns could self-destruct in the future. Indeed, this is the logical reason why I don't take these "anomalies" as seriously as many of my academic colleagues.

Suppose one of these predictable patterns has been quite dependable and that investors could have earned unusually large returns by exploiting it. For example, assume there *is* a truly dependable January effect— that the stock market will rally in the first five days of January. What would an investor do? She would buy on the last day of December and sell on January 5th. But then she would find that the market rallied the last day of December and because there was so much selling on January 5th, she would have to sell on January 4th to take advantage of this effect. Thus, to beat the gun, investors would need to buy earlier and earlier in December and sell earlier and earlier in January, and eventually the pattern would self-destruct. Any truly repetitive pattern that can be discovered in the stock market and can be arbitraged away will do the same.

Evidence of Market Efficiency: The Performance of Professional Investors

The true test of whether indexing is a viable investment strategy is to compare the results of professional investment managers with those that can be obtained by a passive indexing strategy. Exhibit 4 compares the record of professional mutual fund managers with the Wilshire 5000 Index (available for purchase by individuals as the Vanguard Total Stock Market Index). All years are included after 1973, the date of the original publication of *Random Walk*. It is clear that in most years the index outperformed the vast majority of professional managers. On average, over two-thirds of active managers have been outperformed by the broad stock market indexes.

Exhibit 4   Percentage of All General Equity Funds Outperformed
             by the Wilshire 5000

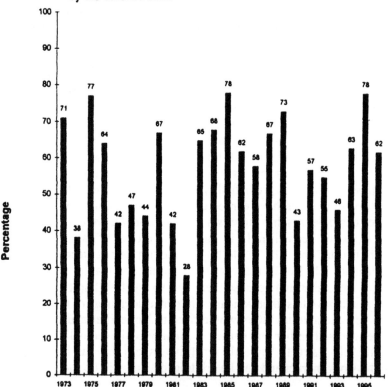

Exhibit 5 presents the recent 10-year record of active mutual fund managers against the Standard & Poor's 500 Stock Index (publicly available from a number of mutual fund complexes). We see that over 80% of the active managers were outperformed by the S&P Index. Moreover, the return for the average manager was about two percentage points *below* the index return. Exhibit 6 looks at the results in a global context against an index of both U.S. and international stocks. Again we find that most managers have underperformed the index, and the number that have out-performed the index by a meaningful amount (four percentage points or more) can be counted on the fingers of two hands. Exhibit 7 shows that institutional fund managers as a group have failed to beat the S&P 500 even before expenses.

Exhibit 5   Growth and Value Equity Mutual Funds vs. S&P 500 Index*
10 Years Ended December 31, 1995

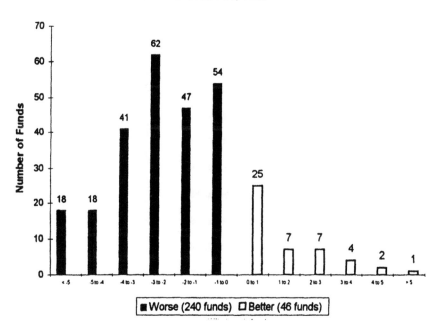

Performance relative to S&P 500 Index (percentage points).
*All funds are shown net of expenses.
Source: The Vanguard Group.

Exhibit 6 Quantidex Global Stock Index (QGSI) vs. 658 Stock Mutual Funds:
1/1/87–12/31/96

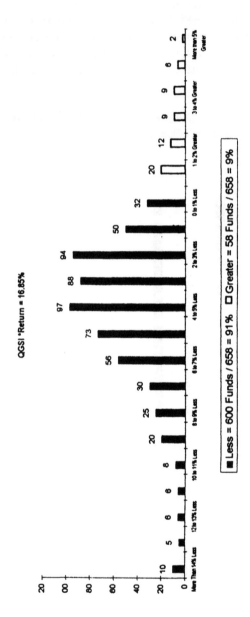

QGSI *Return = 16.85%

■ Less = 600 Funds / 658 = 91% □ Greater = 58 Funds / 658 = 9%

*Annual compound return.
Data source: Morningstar.
Chart source: Daniels and Alldredge Investment Management Inc., publishers of the
QUANTIDEX® Global Indices.

Exhibit 7   Proportion of Institutional Managers Beating the
S&P 500 Total Return

1995	29%
1993-95	32%
1991-95	47%
1986-95	33%

Returns for both the S&P 500 and institutional funds are calculated before expenses. Since institutions can obtain indexed results with an expenditure of only a few basis points, the numbers above understate the advantage of indexing.

Not only is extraordinary performance rare, but there is also no way to judge in advance who the superior managers will be in the future. Past performance is not a reliable guide—it is not possible to select a manager with superior skill by picking those managers with above-average past records. For example, the top 20 equity mutual fund investment managers of the 1970s significantly underperformed the average manager as well as the broad stock market during the 1980s, and the top managers of the 1980s have failed to beat the indexes thus far in the 1990s. A recent study of mine (1995) found that it was impossible to generate superior long-run performance by purchasing equity mutual funds with superior recent performance. One of the many tests I ran was to examine the performance of the top-rated funds in subsequent periods. Exhibit 8 looks at the record of the *Forbes* "honor roll" funds during a 16-year period. To earn a place on the honor roll, a fund not only had to have an extraordinary long-run performance record (usually based on total returns measured over a 10-year period) but also had to meet certain consistency goals. Performance is measured in both up and down markets, and funds must be at least top-half performers in down markets to qualify for honor status. Thus, the *Forbes* method guards against the selection of only high-risk funds following a sharp rise in the overall market. It is interesting to ask if investors could have achieved superior returns by buying these "consistent performers."

In the analysis, we ignore any load charges that might be imposed on the purchase of these mutual fund shares. Exhibit 8 gives the year-by-year performance of the *Forbes* honor roll funds. We note that in the first eight years of the experiment, the honor roll funds did do substantially better than the S&P Index; over the last eight years, however, they did substantially worse than the index. Over the entire 16-year period, the honor roll funds underperformed the S&P 500 Stock Index. Similar results were obtained in an analysis of the Morningstar rankings.

Nobel Laureate Paul Samuelson (1989) sums up the difficulty of attempting to select winning funds in the following parable. Suppose it were demonstrated that one out of 20 alcoholics could learn to become a moderate social drinker. The experienced clinician would answer, "Even if true, act as if it were false, for you will never identify that one in 20," and in the attempt, the rest of the 20 may be ruined. Samuelson concluded that investors should forsake the search for such tiny needles in huge haystacks.

Exhibit 8   Subsequent Performance of Forbes "Honor Roll" Funds

Following Year Year on Honor Roll	Following Year Total Return Honor Roll Funds (excluding loads) (%)	Total Return S&P 500 (%)
1975	17.95	23.81
1976	2.31	-7.19
1977	9.19	6.52
1978	36.32	18.45
1979	29.29	32.45
1980	-2.70	-4.88
1981	24.15	21.50
1982	21.60	22.50
Average annual 8-year return (1975-1982)	16.57	13.32
1983	-7.45	6.22
1984	24.19	31.64
1985	10.66	18.62
1986	2.25	5.18
1987	14.96	16.50
1988	24.83	31.56
1989	-8.60	-3.11
1990	29.96	30.39
Average annual 8-year return (1983-1990)	10.46	16.43
Average annual 16-year return (1975-1990)	13.48	14.86

Criticism of Too Narrow a Definition of Indexing

For all the attractions of indexing, however, there are valid criticisms of too narrow a definition of indexing. Even a strong supporter of passive investment strategies, such as myself, believes there is an important (indeed, even a critical) role for financial analysis in devising appropriate investment strategies for individual and institutional investors. For example, many people equate indexing with simply buying the S&P 500 Stock Index. Critics argue, with some justification in my view, that the "large-cap" domestic stocks which dominate the S&P 500 have enjoyed extraordinary performance in recent years. The unusually large recent superiority of the S&P 500 (it beat 85% of actively managed equity funds in 1995 and 75% in 1996) is unlikely to continue. Many traditional financial analysts argue that better values may well exist today in "small-cap" stocks, in foreign stocks, or in real estate equities. But this is not an argument against indexing since index funds currently exist that mimic the performance of various S&P, Wilshire, and Russell Indexes of small-cap stocks, the Morgan Stanley Capital Index of European, Australian, and Far Eastern (EAFE) Securities, indexes of emerging markets securities, and real estate trusts (REITs). Moreover, these index funds have also tended to outperform actively managed funds investing in similar securities. For example, Exhibit 9 shows that even in emerging markets the case for indexing remains strong.

Exhibit 9 Percentage of Actively Managed Emerging Market Funds Underperforming the MSCI Emerging Markets Index

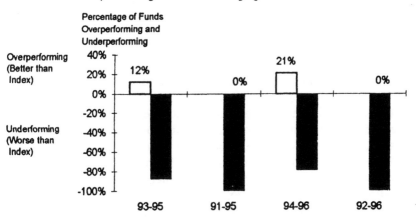

Source: Lipper Analytical Services and The Vanguard Group.

It may seem paradoxical that indexing should be a viable strategy even in the smallest emerging foreign markets. It is certainly plausible that such markets are far less efficient than large-capitalization U.S. stocks, on which I rested the efficiency argument for indexing. But it is precisely the relative inefficiency of trading in these markets that makes passive management appropriate even here.

Transactions costs, including various stamp taxes and bid-asked spreads, are several times larger in emerging markets than in developed markets. Moreover, trading is very thin, and it can be prohibitively expensive to make wholesale shifts between individual securities within markets or between one market and another. In addition, expense ratios charged by active managers far exceed the costs in developed markets. Finally, in many emerging markets that are still quite undeveloped, there are few eligible securities from which to choose. Thus, even in markets where pricing is less than perfectly efficient, a passive strategy has much to recommend it.

The most important determinants of the risk and return for individual and institutional portfolios are the decisions made with respect to asset allocation. Decisions regarding stocks, bonds, and cash; allocations between domestic and foreign equities or large- and small-cap stocks; and the proportion of the portfolio allocated to real estate and other assets— play the biggest role in influencing portfolio performance. They are far more important than the selection of individual securities.

And this is where financial analysis is critically important. The financial analyst must not only judge the attractiveness of various asset classes but also pay particular attention to the way these classes are combined so as to minimize the overall risk of the portfolio. Portfolio theory teaches us, for example, that adding very risky asset categories can in certain circumstances actually *reduce* the risk of the portfolio and substantially improve the terms of the risk/return trade-off available to investors. The amount of risk reduction benefit will depend in turn on the covariance between the asset category that is added and the core portfolio of domestic stocks. For this reason, financial analysts need to consider the role of emerging markets equities and real estate trusts, because these asset classes tend to have low correlations with (tend to move independently of) domestic stock indexes, such as the S&P 500.

Financial analysts also need to tailor their recommended portfolio allocations to their clients' risk tolerances and capacity to suffer loss. The widow in ill health needs a different portfolio than that of the young businesswoman investing for retirement. The pension fund requiring large payouts in the immediate future to fund an early-retirement program needs a different portfolio than the pension fund of the rapidly growing company with very young workers. Probably the biggest investment mistakes are made by people who mismatch their portfolio allocations with their risk tolerances and requirements.

Indexing allows investors to buy securities of all types with no effort, at minimal expense, and, where relevant, at considerable tax savings. But financial analysts have a critical role in tailoring a portfolio to the objectives, requirements, and risk tolerances of both individual and institutional investors.

References

Banz, R., "The Relationship Between Return and Market Value of Common Stocks," *Journal of Financial Economics*, 1981, 9, pp. 3-18.

Basu, S., "The Relationship Between Earnings Yield, Market Value, and Return for NYSE Common Stocks: Further Evidence," *Journal of Financial Economics*, 1983, 12, pp. 129-156.

Campbell, John and Robert Shiller, "The Dividend-Price Ratio and Expectations for Future Dividends and Discount Factors," *Review of Financial Studies*, 1988, 1, pp. 195-227.

DeBondt, W.F.M. and Thaler, R.H., "Does the Stock Market Overreact?" *Journal of Finance*, 1985, 40, pp. 793-805.

Dickson, Joel M. and John B. Shoven, "Taxation and Mutual Funds: An Investor Perspective," NBER: Tax Policy and the Economy, 1995 (9) p. 151.

Fama, Eugene F. and Kenneth R. French, "Dividend Yields and Expected Stock Returns," *Journal of Financial Economics*, 1988, 22, pp. 3-25.

_____, "The Cross-Section of Expected Stock Returns," *Journal of Finance*, 1992, 47, pp. 427-465.

_____, "Size and Book-to-Market Factors in Earnings and Returns," *Journal of Finance*, 1995, 50, pp. 131-155.

Fluck, Zsuzsanna, Burton G. Malkiel, and Richard E. Quandt, "The Predictability of Stock Market Returns and the Efficient Market Hypothesis," *Review of Economics and Statistics*, Vol LXXIX, No. 2, May 1997, pp. 176-183.

French, Kenneth, "Stock Returns and the Weekend Effect," *Journal of Financial Economics*, 1980.

Haugen, Robert and Josef Lakonishok, *The Incredible January Effect*, Burr Ridge, IL: Irwin, 1988.

Lakonishok, Josef, Andrei Shleifer, and Robert W. Vishny, "Contrarian Investment, Extrapolation, and Risk," *Journal of Finance*, 1994, 49, pp. 1541-1578.

Lo, Andrew and A. Craig MacKinlay, "Stock Market Prices Do Not Follow Random Walks: Evidence from a Single Specification Test," *Review of Financial Studies*, 1990, 3, pp. 175-208.

Malkiel, Burton G. *A Random Walk Down Wall Street*, 1st edition. New York: W.W. Norton, 1973.

_____. "Returns from Investing in Equity Mutual Funds, 1971-1991," *Journal of Finance*, June 1995, pp. 549-572.

Poterba, James and Lawrence Summers, "Mean Reversion in Stock Returns: Evidence and Implications," *Journal of Financial Economics*, 1988, 22, pp. 27-60.

Samuelson, Paul A., "The Judgment of Economic Science on Rational Portfolio Management: Indexing, Timing, and Long-Horizon Effects," *Journal of Portfolio Management*, Fall 1989, pp. 4-12.

Shiller, Robert J., "Stock Prices and Social Dynamics," *Brookings Papers on Economic Activity*, 1984, 2, pp. 457-510.

_____. "Do Stock Prices Move too Much to Be Justified by Subsequent Changes in Dividends?," *American Economics Review*, 1981, 71, pp. 421-430.

_____. "Price-Earnings Ratios as Forecasters of Returns: The Stock Market Outlook in 1996," unpublished manuscript, July 21, 1996.

CHAPTER 2

Benchmarks: Definitions and Methodologies

Albert S. Neubert
Director, Domestic Indices
Standard & Poor's

The investment strategy of indexing starts with a most basic and critical decision and that decision involves the selection of the underlying index that will serve as the basis for an investment portfolio. For any given asset or sub-asset class of securities, there is often a number of indexes available to the investor. Within equities, and particularly domestic equities, there are literally thousands of indexes available from which to choose. This chapter will concentrate on examining the issues critical to the investor in selecting a domestic equity index for passive investment purposes, although many of the same issues will be relevant for other asset class indexes as well.

First, we need some definitions to help clarify the discussion. When we say asset class, we mean any group of securities that behaves similarly. Conversely, a group of securities that behaves differently, or has a low correlation with other groups of securities, or asset classes, is itself an asset class. If the correlation between two groups of securities is relatively high, it is still possible for there to be two separate and distinct asset classes if they have statistically different standard deviations. Simply stated, an asset class will have different return and (or) risk characteristics than other asset classes. Lesser degrees of differentiation can constitute sub-asset classes.

An index is a statistical methodology used to measure changes in the value of something over time. An index of equity securities can be used to measure changes in the value of the group of securities included in the index. If the index is designed to represent the securities within an asset class, then the index could be considered a benchmark for the asset class. Benchmarks are used most often to measure the performance of an investment in one or more securities, and not always within the same asset class.

Equity indexes that serve as benchmarks can also form the basis for direct investments, such as index funds. Other direct index investment vehicles include derivative products, such as futures, options, index-linked warrants, notes, bonds and swaps but, they are not necessarily based on benchmark indexes. This is what distinguishes equity indexes from benchmark indexes for various equity asset and sub-asset classes. Some indexes are created simply to serve as the basis for derivatives. The construction and calculation methodology for a benchmark index and a derivatives-based index can be very different because of their market usage. Typically, indexes that are created to be the basis for derivatives tend to have a much narrower focus than an asset class and often are constructed with an emphasis on liquidity.

It is also important to note that not all benchmarks are true indexes. in the statistical sense. The widely followed Dow Jones Industrial Average is just that—an average—for the prices of the 30 issues that make up the benchmark. The time series of daily calculations for the Dow Jones Industrials are made comparable through adjustments to the divisor for stock splits and changes in the constituents. However, the time series is not "indexed" to a base period for comparison purposes.

Despite the fact that the Dow Jones Industrials Average is technically not an index, it is one of the most popular ways of gauging the performance of the U.S. equities markets. The other market indicator that is also widely used as a barometer of domestic equity performance is the S&P 500 Composite Stock Price Index, a statistically true index. Only more recently have other indexes been used to varying degrees by investors to measure U.S. stock movements, including such measures as the Wilshire 5000, the Russell 1000, 2000, and 3000 Indexes, and the NASDAQ Composite Index.

When it comes to investing through indexing or by using index derivatives, the set of indexes most commonly used by investors is somewhat similar to the stock market indicators mentioned above, but there are some notable differences. In particular, the Dow Jones Industrials and NASDAQ Composite are almost never used as indexing vehicles. Both. the Dow Jones Industrials and the NASDAQ Composite only recently became the basis for exchange-traded derivatives contracts. Why is it that some market indicators are more popular than others depending on the usage? There are a number of reasons that investors gravitate to certain indicators within the domestic equities market. Much has to do with the usage, because indicators used for direct or indirect investments often require a different set of characteristics than those used only for performance measurement purposes. On the other hand, the length of history for an indicator is often very useful to many investors. This is the single most important reason that the Dow Jones Industrial Average is so widely used and accepted as an indicator of U.S. stock price performance. Dow Jones started calculating and disseminating the predecessor to the modern Industrial Average in 1896, fully 27 years earlier than the next most popular market indicator series—the S&P 90 Stock Composite Index, the forerunner to the S&P 500.

Let's examine factors that are important to investors using domestic stock market indexes (All references will be made to statistical indexes from this point on, because the Dow Jones Industrials methodology is the only major indicator using a non-index calculation technique) for the reasons mentioned and see what characteristics need to be captured within the index series in order to satisfy the needs of those same investors. First, there are four key aspects to the business of producing a market index. They involve the (1) compilation, (2) calculation, (3) maintenance, and (4) dissemination of the indicator series. Imbedded within the four processes is the quantity and quality of basic and value-added supporting data, including dividends, earnings, and other relevant fundamental and statistical information. This could be called the "completeness" of the product offering by the market index provider.

By compilation we mean the manner in which the constituent securities are selected for inclusion in the index and the data accumulated to calculate the index. Constituents can be chosen either by sampling from the population or by including the entire population. The method chosen will vary for a number of reasons. If the population is very large, such as the U.S. equities market, it may be cumbersome—primarily because of the maintenance process—to choose to include the entire population of securities in an index. However, if an index is being constructed to measure a sub-asset class, such as an industry group or economic sector group of securities, then it might be quite practical to include all of the available securities. Also, the data availability, market usage, calculation, and maintenance methodology will all influence the security selection process.

If the index is going to be used as the basis for indexing and (or) derivatives, then it is important that the constituent securities be reasonably liquid. Sometimes, the entire population might satisfy this criteria, as mentioned above in cases where a sub-asset class is being considered for the construction of an index.

Liquidity is important to the indexer because it affects transactions costs and (or) tracking error. If an index has many securities, including some that are very illiquid, the index fund manager may make the decision to not include the illiquid securities in order to minimize transactions costs. However, the fund manager gives up the risk and return characteristics of those omitted securities, and this may introduce what is known as "tracking error" into the investment. Typically, the mandate for an index fund manager is to match the returns of the target index as closely as possible. Tracking error refers to the difference in returns between the indexed portfolio and the underlying index.

A similar situation exists for index derivatives' users. If the indicator that is being used as the basis for a derivatives' product has illiquid securities in its composition, then it will be difficult, if not impossible, to conduct an effective arbitrage against the basket of underlying securities. Arbitrageurs are important to the efficient pricing and liquidity for derivative products. In the case of OTC derivatives, where no exchange-traded derivative exists for an index series, it is essential that the constituent securities be liquid because trading the basket of securities that make up the index will be the derivatives dealer's only manner in which to hedge the product. Illiquid securities cause the cost and risk of the hedge to rise.

Compilation involves much more than the constituent selection process. Once the constituents have been selected, the data used to calculate the indicator series must be accumulated. For example, a capitalization-weighted index methodology would require the input of shares to compute market values. This raises the question of what kind of shares would be used in the calculation process as well as their source.

In the case of the S&P 500 and other Standard & Poor's indexes, common shares outstanding are used to calculate the constituent weights. These shares do not include treasury stock or common stock equivalents. In effect, the common shares outstanding are similar to those used to compute the constituent's basic earnings per share. The timing of the calculation of the common shares outstanding is the main difference between the Index shares and those used by the constituent to calculate its basic earnings per share. Other differences include the use of moving average shares or weighted average shares for a reporting period versus a point-of-time calculation for Index shares.

There are numerous databases that carry shares, but they may not match the requirements for the index series. Quite often, calculators of indexes are forced to make concessions on the data inputs because of the laborious task of checking and (or) converting data to suit a specific requirement. At Standard & Poor's, the shares that are used to calculate the S&P 500 and other indexes are originated in an internal database that is used to supply other products and services. The shares for over 9,000 issues are updated daily from public filings, such as company 10Ks, 10Qs, and press releases. The common shares outstanding used for the index calculations are tagged and further reviewed on a weekly basis by analysts specifically assigned to the task of monitoring the index weights.

All indicators, whether they are benchmark indexes or narrow-based averages, require pricing in their calculations. As with the weighting factors used to calculate many index series, pricing is another critical element in the process and one that is completely dynamic during trading hours. For domestic equities, pricing originates with the major and regional stock exchanges. Pricing that originates with an exchange is known as primary exchange pricing. However, an index series could also use composite pricing, which incorporates all exchanges on which any issue is listed for trading. The differences are usually not that great, but in a world in which one basis point of performance is critical, it takes only a minute difference in pricing between a primary or composite price to affect the calculation of an index return.

Index calculation starts with a decision on methodology. There are three methods that are commonly used to calculate index series: (1) price-weighted, (2) equal-weighted, and (3) capitalization-weighted. For the purpose of creating an index that can serve as the basis for indexed portfolios, the capitalization-weighted methodology is generally preferred. This is because the turnover is lowest under the capitalization-weighted methodology, whereas the other methods require constant rebalancings of the holdings. However, the rebalancing issue may be overcome if the particular weighting methodology more accurately reflects valuation of the constituent securities.

The calculation of any index starts with the selection of a base period. The base period is the initial value for the index as it represents the underlying basket of securities. Quite often, the base period is a single point in time, and for most equity market indexes it is the last trading day of a particular year. Although the single-day base period is most often used, primarily a result of simplicity, a more accurate way of reflecting a starting value would be to select a representative period of valuation. For example, the base period for the S&P 500 is an average of the total market values for the 500 constituents over the period from 1941 to 1943 on a monthly basis.

Another decision must be made to determine the starting index value, or base-period market value. Again, this will be dictated by the end-use for the indicator series. The most common starting index value is 100, and with good reason. Because an index is a statistical tool designed to translate changes in value of a basket of goods over time, it is important that the measuring device—the index—be easy to understand. In the case of a capitalization-weighted equity index, the index values convert changes in market value for the constituent securities over time into a meaningful time series. When a base-period index value is set at 100 and the index moves to 200 at some point in the future, it means that the underlying basket of securities has increased in value two-fold, or by 100 percent. This exercise demonstrates the need for simplicity in designing the indicator series.

Index maintenance can be critical to the index fund manager because it can help reduce the number of decisions that lead to transactions and, hence, tracking error. It is a process involving the implementation of rules for constituent selection and weighting, and ensures that the statistical integrity of the index series is preserved. For example, if the shares outstanding used to calculate a component's weight in an index is incorrect, or has not been updated routinely, then the final index values will not accurately reflect the market valuation for the constituent. This concerns the index fund manager, because the manager holds a real basket of securities and changes that affect the underlying index must be dealt with in some sort of consistent manner in order to minimize tracking error. The rules for maintaining an index are not necessarily perfect for minimizing transactions costs to the indexer, but it is their consistent application that permits index fund managers to function within a reasonable framework for replicating the target index returns.

Corporate actions, including mergers, acquisitions, bankruptcies, spinoffs, restructurings, stock splits, dividends, and share changes are examples of many of the common events that must be managed by the index provider. Rules to handle these must be established and then maintenance guidelines followed for implementation. The maintenance process is what allows these actions to be processed within the index calculation operation in such a manner that the final product—index returns—are unaffected by non-market related changes to constituent weighting factors.

Some corporate actions are more significant than others. Typically, the most significant changes are those that involve constituents. Ideally, the basket of securities that make up an index would never change but, that would not likely reflect the real world of mergers, acquisitions. restructurings, bankruptcies, or changes in the importance of various industries or economic sectors over time. Also, the objective of the index series might necessitate changes to the constituent list. This would occur if the index were constructed using specific size parameters (for example. market values) to determine boundaries for an equity asset class such as small- or large-capitalization stocks.

There are a number of ways that constituent changes can be managed by the index provider. If an index were compiled using market value guidelines, then some sort of periodic rebalancing would be required to account for market movements. There may be a requirement to keep the total number of constituent securities within an index at a certain level or, conversely, the number of constituents may be allowed to fluctuate. Each methodology requires rules for implementing constituent changes that are designed to keep the index aligned with its overall objectives. It is the consistency of the application of the rules that differentiates the quality of the final index product.

The final step in the production of an index is dissemination—the manner in which users can access the index values and supplemental information. The frequency of calculation is a key determinant of the dissemination methodology. Real-time calculations, which means calculations being performed as rapidly as computer processing speed allows, are usually disseminated over major quotation vendors. including Automated Data Processing, Bridge Data, Reuters, or Bloomberg. Indexes that require real-time calculations often serve as the basis for exchange-traded derivatives contracts.

Less frequent calculations, such as end-of-day, weekly, or monthly computations may not require that major quote vendors disseminate the information. With these types of index calculation frequencies. it may only be necessary to distribute the information through newspapers. broadcast media, or proprietary subscription services. However, for any index product to gain wide acceptance and usage, it is imperative that the index data be broadly distributed.

Now, let's turn our attention to defining the domestic equity marketplace. When we use the Dow Jones Industrial Average, the S&P 500 Composite Stock Price Index, or the NASDAQ Composite Index, what performance are we measuring? By defining the domestic equity market and analyzing its structure, we can develop a framework to better understand the various equity market indicators.

In order to undertake our exercise, we'll need a comprehensive database of U.S. stocks. There are a number of databases that carry information on U.S. stocks, and most contain anywhere from 7,000, or more, issues in them. At Standard & Poor's, the Stock Guide Database, which provides the information published in the widely used *S&P Stock Guide* for investors and is used as the source for data inputs to the S&P 500 and other S&P Indexes, contains over 9,000 securities. The 9,000 securities are listed for trading on either the major national exchanges, the regional exchanges or the major Canadian exchanges.

With over 9,000 securities, the S&P Stock Guide Database covers most of the securities that are listed on the U.S. and Canadian equities markets. However, not all of the securities that are traded in the U.S. market are U.S. stocks, and the Canadian issues that trade on Canadian exchanges are easily eliminated from an analysis of the domestic equity market. Also, many of the other issues listed for trading on the U.S. exchanges would not be considered by investors as logical selections for an investment allocation to domestic equities. These include closed-end funds, royalty trusts, real estate investment trusts, and partnerships. As a result, the database needs to be screened for the various classes of securities in order to produce an appropriate universe of U.S. common stocks from which an investor would ideally chose to build a portfolio.

As of September 30, 1997, there were 9,019 issues in the Stock Guide Database (See Table 1). Screening for foreign companies removed a total of 679 stocks, 221 of which were Canadian. The other 458 foreign companies are listed as American Depositary Receipts or Shares. There were 544 closed-end investment companies, 48 limited partnerships, 254 real estate investment and other royalty trusts that also were screened from the Database total.

An additional 1,193 NASDAQ Small-Cap companies were removed from the Stock Guide Database universe for a slightly different reason. Despite the fact that these are domestic equities, they are so small and illiquid, most institutional investors would never invest in this segment of the market. As we will see, there are still a very large number of small-cap securities left in the domestic equity database after these are removed.

After the screens have been applied, we are left with a domestic equity population of 6,301 securities with a total market value of $10.168 trillion (See Table 1). A total of 2,718 issues, with a combined market value of $4.267 trillion, were removed from the starting Stock Guide population. The domestic equity population of 6,301 securities represents the constituent selection base used to maintain the S&P 500, MidCap 400, SmallCap 600, SuperCap 1500, and other S&P indexes.

Table 1 S&P Equity Universe Decile Description
as of September 1997 (in millions of dollars)

		ADRs/Foreign Companies	Canadian Companies	Limited Partnerships	Mutual Funds/ Investment Companies	REITS/Land Companies	NASDAQ Small Cap	Domestic Common Equity Universe	Grand Total
Decile1	Number of Companies	101	10	—	—	—	—	207	318
	Total Market Value	3,051,060	134,896	—	—	—	—	6,107,382	9,293,338
	Average Market Value	30,209	13,490					29,504	29,224
Decile2	Number of Companies	47	10	1	—	1	—	227	286
	Total Market Value	295,175	52,629	5,220	—	5,164	—	1,346,538	1,704,726
	Average Market Value	6,280	5,263	5,220		5,164		5,932	5,961
Decile3	Number of Companies	38	12	1	2	7	—	244	304
	Total Market Value	120,637	38,839	3,138	5,182	22,299	—	755,715	945,809
	Average Market Value	3,175	3,237	3,138	2,591	3,186		3,097	3,111
Decile4	Number of Companies	45	15	2	7	13	—	284	366
	Total Market Value	81,042	27,944	3,800	13,179	24,472	—	517,702	668,140
	Average Market Value	1,801	1,863	1,900	1,883	1,882		1,823	1,826
Decile5	Number of Companies	24	12	4	11	21	1	319	392
	Total Market Value	28,818	14,435	4,811	12,535	24,227	1,186	366,203	452,215
	Average Market Value	1,201	1,203	1,203	1,140	1,154	1,186	1,148	1,154
Decile6	Number of Companies	30	7	5	19	22	1	383	467
	Total Market Value	24,473	5,266	3,855	15,352	18,059	830	304,427	372,261
	Average Market Value	816	752	771	808	821	830	795	797
Decile7	Number of Companies	25	15	5	41	38	3	445	572
	Total Market Value	12,856	7,787	2,643	21,442	20,905	1,573	238,657	305,863
	Average Market Value	514	519	529	523	550	524	536	535

continued on next page

Table 1 S&P Equity Universe Decile Description
as of September 1997 (in millions of dollars), cont'd.

		ADRs/Foreign Companies	Canadian Companies	Limited Partnerships	Mutual Funds/ Investment Companies	REITS/Land Companies	NASDAQ Small Cap	Domestic Common Equity Universe	Grand Total
Decile8	Number of Companies	28	17	4	76	42	4	594	765
	Total Market Value	9,963	5,800	1,260	24,650	14,926	1,331	198,897	256,826
	Average Market Value	356	341	315	324	355	333	335	336
Decile9	Number of Companies	33	26	7	134	27	27	1006	1,260
	Total Market Value	6,278	4,932	1,293	24,085	5,508	4,563	187,412	234,070
	Average Market Value	190	190	185	180	204	169	186	186
Decile10	Number of Companies	87	97	19	254	83	1,157	2,592	4,289
	Total Market Value	4,224	4,296	1,024	16,800	3,859	26,381	145,155	201,739
	Average Market Value	49	44	54	66	46	23	56	47
Total Number of Companies		**458**	**221**	**48**	**544**	**254**	**1,193**	**6,301**	**9,019**
Total Market Value		**3,634,527**	**296,823**	**27,044**	**133,225**	**139,418**	**35,864**	**10,168,087**	**14,434,989**
Average Market Value		**7,936**	**1,343**	**563**	**245**	**549**	**30**	**1,614**	**1,601**

The total domestic equity population still represents the asset class only in its broadest form and, thus, it needs further refining in order to perform a more detailed analysis of specific asset classes and the indicators used to measure them. This is accomplished by creating a histogram for the domestic equity population. The population is aligned into ten equal market value groupings and securities placed into the deciles ranked from highest to lowest market value. However, it is necessary to make an adjustment in placing the securities within the deciles. The deciles are filled by first populating them only with the New York Stock Exchange-listed issues with the highest market values being placed into the first decile and the smallest market value securitys going into the tenth decile. After the deciles have been filled with the New York Stock Exchange issues, the American and NASDAQ stocks are added to the appropriate deciles, completing the distribution. If this adjustment were not performed, the distribution would be unduly skewed to the very large amount of small-capitalization companies that dominate the NASDAQ National Market System.

After the market value histogram has been completed, the next step is to form the decile groupings that will help to define the large-, mid-, and small-cap asset classes and to calculate some simple descriptive statistics to make comparisons with the various market indicators. In a distribution of securities ranked by market value, it is best to use several measures of central tendency to get a good sense of any skewness that might be present. To accomplish the task, the mean, median, and weighted-mean market values are calculated for each of the decile groupings in the histogram that define the asset classes. The weighted-mean market value is useful to the equity portfolio manager because it will reflect the influence of market value size on the performance of an index or, in this case, the decile groupings of securities. The breakpoints for the market-value classifications are deciles 1-2 for large-capitalization stocks, 3-5 for mid-caps, and 6-10 for small-caps.

Using data as of September 30, 1997, there were 434 stocks that were placed into deciles 1-2 (See Table 2). The total market value for the large-cap deciles was $7.5 trillion. The weighted-mean market value for the large-cap segment was $51.4 billion, the mean $17.2 billion, and the median $8.3 billion. The very large weighted-mean market value for the segment indicates the powerful influence of huge companies such as GE, Coca Cola, Microsoft, and Exxon on the large-cap population. In fact, it could be argued that the large-cap segment be divided into two, creating a new asset class of "super-capitalization" companies.

Table 2 The S&P Indexes as of September 30, 1997

	SGDB 1-2	S&P 500
Number of Companies	434	500
Total Market Value	$7.5 Trillion	$7.3 Trillion
Wtd. Mean Market Value	$51.4 Billion	$52.6 Billion
Mean Market Value	$17.2 Billion	$14.7 Billion
Median Market Value	$8.3 Billion	$6.6 Billion

In effect, the large-cap segment and the domestic equity population, when measured in total, is dominated by a relatively small number of extremely large stocks. This situation is not unusual around the world, where many of the developed nations' equities markets are also dominated by a relatively small number of super-sized companies.

The dominance of a relatively small number of very large companies in the domestic equity market has a major impact on many of the broad stock market indicators available. The reality is that all of those indexes using a market-value weighted calculation methodology are almost equally influenced by the super-sized companies, regardless of how many securities are covered in the indicator. This includes the Russell 3000, the Wilshire 5000 (Wilshire Associates includes over 6,000 stocks in the Wilshire 5000), and the S&P 1500 SuperComposite indexes.

The use of a different calculation methodology can radically alter the effects of size as measured by market value. For example, the Dow Jones Industrial Average uses a price-weighted calculation methodology that implicitly gives greater weight to the highest priced securities in the indicator. This causes the Dow Jones Industrial Average, which is comprised mainly of companies in deciles 1-2, to be more sensitive to movements in securities with the highest prices per share as opposed to those with the greatest market values.

The middle-capitalization decile grouping for the domestic equity market is defined by deciles 3-5. As of September 30, there were 847 issues that fell into the mid-cap segment (See Table 3). The total market value for the segment was $1.6 trillion, about one fifth of the capitalization of the large-cap segment and, yet, with almost twice as many stocks. Even more dramatic a difference between the large- and mid-cap segments can be found when comparing the weighted mean market values. The mid-cap weighted-mean market value was $2.3 billion, less than one-twentieth the size of the large-cap weighted mean. With a mean market value of $1.9 billion and a median market value of $1.7 billion, it is apparent that the distribution for mid-cap stocks is much "tighter," i.e.. there are no extremely large stocks that dominate the segment, or equivalently, an index or portfolio of mid-cap stocks.

Table 3 The S&P Indexes as of September 30, 1997

	SGDB 3-5	S&PMidCap 400
Number of Companies	847	400
Total Market Value	$1.6 Trillion	$878.8 Billion
Wtd. Mean Market Value	$2.3 Billion	$3.4 Billion
Mean Market Value	$1.9 Billion	$2.2 Billion
Median Market Value	$1.7 Billion	$1.8 Billion

Not surprisingly, because the mid-cap segment, as well as the small-cap deciles, have discrete upper boundaries, the distributions tend to be tighter as companies that get larger over time graduate to higher deciles. In the large-cap deciles, there is no upper limit and, therefore, companies can, and do, get very, very big, resulting in the skewed distribution that we observe.

The small-capitalization segment of the domestic equity market is not as neatly defined as the large- and mid-cap deciles. That is because there are about as many definitions for the small-cap population as there are small-cap stocks. One problem is that many portfolio managers that specialize in small-cap stocks tend to hold onto "winners" in their portfolios, including stocks such as Intel and Microsoft, which were small-cap stocks not that long ago, causing the median market value for holdings by small-cap managers to be surprisingly high. The small-cap segment also contains most of the stocks in the total domestic equity population, and the range of market values within the segment is significant and, as a consequence, it is often divided into two subsets.

The total small-cap segment comprises deciles 6-10, with a market value of $1.1 trillion as of September 30, 1997 (See Table 4). Deciles 6-10 contained 5,020 stocks out of the total population 6,301 issues in the domestic equity population. The total small-cap population is then broken down into two subsets according to their institutional "investability," i.e.. the liquidity of the stocks, with deciles 6-8 being considered institutional small-cap and deciles 9-10, micro-cap. Deciles 6-8 contained 1,422 stocks and had a total market value of $742 billion, while deciles 9-10 had 3,598 issues, with a combined market value of $333 billion.

Table 4 The S&P Indexes as of September 30, 1997

	SGDB 6-8	SGDB 9-10	SGDB 6-10	S&P SmallCap 600
Number of Companies	1422	3598	5020	600
Total Market Value	$742.0 Billion	$332.6 Billion	$1.1 Trillion	$369.6 Billion
Wtd. Mean Market Value	$596.6 Million	$142.6 Million	$456.1 Million	$922.1 Million
Mean Market Value	$521.8 Million	$92.4 Million	$214.1 Million	$616.0 Million
Median Market Value	$482.8 Million	$73.5 Million	$123.0 Million	$514.8 Million

A quick examination of the summary statistics for the two small-cap subsets indicates why it is logical for the division. The weighted-mean market value for deciles 6-8 was $597 million, while for deciles 9-10 it was $143 million. Similarly, the mean market values were $522 and $92 million, respectively, while the median values were $482 and $74 million, respectively.

Clearly, measuring the performance of small-cap stocks presents a number of challenges because of the very large number of securities and the diversity in size within deciles 6-10. Even by segregating the small-cap population into two subsets leaves two fairly large groupings of stocks. Now it is more apparent as to why the NASDAQ small-cap universe is removed from the grand total of issues listed within the S&P Stock Guide Database. These issues would create another subset of micro, or "mini-micro" stocks.

With the domestic equity market defined, we can now examine some of the issues associated with building indexes to measure the various asset classes. Also, the analysis can be extended to some of the major market indicators that are used today.

Perhaps the single most relevant issue to the construction of new and existing indexes is the segmentation of the total population into the three primary asset classes of large-, mid-, and small-capitalization stocks. The "borders" between the classes will always cause some "friction" in the compilation process. That is, the decile breakdowns are very attractive in their simplicity, defining the market neatly at a point in time. The reality is that the market values for the 6,301 stocks in the domestic equity population are constantly changing. That means any index providers who set as their objective the performance measurement of a specific stock group, such as the mid-cap segment, are faced with stocks that "drift" in size between segments. Thus, the index management process plays a crucial role in determing how often to rebalance the constituents within an index or whether sampling makes more sense to help smooth the effect of drift. The small-capitalization segment of the market presents index providers with a particular dilemma because of the large number of securities and the differences between the largest and smallest within the classification. Also, there are many small-cap stocks that trade infrequently and not at all for long periods of time, which makes building indexes for direct and indirect investment much more difficult.

The Standard & Poor's family of domestic equity indexes are market value-weighted benchmarks that utilize a sampling methodology to address the effect of market value drift and its resulting impact on turnover. The S&P 500 is by far the most well known of the market benchmarks and has the longest history of any of the S&P Indexes. The S&P 500 was created in 1957, although its predecessor index has a history that dates back to 1923. The original S&P Index contained 233 stocks, representing 26 industry groups.

The objective of the original 233-stock index and the modern S&P 500 is to represent the U.S. stock market by capturing the performance of the most important industry groups in the domestic economy. The S&P Indexes represented a major portion of the domestic equity market's total capitalization—85% or more—for many years going into the 1970s, when the percentage began to fall as the population of U.S. stocks increased.

By the later half of the 1980s, the S&P 500's representation of the total domestic equity population had fallen to about 70% and, consequently, it could no longer be considered the definitive "market" index. As a result, S&P decided to broaden the coverage of the market by introducing a mid- and small-cap index and, then, combining the three indexes to form a new composite market benchmark. The S&P MidCap 400 was launched in 1991, followed by the SmallCap 600 in 1994, and the SuperComposite 1500 in 1995.

With the SuperComposite 1500 now representing the institutionally investable domestic equity market, the S&P 500 should be viewed as the large-cap component of the S&P family of equity index benchmarks. In fact, comparing the S&P 500 to deciles 1-2 (see Table 2 on page 30) of the Stock Guide Database large-cap segment, we can see why the S&P 500 is truly representative of large-cap stock performance. The S&P 500 had a weighted-mean market value of $52.6 billion as of September 30, 1997, which compared to a weighted-mean market value of $51.4 billion for deciles 1-2. The other descriptive data, the mean and median market values, provide similar comparisons. The mean and median for the S&P 500 were $14.7 and $6.6 billion, respectively, while for deciles 1-2 they were $17.2 and $8.3 billion, respectively.

The MidCap 400 and SmallCap 600, likewise, compare favorably with their respective segments. For example the weighted-mean market value for the MidCap 400 was $3.4 billion (see Table 3 on page 31), with a mean of $2.2 billion and a median value of $1.8 billion, respectively. For the mid-cap segment of the Database, deciles 3-5, the weighted average market value was $2.3 billion, the mean $1.9 billion, and the median $1.7 billion.

The S&P SmallCap 600 must be compared to deciles 6-8 (see Table 4 on page 32), the institutionally investable portion of the small-cap population and the segment it was designed to represent. The SmallCap 600 had a weighted-mean market value of $922 million as of September 30, 1997, which was higher than the $596 million for the deciles 6-8. This reflected the run-up in technology and other "hot" issues within the Index and the fact that S&P keeps turnover low as a result of the sampling methodology. Interestingly, the higher weighted-mean market value compares extremely well with the typical mutual fund devoted to small-cap stocks, a reflection of portfolio managers' holding onto winners. The mean and median market values for the SmallCap 600 compare more favorably to the 6-8 decile grouping. The mean and median market values for the SmallCap 600 were $616 million and $515 million, respectively, while the mean for deciles 6-8 was $522 million and the median, $483 million.

The S&P 1500 SuperComposite achieves S&P's stated goal of measuring the broad market, in terms of total capitalization. As of September 30, 1997, the S&P 1500 represented about 85% of the total domestic equity market value (See Table 5). Because the S&P 1500 contains 4,801 fewer securities, mostly small and micro-cap, the descriptive statistics are not directly comparable to the Stock Guide Database domestic equity universe.

The NASDAQ Composite Index measures the performance of the NASDAQ marketplace, its stated objective. Note that this is not an asset or sub-asset class but, instead, a valuation of all the securities listed on an exchange. It is a market-value weighted index, with a total market value of $1.5 trillion as of December 31, 1996. The NASDAQ Composite Index has data available historically to 1971. The Index was comprised of 5,577

Table 5 S&P Indexes as of September 30, 1997

	SGDB Universe	S&P 1500
Number of Companies	6301	1500
Total Market Value	$10.2 Trillion	$8.6 Trillion
Wtd. Mean Market Value	$38.1 Billion	$45.3 Billion
Mean Market Value	$1.6 Billion	$5.7 Billion
Median Market Value	$188.9 Million	$1.4 Billion

securities at year-end. However the Index's performance is dominated by the largest stocks listed on the NASDAQ market. For example, with stocks such as Microsoft and Intel, the NASDAQ's top 100 companies accounted for almost half the Index's total market value. That makes the Index's performance somewhat of a hybrid, reflecting the large-cap NAS-DAQ stocks' performance most of the time and the 5,000-plus small-cap NASDAQ stocks' performance in aggregate on rare occassions. However, the benchmark provides the investor exactly what the NAS-DAQ marketplace behaves like on a market value-weighted basis.

The Dow Jones Industrial Average does not fit within the framework of our analysis because of Dow Jones' calculation methodology. The use of a simple arithematic average for calculation means that the weighting methodology is implicitly based on the price of each of the constituents. As was pointed out earlier, the Industrial Average can be severely affect-ed by the price movement of any constituent—not necessarily the largest either—on any given day. That it why it is not unusual for the Dow Jones Industrials to be down on a particular day while the rest of the "market" is up. It is also the reason that the Industrial Average is not used as a benchmark for performance measurement by professional investors. The capitalization-weighted methodology predominates in that market as evi-denced by the more-than 90% of money managers, pension plan spon-sors, and consultants who use the S&P 500 and other S&P indexes.

Clearly, understanding what goes into the creation and dissemination of a stock market index can have a significant impact on its usage. The many thousands of domestic equity indexes available as measures for performance or, more importantly, that serve as the basis for index funds. means that investors should spend some time in evaluating the quality of the product on which they will be dependent. We have attempted to pro-vide a rational approach to evaluating indexes and hope that investors will find the process useful and rewarding.

The First Index Mutual Fund

John C. Bogle
Founder and Chairman of the Board
The Vanguard Group

Introduction

In April 1995, just three years ago, Vanguard published a booklet that we had the temerity to title "The Triumph of Indexing." The booklet described the whys and wherefores of the remarkable success of the concept of indexing, as manifested in the investment performance of Vanguard Index Trust—the first index mutual fund—and the development of the Vanguard family of index funds. It included the Chairman's Letters I had written for the 1994 Annual Reports of Vanguard's six index funds, then composed of 21 separate portfolios—14 portfolios of various classes of U.S. stocks, international stocks, high-grade bonds, and balanced (stock/bond) investments, and seven portfolios focused on tax-managed or life-strategy (asset allocation) goals. By then, total assets of the Vanguard index funds had reached $18 *billion*, a remarkable growth from $11 *million* when we formed the first (Index 500) portfolio of Vanguard Index Trust in 1975.

In the introduction, I noted the remarkable success of index investment strategies over the long term, even as I disclaimed the notion that the recent performance of the Standard & Poor's 500 Composite Stock Price Index—outpacing more than 85% of all actively managed equity mutual funds during the previous three years—was either sustainable or repeatable. Nonetheless, I looked forward to accelerating growth for indexing as growing numbers of investors came to recognize that "the index fund is the proverbial better mousetrap . . . a very efficient and productive means of investing in the securities markets . . . providing extraordinarily broad diversification at extraordinarily low cost."

And accelerating growth, as it turned out, was just what came to pass. In the subsequent two years, Vanguard index assets have increased more than fourfold to a total now approaching $100 billion, including nearly $50 billion in the original 500 Portfolio. Indeed, standing alone, without counting the other $200 billion of "conventional" fund assets now managed by Vanguard, the Vanguard index funds would rank as the seventh largest complex in the entire mutual fund industry. What is more, our original concept, having met with such a fine reception from investors, is finally (and, I suppose, inevitably) being copied by many other fund groups, albeit neither with much enthusiasm nor with particularly attractive operating cost levels (other than through fee waivers that are but temporary) for investors. Be that as it may, however, we have come a long way since "Bogle's folly"—a phrase I heard all too often from the late 1970s through the early 1990s—first saw the light of day in 1975.

In an ideal world, the basis for the growth of index mutual funds would have been the gradual, if grudging, acceptance of the simple theory that underlies index investing: Investors as a group cannot *outperform* the market, because they are the market. And from that theory flows the reality: Investors as a group must *underperform* the market, because the costs of participation—largely operating expenses, advisory fees, and portfolio transaction costs—constitute a direct deduction from the market's return. Unlike actively managed funds, an index fund pays no advisory fees and limits portfolio turnover, thus holding these costs to minimal levels. And therein lies its advantage. That, essentially, is all you need to know to understand why index funds must provide superior long-term returns.

This self-evident reality, of course, wouldn't matter if experienced professional money managers were able to take advantage of tyros and amateurs. But in highly efficient markets, that doesn't happen. It doesn't happen because it is the professionals who set the prices that are paid by expert and novice alike. And the record is clear that most major financial markets are indeed highly efficient. The body of evidence-some would say *brute* evidence—is so abundant as to defy substantive rebuttal. The facts are: (a) most professional managers fail to outpace appropriate market indexes, and (b) those who do so rarely repeat in the future their success in the past.

Alas, these compelling propositions account for but a fraction of the recent growth of index funds. Rather, the extraordinarily favorable performance of the S&P 500 Index funds—performance we disclaimed in "The Triumph of Indexing" early in 1995—has not only continued, it has gotten even better during the remainder of 1995, in 1996, and so far in 1997. Sorry to say, index funds are "a hot product"—*The Wall Street Journal* described Vanguard's 500 Portfolio as the "industry darling"—and a significant portion of index fund asset growth appears to be coming from short-term investors who are mutual fund traders seeking quick returns, rather than long-term investors persuaded by the simple theory and the remarkable opportunity for the optimal long-term returns that indexing offers to investors who "stay the course."

But, as this history of the first index fund—the 500 Portfolio of Vanguard Index Trust (initially operating under the name First Index Investment Trust)—recounts, the first 23 years have had many ups and downs, many challenges and many opportunities. Today, index funds are changing the way investors look at mutual funds—focusing more than ever on the critical issues of cost and diversification. Even if today proves to be, as well it might, a momentary peak in popularity for the remarkably popular and successful index funds based on the S&P 500 Index, I believe the fundamentals of low-cost indexing are so strong as to prevail over the long pull. Having survived early defeat, as I note at the end of this story, the index fund can also survive victory.

Nearly six years ago, on January 15, 1992, at a speech for the Newcomen Society entitled "Vanguard's First Century," I reflected on the role of indexing in the mutual fund field. At that time, the Vanguard Index Trust 500 Portfolio had risen to become the seventh largest of all U.S. equity funds. I predicted that "market indexing will come into its own as a major force . . . and that Vanguard will at long last confront some competition." Surely that prediction has now been justified.

I also predicted that "by the turn of the twentieth century, our 500 Portfolio will be the largest equity mutual fund in the world." Now that "the first index mutual fund" is the second largest of all equity funds, and rapidly gaining ground on the leader, that prediction doesn't seem quite so far-fetched.

I believe it will come to pass, on schedule.

John C. Bogle
July 23, 1997

The Beginning

Here is what happened and how it happened.[1]

I suppose the beginning of the first index mutual fund goes back to 1949. When I was a junior at Princeton University looking for an idea for my senior thesis, I sought a topic that literally no one had ever written about in a serious academic paper. I stumbled upon an article in *Fortune* magazine (December 1949) entitled "Big Money in Boston." It was the first time I had ever thought about the mutual fund industry. When I read that "mutual funds may look like pretty small change," but constituted a "rapidly expanding and somewhat contentious industry" that could be of "great potential significance to U.S. business," I knew I had found my topic.

After a year-and-a-half of research and writing this thesis, prepared by a callow and idealistic young scholarship student working his way through a great University, I concluded with several main themes, including suggesting that the industry's future growth could be maximized by a "reduction of sales loads and management fees"; that "fund investment objectives must be stated explicitly"; that mutual funds should avoid creating "the expectations of miracles from management"; and (based on the evidence I had ascertained) should "make no claim for superiority over the market averages." Others have interpreted these thoughts as a precursor of my later interest in matching the market with an index fund. Honestly, I don't know whether they were or not. Today, nonetheless, if I had to name the moment when the seed was planted that germinated into the presentation of the first index mutual fund to the Vanguard Board in 1975, that would be it.

The basic ideas go back a few years earlier. In 1969–1971, Wells Fargo Bank had worked from academic models to develop the principles and techniques leading to index investing. John A. McQuown and William L. Fouse pioneered the effort, which led to the construction of a $6 million index account for the pension fund of Samsonite Corporation. With a strategy based on an equal-weighted index of New York Stock Exchange equities, its execution was described as "a nightmare." The strategy was abandoned in 1976, replaced with a market-weighted strategy using the Standard & Poor's 500 Composite Stock Price Index. The

---

[1]Based on my Princeton senior thesis, presentations to the Vanguard Board of Directors, extensive notes taken as the events occurred, 22 consecutive Chairman's Letters in Vanguard Index Trust Annual Reports, and my speeches over the same period.

first such models were accounts run by Wells Fargo for its own pension fund and for Illinois Bell.

In 1971, Batterymarch Financial Management of Boston independently decided to pursue the idea of index investing. The developers were Jeremy Grantham and Dean LeBaron, two of the founders of the firm. Grantham described the idea at a Harvard Business School seminar in 1971, but found no takers until 1973. For its efforts, Batterymarch won the prize for the "Dubious Achievement Award" from *Pensions & Investments* magazine in 1972.[2] It was two years later, in December 1974, when the firm finally attracted its first client.

By the time American National Bank in Chicago created a common trust fund modeled on the S&P 500 Index in 1974 (requiring a minimum investment of $100,000), the idea had begun to spread from academia— and these three firms that were the first professional believers—to a public forum.

Gradually, the press began to comment on index investing. A *cri de coeur* calling for index funds to be formed came from each of several intelligent and farsighted observers.[3] I still have those articles that I read nearly 23 years ago; they read just as well today.

The first article was "Challenge to Judgment," by Paul A. Samuelson, Professor of Finance at Massachusetts Institute of Technology. In *The Journal of Portfolio Management* (Fall 1974), he pleaded "that, at the least, some large foundation set up an in-house portfolio that tracks the S&P 500 Index-if only for the purpose of setting up a naive model against which their in-house gunslingers can measure their prowess. . . . Perhaps CREF (College Retirement Equities Fund) can be induced to set up a pilot-plant operation of an unmanaged diversified fund, but I would not

---

[2] A fine history of the Wells Fargo effort is presented in Peter Bernstein's *Capital Ideas* (Macmillan, Inc., 1992). The Batterymarch story is told in *Program Trading* (J.K. Lasser Institute, 1987), by Jeffrey D. Miller.

[3] I should note that one of the earliest calls for indexing came from a book that I did not read until some years later: *A Random Walk Down Wall Street*, by Princeton University Professor Burton S Malkiel (W.W. Norton, 1973). Dr. Malkiel suggested "A New Investment Instrument: a no-load, minimum-management-fee mutual fund that simply buys the hundreds of stocks making up the market averages and does no trading (of securities). . . . Fund spokesmen are quick to point out, 'you can't buy the averages.' It's about time the public could." He urged that the New York Stock Exchange sponsor such a fund and run it on a nonprofit basis, but if it "is unwilling to do it, I hope some other institution will." In 1977, four years after he wrote those words, he joined the Board of Directors of First Index Investment Trust and the other Vanguard funds, positions in which he has served with distinction to this day.

bet on it. . . . The American Economic Association might contemplate setting up for its members a no-load, no management-fee, virtually no-transaction-turnover fund" (noting, however, the perhaps insurmountable difficulty that "there may be less supernumerary wealth to be found among 20,000 economists than among 20,000 chiropractors").

Dr. Samuelson concluded his "challenge to judgment" by explicitly calling for those who disagreed that a passive index would outperform most active managers to dispose of "that uncomfortable brute fact (that it is virtually impossible for academics with access to public records to identify any consistently excellent performers) in the only way that any fact is disposed of-by producing brute evidence to the contrary." There is no record that anyone tried to produce such brute evidence, nor is it likely that it could have been produced. But Dr. Samuelson had laid down an implicit challenge for *somebody, somewhere* to start an index fund.

A year later, Charles D. Ellis, President of Greenwich Associates, wrote a seminal article entitled "The Loser's Game" in *The Financial Analysts* Journal for July/August 1975. Ellis quickly offered a provocative and bold statement: "The investment management business is built upon a simple and basic belief: Professional managers can beat the market. That premise appears to be false." He pointed out that over the prior decade, 85% of institutional investors had underperformed the return of the S&P 500 Index, largely because "money management has become a Loser's Game. . . . Institutional investors have become, and will continue to be, the dominant feature of their own environment . . . causing the transformation that took money management from a Winner's Game to a Loser's Game. The ultimate outcome is determined by who can lose the fewest points, not who can win them." He went on to note that "gambling in a casino where the house takes 20% of every pot is obviously a Loser's Game."

Finally, Ellis went to the underlying economics of the matter: If equities provide an average return of 9% a year, and a manager generates 30% portfolio turnover at a cost of 3% of the principal value on both the sales and the reinvestment of the proceeds (a reduction in return equal to 1.8% of assets per year) and charges management and custody fees equal to 0.2% (low!), the active manager incurs costs of 2%. Therefore, he must achieve an annual return of +11% before these costs—that is, 22% above the market's return—just to equal the gross market return. (That 2% aggregate cost remains pretty much the same—although of a somewhat different composition—for mutual funds in 1997, 22 years later.) While Ellis did not call for the formation of an index fund, he did ask: "Does the index necessarily lead to an entirely passive index portfolio?" He answered, "No, it doesn't necessarily lead in that direction. Not quite. But if you can't beat the market, you should certainly consider joining it. An index fund is one way." In the real world, of course, few managers indeed have consistently been able to add more than those two percentage points of annual return necessary merely to match the index, and even those few have been exceptionally difficult to identify in advance.

The third article, by Associate Editor A.F. Ehrbar, appeared in *Fortune*, the magazine that in 1949 had provided me with my original inspiration to write about mutual funds. In July 1975, in an article entitled "Some Kinds of Mutual Funds Make Sense," Ehrbar concluded some things that seem pretty obvious today: "While funds cannot consistently outperform the market, they can consistently underperform it by generating excessive research costs (i.e., management fees) and trading costs. . . . It is clear that prospective buyers of mutual funds should look over the costs before making any decisions." He concluded that "funds actually do worse than the market." He had little hope that the mutual fund industry would rush to fill the gap created by the new view that cost is the principal reason that investors as a group are unable to outpace the market index.

Ehrbar despaired about the remote likelihood that an index mutual fund would be created very soon, noting that "there has not been much pioneering lately. While the mutual-fund industry has not provided an index fund, the American Bank of Chicago has put together a common trust fund that aims to match the performance of the S&P 500 Index." (He failed to note that, with an annual fee of 0.8%, it could not possibly do so.) But he described the best alternative for mutual fund investors: "a no-load mutual fund with low expenses and management fees, about the same degree of risk as the market as a whole, and a policy of always being fully invested." He could not have realized that he had described, with some considerable accuracy, the first index mutual fund, soon to be formed. But that is exactly what he had done.

Confronted with those three articles, I couldn't stand it any longer. It now seemed clear that the newly formed Vanguard Group (then only a few months old) ought to be "in the vanguard" of this new logical concept, so strongly supported by data on past fund performance, so well known in academia but acknowledged by few in the industry. It was the opportunity of a lifetime: to at once prove that the basic principles enunciated in the articles could be put into practice and work effectively, and to mark this upstart of a firm as a pioneer in a new wave of industry development. With luck and hard work, the idea that began to germinate in my mind in 1949 could finally become a reality.

The Introduction of the First Index Fund

When Vanguard was formed, it represented a unique departure from the typical industry form of organization—a privately (or publicly) owned mutual fund management company, in which the profits from fees paid by fund shareholders were garnered by the individuals owning the investment manager—to a "mutual" type organization in which the fund shareholders owned the manager, with those profits reverting to them. The Vanguard Group was owned by the funds it administered. It would operate on an *at-cost* basis, the better to put the shareholder in the driver's seat (rather than reposing in the back seat, with the management company driving the car for a fee). Such a structure, we reasoned, would enable Vanguard to deliver extremely low operating and management costs to shareholders. We said "costs matter" then, and we have repeated it ever since.

Vanguard began operations on May 1, 1975, with a limited charter: to direct the day-to-day administrative, financial, and legal operations—but neither the investment management nor the marketing activities—of what had been previously known as the Wellington Group of Funds. (Responsibility for those two activities would remain with Wellington Management Company.) We were a tiny enterprise, but we had great visions of the future, and we wanted to do everything we could within our narrow mandate. We concluded that we had a remarkable opportunity to run an unmanaged, low-cost index fund and to have the market to ourselves for at least a few years. No one else wanted to start a low-cost (indeed, 'at-cost') mutual fund. After all, a sponsor's objective in forming a mutual fund is to increase assets under management, thereby increasing the advisory fees and thus the profits the firm earns. For better or worse in the fund business, that is "the American Way."

There were but three persons on our tiny staff—in essence, our entire strategic team—in a position to develop the investment concepts and the marketing plan for the index fund: myself, James S. Riepe (a truly remarkable young man whose promise in 1975 has been realized; today he is one of the most highly regarded leaders in the mutual fund industry, a managing director of T. Rowe Price and former Chairman of the Investment Company Institute), and a young Princeton graduate and Wharton School M.B.A., Jan M. Twardowski (now President of Frank

Russell Securities Company), who did the awesome statistical work required for us to make our case with completeness, accuracy, and professionalism.

As the summer of 1975 began, the three of us enthusiastically set to work to make the case for an index fund, making the formal proposal to the Directors at the Board meeting on September 18, 1975. At the meeting, most of the discussion focused on whether this unique venture would be within the mandate that precluded our new company from engaging in investment advisory or marketing services—a mandate that had been won only after a considerable internal struggle. But we were able to persuade the Board that no advice would be involved and that a public underwriting could be handled by an outside syndicate of brokerage firms. The Directors accepted this tenuous logic and approved the idea. The Declaration of Trust for First Index Investment Trust was filed on December 31, 1975.

In our final proposal to the Directors, in April 1976, we nervously prepared a draft prospectus. I sent the Board the articles referred to above and projected the costs of managing an index fund to be 0.3% per year in operating expenses and 0.2% per year in transaction costs. Since fund annual costs at that time appeared to be about 2.0%, I concluded that an index fund should reasonably be expected to provide an annual return of +1.5% above a managed fund.

Ever vigorously selling the idea, we also presented a table showing that $1 million invested at an assumed market return of 10% would be worth $17.5 million after 30 years, while a similar investment at 8.5% (using the 1.5% cost differential) would have been worth but $11.5 million. The cost saving resulted, I noted, in a $6 million payoff that was a mere *six times* the original amount of the initial investment. (To this very day, I use that example in my work at Vanguard.) "Great rewards grow from small differences in cost" was my simple thesis. I reinforced that concept with the historical record, showing that the average annual return of all mutual funds for the period 1945–1975 had been +9.7%, compared to +11.3% for the S&P 500 Index. The difference of +1.6%—actually, as it happens, slightly greater than the +1.5% illustrated in my compound interest table—represents, to this day, a reasonable, if conservative. approximation of the long-term advantage of an index fund.

The Board recognized that an index-style mutual fund would break new ground. Unlike a pension account or pooled trust fund, it would have to deal with daily cash flows and the costs of handling thousands—perhaps hundreds of thousands—of shareholder accounts. Our initial plan described how we proposed to minimize commission costs on portfolio transactions and develop fund operational efficiencies that would not defeat our ability to closely match the index.

After getting our responses to the questions they raised over the next few months, the Directors in May 1976 approved the filing with the Securities and Exchange Commission of a prospectus and offering statement for First Index Investment Trust. (The name we chose withstood challenge from the Commission staff and from a number of adversaries.) Now it was my job to find some way Vanguard—this new "at-cost" enterprise—could raise the capital to start an index fund without our spending any money. (We couldn't afford to!) Our objective, I brashly wrote to the Board, "will be to underwrite an index fund in the $50 million to $150 million range."

The Underwriting of the First Index Fund: 1976

In those early days of our history, the Vanguard funds were "load funds," sold exclusively through brokers. Sales of mutual fund shares were hard to come by following a near -50% drop in stock prices in 1973–1974. We needed a "one shot" underwriting so that the new fund had the critical mass of assets needed to own hundreds of stocks. So we immediately set to work trying to enlist a top group of national brokers, including Bache Halsey Stuart (now Prudential Securities), Paine Webber Jackson & Curtis, and Reynolds Securities, to manage a public offering. After a fair amount of persuasion by us, they all came aboard, but conditioned their agreement on our persuading a fourth major firm to join them. That firm turned out to be Dean Witter & Company, which became lead manager. We had enlisted the four strongest mutual fund brokers on Wall Street. And at Dean Witter, I found a real champion for the idea. Roger Wood was that man. He was an executive in Dean Witter's Initial Public Offering group. He believed in the Trust and firmly assumed leadership of the underwriting.

As we assembled the underwriting group, our confidence that we would enjoy a successful initial offering soared when *Fortune* magazine's June edition appeared. A banner headline announced "Index Funds—An Idea Whose Time Is Coming," followed by a remarkable *six-solid-page* article by the persistent editor A.F. Ehrbar. He announced that "index funds now threaten to reshape the entire world of professional money management." Focusing entirely on pension funds, he wrote that "their present management is terrible. Instead of doing as well as the market averages, the corporate executives charged with the responsibility for pension funds have turned the funds over to a group of experts who systematically do worse"—even, he added, "before fees are deducted." Ehrbar then buttressed his position with a formidable stream of rigorous data and a detailed exposition of index theory, and set forth and then rebutted each possible objection. It was a powerful elixir for Jim Riepe, Jan Twardowski, and me.

It may not have been a turning point, but it gave us the strength we needed to carry on.[4]

Jim Riepe and I participated in "road shows" in a dozen cities around the country, but the brokerage-firm registered representatives (today, account executives) did not seem particularly taken with the idea of a fund that said, in essence, that their profession—selecting well-managed funds for their clients-was "a loser's game." Nonetheless, our underwriting group was able to raise enough money to provide the seed capital we needed. At the closing of the public offering, we had raised $11.4 million—a far cry from our initial objective of $150 million, but enough to get the fund started. First Index Investment Trust began operations on August 31, 1976. From that modest base its assets would grow at a remarkably steady annual compound rate of 53% during the next two decades, taking assets to $42 billion on June 30, 1997 (See Figure 1).

The initial press reception to the announcement of the underwriting had been reasonably good, but bereft of a single hint that the index fund represented—as Jim, Jan, and I believed—the beginning of a new era for the mutual fund industry. The most enthusiastic press comments came from Professor (and later, Nobel Laureate in Economics) Paul Samuelson. Writing in his *Newsweek* column in August 1976, he expressed delight that there had finally been a response to his earlier challenge: "As yet there exists no convenient fund that apes the whole market, requires no load, and keeps commissions, turnover and management fees to the feasible minimum."

---

[4]Incidentally, reread today, 22 years later, the Ehrbar article still carries a freshness that suggests it had just been written. However, the full realization of the threat of indexing to "reshape the entire world of money management" still remains on the horizon.

Figure 1

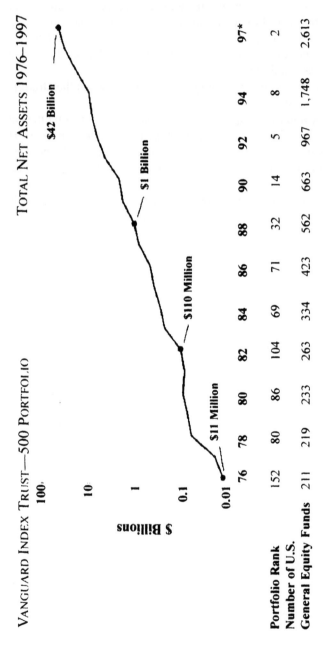

VANGUARD INDEX TRUST—500 PORTFOLIO

TOTAL NET ASSETS 1976–1997

	76	78	80	82	84	86	88	90	92	94	97*
Portfolio Rank	152	80	86	104	69	71	32	14	5	8	2
Number of U.S.											
General Equity Funds	211	219	233	263	334	423	562	663	967	1,748	2,613

*Through 6/30/97

Now such a fund lay in prospect. "Sooner than I dared expect," he wrote, "my explicit prayer has been answered. There is coming to market, I see from a crisp new prospectus, something called the First Index Investment Trust." He conceded that the fund met only five of his six requirements: (1) availability for investors of modest means; (2) proposing to match the broad-based S&P 500 Index; (3) carrying an extremely small annual expense charge of only 0.20%; (4) offering extremely low portfolio turnover; and (5) "best of all, giving the broadest diversification needed to maximize mean return with minimum portfolio variance and volatility." His sixth requirement—that it be a no-load fund—had not been met, but, he graciously conceded, "a professor's prayers are rarely answered in full."

As it was to happen, Dr. Samuelson's final prayer would be answered just six months later. But until then, given our obvious need to enlist broker support for an underwriting, the Trust carried an initial sales charge (low by mutual fund standards in those days—6% on smaller investments, tapered down to 1% on investments of $1 million or more). However, Vanguard was soon to change its distribution strategy. In February 1977, after an extremely contentious Board meeting at which the day was carried by a close vote of 8 to 5, the funds in The Vanguard Group, after nearly a half-century of participation in a dealer-distribution system operated by Wellington Management Company, terminated Wellington's contract and eliminated all sales charges. The Directors of First Index Investment Trust and the other Vanguard funds had overturned their initial ban on Vanguard's providing distribution services and made an unprecedented conversion to a "no-load" distribution system.

But there remained a multitude of strident critics of indexing. They were well described by Rex Sinquefield of American National Bank, an early advocate of the concept. Writing in *Pensions & Investments* he said: "As talk of market (i.e., index) funds moves from the discussion of debate, the exchange is often enlivened but seldom enlightened. Critics of these funds have suggested that market funds are a 'cop-out' and a search for mediocrity. Some have said they are downright un-american. Few, if any, investment concepts have been the object of so much scornful ridicule. The vitriol and paranoia permeating so much of the criticism reveals a profound misconception of the role that market funds should play in institutional portfolios." [Amused by the opposition, Steven C. Leuthold, an astute investment adviser, published a cartoon spoofing the detractors of index funds. It was captioned INDEX FUNDS ARE UNAMERICAN! (See Figure 2.)

Figure 2

Courtesy of the Leuthold Group.

When Sinquefield wrote those words in 1975, we had not yet filed our Fund—designed for individual investors—and when we did, in mid-1976, the criticism was hardly muted. It was described as "Bogle's folly" more than once. Fidelity Chairman Edward C. Johnson III doubted Fidelity would soon follow Vanguard's lead. "I can't believe," he told the press, "that the great mass of investors are [sic] going to be satisfied with just receiving average returns. The name of the game is to be the best."

Another competitor put out a flyer asking rhetorically, "Who wants to be operated on by an average surgeon, be advised by an average lawyer, or be an average registered representative, or do anything no better or worse than average?" Pointing out that the word "average" meant "mediocre," it continued, "we don't think that describes what most people want from their professional managers." The flyer, of course, failed to acknowledge that few mutual funds had been able to achieve 'average market returns." (As a group, in fact, they were falling short by −1.6% a year.) The fund manager struck hard at the concept: "We are going on record now because of the wave of publicity about index funds-funds that, by their charter, need to do no better than the average. As professionals, we reject the thought of settling for the averages. Whatever road other fund managers may take, we are going to continue to strive for excellence." (For the record, this fund had consistently lagged the index before, and has maintained this unimpressive standard ever after.) The flyer concluded with an appeal intended to be inspirational: "No one came up with a handful of dust when he reached for the stars." Clearly, as it was to turn out, most investors were to continue to do just that!

The expected reaction to any new idea—the electric lightbulb, the tank, the telephone, the airplane, to mention just a few—is that it won't work: skepticism about the idea, condemnation upon the formation, attack when the idea becomes reality. Given the radical shortfall from our optimistic $150 million target in the underwriting, we were less than ecstatic about the final *figure*. But, Jan, Jim, and I were indeed ecstatic at the critical *fact*: We had our index fund! We had $11 million, and we promptly invested it in the stocks in the S&P 500 Index.

The first index fund now existed. By December 31, 1976, assets had grown to $14 million—ranking the fund #152 in assets among 211 equity funds.

The Early Development of the First Index Fund: 1977–1982

We had hoped to immediately invest in all of the stocks in the S&P 500 Index in their exact proportions. However, given our limited assets and the transaction costs that would have been involved in buying all 500 stocks, the initial portfolio included just 280 stocks—the 200 largest stocks (representing almost 80% of the weight of the Index) plus 80 stocks selected by various optimization models to match the profile of the remaining 220 stocks in the Index, using industry groups, market capitalizations, price/earnings ratios, and the like. Jan Twardowski, designated as the fund's first portfolio manager, did an inspired job of running it. Under his direction, the successful tracking of the Index return that the fund has maintained to this day began, even with a marginally under-diversified portfolio and the significant transaction costs involved in those ancient days when commissions—notably on smaller lots—were much higher than they are today, and when there was no computer technology to facilitate the optimization process.

But we were off and running, and that was all that mattered. In the Trust's first Annual Report, for the "stub" year 1976, issued on January 30, 1977, we could proudly say that "First Index Investment Trust is the first and only investment company that offers an index-matching account . . . responding to the clear statistical evidence that, for the professional and amateur investor alike, matching the Standard & Poor's 500 Index has been a tremendous challenge. We see growing markets for the Trust. as increasing thousands of investors come to utilize the index fund for the 'core' of their common stock investments." (In mid-1997, 20 years later. I cannot help reflecting that none of us could have ever imagined the substantial uptrend in stock prices that would follow, to say nothing of the continuous growth in the assets of our then-tiny index fund baby.)

The Trust's disappointing initial reception was followed by an equally disappointing ongoing acceptance in the marketplace. Despite (or. more likely, because of) the fact that First Index Investment Trust had eliminated sales commissions in February 1977, any sustained inflow of investor capital would have to await some seasoning and some "proof of the pudding" in the fund's performance. In mid-1977, with the Trust's assets languishing at the $17 million level, I sensed an opportunity to increase them substantially. Among the other mutual funds Vanguard was administering was Exeter Fund, an exchange fund (owned by investors who had exchanged low-cost securities for a diversified portfolio). with assets of $58 million. It could not offer new shares for sale and would ultimately have to be merged into another fund. In September. I presented a recommendation to merge it into First Index. After a heated debate, with Wellington Management urging a merger into Windsor Fund, the Board approved my proposal. The Trust's assets more than quadrupled, to $75 million. And at last it had the resources to own all of the 500 stocks in the Index.

Performance languished too. After performing so sensationally in 1972–1976, outpacing nearly 70% of all equity funds (See Figure 3 on page 54), the Index went into a disappointing spell. It outpaced only about one-fourth of the funds during 1977–1979. (This sort of reversal in form, which seems to plague all new fund concepts, is hardly surprising.) But we were about to move into a new decade, in which the Index would begin by outperforming nearly one-half of all traditionally managed equity mutual funds in 1980–1982. Far better days lay on the horizon, but they were not yet visible.

Even so, in an industry where growth was the exception and not the rule, we eked out an increase in assets (thanks to the Exeter merger), and we were encouraged. As 1982 drew to a close, the assets of the first index fund topped $100 million, ending the year at $110 million—ranking #104 among 263 equity funds.

Index Growth Continues: 1983–1986

A boom in the stock market began in late 1982—a boom, indeed, that has continued for 15 years, almost without interruption to this day. Vanguard Index Trust (the name was changed from First Index Investment Trust in March 1980) participated nicely, and the Trust's record was excellent compared with that of managed funds, outperforming nearly three-quarters of all equity funds during 1983–1986.

During this period, the index fund at last had started to catch the fancy of investors. Wells Fargo started the second index mutual fund (Stagecoach Corporate Stock Fund) in 1984. But burdened as it was with an expense ratio of almost 1% a year, it has never succeeded in the marketplace. (At that cost level, it was an oxymoron; it would inevitably fall far short of the performance of the very index it was designed to emulate.[5]) In 1985, two more index funds were formed, offered to institutions rather than individual investors. And while nine new index funds were formed in 1986, they were an odd bunch. Two invested in small-company stocks (in Japan and in the United Kingdom) and no independent

---

[5]That high cost was recently justified by a Wells Fargo spokesperson as a "so we can make a lot of money. The fund is a cash cow."

Figure 3

GENERAL EQUITY FUNDS OUTPERFORMED BY THE S&P 500 INDEX

1972–1997

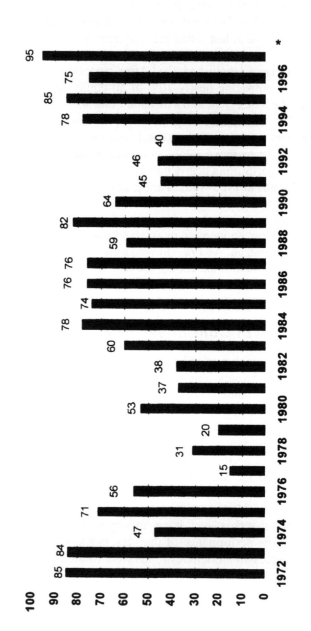

*Through 6/30/97

indexes existed for them. (In fact, these were quantitatively managed sector funds, and these sectors have since provided rather shabby returns to investors.)

The major equity index offering of 1986 was Colonial Index Trust, which carried a sales load of 4.75%. In effect, the public was being offered an index fund that began "behind the eightball"—the amount of the initial sales commission—and, due to an annual expense ratio of about 1.50%, would fall further behind the eightball with each passing year. (The marketplace proved discriminating, and the fund drew limited investor assets, putting itself out of business in 1993.)

Despite these harbingers of success, indexing remained a tiny portion of equity mutual fund assets—less than 1/2% of the total at year-end. There were much stronger signs of life in the private pension fund arena, where indexing had attracted nearly 15% of assets. So the uptrend was taking shape.

As 1986 came to a close, another important step forward for indexing took place: the formation of the first bond index fund for individual investors. (A bond index fund for institutional investors had been started earlier in the year.) There was no question in my mind that bond index funds would come to meet a major need in the marketplace, because most bond mutual funds were grossly overpriced, often carrying both high expenses and excessive sales charges. A low-cost, no-load index fund seemed certain to fill some of that void.

With the formation of Vanguard Bond Market Fund, Vanguard was again the pioneer. (The SEC would not permit the use of the name "Vanguard Bond Index Fund," since the Commission staff could not accept the notion that an index fund could own a relatively small number of individual bonds and hope to closely replicate the performance of an index that included 4,000 bonds.) Vanguard had been laying the groundwork for a bond index fund during much of 1986, but the final inspiration—this is true—came when *Forbes* magazine, writing about second-rate returns and high costs of most fixed-income mutual funds, expressed a crying need for a low-cost bond index fund. The magazine plaintively asked, "Vanguard, where are you when we need you?" Thus, yet another *cri de coeur*—an echo of the pleas of Paul Samuelson and Charles Ellis-provided the final impetus. Once again, we responded. In the ensuing years, our bond index fund was to prove both an artistic and commercial success, admirably tracking the Lehman Brothers Aggregate Bond Index and becoming one of the ten largest bond mutual funds by the end of its first decade.

As 1986 drew to a close, the assets of the first stock index fund had quintupled in only four years, approaching the $500 million milestone-ranking #71 among 423 equity funds.

The March to the $1 Billion Milestone and Beyond: 1987–1990

During the 1987–1990 period, the conceptual framework of the Vanguard index fund "family" was established, and the implementation of the strategy began. Early in 1987, we decided that an index fund modeled on the S&P 500 Index, good as it was, was in some sense not good enough. To be sure, it provided a means to match approximately 75% of the U.S. stock market (the portion of the market represented by the stocks in the S&P 500 Index at that time). It would thus have a powerful tendency to match, with near perfection, the return of the entire stock market over the long term. But it did not include stocks with medium-size and small market capitalizations. There were, however, good theoretical and practical reasons to have an index fund that owned such equities, so as to offer investors complete diversification in the form of ownership participation in the entire U.S. stock market.

At first, we considered converting the 500 Portfolio into such an all-market portfolio, but finally rejected that idea and decided to form an "Extended Market" portfolio covering the "non-500" portion of the market by replicating the Wilshire 4500 Equity Index. Owning all 4,500 issues would have been prohibitively expensive, so we decided to own the 2,000 largest stocks, and use optimization models based on industry diversification, relative price/earnings ratios, etc., to select 800 additional issues. The Extended Market Portfolio was designed and registered with the SEC in August 1987. It would be the second member of the Vanguard index fund family, a burgeoning group that would number 26 in mid-1997. (See Figure 4.)

Pending the launch, scheduled for December 1987, we made a rather fortuitous management move. We decided that two equity index funds—particularly because one had to rely on sophisticated optimization procedures—would require the attention of a professional investment administrator, and had the good fortune to hire George U. (Gus) Sauter, who joined the organization early in October, just two weeks, as it happened, before the Great Crash of October 19, 1987. Perhaps surprisingly, that crash, devastating as it was for stock prices, proved inconsequential in the history of indexing. Both the average equity mutual fund and the S&P

Figure 4

Assets Of The Vanguard Index Fund Family 1976-1997

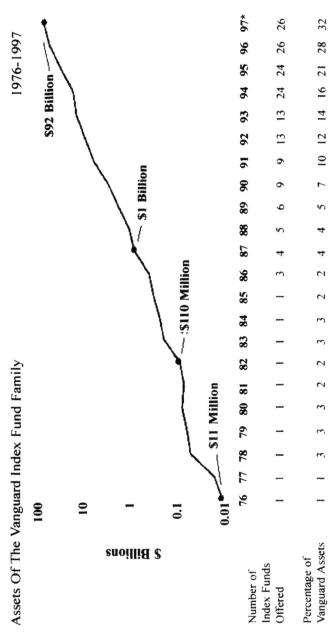

	76	77	78	79	80	81	82	83	84	85	86	87	88	89	90	91	92	93	94	95	96	97*
Number of Index Funds Offered	1	1	1	1	1	1	1	1	1	1	3	4	5	6	9	9	13	13	24	24	26	26
Percentage of Vanguard Assets	1	1	3	3	3	2	3	3	2	2	4	4	5	7	10	12	14	16	21	28	32

*Through 6 30 97

500 Index plummeted something like 30% from the August high to the October low. However, when 1987 came to a close, the Index provided a positive total return of +5.1% for the year, outperforming 76% of all equity funds. Not a sterling gain to be sure, but competitively outstanding.

Vanguard Small Capitalization Stock Fund had been run as an actively managed fund by an external investment adviser. After a long series of fine years, the Fund had provided distinctly inferior results during 1985-1988. In 1989, we impulsively terminated the advisory contract, converting it into a small-capitalization index fund. The SmallCap Portfolio of Vanguard Index Trust was underway, starting with the existing asset base of $30 million. It was to provide fairly consistent competitive returns relative to other blended growth/value small-cap funds, and, under Gus Sauter's direction, it did a remarkable job of matching the Russell 2000 Index of small stocks. The SmallCap Portfolio had become the sixth Vanguard index fund.

During 1990, the growth in the Vanguard index family accelerated again. We considered an international fund modeled on the Morgan Stanley Capital International Europe, Australia, Far East (EAFE) stock index. But we were concerned about the substantial risk of a bubble in the Japanese stock market at that time. In June, we came to grips with the dilemma by starting *two* international funds—one indexed to the European portion of the EAFE Index and the other to the Pacific portion. Fortuitous or smart, our previous evaluation of the Japanese market proved correct, and the decline that began in 1989 has continued to the present day. Nonetheless, we have tracked both indexes with extraordinary precision despite the substantial portfolio turnover costs, stamp taxes, and limited liquidity (relative to the U.S.) in many foreign markets.

In July, we took another step designed to keep us fully competitive in the still-tiny index component of the marketplace (only about 1% of all stock fund assets). We formed Vanguard Institutional Index Fund, modeled on the S&P 500 Index and designed for institutions with substantial assets. To achieve the administrative economies involved, we set a minimum initial investment of $10 million per account. We were quickly able to offer the Fund at an annual expense ratio of just 0.07%, compared to 0.20% for our basic 500 Portfolio. (The expense ratio of the average stock fund was then about 1.30%.) At that expense level, we could be a strong competitor for institutional accounts in the $10–$75 million range. That new fund—little noted by the press or by mutual fund industry observers—has distinguished itself over the ensuing years. Today its assets are $13 billion. Thanks to Gus Sauter's skills, it has succeeded in precisely matching the total return of the theoretical (and cost-free) Index itself, despite the Fund's necessary operating and transaction costs.

Nineteen Ninety also saw the first stirrings of stronger competition entering the index field. Fidelity, despite its commitment to aggressive active management, started two stock index funds, both modeled on the S&P 500 Index, and a U.S. bond index fund. However, Fidelity's heart did not seem to be in those introductions. One stock index fund was part of its then-new Spartan Fund series, designed for wealthy individuals and requiring a $25,000 minimum initial investment. The two other funds were institutional funds, requiring minimum investments of $1 million.

As 1990 ended, 43 index funds were in operation, but indexing was hardly a household concept. Many funds were designed solely for institutional investors. Some were not truly index funds at all, simply operating in discrete market segments (e.g., Japanese small company value stocks). Others were quantitative funds, run by computer programs making individual stock selections designed to resemble the industry composition and risk profile of an index, but with the goal of enhancing its returns.

Vanguard had started the first such quantitative fund, Vanguard Quantitative Portfolios, late in 1986. In the decade-plus since then, however, the fund has found it a tough challenge to significantly outpace the market. It has outpaced the Vanguard 500 Portfolio by a modest +0.2% a year (+15.2% versus +15.0%). But the average traditionally managed competitor proved a pushover, and during its ten-year lifetime Quantitative (now known as Vanguard Growth and Income Portfolio) has outpaced about 90% of all growth and income funds.

The S&P 500 Index again outpaced three-quarters of all equity mutual funds in 1987–1990, continuing its impressive relative performance in 1983–1986. Indexing continued to make inroads in the institutional arena, increasing from 15% to 20% of pension assets. And in the mutual fund field, its tiny penetration finally showed signs of life, leaping from 1/2% to 2 1/2% of equity fund assets. With assets of $2 billion as the period ended, the Vanguard 500 Portfolio remained the largest index fund, and now ranked #14 in size among 663 equity mutual funds.

The Evolution of an Index Strategy: 1991–1993

As 1991 began, real competition in the index arena was nowhere to be found. Few competitors had entered the field, and those that did so entered at prices that gave Vanguard first call on the assets of investors seriously considering indexing. (Average expense ratios were in the 0.50% range versus 0.20% for Vanguard Index Trust.) Vanguard, meanwhile, was broadening the concept of indexing even further. We were about to make it more convenient to own the total stock market. Previously, an investor could do so only by making a joint purchase of appropriately weighted investments in the 500 Portfolio and the Extended Market Portfolio. Vanguard Total Stock Market Portfolio, with the objective of matching the Wilshire 5000 Equity Index, was born in April 1992. Vanguard Balanced Index Fund was formed a few months thereafter, based 60% on the Wilshire 5000 Equity Index and 40% on the Lehman Brothers Aggregate Bond Index. The number of index funds in the family had reached nine.

In a 1990 speech to the Financial Analysts of Philadelphia entitled "Acres of Diamonds," I described the expansion Vanguard expected in the indexing business and had the temerity to say: "The introduction of index funds focusing on growth stocks and value stocks awaits only the availability of a Growth Index and a Value Index." Sure enough, in May 1992, Standard & Poor's developed the S&P/BARRA Growth and Value Indexes; six months later, our Index Trust Growth and Value Portfolios were launched. So, as 1992 came to a close, the Vanguard index fund family had expanded to eleven members. Still, the industry seemed unimpressed. None of the major firms joined the fray, but an additional 35 index funds (or quasi-index funds) were formed, bringing the total to 78.

The 1991–1993 period did not favor the S&P 500 Index, the focal point of both those who praised indexing and those who condemned it. Small-cap funds performed very well, and the large-cap S&P 500 Index outpaced only 45% of the professionally managed equity funds during those three years. We put quotes around the word "only" in our annual reports, in order to emphasize that outperforming 45% of all managed equity funds was a far cry from disaster. (For the record, the Wilshire 5000 Equity Index, a better representation of the portfolios of equity mutual funds, outperformed about 55% of all funds during the same period.) These were hardly the glory days of indexing, but they were not bad, and the funds continued steadily to gain ground.

In the mutual fund industry, the share of equity fund assets represented by index funds rose from 2 1/2% to 3 1/2% during 1991–1993—a small impact to be sure, but a 40% gain. And in the pension fund area, indexing grew to claim fully 25% of assets. At the end of 1993, assets of the Vanguard index family had reached $18 billion, 14% of the assets under Vanguard's supervision. Assets of the 500 Portfolio rose fourfold, to $8.3 billion, and it ranked as the eighth largest equity fund.

The Triumph of Indexing: 1994–1996

As it turned out, the 1991-1993 period provided "the pause that Refreshes" for superior index returns. Following the normal regression to the mean (*before costs*) that seems an eternal rule in the securities markets, index funds began to solidly outperform the active managers again. The pause had proved to provide a solid base for an upward trend to the long-term mean of above-average returns (*after costs*).

Although we didn't know it at the time, a halcyon era lay before us as 1994 began. While the stock market stumbled during 1994 and the average mutual fund declined, the 500 Portfolio turned in a gain of +1.3%. When the year ended, it had outpaced 78% of all equity funds. The bull market returned with a vengeance in 1995, and the S&P 500 Index provided a remarkable return of +37%, outpacing 85% of all general equity funds. In 1996, the bull market continued, and the Index (+23%) outpaced 75% of all managed equity funds. For the three years combined, 91% of the managed funds would lag an unmanaged index fund.

The expansion of Vanguard's index fund family continued apace with the creation in March 1993 of the industry's first specific-maturity bond index funds. The Long-Term Bond, Intermediate-Term Bond, and Short-Term Bond Portfolios of Vanguard Bond Index Fund were modeled after the comparable segments of the Lehman Brothers Aggregate Bond Index. They too affirmed the principle that low cost was the critical ingredient in shaping bond fund returns.

Late in 1993, yet another Vanguard index fund was on the drawing board. With determination that overcame our timidity, we decided to add an emerging markets portfolio to our International Equity Index Fund, in order to complete our entry into the international markets. Our determination was based on the long-term utility of such a portfolio; our timidity on the fact that the emerging markets had soared to what seemed speculative heights. As a result, heavy risks were evident as the year drew to a close and we formed the Portfolio. Happily, procedural and regulatory issues delayed our offering until May 1994, by which time the bubble in the emerging markets had burst. If "timing is everything," we had the fates with us in the introduction of the Emerging Markets Portfolio, our fifteenth index portfolio.

Despite our enthusiasm for and confidence in the index concept, we had been hesitant to exploit one of its major, if tacit, advantages: the tax advantage. By virtue of holding a passively managed portfolio, an index fund should tend to have very low portfolio turnover, and thus retain unrealized capital gains rather than realizing them and distributing them, subjecting shareholders to substantial taxes. The supposition proved correct. According to a comprehensive study of fund performance over 15 years by Stanford University economists John B. Shoven and Joel M. Dickson, our Vanguard index fund outpaced 92% of all equity funds on an *after-tax* basis, even better than its superiority over 80% of funds on a pretax basis. Yet, because large share redemptions could force an index fund to realize gains, we were reluctant to emphasize the benefit.

In 1993, we began the development of a new index fund concept that would optimize its potential tax advantage. We formed not one, but three, index-oriented funds that would levy a transaction fee on shareholders who redeemed within a year (2% penalty) to five years (1% penalty). The idea was to appeal to long-term investors and avoid the "hot money" of speculators. Vanguard Tax-Managed Fund included: (1) a Growth and Income Portfolio, designed to track the S&P 500 Index, but with the ability to vary slightly from the Index by selling stocks that had an unrealized loss, in order to offset capital gains that may have been realized by other sales, thus minimizing realized capital gains; (2) a Capital Appreciation Portfolio, designed to hold low-yielding stocks, using the Russell 1000 Index as a rough tracking standard, thus minimizing taxable income as well; and (3) a Balanced Portfolio, with assets divided 50/50 between the low-yielding stock portfolio and tax-exempt municipal bonds. The Tax-Managed Portfolios were introduced early in September 1994.

Just three weeks later, we began the offering of four LifeStrategy Portfolios, each with different allocations to stocks, bonds, and short-term reserves. They were designed to invest in appropriately weighted portfolios of existing Vanguard index funds. The equity ratio targets established for the four portfolios were: Income, 20% of assets; Conservative Growth, 40%; Moderate Growth, 60%; Growth, 80%. The balance was composed of various bond index portfolios. The LifeStrategy Portfolios also utilized Vanguard Asset Allocation Fund, formed in 1988, which provided a portfolio of U.S. Treasury bonds and indexed stocks. We had selected as its investment adviser Mellon Capital Management of San Francisco, led by William Fouse. This fund combined his pioneering work in indexing and in tactical asset allocation, dating back to 1971, with our pioneering work in index mutual funds, since 1975.

Two additional Vanguard index funds were approved by the Board of Directors in late 1995. The Total International Portfolio was offered in April 1996 as a "fund of funds," a composite of our underlying European, Pacific, and Emerging Markets Portfolios. A REIT (real estate investment trust) fund, providing a low-cost way for investors to diversify into the real estate asset class, was launched in May. With our five index-based asset allocation funds and the 21 regular index funds, the Vanguard index family had grown to 26 funds.

During 1994–1996, the index fund concept would become firmly established in the minds of serious investors, and would gain considerable attention in the press. The relative consistency of index performance became apparent. In the 20-year history of the 500 Portfolio of Vanguard Index Trust, through 1996, *Morningstar* had placed the Portfolio in the first quartile among all mutual funds seven times, the second quartile five times, the third quartile seven times, and the last quartile but once (in 1977, the Portfolio's first full year of operation), a record of performance consistency matched by only a handful of equity mutual funds during those two decades.

The first five years of the 20-year period began on a negative note, when the Portfolio's return actually fell short of the average competitive mutual fund by -4.8 percentage points per year. This was likely a simple regression to the mean from the well-documented extraordinary +4.7 percentage point annual superiority of the Index itself during the previous five years. (Clearly, the 500 Portfolio should have begun either five years earlier or five years later!) In the next five years (1981–1986), the Portfolio posted a +3.0 percentage point annual superiority, followed by a +2.1 percentage point annual margin in the next five years, then closing with a further +2.6 percentage point annual advantage in the final five plus years. In all, the S&P 500 Index achieved a margin of superiority of +1.1 percentage points over the average equity fund (a figure that does not take into account the returns of funds that have since gone out of existence-the presumably poorer-performing funds). The S&P 500 Index also led the Portfolio by +0.40 percentage points, largely as a result of operating costs, especially in the Portfolio's formative years. (See Figure 5.)

Given the mean regression of the equity fund returns in the first five years, this total result clearly understates the accomplishments of an index strategy. In fact, over the last 15 years, the Portfolio's margin over the average equity fund was a stunning +2.7 percentage points annually.

Figure 5

20 Years Of Indexing

	S&P 500 Index	VIT–500 Portfolio	**Annualized Returns** General Equity Funds*	Index versus VIT–500	Index versus GEFs
1976–81	8.1%	7.6%	12.4%	+0.5%	–4.3%
1981–86	19.8	19.3	16.3	+0.5	+3.5
1986–91	15.4	15.0	12.9	+0.4	+2.5
1991–97**	17.7	17.5	14.9	+0.2	+2.8
1976–97**	15.2%	14.8%	14.1%	+0.4%	+1.1%

*Morningstar general equity funds.

**Through 6/30/97.

Such a return premium, accomplished as it was with such consistency, has surely justified the concept of index investing.

As 1995 began, I wanted to let the world know unequivocally that indexing was here to stay, and we prepared a booklet entitled "The Triumph of Indexing." Using excerpts from my Chairman's Letters in the 1994 Annual Reports, I proclaimed: 'Index funds have come of age," and cited former star Fidelity Magellan Fund manager Peter Lynch's 1990 statement that "the public . . . would be better off in an index fund."

Soon after "The Triumph of Indexing" was published, a signal event occurred. *Money* magazine dedicated much of its August 1995 issue to the success of indexing. The cover depicted Vanguard Core Management head Gus Sauter, along with two luminous active money managers. A lead editorial by Executive Editor Tyler Mathisen embraced the index concept and called on readers to "make a complete reorientation of your expectations as an investor." He described the index fund advantages of low operating cost, low transaction costs, and low exposure to capital gains taxes as "a trio as impressive as Domingo, Pavarotti, and Carreras." The head-line on the editorial generously declared: "Bogle wins: Index funds should be the core of most portfolios today," and ended with a personal salute, "So here's to you, Jack. You have a right to call it the Triumph of Indexing."

Money, like Saul on the road to Damascus, had experienced an epiphany. And so had many investors. Index assets in the Vanguard complex soared, reaching nearly $70 billion on December 31, 1996. The 500 Portfolio of Vanguard Index Trust, which on August 31, 1996, had reached the 20th anniversary of its initial public offering, soared to new heights, with assets reaching $30 billion at year-end. It was now the third-largest equity mutual fund in the world, larger than all but two of 4,000 U.S. equity funds. It would become the second-largest before January 1997 ended.

The Industry Finally Responds

Many observers thought that it was premature to declare "the triumph of indexing" in 1995. What followed thereafter made it clear that—at least through mid-1997—"triumph" was not too strong a word. Continued superior index fund performance and burgeoning investor acceptance were to give us still further encouragement that the simple concepts I had described in my Princeton thesis in 1951, and the basic insights of forward-thinking financial professionals that inspired me in the mid-1970s and had ushered in the first index mutual fund, were here to stay. The initial response of other firms in the mutual fund industry to the idea of indexing was tepid to a fault. Industry giant Fidelity Investments had poured cold water on the idea in 1976, but had finally been compelled to offer an index fund 14 years later, in 1990. Organized under the Spartan label in 1990 (with a $25,000 minimum initial investment), it had gone nowhere. Its name was changed to Fidelity U.S. Equity Index Fund in 1992, with a $3,000 minimum. Even the newly named fund was offered with little enthusiasm, however, and carried a rather high expense ratio of 0.45% per year. Fees were waived, however, for "a temporary period of time" to 0.25% in order to establish some low-cost credentials.

Dreyfus, ever the marketer and then the second-largest firm in the field, had begun the Peoples Index Fund (based on the S&P 500 Index) in 1987—it carried a relatively high 0.50% annual fee—and followed it with a similar fund for institutional investors in 1990, a bond market fund in 1993, and a mid-cap fund in 1995. Earlier, it had formed a series of managed index-oriented target funds run by Wilshire Associates. T. Rowe Price, another industry leader, climbed aboard the seemingly inevitable bandwagon in 1990 with an S&P 500 fund for institutions. The spate of institutional funds was a recognition that index funds were becoming almost an essential investment option in the burgeoning corporate 401(k) thrift plan market. But none of the other major fund groups tested the index fund waters. Without serious competition, Vanguard experienced a steady increase in its market share of index mutual fund assets, accounting for about 70% of the assets of index funds offered to individual investors as 1997 began.

In January 1997, the acceptance of index funds accelerated. Fidelity, for years unwilling to endorse the concept, stated its intention to offer three more index funds, bringing its total offerings to individual investors to four. The offerings, again under the Spartan (high minimum purchase) label, included a total stock market fund, an extended market fund, and an international equity fund. Each would apparently carry a relatively high expense ratio, but management fees would be temporarily capped so as to limit the expense ratio to about 0.25% annually through 1999. By mid-year, Fidelity had further reduced the temporarily low fee to 0.19%. In addition, the firm determined not to administer the funds itself, but to have Bankers Trust Company do so. The presumption is that the fee was negotiated vigorously, and is probably about 0.01%.

Merrill Lynch, long a reluctant dragon, also announced its intention to join the parade. Since an index fund should have a natural cost (including the tiny costs of handling the fund's investments, plus the substantial costs of handling the fund's operations) of only about 0.20% to be competitive, Merrill would offer it only as part of an asset management account that carries a 1.5% advisory fee. Such a fee would, of course, defeat the whole purpose of low-cost indexing. The reception of the idea by the marketplace will be interesting to witness.

The long reluctance of major mutual fund managers to form index funds doubtless comes from two major sources. First, indexing is a business in which it is very difficult for an adviser to earn profits. To state the obvious, no investment advice is needed, and none should be paid for. While the marketplace might permit a modest profit, it is hard to see how, in the long run, annual expense charges could exceed 0.25%, at least as long as Vanguard continues to set the standard at 0.20% per year (or lower—0.06% is the current expense ratio of Vanguard Institutional Index Fund). Higher charges would seem to be unjustifiable to an investor with any native intelligence or for that matter with any fiduciary responsibility. Given that a generic index fund—operated at cost and without profit to its sponsor—is close to a pure commodity, a higher price should not be possible in a competitive marketplace. However, the industry will doubtless struggle to match lower prices by using temporary fee waivers, with fees edging up over time, hoping that the investors won't notice. Although some investors with substantial gains might be "locked-in" when expenses rise, fee ratcheting would seem to be a risky long-run strategy.

If lack of profit potential for the adviser in the mutual fund business causes reluctance to embrace indexing, it must be recognized that *mutual funds* exist solely to make money for their investors-implying minimal costs-but mutual fund *management companies* exist importantly, if not primarily, to make money for their advisers-implying that they should charge the highest costs that traffic (i.e., the market) will bear. The two motives obviously come in conflict. Indeed, they fly in the face of St. Luke's wisdom that "no man can serve two masters." But no matter; the industry rolls merrily along.

In addition to the infinitely small profit potential for advisers to index funds, there's the matter of professional pride. Mutual fund advisers build organizations of brilliant, attractive, well-educated MBAs (often from Harvard, Wharton, and the like) who strive to outpace the market. The fact that they have not been able to do so as a group apparently doesn't faze those who are able to do so at least once in a while. But for a firm to summon its highly paid professional money managers, security analysts, and research analysts to a meeting and tell them that they are going to be competing with an in-house index fund certainly would be a difficult bridge for many managers to cross. Indeed, when Fidelity announced its index fund expansion early in 1997, indicating it was beginning to take the subject with the seriousness it deserves, the firm reiterated the belief that its actively managed funds could once again outperform the market. It was offering index funds, it said, simply because some investors were demanding them. (Given that odd reasoning, it is fortunate for the world that most investors aren't demanding a participation in the Brooklyn Bridge.)

Nonetheless, it turns out that, in both academic theory and real-world practice, index funds have conclusively demonstrated the reality of the financial markets: *All investors as a group*, including a huge component of large institutions with professional managers and skilled individual investors owning carefully selected stocks, *are the market*. And since all investors as a group are the market, there is no way that they can *outpace* the market.

That elemental fact holds true *before* the costs of investing. After costs, the returns of all investors inevitably lag the market by the amount of the cost. These two simple syllogisms hardly defy rationality, and in the last analysis it is amazing that the principle has been resisted or mis-understood for so very long. In short, it doesn't take modern portfolio theory, or a belief in "efficient markets," or quantum mathematics to prove the index thesis. It requires no more than common sense.

Given the results achieved by active managers over the past 20 years plus the results mutual funds achieved over the prior 30 years that I illus-trated for the Vanguard Directors in 1976, we now have more than a half-century of real evidence. Based on that evidence alone, it would seem inevitable that the growth of indexing will be widespread, will accelerate, and will become pervasive in the mutual fund industry, where, despite the public attention being given to index funds, only 6% of equity assets are currently indexed. (See Figure 6.) Among pension plans, however, in the presumably wiser institutional market, at least 25% of equity assets already are indexed.

Early in 1997, index funds were "in the news." On January 28, they were recognized with major front page articles in both *The New York Times* and *The Wall Street Journal*. At almost the same time, both *Time* and *Newsweek* also ran solid and favorable indexing stories. All of the stories focused on the remarkable performance of index funds relative to actively managed funds, but some seemed to miss the fundamental point about indexing: There is no magic to it. It is simply a reflection of a basic

Figure 6

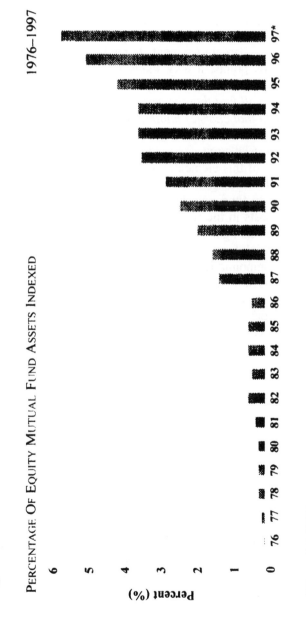

PERCENTAGE OF EQUITY MUTUAL FUND ASSETS INDEXED

1976–1997

*Through 6 30 97

formula that can be expressed as *gross market returns* minus *cost* equals *net returns*, the returns that are shared by all investors as a group. Put another way, as I've said a thousand times, *costs matter.*

A bit later in 1997, when the Annual Report for 1996 of Berkshire Hathaway Corporation was published, Warren E. Buffett, probably the most successful long-term investor in America, added another strong affirmation: *"Seriously, costs matter.* For example, equity mutual funds incur corporate expenses—largely payments to the funds" managers-that average about 100 basis points, a levy likely to cut the returns their investors earn by 10% or more over time. . . . *Most investors, both institutional and individual, will find that the best way to own common stocks is through an index fund that charges minimal fees. Those following this path are sure to beat the net results (after fees and expenses) delivered by the great majority of investment professionals. "*

As the implications of this elemental mathematical formula are recognized, the impact of indexing will permeate the entire mutual fund field. The average equity fund now has an expense ratio of more than 1.5% and transaction costs in the range of at least 0.5%—a shortfall of two percentage points a year against the market's return. In a world where investors increasingly think long term, the implications of the magnitude of this fiscal drag on compound returns will become clear. Investors will inevitably begin to focus on index funds—not because they performed so brilliantly in 1994–1996 and again in early 1997, but because their performance, over a long period of years, has consistently met a high standard of adding value. As a practical matter, the amount of that extra value is almost precisely what theory would indicate.

Will The Past Be Prologue to the Future?

Currently, too many mutual fund investors have an investment horizon limited to weeks or months. Redemptions of equity funds and exchanges among them take place with extraordinary frequency. Turnover in holdings of mutual fund shares is comparable to the turnover in individual common stocks. In important measure, the mutual fund business has become a casino, with the focus on the short term. Just as the stock market is a zero sum game (albeit one that has provided a positive bias and therefore a zero sum *relative* game), so the fund casino is a zero sum game, but *only* before the house takes its "handle" of as much as 20% of the amount earned (i.e., a cost of 2% of assets would consume 20% of a 10% return). In the short run, that may not matter, but in the long run it will. And, assuming that today's investors will begin to invest in a 401(k) plan or an IRA before they are age 25, and will be living off the fruits of their accumulations even after they reach age 75, then something like a half-century will prove to be a normal time horizon for virtually all U.S. investors.

What difference would an index fund make over 50 years? Well, let's postulate a +10% long-term annual return on stocks. (It may not be that large during the coming decade, and even a positive return over any given decade is hardly assured.) If we assume that mutual fund costs continue at their present apparent level of about 2% a year, an average mutual fund would return 8%. This 2% spread is very close to that of the past 15 years, during which the Vanguard 500 Portfolio provided a 2.2% margin of return over the average equity fund (or, more accurately, the better performers that survived the period), if higher than the 1.6% margin provided by the S&P 500 Index itself during the 30 years covered in my presentation to the Vanguard Directors in 1976. In any event, extending this compounding out in time on a $10,000 initial investment, the market (at 10%) would produce $1,170,000 after 50 years; the mutual fund (at 8%) would produce $470,000. The difference in return between the two— 700,000—is an unbelievable 70 *times* the initial stake of $10,000.

Looked at from a different perspective, our hypothetical fund investor has earned $1,170,000, donated $700,000 to the mutual fund industry, and kept the remainder of $470,000. The financial system has consumed 60% of the return, the fund investor has achieved but 40% of his earnings potential. Yet it was the investor who provided 100% of the initial capital; the industry provided none. Confronted by the issue in this way, would an intelligent investor consider this split to represent a fair shake? Merely to ask the question is to answer it: "No."

To be sure, as Coleridge reminds us, "history is but a lantern over the stern." And many changes lie in prospect during the years ahead. Some could reduce the substantial extra margin of return earned by an index fund in the past. At least four possibilities exist:

- Equity mutual funds could start to become fully invested. Cash has always been a drag on return for the long-term equity investor, yet most mutual funds hold 5% to 10% of their portfolios in cash, presumably largely for liquidity purposes. As long as stocks yield more than money market instruments, this is in itself a substantial drag. While such reserves dampen a fund's short-term volatility, they reduce its long-term return. I hold the simple view that a one percentage point increase in standard deviation for the mutual fund, say, from 15% to 16% per year by being fully invested, is *meaningless*. But a one percentage point increase in return, say, from 9% to 10%, is *priceless*. Also, there really wouldn't seem to be much point in paying an adviser 1.5% a year to manage a cash reserve position earning an average yield of, say, 4.5%.

• Mutual fund advisory fees could come down. This is possible, if hardly likely, as the competitive implications of low-cost, unmanaged index funds become known, and actively managed and high-cost funds realize they have to cut their fees in order to reduce the "fiscal drag" on performance that these fees represent. Lower fees could also come about as somnolent independent directors, if such there be, of mutual funds finally awaken and cut fees paid to fund managers when they reach excessive levels.

• Other fund costs could be slashed. Far too large a portion of fund expenses is dedicated to areas that provide no benefit whatsoever to mutual fund shareholders, including marketing, advertising, and excessive administrative and communications costs. Such expenses may help funds to reach giant asset size, but all too often the principal benefits of size accrue to the adviser, not the fund shareholder. (Indeed, it can easily be seen as a detriment to the shareholder.) As an informed guess, I'd expect that no more than 10% to 15% of the expenses paid by mutual fund shareholders go to the professional money portfolio managers and research analysts that, as a group, are purported to provide the returns that the shareholders seek—in all, of course, net returns that have been well below those earned by low-cost, unmanaged index portfolios.

• Fund turnover could decline. There's little question but that the turnover of mutual fund portfolios today is excessive. In the old days (the 1950s, for example) mutual fund annual portfolio turnover rates were usually in the 20% range. Today, average turnover runs up toward 100% a year-and far higher for some funds.

  Put another way, the average holding period of a security is only about one year. Since this turnover is costly, the wise manager attempting to outpace an index will one day more carefully quantify the costly impact of portfolio turnover. (Doing a static analysis of the portfolio at the beginning of the year, assuming that no turnover took place during the year, is an interesting—and usually humbling—exercise. Such studies frequently show performance that is better than that of the actively managed portfolio.)

In all, then, there's a real possibility that the advantage that indexing has enjoyed in the past will decline in the future. But there's also a real possibility that the index advantage will *increase*. Consider these two possibilities:

- Based on present trends, mutual fund expense ratios could increase.For reasons lost in history, mutual fund performance is almost universally calculated without considering sales charges. Sales loads were traditionally paid at the time of an investor's initial purchase. But they were not particularly popular, so industry strategy was directed not to reducing them, but to hiding them.

  The net result is that many standard mutual fund front-end sales charges have been eliminated, but only in favor of 12b-1 fees— annual percentage charges made against fund assets to pay for sales commissions and/or distribution costs. Under this scheme, a deferred sales charge is normally collected if the investor redeems shares before the sales load has been paid in its entirety through the annual charge. In the absence of affirmative action by fund managers and directors to drive fees down, the acceleration of this process will itself drive expense ratios higher.

- At an enormous total of $2 trillion today, assets of equity mutual funds are now more than 10 *times* their $160 billion total in 1986, 50 *times* their $34 billion in 1976. There is simply no way to provide outstanding returns for an asset aggregate of this dimension. Mutual funds now own 20% of all individual stocks compared with 8% two decades ago. It must be obvious that the higher proportion of securities owned, the tougher the industry's job.

  What is more, mutual fund managers are units of advisory firms that manage money for other clients. Total equity assets managed by the 300 largest financial institutions include $1.8 trillion of mutual fund equity assets and $4 trillion of privately managed assets—50% of all equities. It is no more than common sense to assume that a pool of this dimension would not have the ability to systematically outperform the remaining pool of $4.5 trillion run by other institutions and individuals.

  Conclusion: It could well be tougher than ever for managers of large amounts of assets to differentiate their performance in an amount sufficient to overcome their fees and operating expenses.

In any event—both for the detractors of index funds and the advocates—caution should be the watchword in looking into the future and extrapolating the substantial margins of advantage that index funds have earned in the past.

From its humble beginning in 1976, the first index fund is now the second-largest equity fund in the mutual fund industry. Assets of the Vanguard 500 Portfolio approach nearly $50 billion; assets of the entire Vanguard index fund family total nearly $100 billion. Without including the $200 billion in other assets managed by Vanguard, this index pool in itself would comprise the tenth-largest mutual fund complex. So indexing has come a long way. But it still has a long way to go. As one who was present at the creation of the first index fund, I can't imagine it won't make that voyage successfully.

Yet, the future is ever uncertain. How great would market liquidity be if, say, one-third of all stocks were to be held by index funds? Has today's dominant index model—the S&P 500—become a self-fulfilling prophesy? And, if so, will a major reversal be self-fulfilling too? Will there be a shift from indexing based on the S&P 500 to indexing based on the entire stock market? Given their 100% invested position, will index funds drop faster in a sharp market decline than other equity funds holding modest reserves, albeit often with different types of stocks? Will S&P 500 Index futures prove liquid *when* (not *if*) a bear market takes over (i.e.. when the bubble, if indeed there is one, bursts)? Even if institutions as a group must lag the markets, will mutual fund managers be able to outpace other managers (net of the fiscal drag of operating costs)? Brute evidence supporting affirmative answers to any of these questions is, so far at least. totally lacking.

All said, the acceptance by investors of the first index mutual fund— during its first 17 years, hardly a monument to anything but determination to prove something—has, a brief four years later, succeeded in defying Lord Keynes's warning that "it is better to fail conventionally than to succeed unconventionally." Arguably, it has finally become not merely an artistic success but a commercial success—for investors, if not for fund managers. In the years to come, my expectation is that the index fund has a strong opportunity to validate Stephen Vincent Bene't's aphorism: "If the idea is good it will survive defeat. It may even survive victory."

So that's the history of the first index mutual fund, from its genesis in the ideals of 1949 to its flowering in the realities of 1997, described by an observer who was present at the creation, and who remains an enthusiast. Doubtless, much interesting history remains to unfold in the years ahead.

Appendix Performance Summary

Portfolio (Inception Date) Benchmark Index	Average Annual Total Returns For Periods Ended June 30, 1997		
	1 Year	5 Years	10 Years
Vanguard Index Trust-500 Portfolio (8/31/76)	34.56%	19.62%	14.41%
Standard & Poor's 500 Composite Stock Price Index	34.70	19.78	14.66
Vanguard Index Trust- Extended Market Portfolio (12/21/87)	18.98%	17.82%	15.75%*
Wilshire 4500 Equity Index	16.99	17.30	15.72*
Vanguard Index Trust- Small Capitalization Stock Portfolio (10/3/60)	18.17%	18.61%	11.20%
Russell 2000 Index	16.33	17.87	11.14
Vanguard Index Trust-Value Portfolio (11/2/92)	30.67%	20.31%*	--
Standard & Poor's/BARRA Value Index	30.89	20.48*	--
Vanguard Index Trust-Growth Portfolio (11/2/92)	38.24%	19.50%*	--
Standard & Poor's/BARRA Growth Index	38.34	19.74	--
Vanguard Index Trust-Total Stock Market Portfolio (4/27/92)	29.29%	18.66%	18.00%*
Wilshire 5000 Equity Index	29.32	19.06	18.38*
Vanguard Institutional Index Fund (7/31/90)	34.79%	19.77%	17.26%*
Standard & Poor's 500 Composite Stock Price Index	34.70	19.78	17.29*
Vanguard Bond Index Fund- Total Bond Market Portfolio (12/11/86)	8.03%	7.04%	8.45%
Lehman Brothers Aggregate Bond Index	8.15	7.12	8.82
Vanguard Bond Index Fund- Short-Term Bond Portfolio (3/1/94)	6.71%	5.87%*	...
Lehman Brothers 1-5 Year Government/ Corporate Bond Index	6.83	5.96*	--
Vanguard Bond Index Fund- Intermediate-Term Bond Portfolio (3/1/94)	7.92%	6.62%*	

Lehman Brothers 5-10 Year Government/ Corporate Bond Index	8.06	6.76*	---

*Performance figures since inception.

Vanguard Bond Index Fund- Long-Term Bond Portfolio (3/1/94)	8.91%	7.29%	—
Lehman Brothers Long Government/Corporate Bond Index	—	9.19	7.49*
Vanguard International Equity Index Fund- European Portfolio (6/18/90)	30.25%	15.08%	12.29%*
Morgan Stanley Capital International Europe Index	30.09	15.30	12.62*
Vanguard International Equity Index Fund- Pacific Portfolio (6/18/90)	-3.98%	10.60%	2.81%*
Morgan Stanley Capital International Pacific Free Index	-4.47	10.53	2.63*
Vanguard International Equity Index Fund- Emerging Markets Portfolio (5/4/94)	13.06%	12.08%*	—
Morgan Stanley Capital International Select Emerging Markets Free Index	13.58	9.72*	—
Vanguard Total International Portfolio (4/29/96)	13.01%	10.49%*	---
Morgan Stanley Capital International Total International Index	13.05	10.34*	---
Vanguard Balanced Index Fund (11/9/92)	20.75%	14.02%*	---
Balanced Composite Index (60% Wilshire 5000 Index and 40% Lehman Aggregate Bond Index)	20.64	14.42*	---
Vanguard Tax-Managed Fund-Balanced Portfolio (9/6/94)**		16.62%	15.49%*
Tax-Managed Balanced Composite Index (50% Russell 1000 Index and 50% Lehman 7-Year Municipal Bond Index)	19.28	16.61*	—
Vanguard Tax-Managed Fund- Growth and Income Portfolio (9/6/94)**	34.68%	28.05%*	—
Standard & Poor's 500 Composite Stock Price Index	34.70	28.03*	---
Vanguard Tax-Managed Fund- Capital Appreciation Portfolio (9/6/94)**	27.76%	25.26%*	---

Russell 1000 Index	32.26	27.08*	—
Vanguard LifeStrategy Portfolios- Income Portfolio (9/30/94)	12.93%	13.28%*	—
Income Composite Index (60% Lehman Aggregate Bond Index. 20% Wilshire 5000 Index. and 20% Salomon Three-Month Treasury Bill Index)	11.66	11.82*	—

*Performance figures since inception.
**Returns exclude 2% fee applied to shares redeemed or exchanged within one year of purchase and 1% fee applied to shares redeemed or exchanged within five years of purchase.

Vanguard LifeStrategy Portfolios- Conservative Growth Portfolio (9/30/94)	16.25%	15.74%*	—
Conservative Growth Composite Index (40% Lehman Aggregate Bond Index. 35% Wilshire 5000 Index. and 20% Salomon Three-Month Treasury Bill Index)	15.04	14.52*	—
Vanguard LifeStrategy Portfolios- Moderate Growth Portfolio (9/30/94)	19.73%	18.50%*	—
Moderate Growth Composite Index (40% Lehman Aggregate Bond Index. 50% Wilshire 5000 Index. and 10% MSCI EAFE Index)	19.07	18.05*	—
Vanguard LifeStrategy Portfolios- Growth Portfolio (9/30/94)	23.07%	21.22%*	—
Growth Composite Index (20% Lehman Aggregate Bond Index. 65% Wilshire 5000 Index. and 15% MSCI EAFE Index)	22.55	20.83*	—
Vanguard Specialized Portfolios- REIT Index Portfolio (5/13/96)**	33.44%	31.95%*	—
Morgan Stanley REIT Index	33.72	32.18*	—

*Performance figures since inception.
**Returns exclude 1% fee applied to shares redeemed or exchanged within one year of purchase.

This brochure can be used in conjunction with the offering of shares of any of the member funds of The Vanguard Group only if preceded or accompanied by a cur-

rent prospectus of each fund whose shares are being offered. Prospectuses contain more complete information on advisory fees, distribution charges, and other expenses and should be read carefully before you invest or send money. Prospectuses can be obtained directly from The Vanguard Group, Valley Forge, Pennsylvania, 19482. The Vanguard fund total return data provided represent past performance, and the investment return and principal value of an investment will fluctuate so that an investors' shares, when redeemed, may be worth more or less than their original cost. The comparative indexes represent unmanaged or average returns on various financial assets that can be compared to the funds' total returns for the purpose of measuring relative performance.

"Standard & Poor's," "S&P 500," and "500" are trademarks of The McGraw-Hill Companies, Inc.
"Wilshire 4500" and "Wilshire 5000" are registered trademarks of Wilshire Associates."
"Russell 1000" and "Russell 2000" are registered trademarks of the Frank Russell Company.

CHAPTER 4

Optimal Indexing

Shucheng Liu*
Senior Consultant, Research Optimization Group
BARRA, Inc.

Aamir Sheikh*
Manager, Derivatives Research
BARRA, Inc.

Dan Stefek*
Manager, Analytics Research
BARRA, Inc.

In a frictionless world, constructing index funds is a simple task. The set of assets underlying the index is identified. A portfolio is constructed with exactly the same weights as the index. As the index weights change, assets whose weights have declined are costlessly liquidated, and those whose weights have increased are costlessly purchased to instantaneously match the changing weights of the index. As the assets in the index make cash payouts, these are reinvested in the portfolio in exactly the same proportion as the index. Conversely, withdrawals from the index fund are honored by costlessly liquidating asset holdings in exactly the correct proportions.

The world, however, is not frictionless. There are costs to trading, and these costs differ across assets. At the same time, management fees for index funds are typically very low, often only about 10 basis points. Frequent portfolio revision without consideration of trading costs will rapidly drive an index fund manager out of business. These costs are important even when tracking capitalization-weighted portfolios whose assets weights adjust automatically as prices change. Managing an index fund involves a delicate balance between trying to closely track the index and keeping costs as low as possible.

---

*The views expressed in this paper are those of the authors. and do not necessarily represent those of BARRA.

In this chapter, we discuss different approaches to achieving this balance. We begin by giving a precise statement of what it means to track an index as closely as possible: minimize the variability of the difference between the fund return and the index return. This variability is referred to as the *tracking error* of the index fund and is measured by the standard deviation of the difference between the fund return and the index return. Forecasting this variability requires a risk model, and we provide a brief discussion of how risk may be accurately estimated. We next turn our attention to different techniques for balancing the desire for a low tracking error against the need for low management costs, beginning with a discussion of the impracticality of exact replication. The alternatives to exact replication focus on using a relatively small set of assets to track the index. These include simple methods, such as stratified sampling, as well as advanced optimization techniques. We include an empirical examination of the relative performance of the different indexing techniques. Not surprisingly, we find that optimization significantly out performs its competitors.

The Objective

The objective of indexing is to minimize tracking error while keeping costs as low as possible and satisfying any other constraints that may be imposed on the fund. Why is minimizing the tracking error the focus of our attention? Why not try to minimize the actual difference in returns, or the average difference in returns?

Unless we exactly replicate the index, the actual difference in returns is not completely in our control. From period to period, it will vary randomly with the returns of the assets that are included in the index but not in the index fund. For example, suppose we try to mimic the behavior of the S&P 500 with a portfolio of 100 of the 500 stocks in the index. The difference in the return of the mimicking portfolio and the S&P 500 will depend on the returns of the 400 excluded assets. These returns are random and beyond our control; thus, the actual difference in the two returns is beyond our control.

What about minimizing the expected (or the long-run average) value of the difference between the returns of the two portfolios? Consider a portfolio for which this expected value is zero (and there are an infinite number of such portfolios) but where the tracking error is large. Although we will match the performance of the index on average, there is a large likelihood that we may substantially underperform the index in a particular period.

Large deviations from the index are undesirable, and they are more likely the greater the tracking error. Hence, it makes sense to target the tracking error. At this point, we can make an exact mathematical statement of our problem. We need to introduce some notation, however. Denote by h_{Ij} and h_j the weights of security j in the index and in the tracking portfolio, respectively, by r_j and r_l the returns of any two securities j and l, and by σ_{jl} the covariance between any two securities j and l. Then the objective in indexing is to pick the weights, h_j, in the tracking

$$
var\left(\sum_j h_j r_j - \sum_j h_{Ij} r_j \right) = \sum_j \sum_l \left(h_j - h_{Ij} \right)\left(h_l - h_{Il} \right)\sigma_{jl}
$$

portfolio to minimize subject to transactions costs or holding bounds. If we let h_I and h be the vectors of holdings in the index and the tracking portfolio, and let Σ denote the matrix of asset covariances, then we may state our problem as minimizing $(h - h_I)' \Sigma (h - h_I)$ while controlling transactions costs and satisfying any constraints imposed on the fund.

A Digression on Risk Modeling

Minimization of the tracking error requires estimates of the variances and covariances of the returns of the securities that are considered for inclusion in the tracking portfolio, as well as for the securities that are in the index. For example, to track the S&P 500 with 50 stocks that are in the index, we would need the covariances between all 500 stocks as well as the variances of all 500 stocks. To track BARRA's ALLUS index, we would need the covariance matrix of all U.S. common stocks. Accurate estimation of the covariance matrix of asset returns is thus an integral part of optimally tracking an index portfolio.

The simplest way to estimate the covariance matrix is to compute the historical covariances among asset returns. This approach, however, is subject to estimation and sampling error and may be unfeasible. For example, estimating the covariance matrix for 7,000 assets requires estimation of over 24 million numbers. Getting a mere 5% badly wrong can induce severe estimation errors when computing portfolio risk. Moreover, it is quite possible that in any given period an automobile stock like Ford exhibits a high correlation with a forest-and-paper products stock such as

Weyerhauser—higher than the estimated correlation between Ford and another automobile stock such as General Motors (GM). The higher correlation between Ford and Weyerhauser is probably simply an artifact of the period used to compute the correlations and is unlikely to persist in the future. Thus, using the historical covariances among securities may indicate that we could track an index containing Ford by replacing Ford with Weyerhauser!

Our intuition that Ford and GM should be more highly correlated than Ford and Weyerhauser provides us with an alternative approach to estimating the covariances among security returns: Ford and GM are exposed to a common factor: namely all the news that affects the automobile industry as a whole. In addition, Ford and GM stock returns are driven by news that is specific to Ford or GM. The degree to which the two stocks move together depends on their sensitivities to the auto industry return and the variability of the auto industry return relative to the variability of returns due to firm specific news. The more sensitive the stocks are to the auto industry, and the greater the variability of the auto industry return, the greater the covariance among the returns of the two stocks, as well as the variance of each stock's return. Moreover, other things being constant, the greater the variability of returns due to firm specific news, the greater the variability of a stock's returns.

We may generalize this intuition by noting that firms with similar characteristics, including industries, tend to have similar returns. For example, returns of large firms tend to be more highly correlated with returns of other large firms than with small firms. There is a size factor in stock returns, and a firm's sensitivity to the size factor is simply a measure of the relative size of the firm.

More formally, we may think of k factors, which may include industry factors, and factors related to firm attributes such as size, book-to-market, and expected earnings growth. Denote by x_{jk} the sensitivity of firm j to factor k, by f_k the realized return on a portfolio that represents factor k (the factor k return), and by u_j the return to asset j due to firm specific events (the specific return). Our model of asset returns may be written as

$$r_j = \sum_k x_{jk} f_k + u_j$$

where the specific returns are, by definition, uncorrelated among assets. This implies that the covariance among the returns of two different assets, i and j, is given by

$$\sum_k \sum_l x_{jk} x_{il} Cov(f_k, f_l)$$

whereas the variance of asset j's return equals

$$\sum_k \sum_l x_{jk} x_{jl} cov(f_k, f_l) + var(u_j)$$

In matrix notation, if we denote by r the vector of asset returns, by X the matrix of asset sensitivities to the factors, by f the vector of factor returns, by u the asset specific returns, by F the covariance matrix of the factor returns, and by Δ the matrix with the specific return variances along its diagonal, then we have

$$r = Xf + u$$

$$\Sigma = XFX' + \Delta$$

Thus, to estimate the covariance matrix of asset returns, we need to estimate the covariances and the variances of the factors and the variances of specific returns.[1]

Typically, the number of factors is far fewer than the number of securities. For example, BARRA's U.S. equity risk model has 68 factors, of which 55 correspond to industries and 13 correspond to firm attributes

---

[1]We also need to compute the sensitivities. In the model as stated, these are computed from fundamental data. In alternative specifications and estimation methods for factor models, these may be estimated via statistical analysis. For example, if we begin by specifying observable factors, such as macroeconomic variables like shocks to interest rates, inflation, etc., then the sensitivities of the assets to the factors may be obtained via regression analysis. Alternatively, we may leave the factors completely unspecified, and estimate the factor covariances, the specific variances, and the sensitivities by factor analysis. Empirical evidence in Connor (1995) indicates that factor models estimated using firm fundamentals outperform those based on macroeconomic factors or statistical factors. Moreover, fundamental models are dynamic because asset risk characteristics and sensitivities change as firm fundamentals change. Statistical and macro factor models have limited dynamic capabilities.

such as size. With 7,000 asset specific variances, this requires computation of 9,346 variance and covariance terms—far fewer than the 24 million estimates needed for individual assets. Thus, the impact of estimation error is substantially reduced. Moreover, assets with similar industry and fundamental characteristics will have greater sensitivities to the same common factors, and therefore the estimated correlations among these assets will be higher than for assets with different industry and fundamental characteristics. For example, this risk model would predict that Ford and GM are more highly correlated than Ford and Weyerhauser. Finally, as the characteristics of an asset change, the asset's sensitivities to the factors change, and the model is able to dynamically capture the impact of the changing asset characteristics on the asset's variance and its covariances with other assets.

For the remainder of our discussion, we will assume that a covariance matrix of asset returns has been estimated. Moreover, we will refer to factor models because they provide insights into how one may optimally track an index.

Techniques for Tracking an Index

Replication

The simplest solution to the indexing problem appears to be to replicate the index, i.e., set the vector of weights h equal to h_I. However, this may be impractical, and the larger number of assets in the index, the less practical exact replication is. The transactions costs incurred in an effort to match an index with a great many assets will quickly eat up available funds—even when the index is capitalization weighted.

Although in principle capitalization-weighted indexes rebalance automatically (as asset prices change, the weights in the index automatically adjust so that the index is capitalization weighted at every instant), in practice there are changes in the weights that require adjusting the number of shares of each asset in the index. Corporate actions, such as the issuance of new shares, alter the amount outstanding of an asset and hence its weight in the index. Similarly, changes in the composition of the index due to mergers and acquisitions or because an asset fails to meet the criteria for inclusion in the index alter the index weights. For the S&P 500, many such revisions may occur in the span of a month, requiring indexers to trade in and out of assets in their portfolios. For larger indices such as the Wilshire 5000 this problem is even worse.

Cash inflows and outflows require more trading. As securities make payouts, such as dividends for common stocks and coupons for bonds, the resulting cash has to be reinvested. Similarly, cash infusions (or withdrawals) require the purchase (or sale) of assets in the exact proportions that they are held in the index. Often, it makes more sense to hold part of the portfolio in cash to handle redemptions and dividends and use futures contracts on the index (if available) to equitize the cash holdings. The benefits to using index futures, however, crucially depend on whether the futures are cheap or expensive relative to the underlying index.

Alternatives to Replication

Replication is a very costly method of indexing, especially for broad-based indexes. There are, however, a number of ways in which we can try to construct portfolios with low tracking error and acceptable transactions costs. These range from relatively simple approaches, such as choosing the largest holdings or the most liquid assets in the index, to extremely sophisticated optimization techniques. Since optimization techniques are constructed to minimize the tracking error *ex ante*, they have to produce the best tracking errors based on forecast risk. As we shall see, however, they also substantially outperform other techniques *ex post*, i.e., when we compute realized tracking error.

Regardless of the tracking method employed, the first step is to choose the number of assets (as well as the universe of assets) to construct the index tracking portfolio. Exhibit 1 illustrates the relationship between the tracking error and the number of assets used to track an index for the S&P 500. The tracking errors in the exhibit are for portfolios constructed using optimization techniques and BARRA's U.S. equity risk model. Not surprisingly, tracking error declines as we increase the number of assets used to track the index. Therefore, when comparing different asset choice and weighting methods we should always compare portfolios based on the same number of assets.

The number of assets in the tracking portfolio depends on the indexer's degree of risk aversion. More risk-averse managers prefer small tracking errors and thus need to hold more assets to achieve that, whereas less risk-averse managers may choose to hold fewer assets and bear the risk associated with large tracking errors. Given a bound on acceptable tracking errors, the number of assets in the tracking portfolio may be increased until that bound is satisfied. Moreover, the number of assets necessary for producing a given tracking error will depend on the technique used for indexing.

Given the number of assets in the tracking portfolio, what techniques may we use to pick these assets so as to track the index, and how do these techniques perform? It is to this issue that we now turn our attention.

Exhibit 1 Tracking the S&P 500

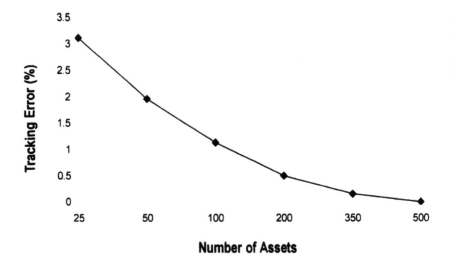

Largest Holdings

The simplest approach to tracking an index is to select the largest holdings and weight them using the scheme prescribed for the index, or to explicitly minimize the tracking error using these assets. For example, if we decide to track the S&P 500 with 50 assets, then we simply pick the 50 largest capitalization assets. We may then form a capitalization-weighted portfolio of these 50 stocks, or, alternatively, we may solve for the lowest-tracking-error portfolio of these 50 stocks.

The logic underlying this approach is straightforward. A large part of the index returns may be accounted for by a relatively small number of high-weight assets; hence it may be possible to capture a large part of the index return by trading in just these assets. The small number of assets keeps tracking costs down, particularly if the assets are liquid relative to assets with lower weights in the index. For example, the 50 highest capitalization stocks in the S&P 500 account for about 47% of the total capitalization of all stocks in the S&P 500, and the largest 200 stocks account for over 80% of the total capitalization. Moreover, liquidity tends to increase with market capitalization, so the larger capitalization stocks are also cheaper to trade.

Unfortunately, this approach lacks risk control. In particular, there is evidence that there is a common factor related to firm size and that large-capitalization stocks tend to move together. A capitalization-based index tracking portfolio makes a large bet on this size factor. In periods when the size factor has a significant return (positive or negative), the tracking portfolio's return will differ significantly from the index return. If the size risk factor has a large variance, the tracking error will be large. Moreover, if the final portfolio is simply a capitalization-weighted portfolio of the largest assets, then it is not even the best portfolio of the chosen assets. It is not constructed to have minimal tracking error of all portfolios of the chosen assets, and there is no consideration of the benefits versus costs of marginal changes in asset weights. Indeed, there is no control of asset specific risk or of the benefits of changing asset weights at the margin when selecting the assets that go into the portfolio.

Stratified Sampling

Stratified sampling attempts to minimize tracking error by building portfolios with exposures to important dimensions of risk that are aligned with those of the index. There are several variants of stratified sampling, differing primarily in the dimensions of risk employed and the technique used to match the exposures of the index and the tracking fund. A common implementation uses sectors and size as risk dimensions. Assets of the underlying index are partitioned into cells of a table with economic sectors (usually nine) along one axis, and size rankings (quartile or deciles) along the other. The desired number of assets is chosen in an attempt to replicate the distribution of weights in the table. This can be done by eye or with the use of a mathematical algorithm. Another scheme involves choosing a small set of assets which match the underlying index along the BARRA factor exposures by using a simple form of optimization which penalizes deviations from the target exposures. Some explicit effort to reduce the number of assets may also be required.

Stratified sampling does provide some risk control, but it is inadequate because risk dimensions other than those used to construct the cells are not considered. Moreover, it suffers from the same lack of consideration of specific risk and of the benefits of marginal changes in asset holdings as does the method that uses the largest weight assets. Explicit risk control, as well as consideration of marginal changes in portfolio holdings, brings us to the topic of optimization.

Optimization

Optimization is the most sophisticated method of building tracking portfolios. The problem is to construct the best tracking portfolio with a given *number* of assets, and it may be formulated as a *mixed-integer* quadratic program. At BARRA, we have dubbed this the "paring" problem, as the goal is to pare away many possible investments to find the optimal basket.

The aim is to find a portfolio with minimum tracking error at minimum cost. Since these goals are generally at odds, a risk aversion parameter, λ, is included to allow one to calibrate the tradeoff between them. Thus, we solve the following problem:

$$\text{Minimize} \quad F(h) \;=\; \lambda\left(h - h_I\right)' \Sigma \left(h - h_I\right) \;+\; TC(h)$$

$$\begin{aligned}
\text{Subject to:} \quad &\text{(i)} \quad e'h \;= 1\\
&\text{(ii)} \quad l_A \;\leq\; Ah \;\leq\; u_A\\
&\text{(iii)} \quad e'z \;\leq\; K\\
&\text{(iv)} \quad 0 \;\leq\; h_i \;\leq\; u_{hi} z_i, \quad\quad i = 1,n\\
&\text{(v)} \quad z_i \;= 0,1 \quad\quad\quad\quad, \quad\quad i = 1,n
\end{aligned}$$

where: n =   number of assets

         h =   vector of portfolio holdings

         h_I =   "   " index holdings

         z =   vector of binary variables

         e =   vector of 1's

         A =   constraint matrix

         l_A, u_A =   lower and upper bounds on the constraints

         u_h =   upper bounds on assets

         Σ =   asset covariance matrix

         λ =   risk aversion parameter

         K =   number of assets to be held in the portfolio

         $TC(h)$ =   convex, piecewise linear transactions costs

We use binary variables to restrict the number of assets in the portfolio. The variable 2 is 1 if asset i is in the portfolio and 0 if it is not. These variables, together with constraints (iii) and (iv) ensure that we hold K or fewer assets in the portfolio. This formulation also allows the portfolio to be constrained in several ways. For example, the holdings of individual assets or the general characteristics of the portfolio may be required to lie in given ranges.

The paring problem is significantly harder to solve to optimality than an ordinary convex quadratic program because of the limit on the number of assets in the portfolio. This restriction poses the formidable combinatorial challenge of finding the best subset of K assets from among a much larger universe. For example, there are over 180,000 possible choices when we try to pick just 10 of 20 assets, let alone 200 out of 7,000.

We have explored three approaches for "solving" the paring problem: branch and bound, genetic algorithms, and heuristics. *Branch and bound* is an integer programming technique for systematically searching the set of possible solutions while trying to exploit information that will reduce the scope of the search. Exhibit 2 illustrates the first few steps of a simple branch and bound approach for the paring problem. At the top node, we solve a much easier problem allowing the z variables to assume any value between 0 and 1. If the solution has no more than K positive holdings, or if the problem is infeasible, we are done. Otherwise, we select an asset, i, with a positive holding and branch on it by creating two new nodes, one in which the asset is forced to be 0 by setting $z_i = 0$, and the other which is chosen to be part of the portfolio by setting $z_i = 1$. The settings established at a node are passed to all its descendants. The process is then repeated at the lower nodes.

Exhibit 2 Branch and Bound for Asset Paring

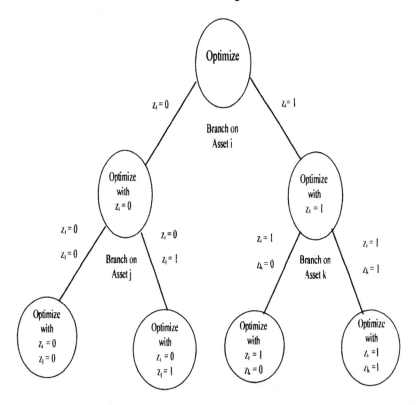

In the worst case, the method is forced to examine all possible combinations of K assets—an enormous number for even a small investment universe. The hope, however, is that information gained at the nodes of the tree during the search will help one avoid investigating many suboptimal paths. How so? The optimization problem solved at a node provides a lower bound on the best one can achieve by pursuing any branch arising from that node (remember that we are minimizing). Moreover, a solution with fewer than K assets at any node provides an upper bound for the original problem. Thus, if the best upper bound for the problem discovered thus far is below the lower bound for a node, we need not examine any branches arising from that node. More sophisticated implementations would include other schemes for obtaining bounds.

Rather than seek *the* optimal solution, we may use an approximate solution technique, a *heuristic,* to find a good solution to the problem in a reasonable amount of time. One such method that works satisfactorily for a range of real problems involves successive optimization. First, we solve the problem without regard to the number of assets in the portfolio. If the solution has no more than K assets, we are done. Otherwise, we discard a certain fraction of the assets in excess of the desired number from the investment universe, beginning with the smallest holdings. The process is repeated until a portfolio containing K or fewer assets is obtained. Some improvement in the quality of the solution can be obtained by dropping assets on the basis of the impact on the objective function. More advanced heuristics may be found in the references.

Lastly, one may use a *genetic algorithm* (GA) to find solutions to the paring problem. Genetic algorithms are search techniques based on the model of evolution and natural selection. To "solve" the paring problem using this approach, we start with a set of portfolios called a population. Portfolios in the population are selected to form a mating pool based on their objective function values, a process called reproduction. Next, in a step called crossover, portfolios are paired up, and with some probability they exchange some assets (genes) to form a new population. In the final step, mutation, genes of the new portfolios are randomly altered with some low probability. The problem is solved by iterating these three steps until a population's composition ceases to change. At that point, the best portfolio in the population is taken to be the solution.

To date, we have found that, for realistic problems, heuristics provide solutions of equal or superior quality at significantly less computational cost. Genetic algorithms require significantly more time than heuristics and generally provide inferior solutions. Similarly, we have found that branch and bound is not currently a practical method of solving the paring problem. In our experience, it generally did not reach optimality before generous computational limits were exceeded, even for small realistic problems. These comparisons may change as future advances are made in these technologies.

Empirical Investigation

How effective are these methods for producing good tracking portfolios? We investigated three ways of tracking the S&P 500 and BARRA's ALLUS indexes, two capitalization-weighted indices. The first approach simply selects the largest stocks in the index and weights them by capitalization. The second method is a variant of stratified sampling, which constructs a portfolio that matches the index as closely as possible along all BARRA risk factors. This scheme achieves almost complete control of factor risk, far more than most implementations. However, no effort is made to reduce specific risk. Lastly, we used the BARRA optimizer (and risk model), which employs a heuristic to reduce the number of assets in the portfolio.

To evaluate these approaches, we used them to track the S&P 500, with 50 stocks, and the ALLUS, with 200. Our backtests were run from January 1, 1973, through December 31, 1996 for the S&P 500, and from January 1, 1987 through December 31, 1996 for the ALLUS. All portfolios were rebalanced monthly. In this study, we focused on achieving the best tracking error possible and therefore omitted transactions costs.

It is interesting to examine the forecast tracking errors of portfolios constructed by each method. Table 1 contains these forecasts[2] for portfolios formed as of August 1, 1993. It further decomposes the tracking error into common factor and specific components. The rationale underlying each method is clearly visible in the numbers. By selecting the largest holdings and cap weighting, we try to make the tracking portfolio look like the index at the asset level, but we pay no attention to factor risk. Consequently, this approach has the lowest specific risk and the largest factor risk. At the other extreme, stratified sampling tries to match the index's exposure to common sources of risk without much regard for trying to match it at the asset level. Thus, it has the lowest factor risk and the highest specific risk. Optimization strikes the a balance between these two considerations, producing the best total forecast tracking error.

Results related to realized tracking error are provided in Table 2. Optimization produces the lowest tracking error over the entire sample and within each subperiod, for both indexes. Stratified sampling comes in second, generally doing better than using the largest stocks. Moreover, the differences in the relative performance of the three methods are substantial, showing the power of optimization techniques coupled with an accurate risk model.

---

[2]These forecasts were produced using BARRA's U.S. equity model

Table 1 Forecast Risk of Tracking Portfolios as of August 1, 1993

Index and Tracking Portfolio	Components of Tracking Error	Approach		
		Largest Holding	Stratified Sampling	Optimization
		(%)	(%)	(%)
S&P 500 with 50 stocks	Total	2.93	2.90	1.98
	specific	1.66	2.90	1.80
	factor	2.42	0.00	0.83
ALLUS with 200 stocks	Total	2.67	2.36	1.02
	specific	0.82	2.36	0.98
	factor	2.56	0.00	0.30

Table 2 Realized Tracking Errors

Tracking	Period	Approach		
		Cap-Weighted	Stratified Sampling	Optimization
		(%)	(%)	(%)
S&P 500 - 50 stocks	7301-9612	3.68	2.56	1.87
	8701-9112	3.58	2.42	2.00
	9201-9612	2.74	3.08	1.69
ALLUS - 200 stocks	8710-9612	2.75	2.11	1.21
	8701-9112	2.73	2.04	1.17
	9201-9612	2.67	2.25	1.21

Conclusion

Successful indexing requires a delicate balance between reducing tracking error and reducing transactions costs. There are a number of ways of achieving this balance. At one end of the spectrum lie straightforward methods, such as simply choosing the largest holdings in the index. At the other extreme lie quantitative methods that combine optimization methods with sophisticated risk forecasts to find the portfolio that minimizes tracking error while keeping transactions costs in check. An empirical investigation of three methods shows that optimization provides substantially better realized tracking errors than its competitors.

Bibliography

Connor, G., "The Three Types of Factor Models: A Comparison of Their Explanatory Power," *Financial Analysts Journal*, May/June 1995, pp. 42-46.

Goldberg, David E., *Genetic Algorithms in Search, Optimization and Machine Learning*, Addison Wesley Publishing Company, Inc., 1989.

Liu, S., and Dan Stefek, "A Genetic Algorithm for the Asset Paring Problem in Portfolio Optimization," *Operations Research and Its Applications*, ISORA 95, pp. 441-449.

Nemhauser, G.L., and Laurence A. Wolsey, *Integer and Combinatorial Optimization*, Wiley Interscience, 1988.

Rudd, A., "Another Look at Passive Management," *Journal of Accounting, Auditing and Finance*, vol. 1, no. 3, Summer 1986, pp. 242-252.

Stefek, D., "Paring," BARRA Equity Research Seminar, June 1993, Section L.

Enhanced Indexing— Without Enhanced Risk?

James C. McKee
Vice President and Quantitative Consultant
Callan Associates Inc.

As the S&P 500 continues to frequently beat traditional active managers, plan sponsors increasingly accept passive strategies as the core component of their overall equity allocation. Not coincidentally, in recent years enhanced index strategies have become a popular substitute for traditional active strategies. Defined by objective, true enhanced index managers minimize the risk of straying far from their benchmark by, in effect, imitating that benchmark. At the same time, they claim to add value to that benchmark.

The paradox to resolve is whether "enhanced" returns disappear as an enhanced indexing strategy behaves more like a passive index. Plan sponsors may wonder whether it is worth hiring active managers to reduce non-market risk to virtually zero when their strategy is essentially to replicate the market benchmark. As managers behave more like an index, are they getting index-like returns or are they consistently adding value? Is it worth doing at all? What are the bets that add value? Or, indeed, is there a free lunch here?

To assess this index-like investment strategy, we first review the playing field and the players in it. Many types of enhanced index strategies exist. Each has its strengths and weaknesses. Next, we look at our measuring sticks. How do we judge whether these managers are adding value after adjusting for any risk? Then, with peer groups of enhanced index managers assembled, we evaluate historical performance and look ahead at what to reasonably expect in the future. Throughout this analysis, the source of manager returns is Callan Associates Inc., which collects manager data directly from institutional money managers.

The Playing Field

Over the last decade, two primary strategies for enhancing performance have evolved in the U.S. equities market. In this study, we will focus on the performance of managers using these two strategies.

Stock-Based Strategy

Managers using a stock-based strategy look at stock fundamentals-earnings, assets, projected growth, and other valuation measures. Then, through various diversification techniques, they explicitly or implicitly minimize sector risk relative to the S&P 500 benchmark while attempting to add value through stock selection. To minimize tracking error (i.e., risk unexplained by the benchmark), these portfolios typically contain between 150 and 500 holdings, which is far more than the 40 to 80 stocks usually held by traditional types of active managers.

Synthetic-Based Strategy Using Enhanced Cash Techniques

This strategy relies on liquid S&P 500 futures to achieve equity exposure while the manager enhances returns on the available underlying cash collateral. A portfolio of S&P 500 futures plus risk-free returns on the futures' cash collateral yield a total return equal to that of the underlying S&P 500 index. To enhance the cash return, these managers make modest bets on duration, credit, or other forms of fixed-income risks.

Money managers also offer many other types of "enhanced indexing" strategies. In this study, we did not evaluate these strategies because either: (1) not enough managers use the strategy to construct a meaningful peer group for evaluation, or (2) they contained too much tracking error to be considered as an "enhanced index" strategy. These strategies include:

"Guaranteed" Enhanced Index Strategy

These managers guarantee an annual premium (e.g., 0.25%) over the S&P 500. This strategy typically includes a liquidity constraint requiring the investor to lock up the portfolio for three or more years (although by paying a penalty fee, the investor can get out). By definition, this strategy has no tracking error but does include credit risk (i.e., the creditworthiness of the underwriter). A sample listing of managers offering a "guaranteed" enhanced index product is presented in Appendix A.

Arbitrage-Based Strategy

In the early 1980s, this enhanced index strategy was a popular technique that extracted an attractive alpha via arbitrage between the derivatives' markets and the underlying stock market. In this arbitrage technique, managers look at the prices for stocks, options, and futures and take advantage of mispricing, simultaneously buying "cheap" and selling "expensive" markets. As these markets became more efficient in the late 1980s, this profitable difference became marginal. Through leveraged and opportunistic investing, though, this strategy still survives. Few of the original investment managers, however, remain. Another arbitrage technique uses convertible securities against the underlying stock to extract an extra return. A sample listing of managers offering these arbitrage-based products is presented in Appendix A.

Equitized Market-Neutral Strategy

In this "portable alpha" strategy, managers hold long/short stock portfolios with effectively zero correlation to the equity market and an S&P futures position to gain equity exposure. However, the results of these managers indicate that, if unconstrained, they often have so much tracking error that they do not really imitate the benchmark—they just simply use the benchmark as their foundation, doubling the alpha of their process through a long/short strategy and leaving a lot of tracking error. Responding to this concern, these managers note that they can limit the market-neutral portfolio to a fraction of the total S&P futures position, thereby controlling tracking error. Only return data for the unconstrained market-neutral strategies, however, was available.

The Yardstick

How do we judge the two primary enhanced index strategies? For this study, we will use three measures:

Tracking Error

Tracking error measures the amount of risk not explained by the market (i.e., the S&P 500). Specifically, it represents the standard deviation of the excess returns of the portfolio relative to the benchmark over a series of time periods. This measure over various time periods allows us to see how consistently managers keep unexplained risk, or residual risk, out of the portfolio. From the enhanced index investor's perspective, less tracking error is better, all other things being equal.

Excess Return

Excess return in this study is defined as a relative return calculated by dividing the portfolio's factored return (e.g., 10% = 1.10) by the benchmark's factored return (e.g., 8% = 1.08) and reverting the resulting quotient back to a percentage form (e.g., 1.10/1.08 = 1.0185 = 1.85%). Unlike excess return defined as the nominal difference between the returns of the portfolio and its benchmark, this relative return measures the true excess performance over time.

Information Ratio

This ratio is defined simply as excess return divided by tracking error. This last measurement is particularly useful for evaluating enhanced index managers. Managers who deliver excess returns with very little benchmark risk will score well with high information ratios.

The Players

What is the money manager lineup? How do we assemble style groups for evaluation? To identify these managers, we examined Callan's universe of all U.S. equity managers reporting composite returns[1] from their separate or commingled accounts. To narrow the focus, we eliminated equity products with tracking error consistently greater than 2% over recent three-year periods.[2] Passive index products, which have tracking error typically less than 1%, were also dropped. The remaining products were divided in appropriate groups based upon their stated investment objective and process. From this screening process, we identified 22 funds using stock-based enhanced index strategies, with over $80 billion in total assets managed against the S&P 500. Looking for synthetic-based strategies using enhanced cash techniques, we identified 10 funds with over $16 billion in total assets managed against the S&P 500. For the list of individual managers included in these peer groups, see Appendix A.

Instant Replay

Elements of Style

How have these two groups of enhanced index managers performed? Using a return-based style analysis,[3] we looked at the "footprints in the sand," determining whether these products have historically behaved like

---

[1] Returns in Callan's equity database are gross of fees.

[2] Because of the strict criteria concerning tracking error, this process undoubtedly filtered out a few potential enhanced indexers reporting a broad composite of returns. These managers who were excluded due to tracking error over 2% might say, "We do enhanced indexing, too. But we let our clients tell us how much benchmark risk they will accept."

[3] This return-based style analysis, based on methodology described in William Sharpe's "Asset Allocation: Management Style and Performance Measurement," in *The Journal of Portfolio Management* (Winter 1992), assigns a sensitivity of portfolio returns to six investment style factors: large-cap growth and value indices, mid-cap growth and value indices, and small-cap growth and value indices. This analysis allows us to identify a set of passively managed indices that best represents the variance of a manager's returns.

the S&P 500 or whether they have capitalization or growth/value tilts. Exhibit 1 presents ellipses defining 80% of the funds within each style group. Measurements along the x-axis represent the degree of growth/value factors affecting performance; measurements along the y-axis reveal tilts toward large- or small-cap exposure.

The smallest ellipse in the chart represents the synthetic-based indexers using enhanced cash, while the next largest ellipse represents the stock-based style. The broadest ellipse covers Callan's Core Equity style group, which consists of about 40 managers whose primary goal is to beat the S&P 500 using sector as well as stock-selection bets; for these managers, tracking error is not the primary concern. In this chart, Core Equity managers clearly show much more style variance than the enhanced index managers. The enhanced cash group is the most narrowly focused, indicating that the managers in this group closely track the index. But who is adding more value?

Cumulative Returns

To examine historical performance, let's first look at the cumulative return history of these managers over the last ten years. We see in Exhibit 2 that over this time the average stock-based and enhanced cash managers added value, before fees, over the S&P 500. In contrast, the Core Equity style group underperformed the S&P 500, let alone both sets of enhanced indexers.

Since these lines are tightly clustered, let's stretch the S&P line flat to look at the relative returns of these groups over the S&P benchmark. From this perspective, shown in Exhibit 3, we cut through the time period bias and identify where the average managers have had their periods of down performance. For example, as we look at the average enhanced cash strategy beginning in 1994, we see that performance has leveled off relative to the benchmark, whereas stock-based performance has followed, to some degree, its own pattern.

For comparative purposes, we threw in a "free lunch." This free lunch is simply the S&P 500 plus an excess return of 1%, annualized year after without any benchmark risk. Below the S&P baseline, we find the Core Equity style group with the Callan Broad Market Index, which represents the top 2,000 U.S. stocks. The poor relative performance of the Callan

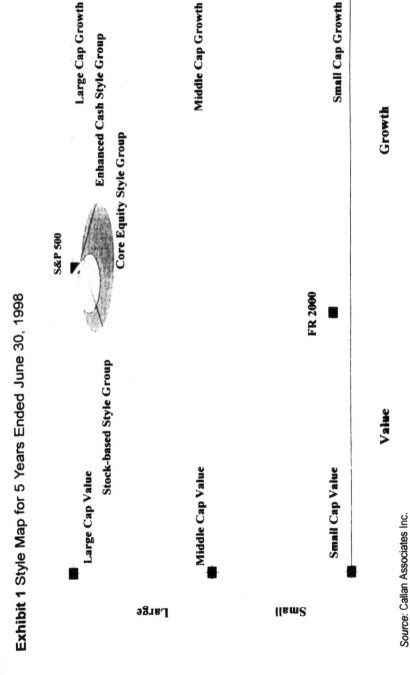

Exhibit 1 Style Map for 5 Years Ended June 30, 1998

Source: Callan Associates Inc.

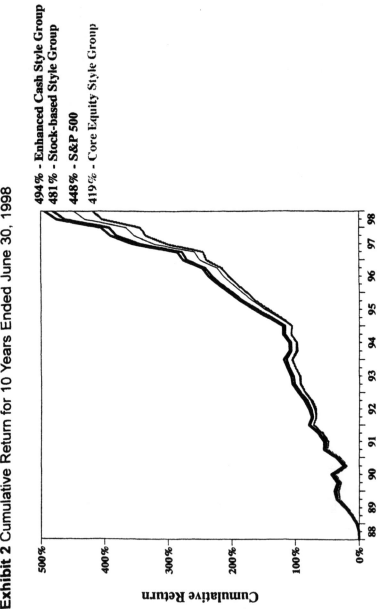

Exhibit 2 Cumulative Return for 10 Years Ended June 30, 1998

494% - Enhanced Cash Style Group
481% - Stock-based Style Group
448% - S&P 500
419% - Core Equity Style Group

Source: Callan Associates Inc.

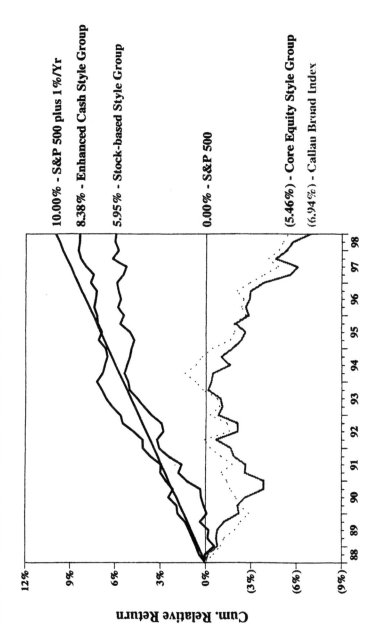

Exhibit 3 Cumulative Relative Returns versus S&P 500

10.00% - S&P 500 plus 1%/Yr

8.38% - Enhanced Cash Style Group

5.95% - Stock-based Style Group

0.00% - S&P 500

(5.46%) - Core Equity Style Group

(6.94%) - Callan Broad Index

Source: Callan Associates Inc.

Broad Market Index through 1990 and after 1993 is primarily attributable to its exposure to small cap stocks. Given the similar pattern of performance, the Core Equity group clearly suffers from the effects of that same exposure via typically equal-weighted stock holdings.

Risk vs. Return

Next we consider the risk or volatility that goes with these styles of returns. In the two-dimensional world shown in Exhibit 4, we see that the enhanced cash strategy is slightly more clustered around the S&P 500 for the five-year period ended June 30, 1998. The free lunch, denoted by the triangle, is directly above the S&P by 1%. As expected, it offers higher returns with no more volatility. During this time period, we see that in aggregate the two enhanced index strategies have fared well relative to the benchmark, although some managers within the groups underperformed. While the enhanced cash group has performed with less downside experience, the stock-based group has had more upside potential. With its typically smaller cap exposure, the Core Equity group evidently had a difficult time beating the benchmark, as shown in Exhibit 4.

Although comparing absolute levels of volatility may indicate similar risk between a portfolio and its benchmark, we need to understand how much of portfolio volatility is not explained by the benchmark. Furthermore, to isolate any time-period bias, we need to evaluate how much this risk fluctuates over time. For these purposes, the measure of tracking error over rolling time periods is helpful.

Tracking Error

Over rolling three-year time periods, we can observe the range of tracking error, or portfolio volatility unexplained by the benchmark. Exhibit 5 shows that enhanced cash indexers have had low residual risk historically; that is, they have consistently been under the 2% tracking error assigned for the screen. While the style group was based on the more recent three-year periods, we can see over time they have consistently maintained the risk under 2%. That is a comforting pattern if you are looking for an enhanced manager who is sticking to the benchmark. For

Exhibit 4 Returns versus Standard Deveiation for 5 Years Ended June 20, 1998

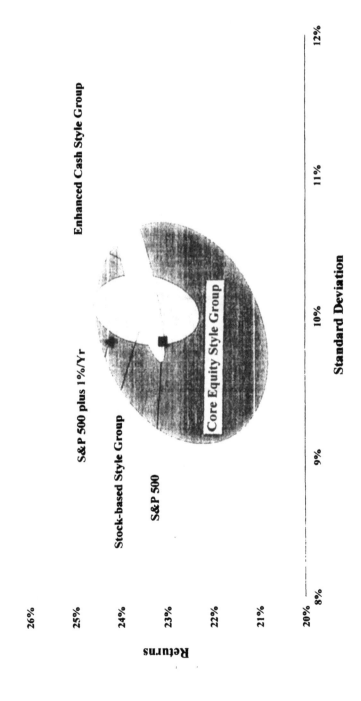

Source: Callan Associates Inc.

Exhibit 5 Tracking Error versus S&P for Rolling 3-Year Periods
Enhanced Cash Style Group

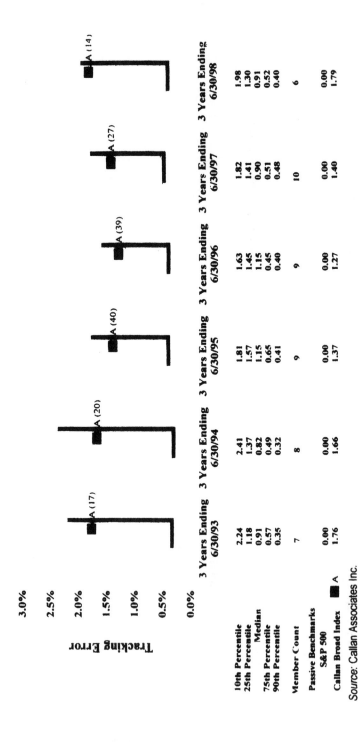

	3 Years Ending 6/30/93	3 Years Ending 6/30/94	3 Years Ending 6/30/95	3 Years Ending 6/30/96	3 Years Ending 6/30/97	3 Years Ending 6/30/98
10th Percentile	2.24	2.41	1.81	1.63	1.82	1.98
25th Percentile	1.18	1.37	1.57	1.45	1.41	1.30
Median	0.91	0.82	1.15	1.15	0.90	0.91
75th Percentile	0.57	0.49	0.65	0.45	0.51	0.52
90th Percentile	0.35	0.32	0.41	0.40	0.48	0.40
Member Count	7	8	9	9	10	6
Passive Benchmarks						
S&P 500	0.00	0.00	0.00	0.00	0.00	0.00
Callan Broad Index ■ A	1.76	1.66	1.37	1.27	1.40	1.79

Source: Callan Associates Inc.

Exhibit 6 Tracking Error versus S&P 500 for Rolling 3 Year Periods Stock-based Style Group

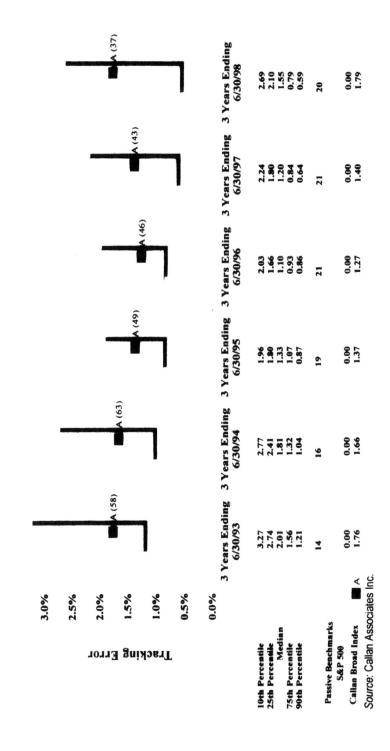

Source: Callan Associates Inc.

a reference point, the chart also shows the tracking error of the Callan Broad Market Index. This reference point gives a sense of how much volatility in the total stock market is unexplained by the S&P 500. For Core Equity managers, the average tracking error over these time periods was 2.91%.

Relative to their enhanced cash counterparts, the stock-based enhanced indexers in Exhibit 6 show systematically more tracking error. Nevertheless, it appears that, as a group, they have been fine-tuning their risk control process and reducing tracking error since 1993.

Excess Return

As we look next at the measure of excess return, we see a pattern evolving for the synthetic-based strategies using enhanced cash. In Exhibit 7, over the recent 3-year periods, the relative return has been declining or eroding. Why did the performance weaken over time, and is there a prospect of further erosion? Since this group has effectively no capitalization or style factor exposure relative to the S&P 500, the performance problem is attributable to an excess return derived from bond market exposure. Rising interest rates in 1994 and 1996 have undermined this strategy. Looking ahead, though, we can expect this group to perform better, assuming interest rates stabilizes or decline, particularly with a positively sloped yield curve.

For the stock-based enhanced indexer shown in Exhibit 8, we see that the excess return is much more wide-ranging, with also a slight erosion in recent periods. We can expect this pattern of widely varying returns to continue since this group extracts its excess return in many uncorrelated ways of stock selection. In other words, its excess return is not dependent, to some degree, on one single variable, like the yield curve. Nevertheless, stock-based enhanced indexers can conceivably be adversely affected as a group if one or more fundamental variable (e.g., forecasted earnings, earnings growth momentum, price momentum) commonly used in stock selection becomes a consistently poor predictor of excess returns.

Exhibit 7 Excess Return versus S&P 500 for Rolling 3-Year Periods
Enhanced Cash Style Group

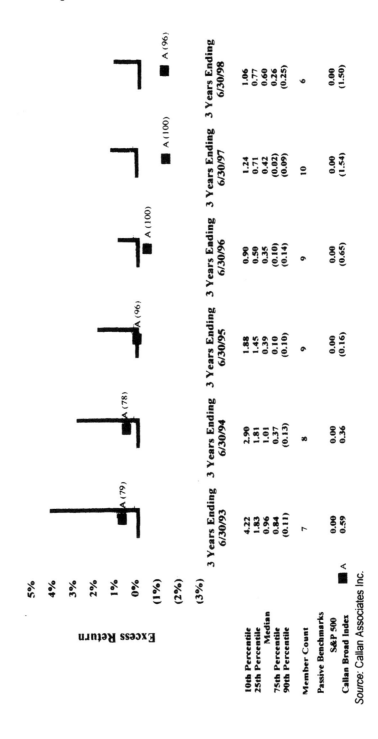

	3 Years Ending 6/30/93	3 Years Ending 6/30/94	3 Years Ending 6/30/95	3 Years Ending 6/30/96	3 Years Ending 6/30/97	3 Years Ending 6/30/98
10th Percentile	4.22	2.90	1.88	0.90	1.24	1.06
25th Percentile	1.83	1.81	1.45	0.50	0.71	0.77
Median	0.96	1.01	0.39	0.35	0.42	0.60
75th Percentile	0.84	0.37	0.10	(0.10)	(0.02)	0.26
90th Percentile	(0.11)	(0.13)	(0.10)	(0.14)	(0.09)	(0.25)
Member Count	7	8	9	9	10	6
Passive Benchmarks						
S&P 500	0.00	0.00	0.00	0.00	0.00	0.00
Callan Broad Index	0.59	0.36	(0.16)	(0.65)	(1.54)	(1.50)

Source: Callan Associates Inc.

Exhibit 8 Excess Return versus S&P 500 for Rolling 3-Year Periods Stock-based Style Group

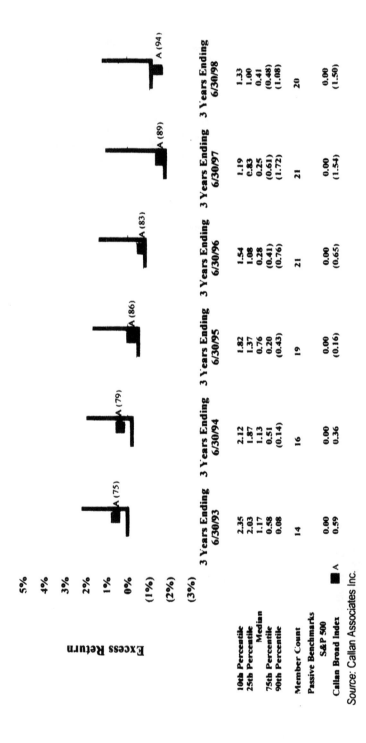

	3 Years Ending 6/30/93	3 Years Ending 6/30/94	3 Years Ending 6/30/95	3 Years Ending 6/30/96	3 Years Ending 6/30/97	3 Years Ending 6/30/98
10th Percentile	2.35	2.12	1.82	1.54	1.19	1.33
25th Percentile	2.03	1.87	1.37	1.08	0.83	1.00
Median	1.17	1.13	0.76	0.28	0.25	0.41
75th Percentile	0.58	0.51	0.20	(0.41)	(0.61)	(0.48)
90th Percentile	0.08	(0.14)	(0.43)	(0.76)	(1.72)	(1.08)
Member Count	14	16	19	21	21	20
Passive Benchmarks						
S&P 500	0.00	0.00	0.00	0.00	0.00	0.00
Callan Broad Index	0.59	0.36	(0.16)	(0.65)	(1.54)	(1.59)

■ A

Source: Callan Associates Inc.

Exhibit 9 Information Ratio versus S&P 500 for Rolling 3-Year Periods
Enhanced Cash Style Group

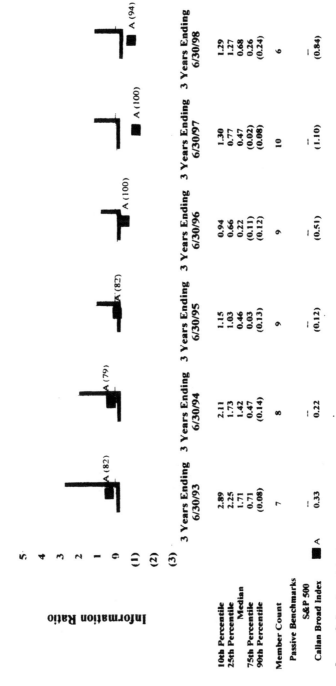

	3 Years Ending 6/30/93	3 Years Ending 6/30/94	3 Years Ending 6/30/95	3 Years Ending 6/30/96	3 Years Ending 6/30/97	3 Years Ending 6/30/98
10th Percentile	2.89	2.11	1.15	0.94	1.30	1.29
25th Percentile	2.25	1.73	1.03	0.66	0.77	1.27
Median	1.71	1.42	0.46	0.22	0.47	0.68
75th Percentile	0.71	0.47	0.03	(0.11)	(0.02)	0.26
90th Percentile	(0.08)	(0.14)	(0.13)	(0.12)	(0.08)	(0.24)
Member Count	7	8	9	9	10	6
Passive Benchmarks						
S&P 500	--	--	--	--	--	--
Callan Broad Index	0.33	0.22	(0.12)	(0.51)	(1.10)	(0.84)

Source: Callan Associates Inc.

Exhibit 10 Information Ratio versus S&P 500 for Rolling 3-Year Periods Stock-based Style Group

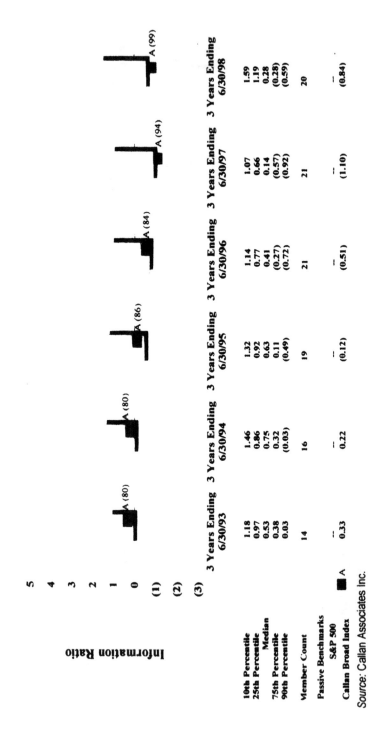

	3 Years Ending 6/30/93	3 Years Ending 6/30/94	3 Years Ending 6/30/95	3 Years Ending 6/30/96	3 Years Ending 6/30/97	3 Years Ending 6/30/98
10th Percentile	1.18	1.46	1.32	1.14	1.07	1.59
25th Percentile	0.97	0.86	0.92	0.77	0.66	1.19
Median	0.53	0.75	0.63	0.41	0.14	0.28
75th Percentile	0.38	0.32	0.11	(0.27)	(0.57)	(0.28)
90th Percentile	0.03	(0.03)	(0.49)	(0.72)	(0.92)	(0.59)
Member Count	14	16	19	21	21	20
Passive Benchmarks						
S&P 500 A	—	—	—	—	—	—
Callan Broad Index	0.33	0.22	(0.12)	(0.51)	(1.10)	(0.84)

Source: Callan Associates Inc.

Information Ratio

Exhibits 9 and 10 display the last measurement, information ratio. Broadly speaking, a value of 1.0 or more indicates that the excess return over the benchmark was created more by skill than luck. Exhibit 9 shows an eroding performance in the enhanced cash strategy. Exhibit 10 shows a more stable range of performance among stock-based enhanced indexers throughout the same time periods.

The Wrap-Up

Looking back, we see discernible patterns of performance among the stock-based enhanced indexers and synthetic-based indexers using enhanced cash. Because non-market risk is substantially controlled, portfolio bets are marginal. Not surprisingly, we find that the historical excess returns have also been limited. While these groups do not hit home-runs, they do hit singles consistently for a winning performance. And when they lose in particular time period, they do not lose by much. Over the 10-year period ended June 30, 1998, the average stock-based enhanced indexer has delivered an annualized 0.58% excess return, while the synthetic-based counterpart's excess return has been about 0.81%.

Management Fees

Relative to passive indexing, one caveat of enhanced index management is higher stated fees, which average about 0.3%[4] per year among peers in each of the two primary strategies. Fees for either of these strategies range from 0.15% to 0.35%, while most passive managers fall below this range. On the other hand, the average stated fee for active, large-cap managers is about 0.5%, with a range from 0.40% to 0.70%. For those investors looking for a passive-like base fee and willing to share excess returns above a certain level, enhanced indexers frequently offer a performance-based fee schedule.

---

[4]Assuming a $50 million account.

Event Risk

Event risk, which describes an identifiable risk causing a strategy to perform differently from its objective, is important to consider. For example, enhanced cash strategies using enhanced cash are exposed to the whims of the Federal Reserve. In 1994, when the bond market was hurt significantly by Fed actions, enhanced cash managers suffered because rapidly rising short-term rates undermined their strategy. Among stock-based enhanced indexers, event risk is more manager-specific. That is, performance relative to the S&P 500 is determined by each manager's proprietary process.

Each stock-based enhanced indexer faces its own type of event risk. For example, price momentum risk among stocks can affect some fundamentally driven models that do not chase faddish stocks, like the "Nifty Fifty" stocks of the late 60s. When "Nifty Fifty" stocks get "niftier" (i.e., defying logic fundamentally), then quantitative techniques that say, "These stocks are overvalued; therefore, underweight them." are going to underperform. Consequently, these unique qualities within the stock-based group require a more detailed investigation to identify superior managers.

Ignoring the means of generating returns, we see that these two strategies offer a choice between a bond market alpha and stock market alpha; that is, interest rate risk versus stock valuation model risk. Arguably, it makes sense to blend diverse styles of enhanced indexers in the portfolio to lessen the impact of these risks.

Limits to Growth?

As more money is placed in these strategies, are there limits to profitable returns on investment? Not likely for strategies using enhanced cash techniques, since the futures and cash markets are extremely liquid. Stock-based strategies are also unlikely to face liquidity constraints, since managers in these strategies invest in individual stocks with amounts not too far from market weights. However, other strategies have shown practical limits on how much money can be invested. For example, the arbitrage style of enhanced indexing using convertible arbitrage depends on profitable differences in pricing that can disappear quickly with large sums of money.

Since the mid-1980s, the basic strategy of arbitraging stocks and futures has suffered a dramatic loss of the original alpha. As the easy profits dried up in the flood of incoming money, this strategy is now dominated by broker-dealers who can trade with leverage and minimal transaction costs. Nevertheless, with significant leverage and tight risk controls, this strategy can still generate attractive excess returns.

Why Do It at all?

This question still requires careful thought. Enhanced indexing is obviously an attractive compromise between traditional core equity and passive index managers. Relative to passive indexing, though, enhanced indexing requires much more due diligence to determine the best fit of investment objectives and guidelines. This marriage of active and passive strategies offers index-like returns with attractive upside potential for a modest fee. Accordingly, this strategy is ideal for two types of institutional investors: (1) those looking for more action in their passively managed portfolios with limited downside risk relative to the S&P 500, and (2) those dissatisfied with fully active managers but not willing to capitulate completely to the passive alternative.

Appendix

Sample Listing of Enhanced Index Products

Managers with Synthetic-Based Enhanced Indexed Products Using an Enhanced Cash Technique

Advanced Investment Management
BEA Associates
Clifton Group Inv. Mgmt. Co.
Harris Investment Management
Lotsoff Capital Management
Mellon Capital Management
New Amsterdam Partners, L.P.
Pacific Investment Management Company
PanAgora
Smith Breeden

Managers with Stock-Based Enhanced Indexed Products

Aeltus Investment Management, Inc.
Alliance Capital Management
Barnett Banks Trust Company
Bankers Trust
Berkeley Quantitative Advisors, Inc.
Brinson Partners, Inc.
BZW Barclays Global Investors
INVESCO (formerly Chancellor Cap)
DSI International Management, Inc.
Fidelity Management Trust Co.
Franklin Portfolio
Goldman Sachs
Independence Investment Associates, Inc.
INTECH
IDS Advisory
Mellon Equity Associates
Mitchell Hutchins Asset Management Inc.
Morgan (J.P.) Investment Mgmt.
PanAgora Asset Management
Parametric Portfolio Associates
TradeStreet Investment Associates
Westpeak Investment Advisors, L.P.

Managers with Arbitrage-Based Enhanced Indexed Products

Camden Asset Management
Noddings Investment Group
UBS Asset Management (New York) Inc.
Ward & Wissner Cap Management
Westridge Capital Management

Managers with a "Guaranteed" Enhanced Indexed Product

Pacific Mutual Insurance
SunAmerica

CHAPTER 6

Choosing a Benchmark

Judy M. Bednar
Director of Passive Investments
Northern Trust Quantitative Advisors

The development of indexes and passive investing follows a pattern of development similar to that of the natural sciences. Initially, the endeavor was focused on the descriptive. The first indexes were constructed primarily to convey the general tone and characteristics of the market. However, just as the natural sciences evolved from the normative to the predictive, indexes began to be used not merely to describe market activity and past events but also as a basis for measuring investment performance, and more recently, as a tool to construct a passively managed portfolio.

Active versus Passive Benchmarks

Because many of the most broadly-referenced indexes are also the oldest, they were developed with only the normative objectives in mind and well before their potential for performance measurement or portfolio construction was envisioned. In choosing a benchmark for passive investing, investors and investment managers must look beyond an index's longevity and popularity and instead consider those factors that affect an index's suitability for a passive investment strategy. Even today, much of the discussion about an appropriate benchmark has taken place within the context of measuring an active investment manager's performance.[1] While certain of these characteristics are applicable to passive investment benchmarks as well, there are other characteristics that are unique to the passive environment. For instance, some obvious requirements for a passive strategy are that the benchmark be established a priori and that it be investible. Additionally, information about the composition of an index, both its constituents and the weights of those constituents, must be accessible to a passive manager. For active managers, the rule is that a benchmark must be a practicable alternative (i.e., an investible alternative); but, while a manager should be able to purchase and hold all the securities included in the benchmark, he or she is unlikely to actually do it. For a passive manager, an inability to hold securities included in the index may significantly constrain his or her ability to meet expectations. Also, active managers select benchmarks to conform to their management style; passive managers conform their style to the benchmark. As a result, the costs and efficiencies attached to using a particular benchmark can be paramount.

Asset Class Exposure

The first requirement in choosing a benchmark for an indexed investment strategy is to determine the market segment to which exposure is desired. Typically, that exposure is part of an overall asset allocation strategy. The benchmark selected should reflect the required market exposure, to the greatest extent possible—neither overlapping other investment allocations nor leaving wide gaps in desired exposure. For example, using a broad market index that covers the entire U. S. equity market may be inappropriate if the investor already has acquired substantial large-capitalization domestic equity exposure through other investments. Conversely, if the investor wishes to maintain a tilt—capitalization, sector, style, etc.—care must be taken not to undermine the tilt through the selection of too broad a benchmark. Thus, the choice of an appropriate benchmark should be made within the context of other investments already made or planned. The investor also needs to be sure that the index chosen actually does provide the factor exposure that is desired. If, for

---

[1]See, for example, J. Bailey, "Evaluating Benchmark Quality," *Financial Analyst's Journal.* May-June 1992. See Also J Squires, ed., Performance Evaluation, Benchmarks. and Attribution Analysis. Association for Investment Management and Research, 1995.

example, the goal is to participate in the "small-cap" effect, not all small-cap indexes may provide that exposure.

When the investor is using an asset allocation model that sets allocations which depend on expected returns, the selection of a benchmark to provide appropriate market class exposure becomes even more critical. To the extent that the benchmark's returns deviate from those of the asset class benchmark used in the model, the allocations derived from the model might not provide the anticipated long-term performance. While this may be less of an issue for large-cap, developed markets, where the correlations between various indexes are high, the differences can be significant for small-cap and emerging market indexes. Even in developed markets, the broader regional or global indexes will demonstrate substantial differences in returns over time because of different country weightings, even though the correlations between the various country indexes is high.

Nonetheless, investors must look beyond the desired asset class exposure and into which index best provides that exposure. As noted earlier, the costs and efficiencies of investing can vary significantly from index to index. Since one of the advantages of passive investing is its lower cost relative to active management, it may be counterproductive to choose a benchmark that obviates that benefit.

Index Methodologies

Careful consideration should be given to the methodology used to construct the index itself. Some indexes are based purely on a ranking scheme that includes all the securities in the market that are within the targeted range of the chosen factor. For example, stocks may be ranked by market capitalization, with all the securities grouped into either "large" or "small" cap. Or, stocks may be ranked by book-to-market, with all the securities grouped into either "growth" or "value." No securities are omitted. Other indexes provide broad coverage of the market or a market sector but do not include all the securities in the sector. Instead, the index itself may be based on a sampling methodology. Such a process is designed to limit the number of securities in the index while still being representative of the sector or market. Such indexes typically are designed to ensure that characteristics of the index, such as industry representation, price-earnings and book-to-market ratios, capitalization, beta, etc., are closely matched to that of the underlying market or sector. When mergers/acquisitions or bankruptcies force a change in the index, additions to these types of indexes are considered to make sure the index retains its representativeness.

The criteria for weighting securities in an index may differ. An index may be price-weighted, equal-weighted, capitalization-weighted, etc. A price-weighted index includes the same number of shares of each stock, and the passive investor would also hold the same number of shares of each constituent. Equal-weighted indexes include the same market value of each security. As prices change, the number of shares required to keep the weights equal would change. Capitalization-weighted indexes include each security at their market capitalization. Changes in shares outstanding would result in a change in required holdings, but price changes would automatically be reflected in relative weights and require no rebalancing. Alternatively, weighting methods can depend on other criteria not directly related to the security prices and shares outstanding. One widely used alternative for country weights in regional/international indexes is to weight by each country's GDP. When economic growth diverges from market movements, holdings must be rebalanced.

Rebalancing frequency also differs from index to index. Some indexes are rebalanced (or reconstituted) only annually. Any changes between the annual rebalancing reflect only mergers/acquisitions, bankruptcies, etc. At the other end of the spectrum are indexes that have no set rebalancing frequency; constituent changes result not only from mergers and acquisitions or bankruptcies, but also from the creation of new companies, significant changes in company size or representativeness, etc. Between the two extremes are indexes that are rebalanced/reconstituted monthly, quarterly, or semi-annually, or combinations of regular rebalancing (for small changes) and occasional adjustments (for significant changes).

Families of indexes created by a single provider are likely to feature parallel construction of the various indexes. For example, large and small-capitalization indexes from the same provider are likely both to be based either on a pure market ranking or on a selection criteria methodology. Indexes for different countries will also use similar construction methodology. In contrast, local market indexes are likely to vary from country to country. Some will use price-weighting, others cap-weighting; the coverage can be broader for some local market indexes than others.

Constituent Selection and Representativeness

With an index that uses a selection process rather than pure ranking, care should be taken to make sure the index matches the underlying market segment for which exposure is desired. Because such indexes do not include all the securities in the market, there is also the risk that the index may miss out on the specific returns of the excluded stocks because of factor biases in the selection methodology. For example, an index that is intended to represent the small-cap sector might not participate in the "small-cap effect" if that return happens to be concentrated in the stocks that were excluded. The investor should also consider whether the selection process used for the index itself injects an unintended element of active decision-making into what is designed to be a passive strategy.

On the other hand, an index that uses a more inclusive process by definition is likely to contain more securities. The number of securities included in the index will affect both a passive manager's ability to track the index and the costs involved. Since custody costs are typically a function of the number of holdings in a portfolio and the number of transactions, the broadness of market exposure provided by an index should be weighed against the higher custody costs resulting from holding a larger number of securities. Such an index may also include more illiquid securities, raising transaction costs. (See the section on Liquidity below.) Although a passive manager may use sampling or optimization to reduce the number of holdings, it will be at the cost of greater tracking variance versus the index and potentially increased turnover as well. An index with a more limited membership may provide the same general asset class exposure with lower attendant tracking variance and/or turnover.

Selection Criteria and Turnover

The methodology used to construct the index can also affect turnover, which can affect returns relative to the benchmark because of the higher costs associated with it. Turnover in the benchmark is typically not a concern for active management, where the assumption is that the expected outperformance will outweigh any costs resulting from higher turnover. Considering that the active strategies themselves produce turnover of 50% to 100% or even higher, the turnover in the benchmark tends not to be noticeable. For passive investors, however, higher turnover will always result in a greater reduction in returns relative to the benchmark, increasing tracking variance. Commissions, bid/ask spreads, and market impact will all contribute to higher transactions costs when an index has higher turnover. The more illiquid the asset class, the more significant the turnover issue becomes. Custody costs, which are constructed to reflect the number of expected transactions, will be higher as well. Finally, higher turnover can significantly reduce the after-tax returns of taxable investors. For all of these reasons, the amount of turnover in the index itself should be carefully considered. Indexes that include all securities within a market segment that meet certain criteria typically have larger turnover than indexes that use a selection process. For example, a small-cap index that bases its constituents solely on market cap ranking, which can change at both the upper and lower bounds when the index is rebalanced, will have significantly higher turnover than a small-cap index that uses a sampling procedure to establish constituents whose characteristics match those of the sector as a whole. Or, for style indexes, an arbitrary inclusion rule based on a particular characteristic, or set of characteristics, may result in significant shifting back and forth between the two styles at reconstitution. Screening rules or ranges can be used to limit turnover from these factors, although the benefit should be weighed against the potential risk of diluting the sector exposure that is being provided by the benchmark index. The large-cap U.S. equity indexes most widely used as benchmarks for passive investment typically have very low turnover, in the range of 5% per year or less. Small-cap indexes, on the other hand, have annual turnover that can range as high as 25% to 30% per year. International indexes are typically in between those two ranges.

Weighting Methods and Turnover

Weighting methods also can have a significant impact on turnover, thereby affecting costs. Capitalization-weighted indexes have the lowest turnover, all else equal, because changes in the relative prices of constituent securities will not require portfolio rebalancing. Any adjustments made to capitalization, such as adjustments for free float, increase turnover whenever the amount of free float changes. An equal weighted index will typically have the greatest turnover associated with it. The turnover will be a function of the distribution of returns of the constituent securities; the more divergent those returns, the more frequently the portfolio will have to be rebalanced to bring the constituents back into alignment, and the greater the size of the rebalancing. International or global indexes that include countries at weights other than their capitalization, such as GDP-weighted indexes, will have to be rebalanced whenever the relative returns in the markets diverge from the relative growth rates in GDP. Similarly, adjusting for changes in crossholdings will add to turnover as well.

Return Calculations and Tracking

A less significant but still important factor that should be considered is the methodology used for calculating index returns. Typically, domestic U.S. equity indexes assume dividends are reinvested on ex-date. Since dividends are not actually paid until several days (or in some cases, weeks) later, the dividends cannot actually be reinvested until they are received (barring the use of derivatives; see below). In a rising market, the investment portfolio will underperform because of this "dividend drag." Some international indexes assume dividends are reinvested monthly and may use a smoothed-dividend assumption rather than actual dividends. While this methodology simplifies returns calculations, particularly in international markets where dividend reporting is less accurate than in the U.S., it creates an additional source of tracking variance. This variance can be significant if the dividend flows themselves exhibit strong seasonal patterns, as is often the case.

Pricing methodologies may also differ. Some domestic U.S. index providers may use primary exchange prices to calculate returns, while others may use composite prices. For securities not traded on the exchanges, or for securities not priced on a given day, last-traded price, bid price, or midpoint of bid and ask price may be used. On international markets, not only may pricing sources or rules be different, but exchange rates used to translate back to the base currency may vary. To the extent that the pricing methodology differs from the prices used to evaluate the portfolio, tracking variance will be introduced.

These difficulties may be addressed by calculating index returns based on the index's constituents, but using prices and dividend reinvestment assumptions that are consistent with the portfolio evaluation. However, care should be taken to ensure that the calculation of the index returns remains objective.

Liquidity

The liquidity of the constituent securities should also be considered when choosing an index. If a significant portion of the index is made up of illiquid securities, the costs involved in trading the securities will reduce returns relative to the benchmark. Both the wider bid-ask spreads and the greater market impact resulting from purchasing illiquid securities will contribute to costs. Although typically any given security is such a small part of the index that its purchase by a passive manager is unlikely to result in significant market impact, there are exceptions. If the index is price or equal weighted, any illiquid securities included must be purchased in the same amounts (shares or market value) as the more liquid constituents. In that case, the purchase by a passive manager may well have market impact if the size of the overall investment is sufficiently large.

Even if the security has only a small weight in the index, there may be a significant "index effect" on the day of its addition to or deletion from a widely used passive benchmark. The demand (supply) at the time of its addition (deletion), resulting from rebalancing to reflect the change, can be many days trading volume for some more illiquid securities. Alternatively, a security may be included at its market cap weight in the index, but the actual amount of the stock available for investment, the "free float", may be much lower. The lower free float may result from large government holdings or holdings by insiders, or from cross-holdings between corporations. There may also be government imposed restrictions on foreign ownership that result in a security in an index being available only at substantial premiums that add to the cost of investment. If the changes are implemented at the same time as they are incorporated in the index, no tracking variance will result. Nonetheless, the investor will have participated in the market impact resulting from index managers' efforts to match the index. Alternatively, changes in the index can be incorporated over a period of time, reducing market impact and participation in the "index effect". However, the tradeoff will be in the form of higher tracking variance versus the index, as the investor is exposed to price risk during the period of adjustment to the index change.

Ownership Restrictions

Governments may also forbid investments in some securities on the grounds of national security, control of national resources, or some other sovereign prerogative. Or, they may limit or control repatriation of dividends or even principal. If a passive benchmark is chosen that includes such securities, the additional tracking risk associated with not holding those securities must be carefully weighed against the potential illiquidity of the investment. Even if no current restrictions are in place, the potential for the imposition of such restrictions should be considered, particularly for investments in emerging markets where changes in the regulatory environment may happen more frequently or unexpectedly.

Derivatives

The investor should also consider the availability of derivative instruments that can provide synthetic exposure or hedges to the indexed investments. Derivatives may be used as either an adjunct to a strategy that invests primarily in the underlying securities or as an independent strategy to provide passive exposure. Even if the manager is providing the bulk of the desired passive exposure through investment in the underlying securities, there is typically cash drag resulting from small residual cash balances, dividend accruals, or other receivables. The tracking variance associated with cash drag can be minimized through investing in derivative instruments. Derivatives can also be used to help manage index changes as well as cash contributions/withdrawals by reducing the number of transactions required to raise cash or invest cash to implement a change or respond to a cash flow.

The availability of derivatives becomes more significant if the assignment is short-term or if the index assignment is within the context of an asset allocation strategy. Index strategies are often used to bridge the gap during a transition between active managers. If the expected horizon of the transition is only a few weeks or a few months, gaining exposure synthetically may be the most cost-efficient approach, particularly if the underlying market is illiquid or has high start-up costs (transactions-based custody fees, etc.). If the investor employs an asset allocation overlay strategy that requires frequent rebalancing, the availability of synthetic instruments may significantly reduce the costs involved.

However, derivative instruments may not be available for some markets, or may be extremely expensive. In other markets, the indexes underlying the derivative instruments may differ significantly in their composition from the investor's chosen benchmark. For instance, international derivative instruments typically are based on a local country index. The most popular international benchmarks, however, include country indexes that may differ significantly from the local market index. As noted earlier, international benchmarks typically create country indexes that are parallel in construction. Local market indexes have grown out of local market custom and are likely to differ significantly in construction from country to country, and by extension, from the country indexes of the international benchmarks. The greater those differences are, the greater the tracking variance that will result from the use of derivative instruments. If the investor is using a regional or global benchmark, the tracking variance due to constituent differences in a given country will be compounded by the absence of any derivative instruments for some countries. While a basket of available derivatives can be constructed to minimize expected tracking variance, the exposure nonetheless may differ significantly from that provided by the benchmark.

Even if derivatives exist, they may not be readily available to a particular investor. U.S. residents, for example, may only purchase C.F.T.C. approved index futures. That reduces the number of futures readily available for their use. Although over-the-counter synthetic instruments can be constructed to provide exposure to markets where listed derivatives are not available or where usage is restricted, those structures have other issues that should be considered.

Taking these factors into account when choosing a benchmark for a passive strategy that will employ derivatives will reduce the likelihood of unexpected outcomes and disappointment.

Investor Goals versus Manager Concerns

It is important to recognize that the investor and the manager have different priorities when establishing a benchmark. The investor's choice is likely to reflect long-established benchmarks for active managers. It may also be motivated by familiarity with an index and the index's popularity, or by the choices made by the investor's peer group. The manager's preference, on the other hand, is for a benchmark that is easy to replicate, with a minimum of tracking variance. Such an index requires less effort to manage, and typically a more attractive end result for the client. The challenge is to establish a benchmark that meets the client's goals while taking into account the issues that affect the manager's ability to provide the expected performance. Considering the criteria discussed here as a basis in the process of selecting a benchmark for passive management will increase the likelihood that expectations will be met.[2]

[2] I would like to thank John Goodwin, Jeremy Baskin, Susan French, and Andrew Buchner for their suggestions and assistance.

CHAPTER 7

The "S&P Effect" Has Moved Beyond the S&P Composite

Claudia E. Mott
First Vice President
Director of Small-Cap Research
Prudential Securities Inc.

Eddie Cheung
Associate Quantitative Analyst
Prudential Securities Inc.

As the amount of assets benchmarked to the S&P Composite has grown, investors have become increasingly aware of a phenomenon known as the "S&P Effect." Essentially, the S&P Effect describes the unusual behavior of stock prices when it is announced they are being added to or removed from the S&P Composite (Composite).

Investors should be aware that the S&P Effect can also be seen in relation to changes in the S&P MidCap (MidCap) and even in the relatively new S&P SmallCap (SmallCap), but inclusion in either index is not a guarantee of future long-term success. Those with short-term trading interests, however, may find the following results of this study of interest.

Assets Under Management Are Rising

The concept of indexing has been in existence for some time; the assets tied to the S&P Composite now exceed $375 billion (Exhibit 1). The S&P MidCap was introduced in 1991, and over its brief history assets indexed to it have already reached $17.0 billion. Since the launch of the S&P SmallCap in Fall 1994, the assets passively managed against the benchmark have reached $3.0 billion (Exhibit 2).

Exhibit 1 Assets Indexed to the S&P Composite Have Grown Dramatically

Indexes Assets Under Management ($ Bil.)

Source: Standard & Poor's Corp.

Exhibit 2 The S&P MidCap and SmallCap Indexes Are Also Attracting Money

Indexes Assets Under Management ($ Bil.)

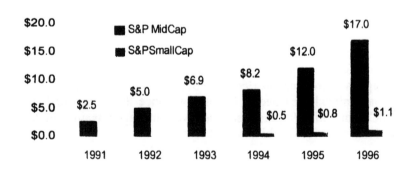

Source: Standard & Poor's Corp.

The Measurement Period Has Changed

Prior to 1989, Standard & Poor's Corp. would announce and implement changes on the same day. But concern over the impact on stock prices caused the company to change this policy. In October 1989, it began announcing changes one week prior to the date they would become effective. Although such scheduling is not always possible, most of the recent changes have followed this pattern. In our analysis, we looked at returns on an absolute and a relative basis, from the announcement date to the effective date (the A/E period) and for one week, two weeks, one month, and three months following the change. Because of the abnormal price change that resulted from Freeport McMoRan's splitting into pieces, we had to exclude it from our analysis.

Management of the Indexes Causes Some Changes

As the three indexes comprise the 1,500-stock S&P Super Composite, the committee that oversees the changes faces many new challenges. In order to keep the indexes in line with their respective market-cap size segments, large companies must be moved from the top into the next larger index, while very small companies must be dropped off the bottom into a smaller index or out of the universe altogether. As the total assets managed against these benchmarks have increased, S&P has made a concerted effort to minimize the disruption to stock prices by keeping turnover within this 1,500-stock universe to a minimum. In our performance tables, we detail the price performance of these various subsets of change: companies added from another index; companies moved to another index; and companies deleted but still trading.

The S&P Effect Is Well Documented

Academics have published numerous studies on the stock market's S&P Effect, and most have concluded that there is some abnormal positive return associated with a stock's being added to the S&P Composite, and stocks deleted from the index tend to experience price declines. In a recent paper, Anthony W. Lynch and Richard R. Mendenhall of NYU found that the additions have had abnormal excess returns of 3.81% in the period from the announcement date through the effective date and that the deletions have lost 12.69% over the same period.

The Small-Cap S&P Effect Started in 1996

In the first two years of the SmallCap index's existence, there was no positive impact on the prices of stocks being added to the index. In fact, on average the additions underperformed the index, and the deletions outperformed. In 1996, however, the companies added to the index outperformed by an average 1.48% during the A/E period (Exhibit 3). But then they proceeded to underperform over each period following inclusion in the index (Table 1). The percentage of companies that outperformed also shows that the A/E periods has the highest percentage of companies that beat the index at 60.0% (Table 2).

Exhibit 3 Additions to the SmallCap Index Don't Outperform in the Short Term

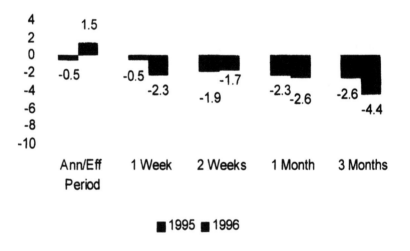

Source: Standard & Poor's Corp., Prudential Securities Inc.

Table 1 'The S&P Effect' Didn't Hit The S&P SmallCap Until 1996

	No. Of Firms	Return Fr. Announcement To Effective Date	Subsequent Return From Effective Date				A/E Period	Relative Performance vs. S&P SmallCap Index			
			1 Wk.	2 Wks.	1 Mo.	3 Mos.		1 Wk.	2 Wks.	1 Mo.	3 Mos.
Additions											
Overall	112	0.98	-1.05	-0.80	0.89	7.61	0.28	-1.20	-1.37	-0.72	1.79
1994	7	1.16	-1.30	-0.64	3.42	17.60	-0.12	-0.81	-0.55	2.76	12.38
1995	45	-0.32	0.08	-0.94	-0.02	4.27	-0.52	-0.54	-1.87	-2.31	-2.58
1996	60	2.11	-1.93	-0.82	-0.73	0.96	1.48	-2.26	-1.68	-2.61	-4.42
Deletions											
Overall	112	1.83	0.60	-0.19	-1.39	-1.31	1.10	-0.25	-0.84	-1.59	-5.93
1994	7	2.48	0.29	-3.72	-4.79	-6.61	1.18	0.08	-2.67	-0.60	-5.97
1995	45	3.18	-3.21	-2.26	-4.95	-8.99	2.91	-3.57	-2.49	-5.62	-14.25
1996	60	-0.16	4.72	5.41	5.57	11.67	-0.78	2.74	2.63	1.45	2.45
Added From Another Universe											
Overall	18	-9.58	-2.10	-1.98	0.10	5.35	-10.22	-2.92	-3.85	-2.97	-0.95
1995	7	-11.66	2.69	0.46	5.70	13.19	-12.71	2.41	-1.23	2.66	4.78
From S&P Composite	6	-13.20	2.86	0.53	7.50	15.38	-14.38	2.80	-1.02	4.55	7.60
From S&P MidCap	1	-2.48	1.69	0.00	-5.08	0.00	-2.70	0.09	-2.49	-8.64	-12.14
1996	11	-7.49	-6.89	-4.42	-5.50	-2.49	-7.73	-8.25	-6.46	-8.61	-6.68
From S&P Composite	8	-9.62	-5.59	-3.26	-8.01	-2.33	-9.94	-6.52	-4.73	-11.19	-11.11
From S&P MidCap	3	-1.80	-10.34	-7.52	-1.32	-2.70	-1.83	-12.88	-11.10	-4.31	-0.76
Moved To S&P MidCap											
Overall	15	4.87	0.24	1.87	5.02	-0.81	4.77	-0.05	0.79	2.80	-6.21
1995	7	4.33	0.08	1.81	-1.46	-3.47	4.77	0.45	1.64	-1.04	-7.70
1996	8	5.42	0.40	1.92	11.49	1.84	4.77	-0.54	-0.05	6.64	-4.71
Deleted But Still Trading											
1995	9	8.96	-8.81	-9.72	-10.84	-12.69	7.93	-9.61	-10.70	-13.17	-19.60
1996	19	-4.25	8.11	8.23	9.62	16.59	-4.92	6.91	6.53	6.69	9.12

Source: Prudential Securities Inc.; Standard & Poor's Corp.

Table 2 Being Added to the S&P SmallCap Isn't a Guarantee of Performance
Success

Percent Of Companies Outperforming S&P SmallCap

	A/E Period	1 Week	2Weeks	1Month	3 Months
Additions					
1995	53.3	48.9	44.4	40.0	40.0
1996	60.0	40.0	45.0	42.1	36.7
Moved To					
S&P MidCap					
1995	85.7	42.9	57.1	42.9	57.1
1996	87.5	50.0	62.5	75.0	42.9
Deleted But					
Still Trading					
Overall	39.3	53.6	42.9	48.0	34.8

Source: Prudential Securities Inc.; Standard & Poor's Corp.

Dropping Into the S&P SmallCap Isn't Necessarily Great for Performance

Companies that were added from another S&P universe have fared very poorly in the A/E period. Stocks that came from the S&P Composite lost an average 14.38% relative to the S&P SmallCap index in 1995, and those dropping into the index in 1996 gave up 9.94%. The differential in the amount of assets indexed to the Composite compared with the SmallCap would account for some of this negative price performance. More shares will potentially be sold as a result of the deletion than will be purchased to fill the positions in the SmallCap. These companies also went on to underperform over the subsequent week, two weeks, month, and three months following inclusion in the S&P SmallCap.

The companies coming to the S&P SmallCap from the S&P MidCap also underperformed in the A/E period in both 1995 and 1996, with relative declines of 2.7% and 1.8%, respectively (Exhibit 4). In 1996, the mid-cap refugees also lagged the SmallCap index in the subsequent four performance periods.

Exhibit 4 Coming From Another S&P Index to the SmallCap Isn't a
Short-term Plus

Average relative return from announcement to effective date

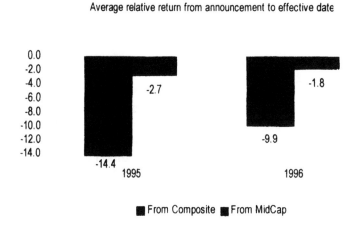

■ From Composite ■ From MidCap

Source: Standard & Poor's Corp., Prudential Securities Inc.

SmallCap Deletions Arise for Three Major Reasons

To keep the market-cap range and the average market-cap characteristics in check, Standard & Poor's must move the larger companies into the MidCap index when the opportunity arises. Conversely, companies whose market values have gotten quite small and are no longer appropriate to the general size range of the index must also be removed. Finally, companies that are being acquired or delisted need to be taken out.

The performance patterns for the deletions from the S&P SmallCap have changed. In 1994 and 1995, the stocks dropped from the index rose in the A/E period but declined in all but one of the periods subsequent to deletion. This past year, however, the companies dropped from the index declined 0.78% relative to the index in the A/E period but went on to perform quite well relative to the benchmark in the subsequent four performance periods.

The lion's share of the good performance can be attributed to the companies that were deleted but are still trading. These stocks dropped almost 5.0% in the A/E period, but they gained almost 7.0% in the week following deletion and were up 9.0% relative to the SmallCap index in the three months following their deletion. This strong performance, however, is not widespread—only 34.8% of the companies beat the index in that three-month period.

Moving to the MidCap Index Gives Stocks a Short-Term Lift

In the past two years, 15 companies have moved from the SmallCap index to the MidCap index. In both years, over 85% of the stocks outperformed the SmallCap index in the A/E period. Such a move is not a guarantee of future success, though. Within the first week of addition to the MidCap index, the percentage of outperformers fell to 42.9% in 1995 and to 50.0% in 1996.

Being Dropped From the Index Isn't the Kiss of Death

Over the past two years, 28 companies have been dropped from the SmallCap index, generally because their market cap has fallen substantially from the point they were included and no longer meets the limits that S&P wishes to maintain. It might be expected that any stock dropped from an S&P index would fall on hard times, but that isn't the case.

In general, such stocks do poorly relative to the benchmark after the announcement, as only 39.3% of the names outperformed during the A/E period, with fewer than 50% beating the SmallCap index over the subsequent two-week, one-month, and three-month periods. But the average returns for the names dropped in 1996 were actually positive, indicating that a few names had some mighty big returns after being eliminated from the index.

The Mid-Cap S&P Effect Seems to Have Peaked

The assets tied to the MidCap index have accumulated at a steady pace since its inception in 1991. The S&P Effect for additions to the MidCap index seems to have peaked in 1994, when 91.3% of the companies beat the index in the A/E period. In that year, the 23 companies added to the index gained an average 5.01% relative to the index (Table 3). In 1996,

Table 3 Additions to the S&P MidCap Show Positive Price Performance Prior to Inclusion

	No. Of Firms	Return Fr. Announcement To Effective Date	Subsequent Return From Effective Date				AJE Period	Relative Performance vs. S&P SmallCap Index			
			1 Wk.	2 Wks.	1 Mo.	3 Mos.		1 Wk.	2 Wks.	1 Mo.	3 Mos.
Additions											
Overall	130	3.18	-1.13	0.17	-0.16	3.12	2.67	-1.39	-0.98	-1.99	-1.19
1991	4	-1.47	-0.92	4.52	2.47	8.76	-1.79	-1.42	0.75	-2.24	0.61
1992	15	4.44	0.61	1.35	-4.22	4.15	3.73	0.21	0.35	-5.81	0.61
1993	15	4.14	-0.20	1.53	5.49	6.47	3.41	0.47	1.46	5.02	3.77
1994	23	4.81	-1.27	-0.97	-3.51	-5.57	5.01	-1.51	-1.32	-3.09	-5.12
1995	37	5.48	-1.71	-0.75	-2.71	1.62	4.29	-2.06	-1.54	-4.36	-4.50
1996	36	1.66	-3.26	-4.64	1.49	3.30	1.38	-4.02	-5.59	-1.44	-2.50
Deletions											
Overall	130	2.72	0.99	0.33	1.76	1.29	4.40	-0.64	-0.63	-0.56	-2.42
1991	4	6.17	-1.25	-1.81	-1.12	4.98	17.92	-1.38	-5.06	-3.13	-4.65
1992	15	4.07	2.05	1.04	4.02	-9.43	3.36	1.63	0.31	1.53	-11.63
1993	15	7.01	-3.00	-5.94	-3.43	-7.43	6.46	-2.49	-6.03	-4.09	-9.59
1994	23	-1.05	5.42	4.15	5.1	4.28	0.85	-2.72	5.07	2.57	9.62
1995	37	-0.06	1.53	2.50	1.84	9.08	-2.04	1.02	1.42	-0.10	0.77
1996	36	0.19	1.17	2.03	4.12	6.23	-0.14	0.08	0.49	-0.15	0.98
Added From Another Universe											
Overall	18	2.88	-0.33	0.52	3.21	-0.32	2.71	-0.44	0.62	2.14	-5.25
1995 From S&P SmallCap	7	4.33	0.08	1.81	-1.46	-3.47	4.53	0.28	1.71	-1.49	-7.65
1996	11	1.44	-0.73	-0.76	7.88	2.83	0.89	-1.16	-0.47	5.77	-2.86
From S&P Composite	3	-6.98	-2.23	-5.85	-1.51	6.97	-8.03	-2.96	-5.26	-3.29	-2.39
From S&P SmallCap	8	4.59	-0.17	1.14	11.40	1.65	4.24	-0.48	1.32	9.17	-3.01

continued on next page

Table 3 Additions to the S&P MidCap Show Positive Price Performance Prior to Inclusion, *cont'd.*

	No. Of Firms	Return Fr. Announcement To Effective Date	Subsequent Return From Effective Date				A/E Period	Relative Performance vs. S&P SmallCap Index			
			1 Wk.	2 Wks.	1 Mo.	3 Mos.		1 Wk.	2 Wks.	1 Mo.	3 Mos.
Moved To Another Universe											
Overall	45	5.60	-1.20	-1.56	-2.24	0.03	4.90	-1.45	-2.28	-3.80	-4.19
1992	5	7.98	2.72	1.63	4.02	-9.43	5.86	2.55	0.76	1.53	-11.63
1993	6	9.94	-1.19	-2.33	-1.06	-2.24	8.93	-0.53	-2.55	-1.45	-3.97
1994	7	0.94	-2.18	-2.86	-5.31	-0.96	1.92	-3.09	-3.74	-4.60	-0.63
1995	14	5.74	-6.36	-6.65	-9.20	-1.72	4.43	-6.09	-6.97	-10.53	-7.99
To S&P Composite	13	6.37	-6.98	-7.16	-9.52	-1.86	5.03	-6.55	-7.39	-10.71	-7.91
To S&P SmallCap	1	-2.48	1.69	0.00	-5.08	0.00	-3.27	-0.12	-1.50	-8.17	-9.12
1996	13	3.42	1.02	2.41	0.34	14.48	3.36	-0.09	1.11	-3.97	3.27
To S&P Composite	10	8.15	-1.49	-1.03	-4.80	8.89	7.32	-2.27	-1.99	-9.95	-5.30
To S&P SmallCap	3	-12.33	9.39	13.90	17.45	29.39	-9.84	7.21	11.46	13.99	23.26
Deleted But Still Trading											
1994	3	-13.69	28.90	19.32	30.05	16.52	-0.73	-11.68	23.50	18.41	33.54
1995	8	-15.51	6.74	9.15	11.41	18.08	-17.40	6.19	7.94	9.49	10.21
1996	8	-2.88	-1.38	0.30	7.35	-10.04	-3.56	-2.82	-1.49	3.58	-3.29

Source: Prudential Securities Inc.; Standard & Poor's Corp.

the percentage of companies that beat the index dropped to 55.6%, and although they still outperformed, the margin dropped to 1.38% (Table 4).

Table 4 Once Announced, S&P MidCap Issues Moved to the S&P Composite Perform

Percent Of Companies Outperforming S&P MidCap

	A/E Period	1 Week	2 Weeks	1 Month	3 Months
Additions					
1991	25.0	50.0	50.0	50.0	50.0
1992	60.0	53.3	46.7	46.7	66.7
1993	86.7	66.7	53.3	66.7	60.0
1994	91.3	21.7	34.8	26.1	21.7
1995	89.2	40.5	45.9	43.2	43.2
1996	55.6	36.1	25.0	44.4	37.0
Moved To					
S&P Composite					
1992	80.0	60.0	40.0	40.0	20.0
1993	100.0	33.3	33.3	50.0	33.3
1994	71.4	28.6	14.3	42.9	57.1
1995	100.0	46.2	23.1	30.8	38.5
1996	100.0	30.0	30.0	0.0	28.6
Deleted But					
Still Trading					
Overall	36.8	57.9	52.6	57.9	50.0

Source: Prudential Securities Inc.; Standard & Poor's Corp.

The additions to the MidCap index tend to perform poorly after their inclusion. The average excess return for the 130 additions are negative in all four of the periods after the effective date that we measured, and the latest years accounted for much of the decline. Over the past three years, the excess return in the first week has gotten progressively worse, and the 1996 additions lost 4.02% relative to the index in the first week (Exhibit 5).

Exhibit 5 Becoming A Member of the MidCap Index Isn't a Guaranty of
Success

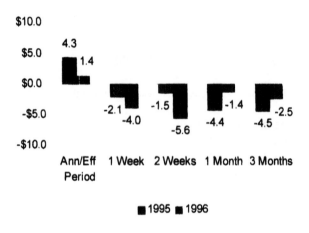

Source: Standard & Poor's Corp., Prudential Securities Inc.

Over the past two years, 18 of the 73 companies added to the MidCap
have come from either the Composite or the SmallCap (as noted previously, those moving up from the SmallCap have tended to perform well
relative to their former universe). The stocks coming from the SmallCap
have also beaten their new universe as well, to the tune of 4.53% in 1995
and 2.88% in 1996. In both years, this outerperformance continued into
the second week post addition.

Stocks Coming From the Composite Have Fared Poorly

Falling out of the Composite was a fall from grace for the three companies added to the MidCap in 1996. The amount of stock being sold by
S&P Composite index funds is not entirely offset by the buying volume
of Midcap indexers, which contributes to the poor performance. These
stocks gave up an average 8.03% relative to the S&P MidCap in the A/E

period and continued to lose ground over the first two weeks as members of the S&P MidCap.

MidCap Deletions Fit Into Four Categories

Stocks deleted from the MidCap index fall into four potential categories. Stocks that have gotten large enough to move up into the S&P Composite or small enough to drop into the S&P SmallCap are two reasons. Some companies are deleted from the indexes entirely; others are removed owing to acquisition or delisting.

The Impact on Deletions Didn't Hit Until 1995

The average return for the 130 stocks that have been deleted from the MidCap index over the past six years is a positive 4.40% for the A/E period. In the past two years, however, the return for deletions has been

negative in the A/E period and positive in most of the periods subsequent to the effective date.

Only two years in which the number of companies moved to the Composite and the SmallCap indexes are worth summarizing–1995 and 1996. As might be expected, being moved up to the Composite is a positive for stock prices, while being dropped to the SmallCap is a negative (Exhibit 6). The stocks moved to the Composite beat the MidCap by 5.03% in 1995 and 7.32% in 1996 during the A/E period, with 100.0% of the companies outperforming in 1993, 1995, and 1996. But in both years the subsequent return relative to the MidCap was negative across all four periods after the effective date.

The four companies that were moved to the SmallCap index gave up ground relative to the MidCap index; the one deletion in 1995 lost an average 3.27%, and the three in 1996 dropped 80 basis points on average during the A/E period. These issues went on to underperform both the Smallcap and Midcap indexes for the two week period after the effective date.

Exhibit 6 Moving From MidCap to Composite is a Positive, to SmallCap
a Negative

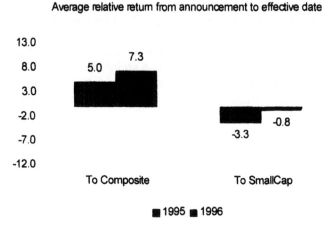

Average relative return from announcement to effective date

■ 1995 ■ 1996

Source: Standard & Poor's Corp., Prudential Securities Inc.

Being Dropped From the MidCap Index Is a Mixed Blessing

Initially, the companies being removed from the S&P MidCap and not moved into another S&P index underperform the benchmark, but the magnitude ranged from a loss of 73 basis points in 1994 to an average relative decline of 17.4% in 1995. Overall, just over 50% of the deleted-but-still-trading companies beat the index over the four periods we measured post deletion.

- These results are quite a bit better than for the former component stocks of the S&P SmallCap.
- In 1994, the three deletions generated positive excess returns in the subsequent two-week, one- month, and three-month periods.
- The eight deletions in 1995 outperformed the S&P MidCap across all four subsequent periods.
- In 1996, the eight companies removed from the index had more varied results–lagging in the subsequent one-week, two-week, and three month periods, but outperforming after one month.

The S&P Effect Has Its Place for the Short-Term-Oriented Investor

The results of this study show that the S&P Effect has its strongest impact on the companies that "moved" up from one index to a larger one. The effect, however, has lasted only during the period from the announcement date through the date the change was made effective. In most cases, this has been a one-week period, but for some issues it has been as short as a day or two.

Reference

Lynch, Anthony W., and Mendenhall, Richard R., "New Evidence on Stock Price Effects Associated with Changes in The S&P 500 Index," New York University, Working Paper Series, 1995.

The S&P 500 is Not Your Father's Index

Thomas McManus
Investment Strategist
Strategy Connection

Despite the recent introduction of exchange-traded derivative securities on the Dow Jones Industrial Average, the Standard & Poor's Composite Index of 500 stocks (S&P 500) remains the "Big Daddy" of stock indexes. Beyond its traditional role as the standard against which most financial institutions measure their U.S. stock market success, the S&P 500 has garnered huge interest on behalf of those investors who aim merely to attain, rather than to exceed, average returns available from U.S. equities.

The "Market Portfolio"

For quite some time, the S&P 500 index portfolio has generally been regarded as "the market portfolio" whenever the attractiveness of U.S. equities is compared with other countries, other asset classes (such as cash, bonds, or real estate), or economic fundamentals (such as Gross Domestic Product, productivity, or corporate profit margins). Why?

Popular market averages coexist primarily because they each serve a particular need. Market watchers remain loyal to their familiar indexes because of their venerable historical records, though new indexes can gain prominence if they provide some unique insight into the workings of an important market sector. Even among investment professionals, an inquiry such as "How's the market?" is usually answered by stating the number of points, up or down, that the Dow Industrials have moved. But if the topic should shift to quarterly performance, or the long-term returns generally available from U.S. stocks, the index of choice is the S&P 500. Presumably, that's because Ibbotson Associates' *Stocks, Bonds, Bills, and Inflation*, long considered the bible of performance measurement, has always depended on the S&P 500 as its proxy for returns on "large company stocks."

Despite the fact that the S&P 500 is predated by the Dow, its broader coverage, capitalization weighting, and availability of historical valuation statistics enable the S&P 500 to overcome its relatively junior status. What's more, as research involving the financial markets developed over the past few decades and theories such as the Capital Asset Pricing Model (CAPM) were born, academics and quantitative practitioners pushed the S&P 500 even further into the limelight as the basis for comparing opportunities and risks adherent to stocks in general. Furthermore, the S&P 500 has also been the preferred economic barometer among practitioners of that dismal science (its momentum is one of the constituents of the oft-quoted index of leading economic indicators) as well as policy makers at the Federal Reserve. Equity valuation—especially as it relates to wealth creation and the resulting impact on consumer attitudes—has recently attracted increased attention at the Fed.

What many observers seem to be missing is that the S&P 500 is not the market portfolio, but instead only a subset. It is my contention that the S&P 500 is more attractive than the market portfolio of U.S. companies, and that its allure—relative to the average company—has been increasing over time.

A Valuation and Performance Standard

In the relevant context, Webster's Dictionary defines *standard* as "something established by authority, custom, or general consent as a model, example or rule for the measure of quantity, weight, extent, value, or quality." Clearly, the definition applies; the S&P 500 has been established, by general consent, as an example for the measure of both the value and quality of the U.S. stock market. Certainly, the vast majority of its constituents, i.e., companies, are based in the U.S., and their aggregate value still represents three-fourths of the entire value of U.S. stocks.

But if you peruse practically any physics textbook, you'll note something else about most of the standards upon which we've built our trust: constancy. Precise definitions of standards helped advance the development of engineering-oriented pursuits; in fewer than 70 years, aviation progressed from the sands of Kitty Hawk to those of the Moon's surface. For more than 100 years now, the metric standard of mass (the kilogram) has been defined by that of a prototype, fashioned from inert materials, carefully protected lest it deteriorate or decay. Our units of time, temperature, length, and intensity are likewise carefully defined. As new methods of measurement are developed, occasionally these standards are redefined to permit even greater precision and less variability.

How Old is Old?

Invariability of the standard, or unit, of measure is not equivalent to constancy of the parameter being measured. For example, even though we've taken great pains to standardize the units of time, qualitative concepts—say, the definition of elderly—has necessarily changed over the years. That's because improvements in our environment, nutrition, and healthcare have increased human longevity. In the U.S., those who've reached the age of 65 can expect to live over five years longer than their antecedents could only 90 years ago.

Given the pace of progress in so many areas of human endeavor, it is somewhat surprising that investors still measure expected returns on financial assets in much the same way as they did generations ago. Unfortunately, our ability to forecast the future still leaves a lot to be desired, so comparing an asset's price to an estimate of its "coupon" (the reward that accrues to the investor) is still the basis for most financial analysis.

Realized returns on stocks and bonds have been very favorable recently, with the stock market enjoying an especially good run. This is no accident; U.S. companies have been extraordinarily conscious of meeting and exceeding investors' expectations. It appears that the large, established companies—the kind that dominate the S&P 500—are in the vanguard when it comes to taking steps toward delivering value to shareholders. Maybe that's because they lug more baggage from a more lethargic era, but I think it's because the larger S&P 500 companies are especially well suited to today's ultra competitive environment.

Over the past few years, the S&P 500 has exemplified the classical definition of a growth company. Both revenues and earnings have grown faster than the overall economy, and the annual total return of 18 percent achieved over both the past 10-year and 20-year periods has been significantly above average as well.

This result troubles some observers who worry that conditions recently have been too good to be true. Over seven decades, the S&P 500 has
delivered barely 11 percent annual returns before inflation's levy, and the
widespread belief that returns are mean-reverting gives rise to concerns
that an extended period of lower-than-average returns is in store.
Conceptually, the power of the mean reversion process relies on basic
economic forces—innovation, competition, and obsolescence—tending
toward equilibrium. Hence the concern regarding the rate of stock appreciation, which depends on dividend growth, which, in turn, ultimately
hinges on the returns available from capital invested in a dynamic, competitive economy.

It's impossible to gauge what portion of the past twenty years of
returns are gains deferred from the previous ten, when stocks and bonds
provided their owners with extremely disappointing rewards, especially
after inflation. But it seems an incontrovertible assertion that a substantial amount of investors' recent good fortune is a payback for the "lost
decade" of the 1970s.

Treasury bond yields rose from 4.2 percent in 1964 to peak near 15
percent in 1981 as they struggled to keep pace with inflation expectations,
but they have trended lower over the past 17 years to the current level
under 6 percent. There's a strong case to be made that bond yields can
drop a good deal further, potentially to 5 percent or even lower. Since
these bonds are generally believed to be risk-free, their expected returns
form the foundation for expected returns on other financial assets. A variety of factors determine whether investors will demand more return or
less from a given stock than a bond would offer (more on this later).
Suffice it to say that if bond yields continue their long journey to lower
levels, the expected return on stocks should decline as well, which is the
same as saying their P/Es should rise.

Meanwhile, earnings power has increased substantially as a result of
the heavy pace of restructuring and consolidation, which together with an
emphasis on boosting productivity have enabled U.S. companies to compete more effectively in an increasingly globalized economy. This
progress is evidenced by recent strength of the U.S. dollar, which for
decades had been falling under the weight of lagging productivity growth.

The S&P 500 is Not the Market, it's an Evolving Portfolio

Often, the S&P 500 is described as an *unmanaged* portfolio. But the selection of companies entering and leaving is anything but random, so I would propose the term *lightly managed* for the portfolio of companies which comprises the S&P 500, whose characteristics can and do change over time.

You will find it helpful to think of the S&P 500 as a vast conglomerate, spanning an amazingly diverse range of businesses. Many observers presuppose the S&P 500 to be a good proxy for the U.S. economy which is admittedly mature, but that leads them to underestimate the S&P 500's potential. In fact, the S&P 500 has increasingly become dominated by a new "Nifty 50," leading-edge companies who have made substantial investments overseas to expand their businesses amidst faster-growing economies, and which have, by shedding underperforming, non-core operations, focused their efforts on developing their most attractive assets. What's more, though the nifty 50 may be the bluest of the blue chips, the remainder of the S&P 500 companies are anything but ordinary. Most are leaders in their chosen fields of endeavor, and many have made great progress toward extending their competitive edge.

Perhaps the epitome of the nifty companies is General Electric ($77), whose Chief Executive Officer (CEO) is Jack Welsh. Over the past 17 years, Jack's role at GE has been akin to that of a portfolio manager, allocating capital among its diverse interests, boosting the contribution from businesses that GE can dominate, and reducing its reliance on areas where it's impossible for the company to differentiate itself. By so doing, he has been increasing the quality of GE's earnings and the sustainability of its franchise, and the market has rewarded this improvement with a higher P/E multiple. This same process is underway at innumerable other companies, including most of those in the S&P 500. So in one sense (at the very least) an S&P 500 index investor owns a portfolio which is being managed very actively and professionally.

Scope of This Study

As previously mentioned, the history of the S&P Composite index extends back to 1925, but this study examines only its evolution since the early 1960s, with the focus being on the past few years. I believe that the S&P 500's transformation over the past 35 years is, in all probability, more dramatic than that of its first 40 but likewise much more significant to today's investors. At any rate, the period under study should be sufficient for most readers to develop a new appreciation for the S&P 500, and to modify their assumptions regarding it as a standard, whether for performance or valuation.

Indexation is No Panacea

The S&P 500 has outperformed the majority of actively managed equity funds over most measurement periods. Adherents to efficient market theory point to this result as proof of the futility of active management, primarily due to its higher expenses. But active management itself is likely not the problem, since stock pickers seem eminently capable of outperforming other benchmarks, such as the Russell 2000. If passive management is a panacea, why are some indexes easier to beat than others?

The underperformance of active equity funds may have been overlooked by many investors over the past few years because the absolute level of returns surpassed even the most bullish forecasts. After all, the Dow Industrials, the NASDAQ Composite, and the S&P 500 each doubled over three years, from 1995 through 1997. But I think that a period of sub-par returns will refocus attention on relative performance, and now may be a good time to reevaluate the benchmark.

It's important to recognize the S&P 500 is almost like two portfolios blended into one. The top 50 companies—in terms of their weight in the S&P 500—comprise half the portfolio, while it takes 9 times as many to make up the other half. The top 50 have been pulling more than their own weight in recent years, and the reasons for this outperformance help shed some light on why the S&P has been such a tough portfolio to beat.

The Evolution of the S&P 500

Today's S&P is not your father's index. Today's S&P 500 is less cyclical and more diversified—both sectorally and geographically—than it was a generation ago. Back then, it was dominated by cyclicals, energy, and utilities, but today it is the global consumer brand franchise companies that hold sway. Just look at today's top 50 S&P companies—more than 50 percent of the total weight—and you can count the traditionally-defined cyclical companies on the fingers of one hand.

Perhaps the most striking evidence of the S&P 500's transformation over time is the comparison of sector weightings today versus those of a generation ago. Interestingly, the P/E commanded by the S&P 500 then (22x) is not much different from today (24x). But today's S&P 500 is much more deserving of that lofty multiple, in my view, despite the fact that government bond yields were lower then (4.5 percent) than today (6.0 percent).

Table 1 This is Not Your Father's Index: S&P 500 Sector Weighting Changes, 1964-1998 (percent)

Sector	1964	1969	1974	1979	1984	1989	1994	1998
Finance	0.0	0.8	0.7	5.7	6.5	8.8	10.4	17.8
Health	2.3	4.5	8.7	5.8	6.4	8.5	9.0	11.6
Cons. Nondurables	10.1	14.1	13.3	10.1	10.9	12.3	12.7	11.3
Cons. Services	6.3	6.6	6.1	6.4	9.1	11.2	9.5	10.7
Cons. Durables	11.3	8.1	4.8	3.7	4.6	3.2	3.5	2.5
Energy	17.8	14.2	19.1	22.7	15.7	12.6	9.8	7.8
Transportation	2.6	2.2	2.2	2.0	2.7	2.0	1.6	1.1
Technology	5.5	12.9	10.1	9.3	14.6	9.5	12.7	13.8
Basic Materials	16.5	12.9	13.6	11.7	8.7	9.4	8.2	4.9
Capital Goods	8.5	10.8	8.2	11.1	10.3	9.3	12.7	8.7
Utilities	19.2	12.9	13.2	11.5	10.5	13.2	9.9	9.8
Grand Total	100.0	100.0	100.0	100.0	100.0	100.0	100.0	100.0

Source: The Strategy Connection, Standard & Poor's

If you combine the weightings of financial, healthcare and technology companies, you'll see that these comprised less than 8 percent of the S&P 500 portfolio in 1964. Their importance has increased so much over the ensuing period that, today, they represent over 40 percent of the benchmark. Corresponding declines have been seen in public utilities, basic industries, consumer durables, and energy. What previously accounted for over two-thirds of the portfolio's value has fallen now to less than one-third. These moves are monumental, and signify much more than a gradual shift of investor preferences over a generation.

The huge migration of capitalization among economic sectors of the S&P 500 portfolio incorporates the major secular trends which have been transforming the overall economy, both in the U.S. and around the world. These trends include globalization and the emergence of global brands, the aging population, the rising importance of the service sector, consolidation, deregulation, privatization, and an exponential growth in the application of technology products and services.

152   CHAPTER 8

Recognizing the substantial differences between today's S&P 500
portfolio and that of thé past, I estimate that the underlying earnings
growth rate for the index has risen to around 10 percent, significantly
higher than typical forecasts in the 5 percent to 7 percent range. The con-
sensus estimates are usually based on assumptions regarding the growth
potential of the U.S. economy and the historical record of earnings
growth for the S&P 500, but neither of these is highly relevant to today's
portfolio. An increasingly significant proportion of income (and more
importantly, growth) is attributable to operations conducted outside the
U.S. and, therefore, outside the purview of U.S. Gross Domestic Product.
Besides, the rapid turnover rate of index components has muddled comparisons; income from today's companies should be compared against
income from the same companies in previous periods, not the income
earned by yesterday's companies.

Managing the Index Portfolio

Over the past several years, the rapid pace of consolidation, restructuring, and new issuance has been keeping the S&P 500 Index committee
extremely busy. The committee is comprised of eight S&P 500 professionals representing various investing disciplines, and they're responsible
for the management and integrity of the index products. Usually, they let
the market determine—through the acquisition process—which companies are removed from the index, although they do conduct periodic "cel-
lar clean-ups" to rid the index of broken companies. Additions are made
with an eye toward the ideal composition of the index: it's meant to be a
fair portrayal of both the stock market and the economy of the United
States, simultaneously, an easily tradable and investable portfolio.

Table 2 The Top S&P 500 Companies: 1964 and 1998

1964 Company	Weight (%)	Cum'l (%)	1997 Company	Weight (%)	Cum'l (%)
AT&T	9.1	9.1	General Electric	3.2	3.2
General Motors	7.3	16.4	Microsoft	2.5	5.7
Std. Oil of New Jersey	5.0	21.4	Coca-Cola	2.3	7.9
IBM	3.7	25.1	Exxon	2.0	10.0
Texaco	3.1	28.2	Merck	1.7	11.6
Du Pont	2.9	31.1	Pfizer	1.6	13.3
Sears	2.5	33.6	Wal-Mart	1.4	14.7

Continued on next page.

Table 2 The Top S&P 500 Companies: 1964 and 1998, *cont'd*

1964 Company	Weight (%)	Cum'l (%)	1998 Company	Weight (%)	Cum'l (%)
General Electric	2.2	35.8	Intel	1.4	16.1
Gulf Oil	1.6	37.4	Royal Dutch	1.4	17.5
Eastman Kodak	1.4	38.8	IBM	1.4	18.9
Std. Oil of California	1.4	40.2	Procter & Gamble	1.3	20.2
Socony Mobil	1.2	41.4	Bristol-Myers Squibb	1.3	21.5
Royal Dutch	1.1	42.6	AT&T	1.1	22.6
Union C & C	1.0	43.6	Lucent Technologies	1.1	23.8
Shell Oil	0.9	44.5	Johnson & Johnson	1.1	24.8
Procter & Gamble	0.9	45.4	Du Pont	1.1	25.9
General T&T	0.8	46.3	Philip Morris	1.1	27.0
Standard Oil Indiana	0.8	47.1	American Int'l. Group	1.0	28.0
Minn. Mining & Mfg.	0.8	47.8	Cisco Systems	0.9	28.9
Ford	0.7	48.6	Walt Disney	0.9	29.8
US Steel	0.7	49.3	NationsBank	0.8	30.7
Monsanto	0.7	50.0	Eli Lilly	0.8	31.5
International Nickel	0.6	50.6	Bell Atlantic	0.8	32.4
Unilever	0.6	51.2	Travelers Group	0.8	33.2
Chrysler	0.6	51.8	SBC Communications	0.8	34.0
Commonwealth Edison	0.6	52.4	Hewlett-Packard	0.8	34.8
Dow Chemical	0.6	53.0	Citicorp	0.8	35.6
Caterpillar	0.6	53.6	Bellsouth	0.8	36.4
Xerox	0.5	54.1	Gillette	0.8	37.1
General Foods	0.5	54.1	Schering-Plough	0.7	37.9
Pacific Gas & Electric	0.5	55.2	American Home Products	0.7	38.6
American Electric Power	0.5	55.7	PepsiCo	0.7	39.3
Coca-Cola	0.5	56.2	Fannie Mae	0.7	40.0
RCA	0.5	56.7	Mobil	0.7	40.7
Phillips Petroleum	0.5	57.2	Ford	0.7	41.4
Consolidated Edison	0.4	57.6	Chase Manhattan	0.7	42.1
JC Penney	0.4	58.0	BankAmerica	0.7	42.8
Conoco	0.4	58.5	Abbott Labs	0.7	43.5
Goodyear	0.4	58.9	GTE	0.7	44.1
Bethlehem Steel	0.4	59.3	Dell Computer	0.6	44.8
Reynolds Tobacco	0.4	59.7	Home Depot	0.6	45.4
Merck	0.4	60.1	First Union	0.6	46.0
Southern Co.	0.4	60.5	Warner-Lambert	0.6	46.7
Avon	0.4	60.9	Chevron	0.6	47.3
Westinghouse	0.4	61.3	General Motors	0.6	47.9
Texas Utilities	0.4	61.7	Unilever	0.6	48.5

Continued on next page.

Table 2 The Top S&P 500 Companies: 1964 and 1997, *con't.*

1964 Company	Weight (%)	Cum'l (%)	1998 Company	Weight (%)	Cum'l (%)
American Home Products	0.4	62.1	Ameritech	0.6	49.0
American Cyanamid	0.4	62.5	American Express	0.6	49.6
Federated Department Stores	0.4	62.9	WorldCom	0.5	50.1
International Paper	0.4	63.3	Morgan Stanley, Dean Witter	0.5	50.6
Weyerhauser	0.4	63.6	Boeing	0.5	51.2
Corning Glass	0.4	64.0	McDonald's	0.5	51.7
Allied Chemical	0.4	64.3	COMPAQ	0.5	52.2
Southern Cal Edison	0.3	64.7	Time Warner	0.5	52.7
Alcoa	0.3	65.0	Allstate	0.5	53.2
Campbell Soup	0.3	65.4	Amoco	0.5	53.6
Firestone	0.3	65.7	Minn. Mining & Mfg	0.5	54.1
National Dairy	0.3	66.0	Schlumberger	0.4	54.6
Public Service Gas & Electric	0.3	66.3	Banc One	0.4	55.0
Norfolk & Western	0.3	66.7	Chrysler	0.4	55.4

Source: Standard & Poor's

When a company is due to be acquired, it's extremely rare for the committee to remove it from the index before the transaction is completed, even if a long-term investment case is no longer justifiable. Seemingly iron-clad merger agreements are sometimes changed, and the committee attempts to avoid the possibility they'll have to reinsert a company soon after its removal. Indeed, to the committee, minimizing future changes to the index is an overriding consideration.

Table 3 A Rapidly Evolving Portfolio: Annual Changes to the S&P 500 Portfolio, 1966-1998

Year	Changes	Turnover (%)
1966	16	3.2
1967	21	4.2
1968	34	6.8
1969	10	2.0
1970	25	5.0
1971	8	1.6
1972	13	2.6
1973	20	4.0

Continued on next page.

Table 3 A Rapidly Evolving Portfolio: Annual Changes to the S&P 500 Portfolio, 1966-1998, *cont'd*[1]

Year	Changes	Turnover (%)
1974	12	2.4
1975	18	3.6
1976	60	12.0
1977	8	1.6
1978	11	2.2
1979	14	2.8
1980	14	2.8
1981	21	4.2
1982	29	5.8
1983	19	3.8
1984	30	6.0
1985	29	5.8
1986	28	5.6
1987	27	5.4
1988	27	5.4
1989	30	6.0
1990	14	2.8
1991	12	2.4
1992	7	1.4
1993	13	2.6
1994	17	3.4
1995	31	6.2
1996	24	4.8
1997	31	6.2
1998*	11	2.2
Total	678	

*Through May   *Source*: Standard & Poor's

Ninety-seven changes to the Composite Index have been made since the end of 1994, altering its complexion considerably. The majority of these have resulted from acquisitions engineered by another company within the index. The acquired businesses, despite being part of a new company, remain in the index and continue to contribute revenues and diversity. But the acquisition makes room for another company in the index, and thus the new additions aren't really replacements in the strict sense. Further, the selection process is hardly random; new S&P 500 constituents are chosen from the ranks of highly successful companies, whose leadership among their respective industries is expected to persist.

Mergers and Acquisitions

Indeed, the consolidation process which has been driving up returns and valuations is hardly new. Back in the mid-1980s, sharply lower costs of debt capital (resulting both from the birth of the junk bond market and declining interest rates) helped finance a leveraged buyout boom. Plenty of companies were removed from the ranks of the publicly traded, and their shares were driven to valuations previously warranted only in the private market. Later, as global competition flared up in many industries, managers sought new ways to raise productivity and margins. Nowadays, most mergers are not going-private deals, but rather a consolidation of similar businesses in a quest for efficiency.

That the government is challenging very few of these deals is notable. Of course, each one causes employees to be displaced, at substantial cost. But the net effect has been a more vibrant economy that's fostered the entrepreneurial climate which is essential to the creation of new opportunities, offsetting the jobs that were forfeited.

The impact on the S&P 500 has been complex. While large, mature enterprises always seem to be on the lookout to acquire promising young businesses, the recent trend of mergers among financial institutions, pharmaceutical companies, firms involved in aerospace and defense, entertainment and telecommunications, together with a whole host of other industries, is clearly beyond the normal pace of consolidation. So, it would be folly for one to claim that this process can continue unabated forever. But at the same time, most of the value created in these deals is not likely to be reversed. Besides, heightened concentration among companies in similar businesses has enabled the S&P index committee to build weightings in certain areas and enhance the growth characteristics of the 500 stock portfolio.

In the context of recent consolidation practices, the best businesses of the combined companies remain within the index, underperforming units are often sloughed off, and the merger benefits—increased productivity and focus—are earned gradually over time. Some companies, like AT&T through its spin-offs of Lucent and NCR, are seeking these benefits through restructuring and deconsolidation instead, but the net effect is often the same. Investors usually acknowledge a portion of the anticipated benefit by awarding higher prices to consolidating and restructuring companies as soon as the plans are announced.

In many cases, such as Disney, Gillette, IBM, Lockheed Martin, Merck, NationsBank, and Wells Fargo, recent acquisitions seem to have helped sustain growth while providing efficiencies. Other acquirers, however, like Aetna, Boeing, Kimberly Clark, and Viacom have yet to fulfill expectations. Thankfully, few deals wind up to be as disappointing as Quaker Oats' purchase of Snapple for $1.6 billion and subsequent sale for $300 million just a few years later.

Table 4 What's Happened to the Stocks "Exiting" the S&P 500?

Reason	1995	1996	1997	1998*	Total	Percent
Acquired and retained within S&P 500	17	11	24	6	58	59.8
Acquired and removed from S&P 500	5	1	1	1	8	8.2
Moved to Smallcap 600 or Midcap 400	5	6	4	2	17	17.5
Dropped from S&P indexes	4	6	2	2	14	14.4
Grand Total	**31**	**24**	**31**	**11**	**97**	**100.0**

*through May   *Source*: Standard & Poor's

On balance, though, the performance and valuation characteristics of the S&P 500 continue to benefit from wealth created through the restructuring and consolidation processes, much of which seems to have been "earned" and, thus, not as subject to confiscation by a bear market as some mean-reversion advocates might claim.

Recent Additions

If you scan the list of new entrants, you'll see that the committee has recently been beefing up the technology weighting by adding Silicon Graphics, Applied Materials, Cabletron, Tellabs, LSI Logic, 3Com, Bay Networks, EMC, Nextlevel, Adobe, Parametric, KLA-Tencor, and Seagate. Likewise, the financial weighting has been boosted, especially considering that most of the companies "lost" through the merger process are actually still contributing to the index. Note new additions: Conseco, Charles Schwab, Equifax, Sun America, State Street, Progressive, Lehman Brothers, Summit Bancorp, and Northern Trust. Mirage Resorts, Cardinal Health, Humana, Worldcom, and Cendant have also recently made their respective debuts. Though not all of the companies added are growth stocks, the majority clearly are. A history of success, however, is not always evidence of continued leadership: U.S. Surgical ($28) was added to the index in 1992 when it was trading at $100-plus.

Development of New Indexes

For more than 50 years, the S&P 500, known as the Composite index, was intended to be all encompassing, spanning the entire U.S. market. Beginning in the early 1980s, however, a trend developed towards investing in smaller companies, a movement born of academic research conducted by the likes of Rolf Banz. Institutions needed new benchmarks to gauge the performance of their small-cap managers apart from the overall market. The consultants at the Frank Russell Company developed the methodology which became the Russell 1000, 2000, and 3000 indexes. Though the first attempt to list futures on the Russell indexes was a failure, the indexes' success as performance benchmarks put pressure on Standard and Poor's to follow suit, by developing first the S&P 400 Midcap (in 1991) and, later, the S&P 600 Smallcap (in 1994).

The Russell indexes are recomposed annually (according to a strictly defined formula) to include the 3000 largest U.S. companies; the two subset indexes, the 1000 and the 2000, are comprised of the top third and bottom two-thirds of the 3000, in terms of the number of companies. No attempt is made to adjust sector weightings; the chips fall where they may. Besides reconstituting the overall index every year, the "border" separating the 1000 from the 2000 is re-opened at that point, resulting in heavy turnover among the Russell indexes.

By contrast, the people at S&P designed their new indexes—the Midcap and the Smallcap—in the likeness of the S&P 500. Gradual turnover is a major goal, liquidity and tradability are important, and sector weightings are managed. The index designers were rightly concerned with the way their new products would interact with the flagship S&P 500. They decided that a given company could not be a component of more than one S&P index, so the S&P universe (now referred to as the Supercomposite) was comprised of 500 companies before June of 1991, 900 companies from June 1991 until January 1994, and 1500 companies hence. However, in terms of market capitalization, there remains a substantial overlap between the three indexes, though recently the committee has been dealing with the issue by orchestrating a gradual migration among them.

Table 5 Some Milestones in the Development of the S&P 500 Composite Index:

1957	S&P Composite enlarged from 90 stocks to 500
1976	Financial stocks added; Utility stocks reduced
1989	Pre-announcement of S&P Index changes initiated
1991	Introduction of S&P Midcap 400 index*
1994	Introduction of S&P Smallcap 600 index*

*The Midcap and Smallcap indexes are not part of the S&P Composite; their introduction is shown because of the impact they've had on the Composite.

Source: Standard & Poor's

To the extent that the junior S&P indexes develop their own entourage of passive investing fans, the "farm team system" (where the best performing stocks graduate to the majors) helps to mitigate the sudden price jump often seen when a stock is added to the S&P 500. Think about it; if mid-cap indexers control 4 percent of a company and big-cap indexers need to own 9 percent, then only 5 percent of the company needs to be bought from active investors when the stock is promoted from the S&P Midcap to the S&P 500. Of course, by reducing the impact of adding a new stock to a portfolio, you can increase the portfolio's expected return.

Table 6 Going For Growth: Changes to the S&P 500 1995-1998

1995		1997	
Added	**Deleted**	**Added**	**Deleted**
Silicon Graphics	Transco Energy	HEALTHSOUTH	Boatmen's Bancshares
General Public Utilities	Pet Inc.	Conseco	Alexander & Alexander
Boston Scientific	National Education	Parametric Technology	Pacific Telesis
Applied Materials	Lockheed	Adobe Systems	Santa Fe Pacific Gold
Lockheed Martin	Martin Marietta	Cardinal Health	Conrail Inc.
Bank of New York	Maxus Energy	Charles Schwab	Morgan Stanley
Laidlaw	Rollins Environmental	Countrywide Credit	USLIFE
CUC International	E-Systems	Equifax	PanEnergy
Loews Corp.	Continental Corp.	Washington Mutual	Great Western Financial
Cabletron	Clark Equipment	SunAmerica	Giddings & Lewis
Darden Restaurants	Oshkosh B'Gosh	Anadarko Petroleum	Santa Fe Energy
Fruit of the Loom	Hartmarx	Apache	Intergraph Corp.
Harrah's	The Promus Companies	NextLevel Systems	General Instrument
Tellabs	M/A Com.	Progressive	U.S. Bancorp
Republic New York	Lotus Development	Owens-Illinois	McDonnell Douglas
Allstate	SPX Corp.	Huntington Bancshares	ENSERCH
Freeport-McMoran Copper & Gold	Skyline Corp.	Mirage Resorts	Noram Energy Corp.
Willamette	Bruno's Inc.	Fort James Corp.	James River
Morgan Stanley	Santa Fe Pacific	State Street Corp.	Nynex

Continued on next page.

Table 6 Going For Growth: Changes to the S&P 500 1995-1998, *con't.*

1995 *(con't.)*		1997 *(con't.)*	
Added	**Deleted**	**Added**	**Deleted**
First Bank System	First Mississippi	Clear Channel Communications	Tandem
US West Communications Group	US West Media Group	KLA-Tencor Corp.	Amdahl Corp.
Federated Dept. Stores	Zenith Electronics	TRICON Global Restaurants	Stride Rite
PP&L Resources	CBS	HBO & Co.	Louisiana Land & Exploration
Comerica	First Chicago	FirstEnergy	Ohio Edison
Humana	NBD Bancorp	Synovus Financial	Salomon
First Chicago NBD	Shawmut National	BB&T Corp.	Beverly Enterprises
LSI Logic	Scott Paper	Cincinnati Financial	HFS
ITT Hartford	ITT Corporation	Cendant	CUC International
ITT Corporation	Morrison Knudsen	Omnicom Group	Fleming Companies
ITT Industries	Zurn Industries	Ameren	Union Electric
3Com	First Fidelity	BestFoods	CPC International

1996		1998 (through January)	
Added	**Deleted**	**Added**	**Deleted**
Case	Pittston Services Group	Lehman Brothers	Barnett Banks
Bay Networks	Capital Cities/ ABC	Consolidated Stores	Echo Bay Mines
Fifth Third Bancorp	Handleman	FDX Holding	Federal Express
Green Tree Financial	Federal Paper Board	Summit Bancorp	Caliber Systems
EMC	Cray Research	Northern Trust	Whitman
General Instrument	First Interstate		
WorldCom	Chase Manhattan Bank		
Chase	Chemical Bank		
AON	Loral Corp.		
Tupperware	Premark Int'l.		
MGIC Investment	U.S. Healthcare		
Battle Mountain Gold	Brown Group		
Allegheny Teledyne	Teledyne		
HFS	Dial		
Seagate	Ogden		
Dell	Varity		
Lucent	Outboard Marine		
Union Pacific Resources	Community Psychiatric		
Cognizant	Yellow Corp.		
MBIA	Consolidated Freightways		
Guidant	Bally Entertainment		
AutoZone	Luby's Cafeterias		
Frontier	Ryan's Family Steak House		
Thermo Electron	Shoney's		

Source: Standard & Poor's

Valuation: The Determining Factors

Almost every forecast of the U.S. equity market outlook today incorporates a disclaimer regarding the high level of valuations extant. But if you examine the well-held views concerning the "expensiveness" of today's market, you'll find that most of them utilize some kind of historical analysis of valuation levels which have existed for the S&P 500 over time. The data exist, so analysts use it. But by failing to account for substantial improvements in the quality of the underlying portfolio that have occurred over time, these analysts underestimate the market's potential and overestimate its risk.

When analysts overlook the lightly-managed nature of the S&P 500 portfolio (by considering it to be the market portfolio), they presume that they can measure the attractiveness of the market by comparing the valuation of today's portfolio versus that of yesteryear. But this amounts to a misuse of the benchmark; one can't measure the market's attractiveness the way one might gauge a teapot's temperature. Water boils at 100°C in 1998, just as it did a generation ago (and ten generations ago). This boiling point hasn't been subject to change over time, though it is subject to change at different altitudes. Careful scientific analysis of water's physical properties under varying conditions—and precise specifications of the thermometer—are responsible for this well-known result.

Perhaps a better analogy for the S&P 500 portfolio is human longevity. As previously shown, people living longer today than in the past because of improvements in the quality of life. It's my view that quality changes in the S&P 500 portfolio are responsible for a great deal of the increase in valuations observed over the past several years. Let's see why, but first we'll have to examine some of the factors which determine value.

Concerns abound regarding today's high Price/Earnings ratios (high P/Es are the same as low E/Ps, or "earnings yields"). Also, people complain about high Price/Book and Price/Sales ratios—likewise, low Book/Price (B/P) and Sales/Price (S/P) ratios. Furthermore, dividend yields (D/P) are commonly regarded as too low, indicating that stocks are overly expensive. Despite the conventional notation, I find it makes much more sense to think of these ratios—and write them—with the P on the bottom. That way, higher is always better, and lower means you get less of what you want—sales, assets, earnings and/or dividends—per dollar invested. Put another way, the lower the numbers, the lower your expected returns.

As I mentioned previously, stock appreciation depends ultimately on dividend growth, though successful investors do well to anticipate changes in dividend policy by trying to gauge a company's ability to pay dividends in the future. Thus, the focus on profits, and the assumption that, unless squandered, earnings today result in dividends tomorrow. But net income is only an approximation of true profitability, so a number of insightful investors—Warren Buffett among them—have devised cash-flow measures that are designed to assess the true return available to an equity investment. Being mere mortals, however, we resort to earnings as the best commonly available measure of profitability, and, likewise, Earnings/Price (E/P) as the expected return of an equity investment.

For companies with attractive prospects, the first year's expected return is usually lower than the return on a Treasury bond (y). That's because the bond's coupon is static until maturity, while the stock's "coupon" is expected to expand over time, at the underlying growth rate (g) of the business. Yet the bond does offer stability (at least as far as the government's ability to redeem it with a stable currency), while the stock's earnings stream is subject to the normal ups and downs of business. For low-growth companies whose current level of profitability cannot be expected to continue, the market usually demands a much higher return in the first year than a bond might provide to compensate for the likelihood that earnings will decline sometime in the future.

Some companies (like automobile and appliance manufacturers, as well as steel and paper producers) are extremely exposed to business cycles, while others (like pharmaceutical companies and diaper manufacturers) are less sensitive to economic swings. Usually, we designate the variability of a future profit stream with the Greek letter sigma (σ). Even when the market is agnostic concerning the direction of earnings in the near term, a volatile earnings profile is less highly prized than a stable one.

Most businesses are subject to the risk of increasing competition within their industry and, eventually, obsolescence of their products or services. So, even if earnings are growing strongly with little variability in the near term, investors ought to be wary of projecting today's rosy picture too far into the future. Just as some bonds are subject to a "call" by their issuers before maturity, all stocks are similarly subject to a call at any time during their lives, which are, theoretically, perpetual. We'll let "t" signify the period until that time in the future when the business is "terminal."

Of course, the market is extremely diverse, comprised of companies in every stage of development, some that are extremely cyclical and others not at all. Some enjoy great unscalable barriers to entry, and others battle daily in the fray of an extremely competitive industry. The range of expected returns is likewise diverse. A recent analysis of the 1,500 companies which comprise the S&P Supercomposite showed expected returns ranging from less than 1 percent to over 20 percent, while the median was around 6 percent, which was the expected return on the Treasury bond yield at the time. Fully half the companies were huddled in the range of 80 percent to 125 percent of the bond yield, while one-fourth of them offered less than 80 percent of the bond's yield, and a similar number more thàn 125 percent.

As I've described it, the ratio of the return on a riskless government bond (y) to a given stock's expected return (E/P) is a function of three factors related to the underlying business: the growth rate (g), the variability of that growth (σ), and the extent, or sustainability, of the company's franchise (t). In mathematical notation, where:

$a = f$ (b) means "a is a function of b."

1) $y/(E/P) = f (g+, \sigma^-, t+)$;

2) $P = (E/y) \cdot f (g, \sigma, t)$;

3) $\dfrac{\delta P}{\delta E} = f (g, \sigma, t)/y = P/E$

The signs in the first equation indicate whether there is a direct (+) or inverse (-) relationship between the given factor and the ratio of the bond yield to the stock's earnings yield. Equation number two is merely a solution for the first equation in terms of P (the stock's price), and the third equation displays the derivative of the second, with respect to E (the earnings). It's an attempt to gauge the relative importance of the various factors on the change in a stock's price for a given change in earnings, and it's identical to the stock's P/E.

All the same factors that affect the yield ratio similarly have an impact on a stock's expected reaction to a given change in earnings, plus one more, the interest rate (y). The lower the interest rate, the higher the impact a given earnings change will have.

But nothing is quite so easy. We have to remember that y is the interest rate on bonds of very low risk, and therefore—to a reasonable degree—represents the cost of capital. If returns in a particular industry are overly abundant—especially if the barriers to entry are not high—competitors will raise capital to create new capacity, and drive down the returns available to pre-existing players. What's more, the added capacity will raise the variability of industry profits by making them more susceptible to economic ups and downs, and cause the future for all market players (especially for those struggling along with sub-par profits) to become cloudy and uncertain. No business is immune from this process, but companies with a clear-cut competitive edge are better protected than others.

So, it should be clear that lower interest rates are a mixed blessing for stockholders. It is true that a lower discount rate applied to a relatively stable or growing stream of profits can only improve its present value and, thus, the stock's price. But a falling cost of capital stokes the flames of competitive frenzy by reducing the height of companies' barriers to entry. That is why exceptionally robust barriers become even more valuable as interest rates decline. No wonder, then, that a relatively small cadre of globally dominant companies—the new "Nifty 50," if you will—is pacing the gains of the S&P 500 overall. By and large, though, the niftiest companies are constituents of the S&P 500 portfolio, and I believe that's the major reason why it's proving to be such a tough benchmark to beat.

All of the foregoing theory relating to the value of stocks relative to bonds is applicable to portfolios as well. That's because a portfolio is effectively a large conglomerate with another layer of management, the Portfolio Manager (PM). What differentiates the PM from a company CEO is the inability to bring about change at the operating unit level; the PM's power is limited to allocating capital among the various units to optimize overall performance. But if either the PM or the underlying business unit managers have been enacting measures to boost growth, reduce variability, and extend the viability of the franchise, then the value of the portfolio will rise because its quality is enhanced. If these changes are occurring at both levels, the improvement is even more powerful. Furthermore, as these changes take place, the track record of the pre-existing portfolio becomes irrelevant. This is what's been happening to the S&P 500.

In the case of the S&P 500, the index committee manages the portfolio, and selects industry leaders to add to the index when given a chance. The heavy pace of mergers, together with the creation of the Midcap and Smallcap indexes, have provided numerous opportunities for the committee to add new companies, which have hailed, overwhelmingly, from the growth arena. The net result has been a portfolio which possesses higher growth, less cyclicality, and more diversification—both geographically and along product lines—than the S&P 500 of old. What's more, managements of the underlying companies have been pursuing a strategy of increasing their own companies' competitive advantage, by exiting uprofitable business lines and focusing their efforts on attractive ones.

Dividend Policy

If there were a Hippocratic Oath for corporate managers, it would begin, "First, destroy no value." In no small part due to their own increased participation in company fortunes through incentive programs involving stock and options, company managements have been exploring all available means to create and deliver value efficiently to shareholders.

In days gone by; cash dividends were seen as an attractive means of rewarding shareholders for their patience and loyalty. But for several reasons, cash payouts no longer represent an efficient transfer of wealth. In fact, for many shareholders (including the very management itself whose responsibility remains to propose dividend policy), regular or special cash dividends actually destroy value, because of the voracious appetite of the tax man.

Over the past several years, a gap has been developing between the tax rates applied to income (including dividends) and to capital appreciation. After the passage in 1997 of a reduction in the capital gains tax rate, this gap has now widened to as much as 22 cents on the dollar for a top bracket taxpayer. So, if you believe (as I do) that the total return of an equity investment is driven by the rate at which value is created, it behooves company management to endeavor to deliver growth through appreciation of the share price rather than the conventional means of increasing cash disbursements through the dividend mechanism.

The chart shows that a lower portion of S&P 500 profits have been paid out as dividends over time. Today's record low dividend yield may indicate a more expensive market than normal, but not to the degree that those who deem to ignore this important change in dividend policy might claim.

Figure 1 S&P 500 Earnings & Dividends: 1925-1998
Sources: The Strategy Connection, Standard & Poor's

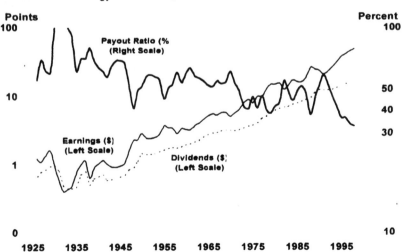

Share Buybacks

As time passes, companies in the S&P 500 have been participating in share repurchase programs to an increasing extent. These repurchases also represent a rising proportion of the total value transferred from companies to shareholders over time. Shareholders who need income can liquidate their holdings gradually and recognize a higher after-tax return when doing so; others who are interested in accumulating a larger position can let the anti-dilutive effect of an ongoing share repurchase program work in their favor.

Competitive Advantage

Michael Porter teaches courses on competitive advantage at the Harvard Business School and has written several books explaining that competitive advantage, if sustainable, is the "fundamental basis of above-average performance in the long run." He shows how companies who deal with competitive forces more effectively than their adversaries, either by pursuing a cost leadership or differentiation strategy, can attain and sustain their competitive advantage. Clearly, the market rewards the companies who possess this kind of advantage with premium valuations, but, in many cases, their stock prices have continued to outperform the market over long periods.

As Porter himself claims, "competitive advantage can't be understood by looking at the firm as a whole." Clearly, then, it would be impossible to measure the amount by which the competitive advantage of the S&P 500 portfolio has increased over time. But if you examine Porter's examples dealing with individual business units, you will soon realize that this approach has been widely adopted among leading businesses—especially S&P 500 companies—over the past ten or more years, and that the restructuring and consolidation processes exist as the most obvious outward indications of progress in this area.

Profit Margins: The Law of Diminishing Returns

Conventional economic theory—the principles of production—explains how traditional manufacturing companies' costs behave as volume increases. Before production can be the least bit profitable, it takes a certain amount of volume to cover fixed costs. As volume increases, the average cost per unit continues to fall, as the fixed costs are amortized over more and more units. At a certain level, production becomes extremely efficient, and thus highly profitable. Sometimes, this is called the "sweet spot." The factory is full, the assembly line is humming, and employee morale is high because workers are effectively utilized and well compensated, but not overworked. Beyond a certain level, things start to go wrong. Component shipments cannot keep up, employee overtime expenses rise, and productivity drops off. Production costs accelerate and profits are squeezed. This is known as the law of diminishing returns.

Most of the traditional manufacturing industries that played such an important role in the makeup of the S&P 500 of yesteryear are subject to the law of diminishing returns. However, a much smaller proportion of today's portfolio is invested in companies whose sweet spot is starkly finite. Today's S&P 500 relies much more on companies whose volume can multiply without violating the kinds of physical constraints that cause margins to suffer as production exceeds conventionally determined sweet spots.

Consider the case of Boeing and Microsoft from the Seattle area. Both are fine enterprises; each one represents the epitome of its industry, possesses a loyal installed base of customers, and delivers products which require a substantial ongoing investment in research and development. Boeing's behemoths, however, require a significant amount of space indoors to construct, placing strict limits on the number of units that can be built simultaneously. If orders pile up, Boeing is tempted to overproduce so as not to lose orders to its erstwhile competitor, Airbus. Even though demand is strong, Boeing cannot hire or train new workers fast enough and parts shortages cause lengthy delays. These problems are compounded by rising absenteeism, as overworked employees take unscheduled vacations to reacquaint themselves with their families.

On the other hand, once Microsoft is satisfied with the code for a new program, it is somewhat immune from the vagaries of diminishing returns. Variable costs are minuscule, and the new product can be easily transported to numerous locations for local manufacture, minimizing shipping costs. For each additional unit sold, average unit costs decline, so margins just keep on expanding once volume passes the key break-even point, where fixed costs are fully amortized.

If you consider that a similar business model—where average costs continue to decline as volume expands—is appropriate for many companies involved in pharmaceuticals, financial services, and technology (both software and hardware), you will realize that these are precisely the kinds of companies which represent such a substantial portion of today's S&P 500. This, I believe, is the main reason that profit margins for the

S&P 500 portfolio have continued to surprise most observers, despite numerous dire warnings 'that a previously existent cycle would reassert itself causing margins to revert down toward historical averages.

The Rise in Service Orientation

The service orientation of the S&P 500 index has increased dramatically over time. Individual companies are often rewarded with higher valuations as they raise the proportion of revenues they receive from providing services (as opposed to producing goods) because the revenues are perceived to be more reliable or persistent. Consumers value the relationship they develop with their service providers, be they banks, brokers, or baby-sitters. Consumer loyalty, developed by delivering exceptional service over time, is a crucially important component of a company's franchise value. Fostering and enhancing that loyalty either through brand awareness or long-term "strategic relationships"—is central to the goal of increasing shareholder value. Today, most companies recognize this concept and are trying to enhance the kind of recurring revenue streams which arise from consumer loyalty. The heavier weightings in financial, healthcare and technology firms within the S&P 500 (now 40 percent of the index as compared to only 8 percent in 1964) serve to underscore this theme; these are precisely the kind of businesses where consumer loyalty is paramount.

The Decline of Regulation

Years ago, most utility companies (including power as well as communications service providers) were protected monopolies. While their pricing and returns were limited by regulatory authorities, at least they enjoyed the benefits of consumer loyalty (even if it was only due to lack of choice)! Transportation companies, too, including airlines, railroads, and the trucking industry, were also subject to regulation, which kept prices high and subsidized inefficiency. The ongoing deregulation wave, which swept through the U.S. economy beginning in the 1970s and continuing through the currently in-process deregulation of communications and electricity providers, has served to accelerate the evolutionary process in the affected industries.

As industries are deregulated, the competitive landscape evolves slowly but relentlessly. Lethargy gives way to enterprise, and inefficient assets are squeezed out of production. Capable management and flexible labor become increasingly important because if productivity and profits don't improve, the company becomes an easy target for acquisition by a more nimble competitor.

Today, these industries have become much more competitive. In many cases, their stocks have been laggards, and thus their weightings have fallen. Presumably, that's because competition benefits consumers rather than shareholders. But the justifiable multiple awarded to current profits has risen even though margins and profit shares may have fallen, for the potential growth of today's profits is more assured within a competitive equilibrium than when these companies were unnaturally protected.

Valuation Implications: The Relative Multiple Trap

If the portfolio represented by the S&P 500 index has indeed undergone a significant improvement over time, as I have claimed, there would be some important implications to the manner in which investors have conventionally assessed value in the stock market.

Figure 2 S&P 500 Price/Earnings Ratio, 1925-1998

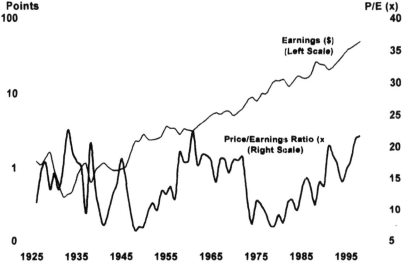

Sources: The Strategy Connection, Standard & Poor's

First, investors would have to modify their assumptions regarding the "market multiple." If the quality (including the prospective rates of growth, as well as the constancy and persistence of that growth) of companies from which the index constituents are selected has improved, or if the means of choosing those components has shifted over time to include more attractive companies, then do not be surprised to see a corresponding decline in the expected return of the portfolio, or, in other words, higher valuations. In this case, historical standards lose their relevance because the historical portfolio is no longer under consideration.

What's more, even if the companies themselves are not undergoing radical changes to improve themselves (or, if you believe that this reinvention process has indeed been the rule rather than the exception over time), then one should realize that the substantial shift of sector weightings experienced by the S&P 500 portfolio over the past generation would—by itself—cause a significant uptick in valuation measures. This result can be observed rather easily by comparing expected returns for companies in various industries, both within and outside the confines of the S&P 500.

Besides gaining a new respect for the current level of valuations for the portfolio which currently comprises the S&P 500, analysts should also be wary of presuming that a particular company's relative valuation might be considered as a constant over time. This is one version of what I view to be the "relative multiple trap." Caterpillar, for example, is an attractive company when compared to the likes of General Motors or Bethlehem Steel. But when you start including faster growing companies with stronger franchises in the comparison portfolio, such as Cisco, Franklin Funds, and Worldcom, Caterpillar's relative valuation is going to suffer, and the stock might appear to be a bargain if you disregard the improvement of the portfolio.

The risks of relative multiple analysis are even greater if you consider that the earnings of the S&P 500 appear less dependent on the pace of the domestic economy than they once were. Conventionally, the expected returns of cyclical companies rise as the market grows increasingly apprehensive regarding the sustainability of growth, and fall as investors become more optimistic about an imminent upturn. Though cyclical companies continue to display this behavior, the weighting of these companies in today's S&P 500 is much lower than before, so their impact on the S&P 500 valuations is thus less significant. The net result is that the cyclical companies stand out more conspicuously when measured against the less-cyclical index, falsely enhancing their apparent attraction.

A New "Nifty" 50

Some observers may regard this study as an argument for the continued outperformance of the super-large capitalization stocks that have come to dominate today's S&P 500. While I have been an early and avid supporter of the emergence of a new "Nifty 50," large companies are not necessarily successful because they are large (although size seems to be an advantage today); they are large because they have been successful, consistently, over long periods of time. To me, it seems right that investors should place a healthy valuation premium on companies that can demonstrate sustainability of their franchises and consistency of their growth opportunities; that premium is likely to rise as interest rates fall and competition intensifies.

A New Paradigm?

Perhaps others may dismiss this study as a treatise on a new paradigm for the economy, a claim that our business environment has improved to such a great extent that it would justify a new valuation plateau. I do believe that valuations can rise substantially, even from these levels, and that a significant portion of the multiple expansion we have seen is explained by falling interest rates and improving fundamentals. That leaves less that must be attributed to an expanding appreciation of equity-like returns, which, of course, depends somewhat on interest rates and fundamentals.

Of course, I recognize the risk in postulating that "things may be different this time." After all, claims that a "new era" existed were heard in the 1920s, not long before the frightening Crash of 1929 and the Great Depression that ensued.

Indeed, innovation and evolution have been enduring elements of economic and market history. Perhaps it's true that the only thing that endures is change. Nonetheless, certain aspects of the increase in the valuation parameters of the S&P 500 are somewhat mechanical, representing procedural changes and technological improvements in the index calculation and measurement process itself. I will leave it for you to decide whether the improvement goes above and beyond the procedural. I believe it does.

All too often, it seems that an unbridgeable schism exists between the active and passive approaches to stock market investing. But each approach has its virtues, and valuable lessons can be learned by spanning the "active versus passive" divide. For active managers, whose success is measured relative to the S&P 500 index, they should understand that benchmark is an important step in the investment process. One crucial aspect of that understanding is accepting the fact that the index has changed dramatically over time. What's more, the index is not "the market." Rather, it is based on a portfolio which is purposely selected to contain the best publicly traded companies in the U.S. Likewise, awareness of fundamental developments can improve passive managers' ability to enhance returns, perhaps by incorporating some aspects of active management.

Table 7 A Blast From the Past: Your Father's S&P 500 (1964 Edition)

Industry	Mkt Cap ($mm)	Weight (%)	Industry	Mkt Cap ($mm)	Weight (%)
Aerospace			**Automobiles**		
Boeing	553	0.14	GM	28,056	7.28
North American Aviation	453	0.12	Ford	2,810	0.73
United Aircraft	427	0.11	Chrysler	2,355	0.61
Lockheed	411	0.11	American Motors	268	0.07
Martin Marietta	387	0.10		**33,489**	**8.69**
General Dynamics	350	0.09			
Curtis Wright	132	0.03	**Auto Accessories**		
Douglas Aircraft	128	0.03	Libbey Owens Ford	626	0.16
Republic Aviation	39	0.01	Rockwell Std.	321	0.08
	2,879	**0.75**	Eaton Mfg.	312	0.08
Airplane Transport			Dana Corp.	292	0.08
Pan Am	397	0.10	Champion Spark Plugs	250	0.06
UAL	387	0.10	Federal Mogul	212	0.05
AMR	373	0.10	Electric Storage	116	0.03
TWA	321	0.08	Clevite Corp.	81	0.02
Eastern	138	0.04	Budd Co.	61	0.02
	1,616	**0.42**	Sheller Mfg.	19	-
Aluminum				**2,289**	**0.59**
Aluminum Co. of America	1,315	0.34	**Auto/Trucks & Parts**		
Aluminum Limited	896	0.23	Fruehauf Trailer	215	0.06
Reynolds Metals	576	0.15	White Motors	168	0.04
Kaiser Aluminum	465	0.12	Mack Truck	103	0.03
	3,252	**0.84**	Divco Wayne	33	0.01
				519	**0.13**

Continued on next page.

Table 7 A Blast From the Past: Your Father's S&P 500 (1964 Edition), *cont'd*

Industry	Mkt Cap [1] ($mm)	Weight (%)	Industry	Mkt Cap ($mm)	Weight (%)
Brewers			**Roofing**		
Falstaff	94	0.02	US Gypsum	650	0.17
Drewry's Limited	11	0.00	Johns Manville	459	0.12
Associated Brewers	7	0.00	National Gypsum	276	0.07
	111	**0.03**	FidiuKote Corp.	127	0.03
Distillers			Masonite	83	0.02
Walker	575	0.15	Jim Walter	61	0.02
Dist. Corp. Seagram's	535	0.14	Ruberoid	56	0.01
National Distillers	333	0.09		**1,710**	**0.44**
Schenley	136	0.04	**Chemicals**		
Publicker	31	0.01	Du Pont	11,076	2.87
	1,610	**0.42**	Union C & C	3,824	0.99
Soft Drinks			Monsanto	2,616	0.68
Coca-Cola	1,993	0.52	Dow	2,259	0.59
Pepsi Cola	397	0.10	American Cyanamid	1,512	0.39
Canada Dry	75	0.02	Allied Chemical	1,356	0.35
Royal Crown	73	0.02	Hercules Powder	838	0.22
Coca-Cola Bottling	54	0.01	Olin Mathieson	535	0.14
Dr. Pepper	41	0.01	Air Reduction	274	0.07
	2,632	**0.68**	Commercial Solvents	106	0.03
Cement			Chemetron	84	0.02
Lone Star Cement	172	0.04	American Pot. & Chemical	80	0.02
General Port.	114	0.03		**24,560**	**6.37**
Marquette Cement	102	0.03	**Coal**		
Lehigh Port.	72	0.02	Consolidated Coal	560	0.15
Penn Dixie Cement	45	0.01	Peabody	401	0.10
Alpha Port.	24	0.01	Pittston Co.	90	0.02
	528	**0.14**	Island Creek	77	0.02
Heating			North American Coal	18	0.00
American Rad & SS	204	0.05		**1,145**	**0.30**
Trane Co.	196	0.05	**Fertilizer**		
Carrier Corp	110	0.03	International Mineral	236	0.06
Crane Co.	64	0.02	Smith Douglas	77	0.02
Fedders Corp.	38	0.01		**312**	**0.08**
Walworth	14	0.00			
Briggs	6	0.00			
	632	**0.16**			

Continued on next page.

Table 7 A Blast From the Past: Your Father's S&P 500 (1964 Edition), *cont'd*

Industry	Mkt Cap[1] ($mm)	Weight (%)	Industry	Mkt Cap ($mm)	Weight (%)
Confectionery			**Drugs**		
Hershey	400	0.10	Merck	1,590	0.41
Wrigley	195	0.05	American Home Products	1,526	0.40
Brach	77	0.02	Pfizer	965	0.25
	672	**0.17**	Searle	906	0.24
Containers (Metal & Glass)			Warner Lambert	759	0.20
Owens Illinois Glass	766	0.20	Sterling	726	0.19
American Can	693	0.18	Bristol Myers	723	0.19
Continental Can	606	0.16	Abbott	616	0.16
Crown Cork & Seal	163	0.04	Parke Davis	461	0.12
Thatcher	59	0.02	Richardson Merrill	342	0.09
National Can	40	0.01	Schering	225	0.06
	2,327	**0.60**	McKesson Robbins	165	0.04
Containers (Paper)				**9,004**	**2.34**
Continental	358	0.09	**Electrical Equipment**		
Lily Tulip	106	0.03	Square "D"	429	0.11
KVP Sutherland	64	0.02	McGraw Edison	328	0.09
Fibreboard	63	0.02	Cutler Hammer	126	0.03
Federal Paper	29	0.01		**883**	**0.23**
Standard Packaging	25	0.01	**Electrical Leaders**		
	644	**0.17**	General Electric	8,403	2.18
Copper & Brass			RCA	1,960	0.51
Kennecott	1,017	0.26	Westinghouse	1,541	0.40
Phelps Dodge	714	0.19	Sperry Rand	427	0.11
Anaconda	572	0.15		**12,331**	**3.20**
Magma	170	0.04	**Electric-Household**		
Inspir Copper	90	0.02	Whirlpool	369	0.10
Copper Range	53	0.01	Sunbeam	303	0.08
	2,615	**0.68**	Maytag	271	0.07
Cosmetics				**944**	**0.24**
Avon	1,545	0.40	**Electronics**		
Revlon	246	0.06	Int'l T&T	1,096	0.28
Chesebrough	221	0.06	Litton Industries	791	0.21
Max Factor	141	0.04	Texas instruments	474	0.12
Helene Curtis	33	0.01	Beckman	113	0.03
	2,187	**0.57**	Raytheon	90	0.02
			Transitron	39	0.01
			General Instruments	37	0.01
				2,639	**0.68**

Continued on next page.

Table 7 A Blast From the Past: Your Father's S&P 500 (1964 Edition), *cont'd*

Industry	Mkt Cap [1] ($mm)	Weight (%)	Industry	Mkt Cap ($mm)	Weight (%)
Biscuit Bakers			**Packaged Foods**		
National Biscuit	801	0.21	General Foods	2,021	0.52
Sunshine Biscuit	119	0.03	Kellogg	862	0.22
United Biscuit	27	0.01	Standard Brands	518	0.13
	947	**0.25**	Beech Nut	358	0.09
Bread & Cake			Gerber Products	351	0.09
Continental Bakeries	112	0.03	Quaker Oats	255	0.07
American Bakeries	37	0.01		**4,365**	**1.13**
General Bakeries	15	0.00	**Gold**		
Ward Foods	7	0.00	Homestake Mining	110	0.03
	172	**0.04**	Campbell Red Lake	93	0.02
Canned Foods			Dome Mines	77	0.02
Campbells Soup	1,298	0.34		**279**	**0.07**
California Packing	337	0.09	**Home Furnishings**		
Heinz Soup	231	0.06	Simmons	74	0.02
Libby McNeil	69	0.02	Mahasco	53	0.01
Stokely Van Camp	53	0.01	Drexel	49	0.01
	1,988	**0.52**	Bigelow Sanford	39	0.01
Corn Refiners			Kroebler	25	0.01
Corn Products	1,211	0.31	Congoleum	19	0.00
Staley Mfg.	78	0.02		**259**	**0.07**
Peneck & Food	73	0.02	**Lead & Zinc**		
	1,362	**0.35**	St. Jos Lead	193	0.05
Dairy Products			Hudson Bay Mining	185	0.05
National Dairy	1,249	0.32	American Zinc	39	0.01
Borden Co.	907	0.24		**417**	**0.11**
Beatrice Foods	339	0.09	**Machine Tools**		
Foremost Dairies	103	0.03	Warner Swasey	89	0.02
	2,597	**0.67**	Cinn. Milling	84	0.02
Meat Packing			National Acme	35	0.01
Swift & Co.	346	0.09	Bullard Co.	15	0.00
Armour Co.	290	0.08	Monarch Machine	11	0.00
Wilson & Co.	124	0.03		**233**	**0.06**
Cudahy	16	0.00	**Agricultural Machinery**		
	777	**0.20**	International Harvester	1,069	0.28
			Deere	621	0.16
			Case	62	0.02
				1,752	**0.45**

Continued on next page.

Table 7 A Blast From the Past: Your Father's S&P 500 (1964 Edition), *cont'd*

Industry	Mkt Cap[1] ($mm)	Weight (%)	Industry	Mkt Cap ($mm)	Weight (%)
Construction Machinery			**Metal Fabricating**		
Catepillar	2,252	0.58	General Cable	307	0.08
Clark Equipment	260	0.07	Revere Copper	116	0.03
Link Belt	111	0.03	Scovill Mfg.	57	0.01
Bucyrus Erie	74	0.02	Calumet + Hecla	40	0.01
Hewitt Robbins	25	0.01	Howe Sound	37	0.01
Jaeger Machines	10	0.00	Mueller Brass	14	0.00
	2,731	**0.71**		**570**	**0.15**
Industrial Machinery			**Metals (Miscellaneous)**		
Ingersol Rand	539	0.14	International Nickel	2,481	0.64
Chicago Pnumatic Tool	160	0.04	American Metal Climax	616	0.16
Gardner Denver	154	0.04	American Smelting	548	0.14
Worthington	85	0.02	Cerro	196	0.05
American Chain	68	0.02	Vanadium	23	0.01
Rex Belt	67	0.02		**3,865**	**1.00**
Blaw Knox	58	0.02	**Motion Pictures**		
Cooper Bessemer	51	0.01	MGM	99	0.03
Bliss E.W.	41	0.01	Warner Bros	92	0.02
Waukesha Motor	24	0.01	Paramount	80	0.02
	1,246	**0.32**	Twentieth Century Fox	65	0.02
Oil Wells			UA	54	0.01
Halliburton	306	0.08	Columbia Pictures	40	0.01
Dresser Industries	153	0.04		**429**	**0.11**
Baker Oil Tools	47	0.01	**Miscellaneous**		
Reed Roller Bit	18	0.00	Eastman Kodak	5,582	1.45
	523	**0.14**	Minnesota Mining & Mfg	2,956	0.77
Specialty Machinery			Weyerhauser	1,386	0.36
American Machine Fdry.	313	0.08	Corning Glass	1,368	0.35
United Shoe Machine	152	0.04	Singer	884	0.23
Excello Corp.	148	0.04	FMC Corp.	876	0.23
Joy Mfg.	85	0.02	Gillette	856	0.22
Leesona Corp.	37	0.01	National Lead	846	0.22
	736	**0.19**	Honeywell	845	0.22
Steam Generating			Grace & Co.	779	0.20
Babcock Wilcox	439	0.11	Pittsburgh Plate Glass	730	0.19
Combustion Engineering	117	0.03	Polaroid	717	0.19
Foster Wheeler	21	0.01	Georgia Pacific	685	0.18
	577	**0.15**	Armstrong Cork	648	0.17

Continued on next page.

Table 7 A Blast From the Past: Your Father's S&P 500 (1964 Edition), *cont'd*

Industry	Mkt Cap[1] ($mm)	Weight (%)	Industry	Mkt Cap ($mm)	Weight (%)
Miscellaneous *con't.*			**Oil - Crude Production**		
Ralston Purina	531	0.14	Amerada	1,053	0.27
Borg Warner	450	0.12	Superior	646	0.17
Timken Roller Bearing	449	0.12	Gen Am Texas Oil	139	0.04
Otis Elevator	358	0.09		**1,838**	**0.48**
Owens Corning	354	0.09	**Paper**		
Textron	275	0.07	International Paper	1,427	0.37
Sherwin Williams	251	0.06	Scott Paper	909	0.24
Bendix Aviation	243	0.06	Crown Zellerbach	863	0.22
Thompson Ramo	222	0.06	Kimberly Clark	585	0.15
	22,289	**5.78**	St. Regis	395	0.10
Office & Business Equipment			Union Bag Co.	273	0.07
IBM	14,337	3.72	Mead	263	0.07
Xerox	2,023	0.52	West Virginia Pulp	230	0.06
NCR	613	0.16	Champion	198	0.05
Addressograph	372	0.10		**5,144**	**1.33**
Burroughs	187	0.05	**Publishing**		
Pitney Bowes	172	0.04	Time Inc.	394	0.10
Amer. Photocopy	55	0.01	McGraw Hill	354	0.09
Royal McBee	26	0.01	Holt & Rhinehart	100	0.03
	17,785	**4.61**	Crowell Collier	90	0.02
Oil - International Integrated			Ginn & Co.	82	0.02
Std. Oil of New Jersey	19,404	5.03	McCall	49	0.01
Texaco	11,870	3.08	Curtis Publishing	27	0.01
Gulf Oil	6,085	1.58	Conde Nast	21	0.01
Std. Oil of California	5,371	1.39		**1,116**	**0.29**
Socony Mobil	4,674	1.21	**Radio Broadcasters**		
Royal Dutch	4,423	1.15	CBS	802	0.21
	51,826	**13.45**	Storer Broadcasting	99	0.03
Oil - Domestic Integrated			Taft Broadcasting	74	0.02
Shell Oil	3,600	0.93	Metro Media Inc.	70	0.02
Standard Oil Indiana	3,003	0.78		**1,045**	**0.27**
Phillips Petroleum	1,784	0.46	**Radio & TV Manufacturers**		
Conoco	1,645	0.43	Zenith	585	0.15
Union Oil of California	1,017	0.26	Motorola	385	0.10
Cities Service	887	0.23	Magnavox	229	0.06
Sinclair Oil	844	0.22	Admiral Corp.	38	0.01
Atlantic Refining	595	0.15	Emerson Radio	24	0.01
Tidewater	443	0.11		**1,262**	**0.33**
	13,817	**3.59**	*Continued on next page.*		

Table 7 A Blast From the Past: Your Father's S&P 500 (1964 Edition), *cont'd*

Industry	Mkt Cap [1] ($mm)	Weight (%)	Industry	Mkt Cap ($mm)	Weight (%)
Railroads			**Department Stores**		
Norfolk & Western	1,238	0.32	JC Penney	1,670	0.43
Southern Pacific	1,048	0.27	Federated	1,500	0.39
Union Pacific	959	0.25	May Dept. Stores	793	0.21
Atcheson Topeka & Santa Fe	808	0.21	Assoc. Dry Goods	309	0.08
Chesapeake & Ohio	651	0.17	Allied Stores	213	0.06
Penna RR	523	0.14	R.H. Macy	205	0.05
Southern Railway	380	0.10	Marshall Field	203	0.05
Gr. Northern	355	0.09	Gimbel Bros.	201	0.05
NY Central	316	0.08	Mercantile	104	0.03
N. Pacific	315	0.08		**5,199**	**1.35**
Seaboard Airline	215	0.06	**Food Chains**		
Atlantic Coast Line	183	0.05	Great Atlantic & Pacific	1,023	0.27
Lou. & Nash.	183	0.05	Safeway Stores	940	0.24
Ill. Central Industries	153	0.04	Winn Dixie	499	0.13
Denver Rio Grande	137	0.04	Kroger	479	0.12
RI & Pac	95	0.02	Jewel Tea	230	0.06
Baltimore & Ohio	93	0.02	Acme Market	174	0.05
Kansas City So. Ind.	87	0.02	Food Fair	153	0.04
Western Pacific	82	0.02	National Tea	150	0.04
West Maryland	73	0.02	Grand Union	134	0.03
Chi. M. St. P & Pac	61	0.02	First National	77	0.02
St. L. & San Fran.	57	0.01	Allied Super	57	0.01
Detroit & Hudson	49	0.01		**3,914**	**1.02**
Chicago Great Western	16	0.00	**Mail Order**		
	8,077	**2.10**	Sears	9,814	2.55
Railroad Equipment			Montgomery Ward	500	0.13
ACF Industries	234	0.06	Spiegel	94	0.02
Pullman	179	0.05	Aldens	79	0.02
West'g. Air Brake	158	0.04		**10,485**	**2.72**
Amsted	118	0.03	**Variety Stores**		
American Brake Shoes	110	0.03	Woolworth	804	0.21
Alco Prod	50	0.01	Kresge SS	283	0.07
General Signal	48	0.01	Grant, W.T.	216	0.06
	898	**0.23**	Murphy GC	101	0.03
			Newberry JJ	46	0.01
			Neisner Bros.	5	0.00
				1,454	**0.38**

Continued on next page.

Table 7 A Blast From the Past: Your Father's S&P 500 (1964 Edition), *cont'd*

Industry	Mkt Cap¹ ($mm)	Weight (%)	Industry	Mkt Cap ($mm)	Weight (%)
Shipbuilding			**Sugar - Beet**		
Newport News	84	0.02	Great Western	63	0.02
Bath Iron Works	14	0.00	Amalgamated Sugar	46	0.01
American Shipbuilding	7	0.00	Holly Sugar	23	0.01
	106	**0.03**	American Crystal	19	0.00
Shipping				**150**	**0.04**
US Lines	78	0.02	**Sugar - Cane Producers**		
American Export	70	0.02	S. Puerto Rico	35	0.01
Moore McCormick	41	0.01	Central Aguire	18	0.00
	189	**0.05**		**53**	**0.01**
Shoes			**Sugar - Cane Refiners**		
Brown Shoes	201	0.05	American Sugar	73	0.02
Genesco	196	0.05	National Sugar	14	0.00
Int'l Shoe	115	0.03	Su Crest Corp.	10	0.00
Melville Shoe	61	0.02		**96**	**0.03**
Endicott Johnson	19	0.00	**Sulfur**		
	592	**0.15**	Texas Gulf Sulphur	512	0.13
Soap			Freeport Sulphur	338	0.09
Procter & Gamble	3,563	0.92	Pan Am Sulphur	104	0.03
Unilever	2,359	0.61		**954**	**0.25**
Colgate Palmolive	506	0.13	**Apparel Manufacturers**		
	6,428	**1.67**	Cluett Peabody	122	0.03
Steel			Kayser Loth	90	0.02
US Steel	2,760	0.72	Bobbie Brooks	71	0.02
Bethlehem	1,599	0.41	Van Raalfe	31	0.01
Armco Steel	955	0.25	Munsingwear	29	0.01
National Steel	823	0.21	Manhattan Shirt	13	0.00
Inland	797	0.21	Reliance Mfg.	8	0.00
Republic	670	0.17		**364**	**0.09**
Jones & Laughlin	534	0.14	**Synthetic Fibers**		
Youngstown Steel & Tube	482	0.13	Celanese	640	0.17
Crucible	88	0.02	American Euka	181	0.05
Wheeling	51	0.01	Beauniat Mills	72	0.02
Colorado Fuel & Iron	41	0.01		**893**	**0.23**
	8,798	**2.28**			

Continued on next page.

Table 7 A Blast From the Past: Your Father's S&P 500 (1964 Edition), *cont'd*

Industry	Mkt Cap[1] ($mm)	Weight (%)	Industry	Mkt Cap ($mm)	Weight (%)
Textile Products			**Electric Companies**		
Burlington	724	0.19	Commonwealth Edison	2,293	0.59
Stevens JP	228	0.06	Pacific G&E	2,012	0.52
Dan River	97	0.03	American Electric	2,002	0.52
Cone Mills	74	0.02	Consolidated Edison	1,688	0.44
Lowenstein	47	0.01	Southern Co	1,553	0.40
Reeves Bros.	26.2	0.01	Texas Utilities	1,531	0.40
	1,195	**0.31**	S. Cal Edison	1,335	0.35
Tires & Rubber			Public Service G & E	1,240	0.32
Goodyear	1,608	0.42	Virginia Electric	1,127	0.29
Firestone	1,284	0.33	Consumer Power	1,095	0.28
Goodrich	529	0.14	Central & SW	1,086	0.28
US Rubber	364	0.09	Detroit Edison	1,044	0.27
Dayco	27	0.01	Philadelphia Electric	980	0.25
	3,811	**0.99**	General Public Utilities	909	0.24
Tobacco & Cigarettes			Middle S. Utilities	827	0.21
Reynolds Tobacco	1,593	0.41	Ohio Edison	760	0.20
American Tobacco	865	0.22	Niagara Mohawk Power	725	0.19
Liggett	326	0.08	Northern State Electric	623	0.16
Lorillard	276	0.07	Illinois Power	576	0.15
Philip Morris	262	0.07	Baltimore G&E	557	0.14
	3,321	**0.86**	Cleveland Elctric Ill.	547	0.14
Vegetable Oil			Allegheny Power	528	0.14
Central Soya	103	0.03	Cinncinnati G&E	473	0.12
Archer Daniels	58	0.02	Duquesne Light	469	0.12
	161	**0.05**	Florida Power Corp.	455	0.12
Cigar Manufacturers			N.E. Electric Systems	398	0.10
Consolidated	259	0.07	Wisconsin Elec. Power	392	0.10
General	81	0.02	NY State Electricity	339	0.09
Bayard	20	0.01	Dayton P&L	305	0.08
Dwg. Cigars	10	0.00	Indiana Power & Light	248	0.06
	369	**0.10**	Delaware	233	0.06
Vending Machines				**28,348**	**7.36**
Auto Retailers	126	0.03	**Natural Gas Distribution**		
Auto Canteen	115	0.03	Columbia Gas	962	0.25
Servomation	86	0.02	People Gas	732	0.19
Universal Match	75	0.02	American Natutal Gas	679	0.18
Vendo Companies	55	0.01	Consolidated Natural	651	0.17
ABC Cons.	48	0.01	Pacific Lighting	509	0.13
	504	**0.13**	Lone Star	382	0.10

Continued on next page.

Table 7 A Blast From the Past: Your Father's S&P 500 (1964 Edition), *cont'd*

Industry	Mkt Cap[1] ($mm)	Weight (%)
Natural Gas Distribution *con't.*		
Brooklyn Union	192	0.05
Oklahoma Natural Gas	158	0.04
Washington G&L	109	0.03
Equitable	107	0.03
Laclede	106	0.03
	4,589.0	**1.19**
Pipelines		
Panhandle Eastern	552	0.14
Northern Natural Gas	537	0.14
El Paso Natural Gas	518	0.13
United Gas Corp.	469	0.12
S. Natural Gas	337	0.09
Miss. River Fuel	159	0.04
	2,572	**0.67**
Telephone		
AT&T	35,076	9.10
General T&T	3,258	0.85
Rochester T&T	90	0.02
	38,424	**9.97**
Grand Total	**385,421**	**100.00**

CHAPTER 9

Performance Track Record versus Active Management

Roderick G. Baldwin
Director, Index Investment Management
Bank of America Capital Management

Introduction

So much has been written on this subject that reviewing it in this relatively short space is a little like summarizing the Old or New Testaments. Nevertheless, I found it most interesting to re-read the more important academic articles of the last four decades. What Jensen said in 1968 about the failure of mutual funds to beat the market on a risk-adjusted basis is still valid today. The same can be said of most of the work of his colleagues over this prolonged period.

A review of the works of journalists in business magazines and newspapers reveals a similar trend towards the growing recognition of the value of indexing for investments. These articles are less rigorous in their academic approach but more relevant to the daily practitioner. Also, there are the easily available databases on mutual funds and pension plans that can be used to quantitatively justify the arguments for indexing large capitalization stocks.

I will review some of the more important and interesting academic and business articles written on indexing. I will also give readers some relevant current data from which they can draw their own conclusions.

Academic Articles On Indexing

"The Losers Game," Charles D. Ellis, *Financial Analysts Journal*, July/August 1975.

Both A. G. Becker and Merrill Lynch noted that pension funds were doing badly as of data available in 1975. This was still true in 1997, as we shall see later.

The money management business is built on the premise that money managers can beat the market, while the fact is they cannot. Money management has become a losers game as more institutional players enter the marketplace. Clearly this trend has grown since the writing of this article. Relative performance at the time Ellis wrote this article was getting worse, not better. The data he cites are:

Time Period	500 Index	Becker Median	Shortfall	
62-74	5.3%	4.1%	-0.8%	Last three market cycles
66-74	2.1%	0.4%	-1.7%	Last two market cycles
70-74	2.2%	-0.3%	-2.5%	Last single market cycles

Ellis discusses the concept of loser's and winner's games, including tennis, war, football, gold, flying, and gin rummy. I think the gin rummy analogy is easiest to understand. Here the argument is that late in the game the discards reveal less information, and the nature of the game changes.

John J. Raskob wrote an article in the 1920s claiming that everyone can be rich. So scores of people got into the game of money management. The bull markets of the 50s and 60s attracted many bright people to the Street. They had been to the best Ivy schools and the Marines and thought this would be the American dream. In short, institutional investors took over the winner's game and made it a loser's game. He uses example of a gold rush where the end result is not pleasant, as there are clearly more people looking for gold than there is gold to be had.

Ellis notes that at that time, institutional traders had gone from placing 30% of trades to placing 70% of trades. Ellis refers to this as a phase change. The pro competes with the pro, not with the amateur, as in 1975 and 1977.

The following formula, with these still valid assumptions, demonstrates his theory:

$$(X * 9) - (30 * (3*3) - (0.20) = 120 (*9)$$

Then solve for X.

1. 9% equals the long-term return on stocks.
2. Turnover of 30% per year, which may be low by today's standards.
3. Average commission costs of 3% of the principal.
4. Management and custody fees are only 20 basis points, or 0.20%.
5. Goal of manager is to beat market by 20%.

$$X = (30*(3+3))+(0.20)+(120+9)/9$$
$$X = 1.8 + 0.20 + 10.8$$
$$X = 12.8/9$$
$$X = 142\%$$

He must earn a gross return before fees of 42% to get 20%. Stated another way, an active manager at 30% turnover must beat the market by 22% to equal the return on the market.

How can managers "beat" the market by this amount when they *are* the market, today and now. Managers know they are losing the money managers' game, but they cannot admit it.

Ellis suggests that "If you cannot beat the market you should consider joining it."

An index fund is one easy way to "beat" the market or at least to counter the null hypothesis sattes that no one beats the market.

Here are Ellis' rules to try to win at the losers' game:

1. Know your policies well and play according to them. Obey your own rules.
2. Keep it simple, as in the "Less is more" concept of Mies Van der Rohe.
3. Concentrate on your defense and be wary of nothing but buy decisions. You should look at what you own *now*, not what they want you to buy;
4. Do not take managing money personally.

Many money managers are bright, articulate people who are not used to losing, even though they may do that. Ellis makes a good analogy: that Chinese finger locks and straightjackets are representative of the game active money managers play. That is, the harder you try to solve the problem, the harder it becomes.

"The reason institutional investing is a loser's game is that in the complex problem each manager is trying to solve, his efforts to find a solution—and the efforts of his many urgent competitors—have become the dominant variables. And their efforts to beat the market are no longer the most important part of the solution; they are the most important part of the problem," Ellis concludes.

Ellis's article is still referred to, and for good reason.

"Can Professional Investors Beat the Market?," Richard A. Brealey, *An Introduction to Risk And Return From Common Stocks,* 2nd Edition, The MIT Press, 1983.

Brealey reviews the academic debate on the idea of semi-strong forms of efficiency and weak forms of efficiency in the stock market. If the market efficiency were semi-strong, there would be more of a chance to beat it.

Do stock prices thus reflect all information and the tireless work of stock analysts, he wonders?

Given that in a perfectly efficient market no manager could achieve consistently superior results, let us see what the record shows:

Quoting the classic study of Michael Jensen in the May 1968 *Journal of Finance,* he showed that 115 mutual funds adjusted for risk over the period 1955-1964 lagged the market by 0.1% before expenses. There was no sign that any manager could show superior returns.

Data by Bogle and Twardowski (January-February 1980), *Financial Analysts Journal,* "Institutional Investment Performance Compared: Banks, Investment Counselors, Insurance Companies and Mutual Funds") showed that 1,200 funds for the period from 1968 to 1977 had these abnormal returns *before expenses:*

a. -1.6% banks
b. -1.1% investment counselors
c. -1.6% insurance companies
d. -1.4 % mutual funds

This data my not be perfect, but it is felt that pros do not make unusual gains at the expense of the hapless investor. It is a "warning" against high ambition by active managers.

He then reviews studies done by Value Line and Wells Fargo Bank, amongst others. There was some very slight positive correlation of +0.14 at Wells Fargo for the stocks' rating and its outcome. This is encouraging, but not an easy thing to translate into gains after transaction cost expenses.

He quotes Jack Treynor's analogy of a fairground game in which players guess how many beans are in a jar. To win you must guess more accurately than all of the other players on average. Thus, you must not only know more than any other single player, but also all other players.

Perhaps, he concludes, if analysts look at off-the-beaten track stocks and focus less on the widely followed stocks, then they might find something new. This idea has come to be accepted, in my opinion, in the analysis of large cap stocks versus underfollowed stocks.

In the end, both the risk level and the tax liability of a fund are the most important things to focus on. I would agree with the author's conclusions. Brinson and Beebower have shown that your asset allocation and risk taken on a fund have far more impact—90%—than the stocks you pick. Also, tax liability matter is always a concern for the taxable fund and often ignored in a world dominated by pension and 401(k) plans.

"The Coffee Can Portfolio," Robert G. Kirby, *Journal of Portfolio Management*, Fall 1984.

Bob Kirby is often quoted as an advocate against indexing. He is articulate and well respected in our industry. He states that the rise of index funds concerns him; but, for many, the index fund is the best route to go insofar as it realizes that the market is efficient and therefore that it is almost impossible to get superior returns. Also, the poor returns of active managers result from their futile transaction costs—and, I would add, their high fees.

He argues that the Standard & Poor's 500 is actively run by managers at Standard and Poor's and one should use the Wilshire 1000 to get 87% of the market. A good idea at the time, and now we have the Standard and Poor's 1500 or the Russell 1000, 2000, and 3000 indices to do just that. Kirby was prescient in his thoughts on the latter but not the former.

Bob Kirby's uses his "Coffee Can Portfolio" to suggest how one should manage money:

1. Buy and hold good stocks to avoid transaction costs.
2. Keep your turnover low. A.G. Becker, a performance measurement firm, says turnover was 74% on average for institutional funds.
3. Sell winners to put back into losers to keep everyone at 2% of the fund.

However, there are problems with this approach:

a. It takes 10 years to see if it works!
b. Who would pay this fee up front to support a good investment organization?

Kirby does not have answers for these significant objections! To my way of thinking, his is the Warren Buffet or Peter Lynch approach with modifications. It is nevertheless an interesting way for Mr. Kirby to suggest how individual's should invest.

Nonacademic Articles On Index Funds

"The Discreet Charm of Mediocrity," *The Economist*, March 7, 1992.

One of a series of articles on the rise of index funds, this one is well written and provides some data from the United Kingdom. It starts by noting how indexing disturbs those who make a living from active fund management, but how one-fifth of UK public assets and one-third of US public assets are nevertheless indexed for the well-known reasons.

The categories the writer ascribes to active managers attempting to downplay indexing are of interest:

1. *Lofty Arguments.* The role of equity markets to allocate capital efficiently is at risk, says William Donaldson, head of the NYSE. Adam Smith's invisible hand is tied behind his back by all this indexing.The strength of the exchanges is weakened as major indexers here and abroad cross trades off of the exchanges. The author notes the international market in foreign exchange, which flourishes with a market separate from the exchanges. Clearly the index firms are merely trying to lower transaction costs.
2. *Bias against small companies.* Isn't the economic vitality of these companies hurt by index funds that buy large capitalization stocks? Not if you consider that at the time one-half of the money at Bankers Trust was in non S&P 500 index funds and that firms

on both sides of the Atlantic are increasingly voting their shares actively, sometimes against the management of large companies.
3. *Old studies of active managers are out of date.* This claim is rebuked by none other than the Frank Russell Company, hired to find good managers for major corporations at a generous yearly stipend. Russell says the past is not a good indicator of the future. Consultants argue that good individual mangers exist but they 1) change firms and 2) attract too much money to remain better than the market. One is thus challenged to find that manager.

"The Coming Investor Revolt," Jaclyn Fierman and Kathleen Smith, *Fortune*, October 31, 1994.

I think this article should be mandatory reading for all corporate plan sponsors.

It starts by noting the growing realization of plan sponsors like John Carroll of GTE that plan sponsors are paying high fees and not getting any better results than the market average. Barton Biggs, of Morgan Stanley's Asset Management Group, said," "I won't help you with this story because I don't want you to write it."

While highly regarded Microsoft made 25 cents after taxes, the Dreyfus Corporation made 26 cents, and John Nuveen made 29 cents. The following chart by Performance Analytics of Chicago shows the dismal record of active managers versus the S&P 500 index for the period ending June 1994. Note the time period. As we know and will see later, the coming two and one half years were even better for large capitalization index funds.

Also of interest is the following data from Morningstar, which shows that paying higher fees in a mutual fund, supposedly to get better returns, does not work.

2,700 Equity Managers, "Overall, Money Managers Have Done a Dismal Job"

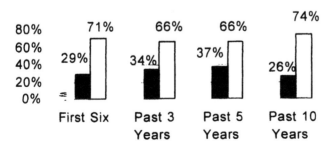

Investors Who Paid More Got Less: 1,281 Mutual Funds

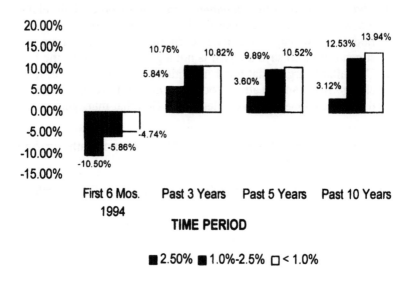

■ 2.50% ■ 1.0%-2.5% ☐ < 1.0%

Investors Who Paid More Got Less: Data on 1,281 Diversified U.S. Stock Funds

	First Six Months of 1994	Past 3 Years	Past 5 Years	Past 10 Years
2.5%	-10.50%	5.84%	3.60%	3.12%
1.0%-2.5%	-5.86%	10.76%	9.89%	12.53%
< 1.0%	-4.74%	10.82%	10.52%	13.94%

Here are some of the authors' reasons for this underperformance:

1. *High turnover or hyperactive trading.* Chasing better stocks or trying to time the market leads to turnover rates of 80% in growth funds and 130% in aggressive funds. Even at lower institutional commission rates this hurts performance due to the bid/ask spread.
2. *Groupthink.* Josef Lakonishok of the University of Illinois feels that this is the problem. A manager must own Wal-Mart because everyone else does. If these stocks fall, they hurt other managers; so the misery loves company concept applies.
3. *Testosterone.* Alan Blanchard, who runs the large Episcopal church pension fund, says this is the problem. "It's heady stuff to have a bunch of well-educated guys descend on your office, laugh at your jokes, and show you a bunch of colorful charts. There's nobody there to say the emperor has no clothes." Unfortunately I think this is true. The article does note that perhaps corporations are paying for comfort, or for someone to take care of them or impress them with their mystique. If so, this is a high cost to the shareholders.
4. *Me-too behavior.* Louis Lowenstein of Columbia Law notes that the idea here is to cover one's self and look respectable. Thus mananagers overdiversify in terms of outside managers, countries, and industries.
5. *Indexing is boring.* James Martin of CREF, which has two thirds of its assets indexed, notes this sentiment. The tortoise does win, and CREF's nonindexed assets returned the same as the indexed money.
6. *Fees hidden.* I find this argument all too valid. Although the average investor acts rationally while shopping for other goods and services, the fees they pay for investment management are deliberately complex to decipher. Mr. Louis Harvey, President of Dalbar Financial Services, a firm that tracks mutual funds among other things, says the "78% of employers had no clue as to what investment management expenses their plans incurred. . . Fees are bundled in 80 different ways."

Most people do not understand the impact of compounding. When they see a 2% expense ratio, they may think it low. Compounded over 10 years, however, it is a lot of money in absolute dollars. The author does not note that the SEC requires fees to be listed in dollars, over several time periods, but this is not quite the same as seeing the fees applied to your investment portfolio over a long term.

"Monkey Business," Dyan Machan, *Forbes*, October 25, 1993.

This amusing, yet still very insightful, article begins with a quote from Bill Fouse, one of the men who truly started the index fund business, saying that money management is ". . . like monkeys trading bananas in trees. The money mangers end up with all of the bananas."

An estimated $9 billion dollars is spent on money management, a losing game, by small investors as well as by the largest, such as Ford and AT&T. "Why bother trying?" is a question Robert Kirby says that he has candidly asked himself a hundred times. Good money managers get hot, receive money, and then regress to the mean, Kirby notes. They fall back to a 0.500 batting average. A few managers, like General Mills, try to fight this trend by giving money to the worst managers as well as the best. Few people are that bold.

An interesting study is noted here by Professors William O'Barr of Duke and John Conley of the University of North Carolina. Anthropologists, they visited nine money management firms to try to determine how money is managed. The results were that the firms would all be better off indexing. This, of course, would have eliminated their jobs of supervising many outside managers of varying styles and reporting to their Boards on the matter. The role of consultants, who also learn high fees in shuffling this money around, is reviewed.

Two major automobile companies are compared. General Motors has 70 money mangers and an internal staff of 70. Despite this large cost, they ranked dead last in the SEI universe of companies with assets over $1 billion. Ford, on the other hand, has only 2 on staff, no consultants or specialty investments, and ranked among the top 15% in the SEI universe.

Keith Ambachsteer, a respected researcher in this area, studied 135 funds with assets of $700 billion. He concluded there was no correlation between performance and money spent on staff, managers, and consultants. The reader should remember that when next asked by a money manager for some business.

"Does Historical Performance Predict Future Performance?," Ronald N. Kahn and Andrew Rudd, *Financial Analysts Journal*, November-December, 1995.

This is one of the more current articles on this subject, by two well-known authors who work for BARRA. It differs from earlier studies in that:

1. It uses Bill Sharpe's style analysis to more accurately categorize funds than their SEC objectives.
2. It includes the effect of fund expenses and fees.
3. It uses data from both Morningstar and Micropal to assure data accuracy.
4. It addresses well the nature of the historical time periods studied.

Although it looks at the persistence effect in fixed income funds, we will ignore that data. Some minor persistence before fees is found, and the reader should pursue this if interested.

A brief review of the 25 years of studies is worth noting:

1. Jensen (1968, *Journal of Finance*) found no persistence in 115 funds for the period 1945 to 1964.
2. Dunn and Theisen (1983, *Journal of Portfolio Management*) found no persistence in 201 institutional portfolios, as opposed to mutual funds, for the period 1973 to 1982.
3. Grinblatt and Titman (1988, working paper, Anderson School of Business, UCLA) did find some persistence in 157 funds for the 1975 to 1984 period.
4. Goetzman and Ibbotson (Winter 1994, *Journal of Portfolio Management*) found persistence in 728 funds in the 1976 to 1988 period.

Style Analysis

Alpha or total return are used in most of these studies. Although this is traditional for that time period, it does not take into effect the correct benchmark for differing funds and may impact the outcome. The authors thus decided to use the style analysis, now incorporated in Morningstar, from the S&P/Barra Value and Growth Indices for the 500, Mid Cap, and Small Cap 600. This leads to what they call, and I concur is, a "level playing field" and is thus a good advance.

Survivorship Bias

Given that unsuccessful funds tend to be merged into other funds or go out of business, this is a serious problem in all of the other studies and has been noted by Ibbotson et al. The authors work around this by using a set of 300 funds for two time periods:

1. In sample: 1/83 to 12/87. This was the period used to determine the 300 equity funds. ͟
2. Period 1: 1/88 to 12/90. The first period.
3. Period 2: 1/91 to 3/92. The second period to see if the performance of period 1 continued.

Period 1 was better for value managers and period 2 for growth mangers. Thus the role of style benchmarks is even more important.

Results

Looking at total equity returns, equity selection returns, and equity information ratios all lead to no signs of persistence from period 1 to period 2. (The equity information ratio is the annualized ratio of residual return to residual risk in the traditional alpha regression equation.) This is confirmed by rigorous statistical testing but is best seen in the following tables.

Total Equity Returns

		Period 2	
		Winners	Losers
Period 1	Winners	62	88
		41.30%	58.70%
	Losers	88	62
		58.70%	41.30%

Equity Selection Returns

		Period 2	
		Winners	Losers
Period 1	Winners	79	71
		52.70%	47.30%
	Losers	71	79
		47.30%	52.70%

Equity Information Ratios

		Period 2	
		Winners	Losers
Period 1	Winners	80	70
		53.30%	46.70%
	Losers	70	80
		46.70%	53.30%

Note that all tables are essentially divided into 50/50 results for period 1 to period 2. The numbers of funds and the percentages are given. Also, chi-squared statistics confirm that the probability of the outcome p is random. The total return data in #1 is not mean reversion but the fact the value did well in period 1 and growth in period 2, so that "winners" became losers. Thus the validity of style analysis is shown again.

Fees and Expenses

A detailed analysis of fees and expenses is done using the Morningstar data. Looking at information ratios (IR) before and after fees shows a 0.36 mean and a 0.12 mean, respectively. Whatever better returns mangers might be able to add is removed by fees and expenses. The authors note that the avoidance of high fees is clearly a viable strategy.

Summary of Results

For 300 equity funds the significance of persistence of the following variables is summarized:

Statistic	Contingency Table	Regression
Total return	No	No
Total + fee	No	No
Selection return	No	No
Selection + fee	No	No
IR	No	Yes
IR + fee	No	No

As noted above, the IR is removed by the fees. Thus, the one "Yes" is removed.

Context of this Study

The authors note several things they did that others had not done over the last 25 years.

1. Style analysis. This removes the tendency of alpha-based studies to show persistence. The impact of value managers versus growth managers in different markets must be addressed, in my opinion.
2. Survivorship bias. It is acknowledged that this is a key factor, and the choice of funds is important for the time periods studied.
3. Fees. Due to improved databases such as Morningstar, it is now possible to look beyond just total returns and see what impact fees have on the investor. As noted, they are negative and should be avoided.
4. Time dependency. The time period reviewed is important. In an efficient market an active manager may acquire a type of superior information, but only briefly before it is discovered by others.

Conclusions

The best alternative is clearly an index fund, as there is no persistence in the above data for equity funds. Low fees, low turnover, and low transaction costs all help the index fund to perform above the median over time.

It is noted that if the investor is able to define his investment objectives well enough, style index funds may be worth looking into. This excellent article ends with the interesting comment, "Only with information beyond historical performance statistics should investors choose active managers." The reader is left to decide what that is.

Stocks for the Long Run: A Guide to Selecting Markets for Long-Term Growth, Jeremy J. Siegel, Richard D. Irwin, Inc., 1994, Chapter 18, "Funds, Managers, and Long Term Investing."

Almost 20 years after the famous Charles Ellis article, "The Losers Game," Jeremy Siegel started his chapter with a quotation from Ellis: "How can institutional investors hope to outperform the market . . . when, in effect, they *are* the market?"

Siegel is a well-known Wharton professor, and his book is currently a popular one. It tries to educate investors about the market by looking at long-term trends, what makes markets move, anomalies, and the importance of asset allocation for the individual.

In addressing the topic at hand, he quickly notes that institutional managers and mutual funds in particular have not done well as shown in the usual studies. His reasons for this poor performance are:

1. The fees that must be paid to the managers. He explains well the compounding impact of these fees over the years;
2. The heavy trading costs that active management entails. The investor must pay the high bid/ask spread in a very efficient market, let alone the commissions;
3. Survivorship bias in the studies is quantified by adding a penalty of one percentage point per year on investors' accounts, according to Richard Ippolito in a 1993 *Financial Analysts Journal* article, "On Studies of Mutual Fund Performance."

Siegel describes in statistical detail how Peter Lynch and the Magellan Fund are the very rare exception. While this fund did beat the market, it took on a standard deviation of 22.11 % versus the market's 12.84% for the 14 years ending in 1992. What is of note in my opinion is the low correlation coefficient of 0.82. This indicates that Magellan was not a closet index fund and clearly took the bets that Siegel has written about.

The following table is a key contribution of Siegel's, and illustrates the difficulty of beating the market. It assumes a beta, or a market risk, of 1.00 and a correlation coefficient of 0.85. More importantly, it assumes you can find a manager who can pick stocks with some "expected excess return." As Siegel notes, the results are surprising—in my opinion, disturbing—for active management. Note that even with a low +1% excess return, the manager would have only a 60.1% chance of beating the market in 10 years, and only 67.1% in 30 years. These are both long investment horizons for either the individual or the institution. Although the results get better with higher expected excess returns, it is noted that there are not many managers around with the insight of Peter Lynch.

Siegel notes that this situation works in reverse. That is, it is just as hard to know for sure that a bad manager is really bad and not just having bad luck.

Expected Excess Return	Holding Period						
	1	2	3	5	10	20	30
1%	53.2%	54.5%	55.6%	57.2%	**60.1%**	64.2%	**67.1%**
2%	56.4%	59.0%	61.0%	64.0%	69.4%	76.4%	81.1%
3%	59.5%	63.3%	66.1%	70.4%	77.6%	85.9%	90.6%
4%	62.5%	67.4%	71.0%	76.2%	84.3%	92.3%	96.0%
5%	65.4%	71.2%	75.4%	81.2%	89.5%	96.2%	98.5%

In closing his chapter, Siegel explains how "excess return over the market" is dragged down by various levels of trading at differing levels of information on excess returns. The conclusion is that once again the individual investor and the institutional investor are both better off holding an index fund. This is largely due to the costs of trading canceling out the benefits of insight on stocks.

"Future Stock, Best Bets for 2096: No More Brokers," Michael Lewis, *New York Times Magazine*, September 29, 1996.

Last fall the *New York Times* published a series of articles on what the world would look like one hundred years from now. Michael Lewis, a former investment banker and author of *Liar's Poker*, was chosen to address the investment world.

In addition to seeing the dollar being replaced by a world currency and many different stocks in the Dow Jones, he makes two logical predictions:

1. Most money will be invested in buy-and-hold stock index funds. The research of 20 years has argued for this, and it will have come to pass. People will choose an investment mix and stay with it via the index funds.
2. Related to the above, brokerage houses and mutual funds will be the railroads of the future. "Merrill Lynch and Fidelity will go the way of the Reading and Penn Central," he opines.

I would like to think that the growth of lifestyle funds, funds that are targeted toward investors at a certain age or with a specific time horizon for investing is a precursor of what he is promising us. Also, it ties into what Jeremy Siegel says in his book.

Data Review

As this book goes to press, there are two major sources of data available to test the theory that large cap funds underperform index funds. These are of course the Morningstar data and the SEI data through December 31, 1996. SEI focuses on corporate pension and 401(k) plans, and Morningstar on mutual funds. Fees are not included in the SEI data but are in the Morningstar data. The Morningstar data is also in the public domain, as there are other ways to check its validity and it represents what the individual can buy or the corporate CFO is offering to its 401(k) participants. I therefore prefer the Morningstar data, but feel that it is worth looking at the SEI data briefly.

SEI DATA to December 1996: Equity Fund Universe

The first table and chart show the universe statistics for equity funds for three quarters and for annual period ending in 1996. Equity funds are that universe of funds as opposed to the equity portion of a balanced fund. The results are, as expected, quite positive for the S&P 500. It is ranked at the 35th to the 25th percentile for the time period covered. Two points should be noted:

1. Fees are not included on the SEI universe. The percentile numbers would be lower and the S&P 500 ranking higher if this were done,
2. All performance numbers are period dependent. This has been a three-year period (1994 to 1996) where the S&P 500 has done very well as investors sought large capitalization stocks.

Equity Funds: Total Fund Rates of Return

DECEMBER 1996

	Five Years	Three Years	Two Years	One Year	Three Quarters	Two Quarters	One
5 TH PCT	19.5	25.0	37.3	29.8	22.0	15.8	11.6
25 TH PCT	15.5	20.0	30.1	24.0	17.2	12.5	8.7
MEDIAN	14.6	17.5	27.6	21.2	14.6	10.3	7.3
75 TH PCT	13.2	14.9	24.5	18.4	12.5	8.1	5.1
95 TH PCT	11.2	10.2	14.0	12.4	7.1	1.4	0.7
S&P500	15.2	19.7	30.1	23.0	16.7	11.7	8.3
RANK	32	32	25	35	29	32	32

EQUITY FUNDS: PERIOD ENDED DECEMBER 1996, S&P 500 PCTILE RANK

SEI Universe: Equity Funds for Market Cycles

In a similar fashion, the SEI Equity Fund universe is presented in the following table and graph for 10 different time periods or market cycles. Keeping in mind the above caveats about fees and period dependency, the following observations can be made:

Equity Funds: Total Fund Rates of Return for Market Cylces, Falling Markets, and Rising Markets

DECEMBER 1996, ©SEI Corp.

	Peak Cycle to 1/81 9/87	Trough to 10/87 Open	Trough to 4/87 6/82	Trough to 7/82 12/87	Rising Market 4/78 12/80	Rising Market 7/82 9/87	Rising Market 1/88 Open	Falling Market 1/77 3/78	Falling Market 1/81 6/82	Falling Market 10/87 12/87
5 TH PCT	23.0	15.4	19.6	23.0	34.7	29.6	18.9	3.9	6.7	-14.8
25 TH PCT	20.2	14.0	14.7	20.7	25.9	27.4	17.1	-4.2	-1.0	-19.3
MEDIAN	18.2	13.0	12.6	18.8	21.9	25.3	16.2	-8.0	-5.5	-21.2
75 TH PCT	16.5	12.1	10.2	17.3	19.2	23.5	15.0	-10.5	-10.4	-23.1
95 TH PCT	13.6	10.4	7.5	14.6	15.4	21.1	14.1	-13.5	-15.3	-26.3
S&P500	18.7	12.8	10.6	20.8	22.8	28.0	16.5	-9.6	-8.7	-22.5
RANK	39	54	72	24	45	18	40	68	66	68

EQUITY FUNDS, MARKET CYCLES, DATA TO

DECEMBER 1996, SEI S&P 500 PCTILE RANK

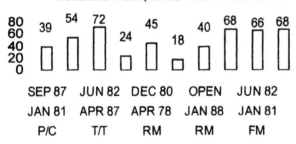

1. One can see the small capitalization effect in column three for the trough-to-trough period of April 1987 to June 1982. Here the S&P 500 ranked lower as small cap stocks did well. In contrast, column four shows a very strong 24th percentile performance for the period of July 1982 and December 1987 where this small cap "anomaly" was not present;

2. All rising markets showed strong S&P 500 performance with percentile ranks of 45, 12, and 40 for the S&P 500;

3. In falling markets the S&P 500 was in the third quartile with 68, 66, and 68 percentile rankings. The most current falling market;
4. The longest time period, from the rising market of January 1988 to date, shows a very strong second quartile ranking of 40th percentile for the S&P 500. This is worth noting as it covers a period not so dominated by large cap stocks as we saw in the above SEI data for periods going back only five years in total.

In summary, I feel that the SEI data makes a strong case for indexing with the data shown here.

Morningstar Data to December 31, 1996

The following table shows selected summary statistics on 1,515 mutual funds for the period ending December 1996. At period end there were 116 aggressive growth, 868 growth, and 531 growth and income funds. In total, there were only 219 funds in this universe 15 years ago and 357 10 years ago. This would reflect some survivorship bias, but also the dramatic increase in the number of mutual funds over this period.

Summary Statistics on 1,515 Equity Mutual Funds from Morningstar, to December 1996

Investment Objective	Tot Ret 12 Mo	Tot Ret Annlzd 3 Yr	Tot Ret Annlzd 5 Yr	Tot Ret Annlzd 10 Yr	Tot Ret Annlzd 15 Yr	Load Adj Ret 12 Mo	Load Adj Ret 5 Yr	Load Adj Ret 10 Yr	Alpha 3 Yr
AVERAGE	19.41	15.55	13.43	13.30	14.32	17.12	12.96	13.05	-2.56
MAXIMUM	51.56	30.92	26.64	21.33	22.36	51.56	26.64	21.33	12.28
MINIMUM	-30.36	-31.99	-22.78	-16.04	-12.79	-30.36	-22.78	-16.04	-44.74
COUNT	1515	973	579	357	219	1515	579	357	971
MEDIAN	19.79	15.97	13.61	13.62	14.95	17.21	13.19	13.27	-2.01
STAND DEV	6.45	4.45	3.99	3.53	3.84	7.14	4.03	3.51	4.05
RANGE	81.92	62.91	49.42	37.37	35.15	81.92	49.42	37.37	57.02
Vanguard Index 500	22.86	19.55	15.06	15.04	16.43	22.86	15.06	15.04	-0.09
Aggressive Growth =116	13.75	13.69	13.66	13.93	13.14	11.26	13.10	13.66	-5.02
Growth =868	19.21	15.30	13.29	13.59	14.63	16.92	12.82	13.34	-2.84
Growth and Income =531	20.96	16.39	13.58	12.65	14.14	18.68	13.13	12.40	-1.53

continued on next page

Summary Statistics on 1,515 Equity Mutual Funds from Morningstar, to December 1996, *con't.*

Sharpe Ratio	P/E Ratio	P/B Ratio	P/C Ratio	5 Yr Earn Gr	Med Mkt Cap $MM	Front Load	Expense Ratio	Defer Load	12b-1	Investment Objective
1.01	25.88	4.73	15.31	22.08	$9,910	4.77	1.42	3.43	0.60	AVERAGE
2.31	54.90	13.60	35.60	58.50	$48,162	8.50	17.69	5.50	1.00	MAXIMUM
-2.98	14.50	1.60	6.60	-5.80	$85	1.00	0.06	0.50	0.05	MINIMUM
973	1573	1573	1573	1573	$1,573	499	1439	395	957	COUNT
1.07	24.30	4.60	14.00	20.90	$8,201	4.75	1.25	4.00	0.50	MEDIAN
0.44	6.15	1.48	4.68	8.91	$8,445	0.97	0.86	1.75	0.34	STAND DEV
5.29	40.40	12.00	29.00	64.30	$48,077	7.50	17.63	5.00	0.95	RANGE
										Vanguard
1.46	23.50	4.90	13.60	17.80	$24,598	0.00	0.20	0.00	0.00	Index 500
										Aggressive
0.57	35.10	6.20	22.30	32.30	$2,575	1.54	1.74	0.95	0.43	Growth
0.95	26.70	4.90	16.00	23.40	$8,582	1.48	1.45	0.81	0.35	Growth
										Growth and
1.23	22.40	4.20	12.50	17.50	$13,905	1.35	1.28	0.82	0.34	Income

A range of statistical data items is given for all funds, followed by the average for the three categories listed above. Note also that the Vanguard Index 500 is used as the proxy for the Standard and Poor's 500 index. The regular index could be used and would show a slightly higher performance. Nevertheless, it is felt that this is a reasonable proxy that the investor can buy.

I feel that to be fair in this analysis it is important to look at the whole universe and the three investment objectives. Too often I read that "1,273 actively managed funds" beat the universe. This is misleading; one should differentiate the funds by their stated objective. Too diverse an aggregate universe makes for a statistically meaningless average, in my opinion. The S&P 500 is a large cap blend fund in terms of style analysis or a growth and income fund in terms of SEC objective.

Although the reader should review the data in the table, the following graphs summarize the findings:

1. Historical Performance by Objectives vs. the S&P 500: In each of the five historical periods shown, the S&P 500 fund had a higher return.

2. Historical Performance by Objectives vs. the S&P 500 Adjusted for Loads: This is the same graph as above, but the returns are adjusted by the fees paid to buy into the fund. This would be the front end or back end load.

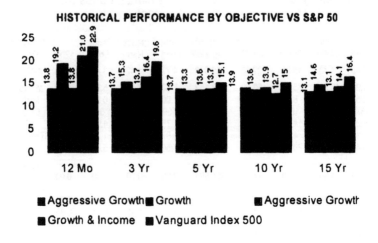

HISTORICAL PERFORMANCE BY OBJECTIVE VS S&P 50

■ Aggressive Growth ■ Growth   ■ Aggressive Growth
■ Growth & Income   ■ Vanguard Index 500

It is worth noting the Morningstar explanation of Load Adjusted Return(s):

Total return, adjusted for front-end loads, and deferred fees. Taxes are not taken into account. Load-adjusted returns since inception date are annualized, not cumulative. In order to meet the requirements of the NASD, the effective date for load-adjusted total returns is as of the most-recent quarter-end. When comparing total-return figures, keep in mind than non-monthly total-return figures are also used in Morningstar Principia.

This figure is adjusted for both front-end load and deferred fees, but not taxes. Because deferred charges generally decline over time, Morningstar calculates load-adjusted total return for each year the charge applies. The load is applied to the lesser of the starting or closing NAV.

Total return is an in-house calculation, based on either NASDAQ or non-NASDAQ electronic transmissions. As of June 1996, these figures are reported as of the most-recent quarter-end, in order to meet the requirements of the NASD.

Here's how we account for deferred fees, to calculate load-adjusted returns: if a fund with a deferred charge of 5% that is reduced to 0% after five years, then its one year performance figure will be penalized by 4%.

For investors that do not reinvest dividends or capital gains, their overall gain will be lower than the total returns shown in these returns. This is because Morningstar's total returns take into account the compounded appreciation and income on the (assumed) reinvested amount.

Note that the same pattern holds—i.e., superior performance for the Vanguard Fund.

3. Historical Performance by Sharpe Ratio vs. the S&P 500 for three years ending December 1996: I think this is most significant, as the ratio for the Vanguard Index 500 is so much higher than the ratios for the average investment objectives. Even allowing for the strong performance of the 500 in this three-year period, the "reward for variability" concept of the ratio shows an almost three-to-one superiority over the aggressive growth fund average. Remember that these are SEC objectives, and many mangers in these categories are allowed to buy into the universe of the S&P 500.

**LOAD ADJUSTED RETURNS BY OBJECTIVE
VS. S&P 500 INDEX**

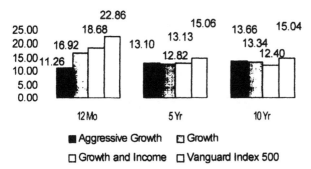

The Morningstar notes on this ratio are helpful:

A risk-adjusted measure developed by Nobel Laureate William Sharpe. It is calculated by using standard deviation and excess return to determine reward per unit of risk. The higher the Sharpe Ratio, the better the fund's historical risk-adjusted performance. The Sharpe ratio is calculated for the past 36-month period by dividing a fund's annualized excess returns by the standard deviation of a fund's annualized excess returns.

Since this ratio uses standard deviation as its risk measure, it is most appropriately applied when analyzing a fund that is an investor's sole holding. The Sharpe Ratio can be used to compare two funds directly on how much risk a fund had to bear to earn excess return over the risk-free rate.

This ratio is calculated for the past 36-month period by dividing a fund's annualized excess return by the standard deviation of a fund's annualized excess returns.

The Putnam Municipal Income fund has a Sharpe Ratio of 2.22, which is the highest or best for the Municipal Bond National category. The three-year standard deviation for Putnam Municipal Income is 3.97.

4. Historical Performance by Alpha vs. the S&P 500 for three years ending December 1996: For the same three-year time period, the Alpha or Jensen measure is displayed for the three objectives and the Vanguard Index 500 fund. Once again a very strong statistical argument is made for the index fund. Note that it has a very small -0.09 alpha. This is statistically identical to the index alpha of 0.00.

S&P 500 VS THREE INVESTMENT OBJECTIVE :

THREE YEAR SHARPE RATIO TO DECEMBER 1996

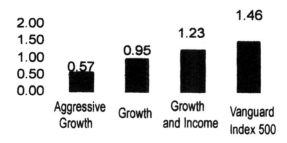

The Morningstar definition is worth also noting:

A measure of the difference between a fund's actual returns and its expected performance, given its level of risk as measured by beta. A positive alpha figure indicates the fund has performed better than its beta would predict. In contrast, a negative alpha indicates the fund's under performance, given the expectations established by the fund's beta. All MPT statistics (alpha, beta, and R-squared) are based on a least-squared regression of the fund's return over Treasury bills (called excess return) and the excess returns of the fund's benchmark index.

Alpha can be used to directly measure the value a mutual fund (and, more specifically, its portfolio manager) adds or subtracts. However, alpha depends on two factors: 1) the assumption that market risk, as measured by beta is the only risk measure necessary, and 2) the strength of the linear relationship between the fund and the index, as it has been measured by R-squared. In addition, a negative alpha can sometimes result from the expenses that are present in a fund's returns, but not in the returns of the comparison index.

All MPT statistics (alpha, beta, and R-squared) are based on a least-squares regression of the fund's return over Treasury bills (called excess return) and the excess returns of the fund's benchmark index. The value of using alpha and beta depends upon the strength of the linear relationship between the fund and the index over the past six months. R-squared measures the strength of this relationship. An R-squared of 100, for example, implies a perfect linear relationship, while an R-squared of zero implies that no relationship exists whatsoever. Additionally, the application of MPT statistics assumes that beta, which is based on market risk, is the only risk measure necessary.

The Norwest Income Investor Class A fund has an alpha of 0.38, a beta of 1.00, and an R-squared of 93.1. The high R-squared lends further credibility to the accuracy of the fund's alpha and beta. The alpha of 0.38 indicates that the fund produced a return 38% higher than its beta would predict.

**S&P 500 VS. THREE INVESTMENT OBJECTIVES:
3 YEAR ALPHA TO DECEMBER 1996**

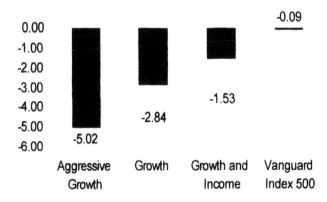

Conclusions

Out of curiosity I looked at the equity data on the following screens using the Morningstar Equity Style Box. Here I looked for the "Large Capitalization Blend" style that is most typical of an index fund. This is in contrast to the Large Value and Large Growth styles. I thought it might be a cleaner, fair comparison. Small and mid cap stocks were excluded over this period that they did so poorly in.

Morningstar looks at the average P/E ratio relative to the S&P 500 and adds it to the average price/book ratio, again relative to the S&P 500. Finally, median market capitalization is used to rank the funds into large, medium, and small. All of this is based on the actual common stocks held at different points in time as reported to the SEC and thus Morningstar. Only 996, as opposed to over 1,500, funds were in this style box as of December 31, 1996. Finally, all index funds were excluded to keep the number of funds lower.

The summary data on their performance shown below.

Summary Results on 996 "Large Blend" Mutual Funds to December 1996*

		Average "996"	Vanguard Index 500	Difference
Annlzd	3 Yr	12.80	19.55	-6.75
Annlzd	5 Yr	12.02	15.06	-3.04
Annlzd	10 Yr	12.48	15.04	-2.56
Annlzd	15 Yr	14.50	16.43	-1.93
Adj Ret	12 Mo	13.88	22.86	-8.98
Adj Ret	5 Yr	11.49	15.06	-3.57
Adj Ret	10 Yr	12.20	15.04	-2.84
Alpha	3 Yr	-3.48	-0.09	-3.39
Beta	3 Yr	0.82	1.00	-0.18
Sharpe Ratio		0.89	1.46	-0.57

MORNINGSTAR Category for Equity Style.

The results make an even stronger argument for indexing. Note that the alpha here is -3.39% fòr these funds versus -1.53% for three years on growth and income funds that we noted earlier. The Sharpe ratio is 0.89 for these funds versus 1.23 for growth and income funds. Other data also supports the outperformance of the Vanguard Index 500 funds. Reasons for this poor showing include the fact that although the funds were equity funds with an average 81% equity position, they did own cash and some bonds, which clearly hurt them in this rising market.

Finally, I screened the same large capitalization blend criteria, and funds with more than 80% in stocks, and more than 95% in United States and Canadian stocks. All index funds were excluded. Only 88 funds passed these criteria. The results are show below. With only 3% cash and 98% invested in the United States and Canada, the numbers look somewhat better for the active managers. The Alpha and Sharpe Ratios are still negative for the former and quite positive for the latter. Only 4 funds had positive alphas. Two of these were closed to new money, perhaps showing that you should stop while ahead. One was, by name, an equity income fund, despite the above screen. The last was Accessor Growth, a five-star rated fund that has done well but has a low asset base of $64 million. The Sharpe ratio gave the same three-year ranking, with only two funds having a higher ratio than the Vanguard Index 500 Fund.

Summary Results on 88 "Large Blend" Mutual Funds to December 1996* with More than 80% in U.S. Stocks

		Average "88"	Vanguard Index 500	Difference
Annlzd	3 Yr	15.86	19.55	-3.69
Annlzd	5 Yr	12.20	15.06	-2.86
Annlzd	10 Yr	12.63	15.04	-2.41
Annlzd	15 Yr	13.56	16.43	-2.87
Adj Ret	12 Mo	18.19	22.86	-4.67
Adj Ret	5 Yr	11.79	15.06	-3.27
Adj Ret	10 Yr	12.40	15.04	-2.64
Alpha	3 Yr	-2.59	-0.09	-2.50
Beta	3 Yr	0.95	1.00	-0.05
Sharpe Ratio		1.10	1.46	-0.36

**MORNINGSTAR Category for Equity Style.*

One could look at the data other ways over other time periods. Use of the best fit regression index is interesting. Suffice it to say that it does not change the conclusion.

(I also now know why textbooks say they will leave it to the reader to pursue the method further.)

Summary

The many studies done over the last 31 years since Jensen's all come to the same conclusion: For large capitalization stocks, it makes sense to index. One wonders why there is still so much active management, but there are many instances where a good solution to a problem exists but is not accepted by the public. Closer to home many, innovations such as money market funds or futures on indices where slow to gain acceptance.

We noted, amongst other things, the camaraderie fostered by having your money manager visit you; the arguments that indexing *really* has not have been proven to work; the publics' ignorance about the fees they are paying; and the fact that it is not fun to talk about your index funds over cocktails. Jack Bogle, in *Bogle on Mutual Funds* (1994, Irwin), comes to somewhat similar conclusions. He argues that indexing is counterintuitive. How could people not beat the index with all those resources, he asks?

It is clearly less profitable. "A great way to manage money, but not a great way to make money," as a former colleague of mine liked to say. Another noted he was moving into index funds when he saw the mutual fund ads that ran during the last Super Bowl. There are a lot of people making a lot of money and operating on the rule that "mutual funds are sold, not bought." Bill Fouse's comments about the bananas and the monkeys comes to mind.

Finally, Bogle notes that hope springs eternal and everyone wants to be among the 20% that beat the market.

Personally, I think we are moving in the right direction. Corporations and state governments have seen the value of indexing. The individual investor is a harder sell, but Michael Thomas is probably right that someday we will *all* be in indexed lifestyle funds.

CHAPTER 10

Overview of the Equity Index Fund Marketplace

Todd B. Johnson
Chief Investment Officer
World Asset Management

Strength of Index Mutual Fund Market

The 1990s are going to be known as "The decade of the index fund." For various reasons, both institutional and retail investors have been flocking to index funds in record numbers. (see Figure 1) At the same time, investors are fleeing this country's largest active mutual funds. The Vanguard 500, for example, has recently risen to the number two spot with assets over $40 billion. Mutual fund investors are learning what pension fund managers have been learning for over 20 years, which is index funds offer investors many advantages. The most significant advantages are lower cost, consistent performance, and better diversification.

The index fund marketplace no longer exclusively belongs to the S&P 500 Index. Eleven years ago, over 93 percent of all index mutual funds tracked the S&P 500 index. Today, though still the dominant equity index fund, the funds that track the S&P 500 now represent 82 percent of the equity index fund market. To understand fully the dynamics of the equity index fund marketplace, you must first understand each of the indices available as equity index funds.

211

Figure 1 Growth of the Equity Index Mutual Fund Assets

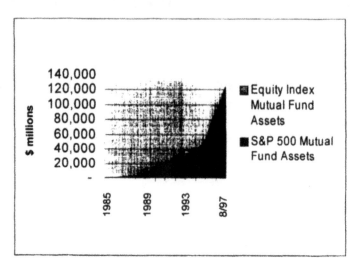

Source: Strategic Insight Simfund

Domestic Indices

Standard and Poor's (S&P)

S&P 500 Index

Today, the S&P 500 Index (S&P 500) is the most chosen index by investors. (see Figure 2) Its reputation, as the most popular index strategy, does not come without merit. The S&P 500 is a broad market index designed to track the movements of the U.S. stock markets. While it contains only 500 stocks out of a possible 7,000, it represents approximately 65 percent of the domestic market.

The S&P 500 consists of 500 stocks chosen for market size, liquidity, and industry group representation. It is a market value (market-cap) weighted index (stock price times number of shares outstanding), with each stock's weight in the index proportionate to its market value. The S&P 500 is one of the most widely used benchmarks of U.S. equity performance and is updated on a daily basis with company additions, deletions, and shares changes. It was created in 1923, and in its original form, the S&P 500 was designed to track the movements of the total U.S. stock markets. Decisions about stocks to be included are made by committee at Standard & Poor's. With over 7,000 stocks trading in the U.S., its emphasis on larger capitalization stocks has effectively turned it into a large cap index. The S&P 500 is the largest and most popular strategy and has several extensions and competitors.

Figure 2 Equity Index Mutual Fund Market Breakdown

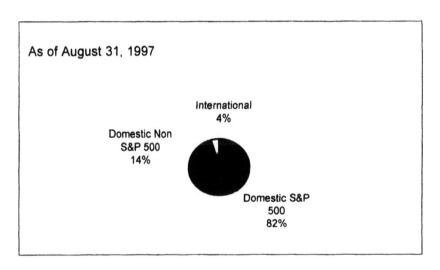

As of August 31, 1997

International
4%

Domestic Non
S&P 500
14%

Domestic S&P
500
82%

Source: Strategic Insight Simfund

S&P 400 MidCap Index

The S&P MidCap 400 index (MidCap 400) was introduced in June 1991. It tracks the stock price movement of 400 companies chosen by committee at Standard & Poor's to represent the mid-sized market capitalization market. None of the companies contained in the MidCap 400, are contained in the S&P 500, or the S&P 600 SmallCap Index (SmallCap 600). Some companies contained in the MidCap 400, however, are larger than those in the S&P 500 and smaller than those in the SmallCap 600. This is a function of the normal drift that takes place between any two markets. The MidCap 400, like the S&P 500, is updated on a daily basis with company additions, deletions, and shares changes.

S&P 600 SmallCap Index

The S&P 600 SmallCap Index (SmallCap 600) was introduced in October 1994 to track the performance of the small capitalization stock market. Companies are chosen by committee at Standard & Poor's for their size, industry characteristics, and liquidity. None of the companies contained in the SmallCap 600 are contained in the MidCap 400 or the S&P 500. Some of the largest companies in the SmallCap 600, however, are larger than the smallest of companies in the MidCap 400 and S&P 500. This is a function of the normal drift that takes place between any two market segments. The SmallCap 600, like the other S&P indices, is updated on a daily basis with company additions, deletions, and shares changes.

S&P 1500 Super Composite Index

The S&P 1500 Super Composite Index (Super Composite 1500) combines the returns for the MidCap 400, S&P 500, and SmallCap 600. The index is market-cap weighted with the S&P 500 making up over 85 percent. of the index. Standard & Poor's began publishing returns for the Super Composite 1500 in January 1995. This index correlates very highly with other popular total market indices, the Russell 3000 and the Wilshire 5000.

S&P Style Indices

S&P/BARRA Growth and Value indices are constructed by sorting the S&P 500 companies based on their price-to-book (P/B) ratios, with the low P/B companies forming the value index and the high P/B companies making up the growth index. Every company contained in the S&P is included in either the growth index or the value index. Each index is reconstructed two times a year to represent 50 percent of the total market value. The MidCap 400 and the SmallCap 600 are also divided to create growth and value indices for mid-cap stocks and small-cap stocks.

Frank Russell Company

Russell 3000 Index

The Russell 3000 Index (Russell 3000) measures the performance of the 3,000 largest publicly traded companies domiciled in the United States based on total market capitalization. The Frank Russell Company uses the market value when it sorts its universe to determine the various indices. Total shares outstanding are adjusted for cross-ownership between firms and shares held by insiders to determine the floating shares and thus the weight. The Russell indices are reconstructed annually to reflect changes in the marketplace. Companies that are acquired, or delisted, are not replaced until the following year.

Russell 1000 Index

The Russell 1000 Index (Russell 1000) measures the performance of 1,000 largest companies included in the Russell 3000 universe. As with all Russell indices, it is market value weighted adjusted for float, and it excludes cross-ownership and shares held by insiders. The Russell 1000 represents approximately 90 percent of the total market capitalization of the Russell 3000. The Russell indices are reconstructed annually to reflect changes in the marketplace; thus, companies that are acquired, or delisted, are not replaced until the following year.

Russell 2000 Index

The Russell 2000 Index (Russell 2000) measures the performance of 2,000 smallest companies in the Russell 3000. It is widely recognized and used to as a small-cap index in the United States. The Russell indices are reconstructed annually to reflect changes in the marketplace; thus, companies that are acquired, or delisted, are not replaced until the following year.

Russell Style Indices

The Russell Style Indices include the Russell 3000 Growth, Russell 3000 Value, Russell 1000 Growth, Russell 1000 Value, Russell 2000 Growth, and Russell 2000 Value indices. These indices are constructed by measuring the performance of the Russell universe of companies and reviewing the price-to-book (P/B) ratios and forecasted growth values. Companies with higher P/B ratios and higher forecasted growth values are included in the Russell Growth Indices while the other companies with lower P/B ratios and lower forecasted growth values are included in the Russell Values indices. A company that is included in the Growth or Value component in the 1000 or 2000 index will also appear as a Growth or Value component in the 3000 index. The Russell Style Indices are reconstructed annually to reflect changes in the marketplace; thus, companies that are acquired, or delisted, are not replaced until the following year.

Wilshire

Wilshire 5000 Index

The Wilshire 5000 Index (Wilshire 5000) is derived from the performance of all publicly traded companies with readily available pricing
headquartered in the United States. Over 7,000 companies are included in
this index. The Wilshire 5000 base is December 31, 1980. The constituents in the Wilshire indices are reconstructed annually, and the
indices are reweighted quarterly.

Wilshire 4500 Index

The Wilshire 4500 Index (Wilshire 4500) is a subset of the Wilshire 5000,
which contains all common U.S. equities, traded on the New York Stock
Exchange (NYSE), American Stock Exchange (AMEX), and Over the
Counter (OTC). The Wilshire 4500 excludes the companies included in
the S&P 500. The constituents in the Wilshire indices are reconstructed
annually, and the indices are reweighted quarterly.

Wilshire Style Indices

The six individual style indices are Large Company Value, Large
Company Growth, Mid Cap Company Value, Mid Cap Company Growth,
Small Company Value, and Small Company Growth. The indices are created by screening each universe for a company's match of the characteristics of each style. The screening criteria for the value index are
price/earnings (P/E) ratio, price-to-book (P/B) ratio, and yield. The
screening criteria for the growth index include sales growth, return on
equity (ROE), and dividend payout. The constituents in the Wilshire
indices are reconstructed annually, and the indices are reweighted quarterly.

International Indices

FT/S&P Actuaries World Indices

The FT/S&P Actuaries World Indices were launched in 1987 and are
owned by FT-SE International Limited, Goldman, Sachs & Co. and
Standard & Poor's. In 1987, the Indices contained approximately 2,400
equities from 23 countries. Today, the indices contain approximately
2,427 equities from 28 countries. Finland was added in December 1987.

Thailand and Brazil were added in November 1994, and Indonesia and the Philippines were added in July 1996. The indices aim to include only equities whose shares are available to foreign investors. The country indices currently aim to include approximately 85 percent of the market capitalization available to foreign investors in each market. Additional countries, which meet the eligibility criteria, may be considered for inclusion in the future.

Morgan Stanley Capital International (MSCI)

MSCI Europe Australia and Far East (EAFE) Index

The Morgan Stanley Capital International Europe Australia and Far East Index (MSCI EAFE) tracks the equity performance of approximately 1,000 companies in 20 foreign countries located in Europe, Australia, and the Far East. It is recognized for measuring foreign equity performance; however, the MSCI EAFE, is a narrow representation of the world, containing only 20 countries and 60 percent of each market.

MSCI World Index

The MSCI World Index (MSCI World) is the EAFE countries plus the United States and Canada, and it contains only 22 developed markets. Even though the MSCI World is broader than EAFE, it only adds Canada (other than the U.S.).

MSCI World All Countries Index

The MSCI All Countries Index represents both developed and emerging markets for a particular region. The index includes approximately 47 countries, of which approximately 9.5 percent are considered emerging markets and attempts to capture only 60 percent of each market.

Index Fund Availability

The world of benchmarks offers many choices, and each benchmark has its strengths and weaknesses. Unfortunately, however, each benchmark is not widely available as a mutual fund investment option. Other than the S&P 500, which has 88 mutual fund products available, the other indices only have a few providers for each. As you construct an actual investment portfolio, you must constrain your choices to those options which are available. Diversification and market representation are important criteria

when evaluating each investment benchmark and investment program.
The number of mutual funds available in this country is large (in excess of 7,000). There are as many, if not more, mutual funds available than there are individual equity securities. As the numbers of equity funds continue to increase, so do the number of index mutual funds, but in much smaller numbers. With the total number of funds available hovering around 7,000, only 160 of them, or two percent, are index funds. With the universe of index funds around 160, over one-half, or 88, directly represent the S&P 500. Of the 17 categories of index funds available to the public, most only have one or two providers representing each of those indices.

The second most widely followed index is the MSCI EAFE. There are 13 funds tracking that benchmark. Adding together all of the different MSCI's benchmarks fund offerings together still only gives 16 fund offerings. The most prevalent small cap benchmark is the Russell 2000 with nine product offerings. Close on its heels is the SmallCap 600 with six offerings. The Wilshire 5000, the broadest index offering, has ten fund offerings.

When comparing these different benchmarks as a percentage of total assets, the numbers become even more staggering; as of August 1997, the S&P 500 had over 82 percent of the assets contained in public mutual index funds. The second largest index followed was the Wilshire 5000 with 4.61 percent; the Russell 2000 has 2.61 percent. All the international benchmarks combined contain less than three percent of the assets invested in index mutual funds. Though the S&P 500 has achieved recognition as the most significant mutual fund vehicle, as demonstrated by both its dominance in the marketplace and its rapid growth, non S&P 500 indexing, such as the SmallCap 600 and International, are seeing tremendous growth. (see Figure 3)

A logical question that may arise when reviewing the popularity of index funds is why there is not more providers of index products. In the United States, there are approximately 30 firms that manage index products for themselves and others. This number pales in comparison to the number of traditional active managers. What also is different is the size of the firms; the top third of firms in the index industry all manage assets in excess of ten billion dollars, and several of the largest firms have assets in excess of one hundred billion dollars. The largest most successful firms have a common trait in that they all offer a mix of index products helping the investor diversify their portfolio. Although the S&P 500, in and of itself, is a diversified investment, a portfolio made exclusively of the S&P 500 would not be considered a diversified portfolio.

Figure 3 Growth of Non S&P 500 Mutual Fund Indexing

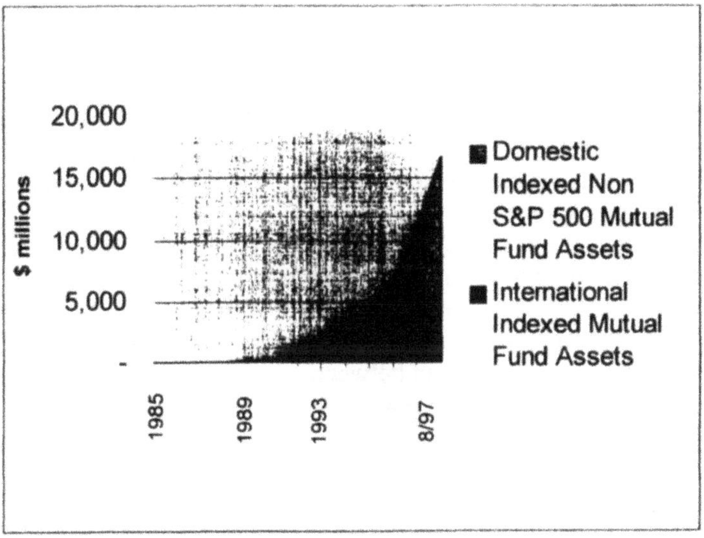

Source: Strategic Insight Simfund

To maintain diversification, you must build a portfolio with a mix of products that represent the marketplace itself. Even though a traditional manager can offer literally hundreds of different products, it is rare to find a combination of those products that add diversification to an investor's portfolio. Building a basket of indexed portfolios, however, does create that diversification. It allows an investor to purchase a basket of dissimilar investments that are built to strict standards and deliver precisely what is required.

Another reason why investment managers do not offer index products more often is that the fees charged are low. It is difficult for an investment manager to have the economies of scale required to maintain a profitable indexing venture. Though several fund families based on additional active products offer index funds, it is becoming increasingly uncommon to find management of those index funds contained within the family. Even Fidelity, a firm with large pools of investment talent and resources, found itself unable to motivate and maintain the investment staff required to manage their index products. They had to search outside to maintain the economies necessary to able to offer a quality product at a reasonable price.

The institutional marketplace for index investment products does not significantly different from that of publicly available mutual funds. Although the ability to customize a product to a client's specific objectives is available on a separate account basis, collective or pooled funds are still the best way to maintain the low cost of management. Institutional investment strategies do differ from those in the retail market. As such, they tend to be more methodical about obtaining diversification. Large pension plans often invest their portfolio in the same proportions as the marketplace.

Even though some additional indices are available to institutions for investment, the number of firms offering credible index products is significantly less. Searching for a traditional active equity product may involve looking at literally hundreds of managers. A complete search of index products will only contain between 15 and 20 managers.

It is important to remember that indexing is not the goal; it is a means to an end. The goal is diversification.

The author would like to thank Strategic Insight Simfund for contributing a significant portion of the mutual fund data used in this chapter.

CHAPTER 11

Implementing Equity Index Portfolios

Andrew Olma
Chief Strategist, Index Equities
Barclays Global Investors

Introduction

This chapter is intended to be a primer for implementing U.S. equity index portfolios. Despite common assumptions about the ease of managing equity index portfolios, it does require an understanding of quantitative modeling techniques and trading. Managing a portfolio to minimize both tracking error and transaction costs is the key challenge of indexing.

Portfolio managers can establish an equity index portfolio by purchasing equities directly. Alternatively, a portfolio manager can secure exposure to a particular index using derivatives. Both methods are discussed in this chapter.

Purchasing Equities Directly

The most straightforward approach to managing an index portfolio is to purchase either a full set or representative sample of stocks in the benchmark index. This approach is generally most appropriate for long-term implementation of an index strategy, particularly when all the stocks in the index are liquid. Ultimately, the decision to choose an equity implementation over derivatives is driven by cost and risk. Purchasing equities directly typically involves greater up-front transaction costs, but fewer risks than most derivative-based strategies. Additionally, once the equity based portfolio is established, the portfolio manager will have to maintain it as the index changes over time.

Portfolio Management Approach

Index funds can be managed as either full replicated, sampled, or optimized portfolios. The approach depends on the liquidity of the constituents of the index, as well as the availability of historical data, and may also vary based on the objective of the portfolio.

Full replication is usually used when the stocks in the index are very liquid, as in establishing a fully replicating S&P 500 portfolio. When an index contains stocks that are less liquid, optimization may be used, but this method requires the existence of a risk or factor model, which in turn requires good historical data for the stocks in the index. A Russell 2000 index portfolio is a perfect candidate for optimization. Sampling is typically used when the stocks in the index are not liquid and historical data is insufficient to be able to properly develop a good factor model. Since many REITs have been issued in the last several years, and creating a factor model covering a full universe of REITs would not be possible, a REIT index portfolio might be built by sampling.

Full Replication Full replication, the most effective way to track an index closely, requires purchasing all stocks in an index in their exact or nearly exact index weights. In a full replication approach, the portfolio manager typically sets a tolerance or bias on the individual stocks in the portfolio. For example, a portfolio manager might choose to manage an S&P 500 portfolio in such a way that no individual stock's weight deviates from its weight in the index by more than X basis points, where X represents the bias. As contributions are made or dividends reinvested, the portfolio manager would seek to minimize the sum of squared biases, as that will generally produce the best tracking portfolio.

Sampling Sampling is one effective way to manage a portfolio when the liquidity of the stocks in an index precludes full replication. For example, in the case of the Wilshire 5000 index, it may be possible to purchase most if not all of the stocks in the index in their proper capitalization weights. However, it is inadvisable to do so because the transaction costs in such a trade will almost certainly guarantee underperformance versus the index.

Sampling provides a way to establish a portfolio position without actually owning all of the stocks in a given index. In fact, in the case of the Wilshire 5000, managing the portfolio so that the larger stocks are fully replicated and the smaller stocks are sampled will produce a lower tracking error than if all the stocks are purchased and maintained in perfect capitalization weights. Generally speaking, the greater the number of securities in the sampled portfolio, the lower the tracking error.

In the sampling approach, all stocks in the index are characterized according to a number of parameters (size, dividend yield, industry, etc.), and the portfolio manager divides the universe of securities into cells based on these parameters. For example, the universe may have a cell containing all technology stocks that have a market capitalization between $300 and $400 million that have yields less than 0.5%. Additional cells might contain financial and healthcare stocks in the same size and yield categories. The cell structure of the universe should be sufficiently fine to ensure that all stocks within the cell are reasonably good substitutes for each other. The portfolio manager assembles the portfolio by "sampling" stocks within each cell to create a portfolio that has fewer stocks than the entire universe, but with characteristics similar to the universe. The weight of each cell in the portfolio should be similar to the cell's weight in the index.

Optimization Optimization uses a more mathematical approach to achieve the same objective as sampling: to build a portfolio that has the same characteristics as the index within a given set of constraints. Optimization requires a risk or factor model describing all the stocks in the index specified along a number of dimensions (e.g., size, beta, yield, economic sector). This is similar to the sampling approach, but the risk model takes into account the covariance between the factors. Consequently, whereas sampling simply requires sufficient data to assign attributes to stocks, optimization requires a history of these attributes to establish the risk/return relationships between them.

Although optimization is a very useful portfolio management tool widely used by both index and quantitative managers, it is important to understand its principal limitation-optimized-portfolios are created based on the assumption that the risk model is a perfect representation of the real world. The risk model, however, is subject to a variety of imperfections. First, no matter how good the risk model is, it is not perfectly specified. That is, the risk model does not perfectly capture all of the risks associated with each stock in the model. Even if it did, risks in the real world are subject to change, and the model is based on historical data which may not accurately reflect the future. Finally, even if the model could accurately reflect changing risks in real time, the portfolio would have to be rebalanced continually to capture those changing risks. This is not intended as an indictment of optimization, but merely to caution that the expected tracking error of any portfolio evaluated against a risk model is likely to be biased low.

Additional Details

In the index world, every basis point counts. To properly track an index, the portfolio manager must pay a great detail of attention to detail.

Cash and Dividend Accruals Because the index contains no cash, all cash in the portfolio should be equitized with futures. Additionally, an often overlooked detail relates to dividend accruals. Most equity indexes assume that dividends are reinvested as soon as they are accrued (i.e., when a stock goes ex-dividend). Unfortunately, in the real world, one has to wait several weeks to several months until the cash is actually paid. Because the index assumes immediate reinvestment and the portfolio does not receive the cash until later, the portfolio will not properly track the index. In a rising market, the portfolio will suffer cash drag and lag the market. In a falling market, the reverse is true.

The portfolio manager needs to purchase futures with a notional value equivalent to the size of the dividend accrual to overcome this problem. Simply put, the portfolio manager should be long in the following number of contracts:

# of contracts = ($ amount to be equitized)/(level of the index * index multiplier)

The number of contracts specified by the above formula should be rounded to the nearest contract (or rounded down if the portfolio guidelines do not permit any leverage). Unfortunately, owing to the significant notional value of a typical stock index futures contract (e.g., the S&P 500 futures contract had a notional value of approximately $400,000 as of April 30, 1997), the resulting portfolio may be over/underequitized by several hundred thousand dollars. Also, the portfolio cash/accrual level must be checked daily, as this value will change when new stocks go ex-dividend and stocks which have gone ex-dividend in the past pay their dividends.

An illustration of the importance of equitizing dividend accruals occurred in 1995, when the S&P 500 was up 37.57%. An index portfolio that did not use futures to equitize dividend accruals would have underperformed the index by approximately 0.08% given that the portfolio might be sitting on an average of 0.20% in dividend accruals.

In cases in which no futures contract exists for the index being replicated, a close substitute should be used. For example, if the portfolio is indexed to the Russell 1000, an S&P 500 contract (or ideally a combination of S&P 500 and S&P Midcap 400 contracts) should be used. Even though these contracts may track different indexes, they will provide lower tracking error to the Russell 1000 than will the cash implied by the dividend accrual. As of this writing, a combination of S&P 500 and S&P Midcap 400 futures could provide tracking error as low as 0.48% against the Russell 1000. This compares to 0.95% for S&P 500 futures alone, or a rather significant 15.38% for unequitized cash. These expected tracking errors will vary a little as changes are made to the index constituents over time.

Corporate Actions/Index Changes Minor corporate actions often result in index changes. For example, a secondary offering of shares will generally have an effect on a stock's weight in an index. The timing of that weight change varies by index and is not necessarily contemporaneous with the actual issuance of shares. However, failing to properly account for an issuance of shares will lead to tracking error. For instance, in the case of a secondary offering, changes in shares outstanding of 5% or greater are accounted for in the S&P 500 on the date of the offering. In the Russell indexes, changes in shares outstanding are not accounted for until the beginning of the following month. If minimizing tracking error is very important, a manager of portfolios against both indexes might wish to trade each portfolio differently.

Index changes may also result from corporate mergers and spin-offs. In the case of a merger, two stocks within an index may become one. Hence, an index like the S&P 500 will add another stock to the index simply to maintain 500 stocks. A spin-off may result in the company being dropped from the index; different indexes have different policies.

Finally, index changes may occur simply because an index provider seeks to make a change. The S&P Index Policy Committee may wish to drop a stock from one of its indexes and replace it with a different one.

Index Reconstitution Some indexes, such as the Russell indexes or the S&P/BARRA Growth and Value indexes, are reconstituted from time to time. In the case of the Russell indexes, at the close of trading on June 30, all stocks no longer eligible for a particular Russell index are dropped, while newly eligible ones are added. This reconstitution may create a significant amount of turnover in the index. A portfolio manager must decide how to best rebalance the portfolio to minimize tracking error on a prospective basis given the changes to the index.

Trading

Trading is the key to effective implementation of an index portfolio. Since the index vendor has already constructed the index, stock selection is not an issue. Additionally, an index does not experience transaction costs, as does a real portfolio. Therefore, minimizing transactions costs is an important attribute of good index fund manager performance.

Transaction costs in the U.S. equity market vary significantly and are typically much less for large, liquid stocks than for small, illiquid ones. Figure 1 shows estimated costs for various segments of the U.S. equity market (the indexes are described in detail in the Appendix).

Figure 1 Estimated Transactions Costs

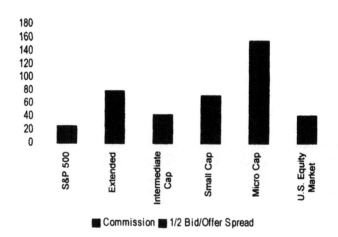

Commission ■ 1/2 Bid/Offer Spread

Trading costs are estimated by combining commissions with one half the bid/offer spread. As shown in Figure 1, commissions are only a small part of the cost. One half the bid/offer spread is used because the true price of a stock is the midpoint of the bid and the offer. To transact, the portfolio manager only pays to go down to the bid or up to the offer. Market impact costs are not shown because they vary greatly with the size of the trade and are difficult to measure. However, one can say that market impact costs will be proportional to the costs shown in the chart. That is, for constant dollar amounts, market impact costs will be greater for small stocks than for large stocks.

Transaction costs are a function of liquidity. Liquidity, in turn, is a function of demand to trade a particular stock or basket of stocks. If the volume in a particular stock is low, the broker/market maker must charge a premium to compensate himself for the risk of holding the stock until the other side of the trade can be found. This results in a wide bid/offer spread, making a stock more expensive to trade. Figure 1 illustrates the significant difference in cost to trade large stocks versus small or micro-capitalization stocks.

Trading Methods

Trading an index portfolio can be accomplished in a number of ways: internal crossing, external crossing, basket trade, basis trade, or some combination of these.

Crosses A securities cross trade is one in which securities are traded without a bid/offer spread and the trade is executed based on the price at a specific time. For example, if two portfolio managers decide in advance to trade 100 shares of IBM at today's market closing price, those shares are said to be crossed.

Internal Crosses Internal crossing is one of the best ways to minimize transaction costs in the implementation of an index fund portfolio. A cross is considered internal if it is a trade done between two clients of the same firm. An index fund manager who manages large portfolios for many clients has a significant advantage in being able to effect large purchases and sales of index portfolios very inexpensively. The likelihood that two or more clients might be trading in opposite directions on a given day is maximized when the index fund manager has a large number of clients. The probability that a client who wishes to cross a large portfolio will be successful is maximized when the index fund manager has significant assets under management.

Typically, an internal cross is done with no execution costs being charged against either the buying or selling accounts. The resulting transaction costs savings can outweigh investment management fees by a significant amount. For example, if the portfolio manager can cross a $50 million S&P 500 purchase against a $100 million S&P 500 sale, he saves the buyer 100% of the transaction cost (approximately $130,000 based on the transaction costs estimates illustrated above). The seller also saved $130,000, which represents half his transaction costs. The potential to internally cross large amounts of stocks is one of the most compelling reasons to place an indexed portfolio with a large investment manager rather than managing the portfolio in house.

External Crosses External crosses are typically executed through one of the third-party crossing networks such as Instinet or POSIT. The crossing network takes trade lists of stocks to be traded from portfolio managers and brokers. The stocks in all the lists are then matched, and resulting executions sent back to the portfolio managers. Instinet crosses occur after the market close, while POSIT crosses occur several times during the trading day. For a small commission, external crossing networks allow a portfolio manager to trade without market impact.

Basket Trade A basket trade is simply a trade in which a broker purchases or sells a basket of stocks rather than a single stock. An example of a simple basket trade would be a broker buying a slice of the S&P 500, with the intended execution occurring at the market open. Basket trades can be executed either on an agency or principal basis.

In an agency trade, the broker acts as an agent and charges a commission for the service without taking a principal position in the trade. In a principal trade, the broker is the counterparty to the trade and typically makes a guarantee with respect to the execution of the trade. The commission in a principal trade is usually higher than in an agency trade to compensate the broker for interposing himself as the counterparty to the trade. The higher commissions for a guaranteed principal trade may also include other costs that the portfolio manager would bear directly if the trade were done as an agency trade, including spread, market impact, and opportunity risk.

Basis Trading A basis trade is an effective way of purchasing or selling a large quantity of stock through the futures market. In a basis trade, the portfolio manager takes either long or short futures positions in a broker's account in the same direction as the intended trade of underlying securities. After the required number of futures contracts are traded, the equities are received from or delivered to the broker.

The mechanics of a basis trade are best described by an example. A portfolio manager needs to buy a $500 million S&P 500 basket under the following conditions:

S&P 500 cash level (previous close) = 820.00
S&P 500 futures fair value = 825.00
Therefore, S&P 500 fair basis = 825.00-820.00 = 5.00
Negotiated basis = 4.75

In this example, the portfolio manager negotiates a basis of 4.75 index points with the intended broker, who will deliver stock to the portfolio manager at a cash equivalent level of 4.75 index points less than the portfolio manager's average futures executions. If during the course of the day the portfolio manager enters into long S&P 500 positions at an average futures price of 827.50, then the broker will fill the order for stock at an S&P 500 cash level of 822.75 (827.50-4.75). At the end of the trade, the portfolio manager has $500 million worth of S&P 500 stock. The broker has a long futures position with a notional value of $500 million hedged with a short stock position of $500 million (see Figure 2).

Figure 2 Basis Trade: An Example

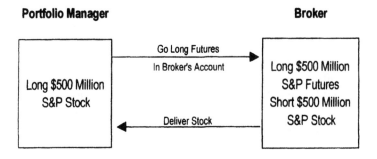

Exchange for Physicals (EFP) An EFP trade is a variant of the basis trade. In this transactioh, the portfolio manager already has futures he wishes to exchange for stock or vice versa. The portfolio manager negotiates a basis with the intended broker. Much as in the case of the basis trade, the negotiated basis will vary from broker to broker and will depend not only on the fair basis but also on the condition of a broker's balance sheet. For example, if the broker has engaged in index arbitrage (by going short futures and long stock), an EFP transaction as described above might allow him to effectively unwind the arbitrage and free up capital for another potentially profitable trade. In such a case, the broker's negotiated basis may be more favorable than fair basis, making the trade particularly favorable for both sides involved (see Figure 3).

Figure 3 An EFP Trade: An Example

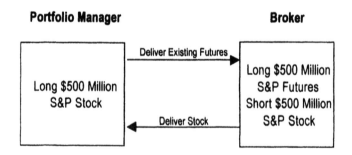

The value at which futures are exchanged for stock is the price of the futures contract at the time the deal is struck, less the negotiated basis. If the S&P 500 futures contract is trading at 827.00 at the time the deal is arranged and the negotiated basis is 4.75 points, then stock is purchased at an S&P 500 cash level of 822.25. In the reverse transaction, where stocks are exchanged for S&P 500 futures, the futures price is determined by adding the negotiated basis to the S&P 500 cash level.

Tracking Error versus Trading Cost

Trading cost should be weighed against tracking error by examining how much it will cost to transact in a particular security versus its contribution to tracking error. Clearly, if the cost of implementing a trade exceeds any improvement to tracking error, then it is pointless to execute the trade. Evaluating this tradeoff is especially important in sampled and optimized portfolios. The transaction costs incurred in reducing tracking error too much can be counterproductive and ensure negative tracking error in the portfolio. This is exactly what would happen if the portfolio manager tried to replicate an index containing illiquid stocks.

Derivative Strategies

The principal advantage of derivative-based strategies is their relative simplicity to implement. In addition, derivative-based strategies can be less expensive to implement than purchasing stocks. The examples below illustrate just a few of the ways derivatives may be used to implement equity index strategies.

Exact Substitution

The simplest way to establish a position in an index using derivatives is to take a long position in futures contracts in the index you wish to replicate. For example, to establish an S&P 500 index portfolio, a portfolio manager simply buys T-Bills and establishes a long position in S&P 500 contracts. As with cash equitization, the number of contracts the portfolio manager needs to go long is:

# of contracts = ($ amount to be invested)/(level of cash index * the contract multiplier)

For example, the S&P 500 index is 819.67, the S&P 500 future is 825.00, the futures multiplier is 500, and the portfolio manager needs to invest $500 million. The correct number of contracts to go long is 1,220:

1,220 = ($500 million)/(819.67 * 500)

Notice that the level of the futures contract is not relevant to determining the number of contracts required. The level of the futures contract relative to fair value, however, is critical in determining whether or not to choose a futures implementation or to simply purchase stocks outright. Generally speaking, a futures implementation would be more expensive than buying stocks if the futures contract was trading above fair value by more than the cost of buying stocks.

To return to the previous example, if the fair basis were 5.00, then the true cost of implementing (apart from any market impact) would be 0.33 index points, which is approximately 4 basis points. Compared to an estimated cost of 25 to 30 basis points for buying stocks in the market, the futures trade is inexpensive.

Tailing The discussion about determining the appropriate number of contracts to use when equitizing cash fails to take into account the daily marks that are paid or received on the futures held. If the portfolio manager is long S&P 500 futures on a day that the market rises, the portfolio will receive the point gain in the index multiplied by $500 multiplied by the number of contracts held. This cash is available for investment at the risk free rate until the futures position is closed out. In essence the portfolio is slightly leveraged. Conversely, if the market falls, the portfolio must pay marks according to the same formula and thus has less cash on which to earn interest. To adjust for this feature of futures contracts, the portfolio manager should "tail" the portfolio by adjusting for the time value of money. The number of contracts held should be adjusted by the formula:

Tailing Factor = $1/(1+r)$, where r equals the risk free rate until the futures position is closed

Consider again the example where 1,220 S&P 500 futures contracts were required for a $500 million portfolio. If the time until the futures are closed out (the next roll) is 90 days, and the risk free rate is 5%, then the tailing factor is 0.9877 ($1/(1+((90/360)*0.05))$). This means that in order to account for the time value of the marks, the correct number of contracts to hold is $1,220*0.9877$, or 1,205. As the futures contracts near expiration, the tailing factor will approach 1, and the correct number of contracts to hold in the portfolio will be 1,220.

Risks There are three important risks to consider when using futures to implement an equity index portfolio: counterparty risk, basis risk, and roll risk.

Counterparty Risk Counterparty risk occurs with respect to both the broker and the exchange clearing corporation. Simply put, the counterparty risk is that one or both of the counterparties will not be able to honor the terms of the futures contract. While such an occurrence might be very rare, its probability is nonetheless greater than zero.

Basis Risk Basis risk is the chance that a futures contract will trade away from its fair value. In fáct, futures contracts seldom trade exactly at fair value, but generally within a range close to fair value. That range is typically as wide as the transaction costs necessary to execute the arbitrage to bring the futures price back to fair value. How a futures contract is trading relative to its fair value is critical in minimizing the transaction costs inherent in establishing the equity index position. In fact, if a futures contract is trading cheap to fair value, the index strategy may actually be established with a negative transaction cost. Even if the portfolio manager ultimately wants an equity-based portfolio, buying futures contracts cheap to fair value and converting them to stock at futures expiration will almost certainly result in negative transaction costs.

Roll Risk Because futures contracts have a definite life, typically expiring on a quarterly cycle, a portfolio manager who wishes to maintain the futures portfolio after futures expiration needs to roll the contracts: essentially shorting the near contract and going long the far contract. These rolls typically take place approximately one to two weeks before futures expiration. The roll risk is simply the price risk inherent in doing these quarterly trades.

Inexact Substitution

The example above deals with a simple situation when there is a futures contract for the index to be tracked. However, in some cases, the portfolio manager may wish to track an index for which there is no futures contract, or the futures contract is so thinly traded as to make it unfeasible to establish a significant portfolio. In such cases, the portfolio manager may simply choose to use a liquid futures contract and tolerate the resulting tracking error. Alternatively, the portfolio manager may use a combination of futures contracts in long only or long/short strategies to minimize tracking error versus the desired index. For example, a portfolio manager wishing to establish a Russell 1000 position using futures could do so by buying a combination of S&P 500 and S&P Midcap 400 contracts. For every $100 of Russell 1000 exposure desired, the portfolio manager could go long $87.10 of S&P 500 futures and $13.80 of S&P Midcap 400 futures (this hedge ratio is subject to slight modification over time as the constituents of the indexes and the risk/return relationships between the indexes change). The resulting portfolio (which is slightly leveraged) would have an expected tracking error of 0.48%.

Swaps

It is also possible to implement an index portfolio using swaps. In a swap, the portfolio manager swaps the return on one index for the return on another index. For example, a portfolio manager may wish to receive the return of the Russell 1000 index. The counterparty to the swap might wish to receive the return on LIBOR plus X basis points on the notional value of the swap. The portfolio manager's cost to implement the strategy is therefore based on his ability to deliver a fixed income return relative to LIBOR plus X basis point benchmark (see Figure 4).

Figure 4 A Swap: An Example

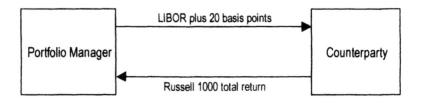

The advantages of a swap are that it can be tailored to the exact needs of the portfolio manager, and the return will exactly match that of the index with no tracking error—thereby eliminating basis risk associated with futures-based strategies. Swaps can also be negotiated to last many years, eliminating/postponing the roll risk inherent in futures strategies. To the extent that the life of the swap is equal to the intended life of the index portfolio, the swap eliminates roll risk for the portfolio manager. If the life of the swap is extended beyond its original term, the "roll risk" is simply that the terms of the swap under the extension are different from the original terms. This is not to say that basis risk and roll risk have vanished entirely: They have simply been shifted to the counterparty. In exchange for bearing these risks, the counterparty will require a higher return to enter into the swap than it would if it did not have to bear these risks. Finally, whereas futures contracts are marked to market daily, the timing of cash flows in a swap agreement is negotiated in advance by the portfolio manager and the counterparty.

The disadvantages of a swap are cost and flexibility. To neutralize its risk, the counterparty to the swap must find another customer to take the other side of the trade. In the event that it cannot do so, the counterparty must manage the risk, which is costly. Additionally, while the swap can be tailored to meet the portfolio manager's exact specifications, its terms cannot be altered easily or without cost.

Summary

The equity index portfolio manager can choose from many portfolio construction alternatives to achieve the desired index return. While a traditional active manager spends the majority of his time deciding which stocks to buy and which stocks to sell, the equity index portfolio manager spends most of his time determining the best method to trade stocks and baskets of stocks. Trading stocks in a cost-effective manner is the key to successful index fund management.

Appendix*

U.S. Equity Market Index—Includes all the stocks in the S&P 500 as well as all other U.S. exchange—traded and OTC common stocks. The index does not include ADRs, closed end mutual funds, stocks priced less than $1, limited partnerships, or pink sheet traded securities. Contains over 6,000 stocks with a market capitalization of $7.9 trillion.

S&P 500 Index—Includes stocks of 500 predominantly large corporations. Represents 71.7% of the U.S. Equity Market Index.

Extended Market Index—Includes all stocks in the U.S. Equity Market Index that are not part of the S&P 500. Contains over 5,500 stocks with a market capitalization of $2.2 trillion. Represents 28.3% of the U.S. Equity Market Index.

Intermediate Cap Index—Includes the largest 1,000 U.S. common stocks in the U.S. Equity Market Index except for those in the S&P 500 Index. Contains 526 stocks with a market capitalization of $1.2 trillion. Represents 14.8% of the U.S. Equity Market Index.

Small Cap Index—Includes stocks that have a market capitalization lower than those in the Intermediate Cap Index, but larger than the smallest 15% of the

---

*All data as of December 31, 1996.

Extended Market Index. Contains over 1,300 stocks with a market capitalization of $723 billion. Represents 9.2% of the U.S. Equity Market Index.
Micro Cap Index—Includes stocks that make up the bottom 15% of the market capitalization of the Extended Market Index. Contains over 3,700 stocks with a market capitalization of $347 billion. Represents 4.4% of the U.S. Equity Market Index.

References

Seigel, Daniel R., and Seigel, Diane F., *Futures Markets*. The Dryden Press, Orlando, FL, 1990.

Tiemann, Jonathan, "Theory of Indexation: Replication or Optimization," *BZW Barclays Global Investors Index Quarterly Currents*, April 1996.

Zurack, Mark, "Applications of OTC Options and Other Structured Products." In *The Handbook of Equity Derivatives*, ed. J.C. Francis, W.W. Toy, and J.G. Whittaker. Irwin, Chicago, 1995.

CHAPTER 12

Adding Value Through Equity Style Management

Bruce D. Westervelt, CFA
Executive Director, Chief Financial Investment
Officer and Director of Research
First Madison Advisors

Why Equity Style Matters

Ninety-seven percent of a portfolio's return is a controlled by style expo-sure. This notion, developed by Nobel Laureate William F. Sharpe, is causing a complete review and rethinking of how portfolios are managed. Since asset allocation is widely accepted as the key determinant of per-formance for an entire fund, the fact that equity style allocation is the key driver of the equity component is not surprising. Naturally, market seg-ments (large, small, growth, and value) have different exposures to "eco-nomic factors," and changes in the economic environment result in dif-ferences in each segment's relative returns. Additionally, distinct differ-ences exist in the fundamentals of these segments, creating differences in relative returns. Exploitation of these differentials is the basis for adding value through equity style management. After a great deal of examination of active management, the empirical data suggest that equity style man-agement offers the largest opportunity to add excess return versus a broad equity benchmark.

Equity Style Allocation Matches Asset Class Allocation in Importance

In a recent First Madison research piece entitled "The Importance of Equity Style Allocation" (January 1997),[1] the opportunity to add value

---

[1] First Madison Advisors. "The Importance of Style Allocation," January 1997.
Additional equity style management data is available from the firm on request:
P. O. Box 1498 Madison. WI 53701.

through allocation was examined. This two-part study analyzed possible returns from asset class allocation and equity style allocation over the 17-year period 1980 through 1996. The opportunity to add value through allocation was assessed by examining the returns generated from allocating assets between four asset classes (long bond, intermediate bond, S&P 500, and cash) as well as the returns generated from allocating assets between four equity styles (large-cap value, large-cap growth, small-cap value, and small-cap growth.

The study found that over the 17-year period, the return of a normal 60% stocks, 35% bonds, and 5% cash portfolio was 14.13%. However, if one could perfectly shift to the best asset class each quarter, the annualized rate of return exploded to 31.99%. The opportunity to add value through asset class allocation was, therefore, the difference of 17.86% (Exhibit 1). Obviously, not all of these returns can be achieved through asset class allocation, but one can see that asset class allocation is important.

Exhibit 1 The Importance of Equity Style Allocation
for the 17 Years 12/31/79 thru 12/31/96

*By taking only the BEST QUARTER for one of the asset classes
each quarter in ASSET ALLOCATION and EQUITY STYLE ALLOCATION
respectively and linking them together, the "potential"
to add extra return through shifting is revealed.*

Asset Allocation:		Equity Style Allocation:	
Long Bond	Intermediate Bond	Large Value	Large Growth
Cash	S&P - 500	Small Value	Small Growth
		* NOTE - Small includes Mid Cap & Small Cap	
Best of Asset Allocation	*31.99%*	*Best of STYLE Allocation*	*30.70%*
VS Traditional 60/35/5 Mix	*14.13%*	*VS Wilshire 5000*	*15.61%*
Maximum Potential From Shifts	*17.86%*	*Maximum Potential From Shifts*	*15.09%*

Conclusion: Style Allocation Rivals Asset Allocation in Potential
Source: First Madison Advisors

The study went on to consider that unless a large difference existed between the returns of various equity styles, no attempt should be made to shift between them. The annualized return of the Wilshire 5000, a broad market proxy, was 15.61% over the 17-year time frame. Perfectly timed shifting among the four equity styles caused annual returns to mushroom to 30.70%. The difference, 15.09%, represented the opportunity to add value through equity style allocation within an equity portfolio. Note, the returns from either ideal asset class allocation or ideal equity style allocation presented above are unreachable optimal scenarios. However, one can see that the magnitude of increased returns from equity style allocation is roughly the same as that of asset class allocation in relative importance and opportunity.

What Consultants Have Known For a Long Time

Historically, when faced with the task of determining if an equity manager was adding value, a consultant had the option of using a broad benchmark such as Standard and Poor's 500 index. However, two or more market cycles (economic cycles) were required to determine if value was being added. This was because the "style" of the manager caused a difference in returns not related to individual security selection (Exhibit 2).

Exhibit 2 Equity Styles Generate Very Different Returns

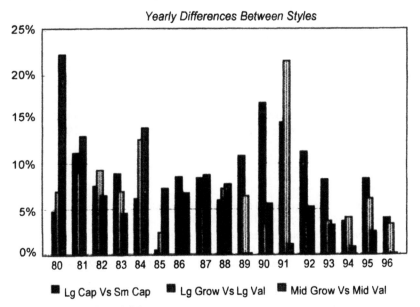

Source: First Madison Advisors

Matching the appropriate segment of the market to the "style" of the manager made the task much easier. The statistical noise of a benchmark not highly correlated to the manager was eliminated, and the number of years required to evaluate the manager was significantly reduced. This recognition of the commonality of returns for the market segments foreshadowed Bill Sharpe's work.

The Academic Way of Thinking

The benchmarking process has not addressed style management other than to indirectly recognize that common factors exist which drive the styles. Style management is very much in line with the theory and empirical evidence that the academic community has uncovered. Robert C. Merton's (1973) Intertemporal CAPM,[2] Stephen A. Ross's (1976) APT,[3] William F. Sharpe's (1992) *Asset Allocation: Management Style and Performance Measurement,*[4] and French and Fama's (1996) "Multifactor Explanations of Asset Pricing Anomalies,"[5] all support the style management process. In a market with new data constantly being assimilated without homogeneous expectations, the persistence (serial correlation) of returns within styles is consistent with a rational market hypothesis.

Recently, Burton G. Malkiel (author of the popular book, *A Random Walk Down Wall Street*), has stated in his research that "there appeared to be a considerable degree of predictability of stock returns on the basis of certain fundamental ratios and variables. Stock returns appeared to be predictable on the basis of such variables as initial dividend yields, market capitalization (size), price-earnings ratios, and price-to-book-value ratios. Of course, return predictability need not imply inefficiency of equity markets. Time series tests of return predictability may reflect rational variation through time in expected returns . . . The apparent robustness of certain predictable patterns has led to a view that our 1970's belief

[2] Merton, Robert C., "An Intertemporal Capital Asset Pricing Model," *Econometrica,* vol. 4, no.5, September 1973, pp. 867-887.

[3] Ross, Stephen A., "The Arbitrage Theory of Capital Asset Pricing," *Journal of Economic Theory,* 13, 1976, pp. 341-360.

[4] Sharpe, William F., "Asset Allocation: Management Style and Performance Measurement," *Journal of Portfolio Management,* Winter 1992, pp. 7-19.

[5] Fama, Eugene F., and French, Kenneth R., "Multifactor Explanations of Asset Pricing Anomalies," *Journal of Finance,* March 1996, pp. 55-84.

in the simplistic efficient-markets constant-returns model was unwarranted."[6] This predictability of returns indicates that trends (serial correlation) in the returns for segments of the market exist.

Capturing Excess Return: Current Fund Composition

Critical to executing an equity style management process is capturing the returns of the intended equity style exposures. Given that equity style exposures generally control the realized returns of equity portfolios, and that the returns for these market segments tend to have persistence in relative performance, favoring (overweighting) market segments can add value. Creating a style-neutral portfolio and ensuring marketlike returns (Exhibit 3) argues toward simply indexing the entire portfolio using a broad market proxy (i.e., the S&P 500 or Wilshire 5000). Actively managing the style exposures of the portfolio is the most logical way to add value as an active process.

Exhibit 3 A Style Neutral Equity Allocation

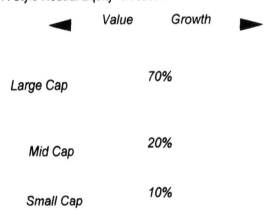

◄   *Value*   *Growth*   ►

Large Cap   *70%*

Mid Cap   *20%*

Small Cap   *10%*

Conclusion: There is a tendency towards average market performance when the equity class is style neutral.
Source: First Madison Advisors

---

[6] Malkiel, Burton G., "Returns From Investing in Equity Mutual Funds 1971-1991," Princeton University, Center for Economic Policy Studies, working paper no. 15, December 1993. pp. 1-2.

Passive management believers maintain that the only way to proceed is with passive portfolios, which have the advantages of low cost and clear definition. Active management believers criticize the use of passive management by pointing out that the opportunity to gain significant extra return from the stock selection is not considered. Whichever position one supports, the question is how to ensure that active style tilts will capture the returns from their respective segments. Naturally, it depends on the nature of the portfolio to which it is applied. The current structure of the aggregate portfolio, and how much this structure will be allowed to change as a practical matter, are important factors.

The three most common structures for funds are a fund composed of multiple active managers; a fund with a core index surrounded by active and/or passive managers; and a single-manager fund with active or passive management. For each of these cases, the introduction of style management will be different; however, the goal—to achieve the gains from style management while minimizing the disruption to the current fund structure—will always be the same.

The Ramifications of Shifting Funds Between Individual Managers

Actively shifting funds between traditional managers is the least efficient way to implement a style-shifting process. When the manager whose allocation is being reduced begins to sell, market impact is incurred while creating a cash build-up at the same time. Conversely, the manager who is receiving the increased allocation is forced to act quickly to be back in the market. Once again, market impact and trading costs are incurred. As funds are shifted between active managers forced to bear interruptions in their investment processes, the validity of the managers' performance assessment comes into question. In addition, removing funds as a reward for good performance (largely a function of equity style) may not be received warmly. Finally, due to their active processes, these managers may not achieve the returns of their assigned market segment. When this occurs, a correct style bet may be completely negated by the failure of the manager to capture his or her respective style.

The Core Index With Multiple Managers

The fund with a core index encompassed by active and/or passive managers is the easiest for introducing equity style management. With a core index configuration, an individual equity style manager can be installed by reallocating a percentage of the index to the manager. The combination of managers is unaffected, and since most equity style managers use passive portfolios to accomplish their equity style tilt, the same efficiency and diversification associated with indexing remains. Conceptually, an investment committee would not be required to change their rational about this portion of the fund. However, at a deeper level, some rather intriguing things happen to the characteristics of the fund.

Often, this type of fund has an overall equity style bias. This affinity for a particular equity style is not likely to change and will turn into quite a bout with the investment committee if attempts are made to do so. The benefit of having a core equity style manager is that the bias remains undisturbed but is modified through time in a favorable way. If, for example, the fund's bias is toward large-cap value, and the equity style allocator is tilted in the same way, the alpha (extra return) is amplified by this larger-than-average weighting to that equity style. Conversely, when the equity style allocator is in a small-cap growth mode, the potential negative impact of the static large-cap value bias is offset. This, of course, would help avoid periods of underperformance for the overall portfolio which would inevitably occur if the shift had not been implemented. The static bias of the fund over time would still have an impact regardless of equity style allocation, but in the short run the fund would tend to generate smoother performance. Moreover, the largest opportunity to add excess return to the aggregate equity portfolio is through shifting equity style exposures over time. At the macro level, the fund will experience subtle benefits from equity style management that go beyond extra return.

The Single Manager Fund

The single-manager equity fund is the most challenging situation. Single-manager funds are generally of smaller size and have biases that are entrenched. Attempting to change the bias or trying to persuade a committee that may not be highly sophisticated of the importance of equity style allocation can be difficult. If the lone manager is questioned as to whether equity style consideration plays an important role in the investment process, the answer uniformly is yes. One should consider that, if this is true, has the manager ever brought this to the board's attention before? In any case, is equity style the true driver of the manager's process? Usually, the only hope of introducing equity style management in a single-manager fund is to wait for underperformance by the manager. Ironically, when poor results occur, the manager is likely to explain the underperformance by saying that the fund's equity style was out of favor at the time. This would be the ideal opportunity to request further clarification of the manager's equity style and how that style led to underperformance. '

On first review, one might be inclined to use the style indexes that are available through various institutions and consultants to implement the strategy. However, when answering the question of how to capture the excess return, the selection of capitalization-weighted style indexes may not be the optimal solution. Assume that AAA Consultant's indexes are known for high turnover and actively managed industry concentrations, while ZZZ Consultant's indexes use only price-to-book for their interpretation of growth versus value. Should one care if custom portfolios are used? If an equity style manager has to deal with arbitrary changes in industry composition over time, the investment model will not be accurate. If an index has high turnover, it will be expensive and can miss the returns of the sector it is designed to replicate (Exhibit 4). If price-to-book, a lagged accounting artifact, is the only criteria for value, the correlation between the value segment and a broad index may be as high as 98%, thereby seriously dampening the equity style shift effort. Many funds would be willing to use futures to accomplish these shifts; however, a quick check on the liquidity of the few index futures that are suitable for style allocation may end that line of thought. Custom indexes that consistently and efficiently replicate style segments can play an important role for effective implementation of an equity style management process.

Exhibit 4 Critical Differences in Equity Style Portfolios

1) If the Turnover Rate of Stocks in the Portfolio is High

   May miss the returns for the market segment.

   Expensive (transaction costs and market impact).

2) Overly Simplistic Value Definition

   Example: Price to Book, often used to separate Growth

   and Value, is a lagged indicator: an "accounting artifact".

3) Industry Concentrations

   Indexes that single out industries as value ignore the

   value stocks of other industries, introducing bias into

   the portfolio.

Source: First Madison Advisors

What Are the Advantages of Custom Portfolios?

Surprisingly, implementation of a style process with straight index portfolios is not the most effective or least expensive way to capture style returns. This seemingly flies in the face of all logic, but after some further exploration becomes readily apparent. As earlier noted, the currently popular methods of style index construction and rebalancing have some significant drawbacks. Number one on the list is turnover. For example, according to BARRA's Performance Analysis software (PAN), on a stand-alone basis the average annual turnover for the past 10 years ended December 1996 for the S&P500/BARRA Growth and Value style indexes was 23% (Exhibit 5). When compared to the PAN calculation for the S&P 500 of 4.4% on a stand-alone basis, one can see that a substantial, incremental increase in turnover of 18.6% exists. Holding both the Growth and Value Indexes is equivalent to holding the S&P 500.

Exhibit 5 Turnover in the S&P-500, S&P-500/BARRA Growth, and S&P-500/BARRA Value Indexes

Turnover was calculated using BARRA's Performance Analysis Software (PAN) and is the summation of the monthly turnover for each year respectively.

	S&P-500 INDEX	S&P-500/BARRA GROWTH	S&P-500/BARRA VALUE
1987	4.14 %	25.51 %	26.87 %
1988	4.81	22.12	24.61
1989	5.22	31.66	31.43
1990	2.78	24.61	27.01
1991	3.72	14.74	14.99
1992	2.43	14.84	16.05
1993	3.93	22.43	21.50
1994	5.47	26.09	21.60
1995	5.84	18.98	22.36
1996	5.97	26.69	26.89
AVG. ANNUAL TURN	4.43	22.77	23.33

Source: First Madison Advisors

The turnover of these indexes, which are rebalanced every six months, is on the lower end of the 'range for the popular style indexes. The problem here is that a large percentage of the stocks held in the indexes reside near the dividing line between growth and value. Consequently, they bounce back and forth between the growth and value indexes. Additionally, when a style shift is implemented by a style allocator (i.e., growth into value), growth stocks are sold that are barely on the growth side, and value stocks are purchased that are barely on the value side. The amount of "bang for the buck" of traded securities is not particularly large for a significant percentage of the portfolio.

Rather than overlay an active process on top of high turnover indexes, a more practical solution is to use a custom portfolio to execute the strategy. To implement the same growth to value shift, the portfolio manager simply focuses on selling the more extreme growth stocks and purchasing the more extreme value stocks. The net result is the achievement of the same level of exposure shift, while generating only about half the turnover. The bulk of the stocks in the "middle" are left untouched. Through this technique, First Madison's four-year, live experience with its Style Allocation product has generated turnover of only 22% annually, while actively shifting styles and adding significant excess return.

Another benefit of the custom portfolio is that it generally reduces risk versus its capitalization-weighted counterparts. Capitalization-weighted indexes are not mean-variance efficient. The relative weighting for each stock in the index is a function of the current price times shares outstanding. Larger capitalization stocks have larger relative weight in the index. This does not consider the way the individual securities interact with one another. When a custom portfolio is not constrained by this weighting scheme, an optimizer is used to create the least variance for the portfolio. By optimizing the relative weighting of each stock, a portfolio may be created that generates the return of the intended style exposure(s) with the least possible variance risk.

Tactical Versus Dynamic Equity Style Allocation

A tactical process does not effectively deal with extreme conditions the way a dynamic process can. This, of course, is when large quantities of excess returns can be captured. By increasing exposure prematurely to an underperforming equity style, the portfolio will have meaningfully reduced opportunity to generate excess return. Tactical equity style allocation requires estimates of economic events and premiums for the market and its segments. Alternatively, dynamic equity style allocation requires only the relative probability of a conditional state being present. Analysts and economists who are in the profession of generating estimates often poke fun at themselves by using the humorous phrase, "Predict, and predict often." Because the interrelationships between economic variables are not stationary, analysts need to update their forecasts constantly. This volume of change in estimates leads to implementation error, resulting in poor performance. A dynamic process that allows the current trends of the market to play a role in the process is less susceptible to estimation errors. An equity style allocation process using custom portfolios and dynamic allocation creates the optimal strategy for capturing excess returns from style.

Conclusion

Equity style allocation is the controlling factor in realized returns for an equity portfolio. Advancement in the process of assessing managers versus their style indexes and peers has enhanced understanding of the key factors that influence performance. However, recognizing equity style management as a source of excess return (arguably, the most significant source) is vital to those who attempt to outperform the market. By combining the driver of active returns (style) with the risk control and cost effectiveness of passive investing, equity style management is destined to become the primary focus for generating excess return in the equity asset class.

Using Style Analysis to Build Completeness Funds

Steve Hardy
President
Zephyr Associates, Inc.

A completeness fund is one of those simple ideas that seem to get complicated very quickly. Here is the simple part: As a plan sponsor, you choose a broad market index, such as the S&P 500 or Russell 3000, as the benchmark for the domestic equity component of your total plan. You then select a number of equity managers with specific styles who also have specific style benchmarks. When you aggregate all of the managers' benchmarks, they may not add up to your broad market benchmark. You therefore have a hole that represents a "style bet." A completeness fund, which is usually a passive portfolio, is constructed to offset that style bet and get the style of your total equity fund as close as possible to the style of your market benchmark. Now your total fund should track the broad market benchmark very closely, and, as long as the individual managers in the aggregate beat their respective benchmarks, your fund will beat the market.

It has never made sense to me to hire active managers and also have a market index fund (typically an S&P 500 fund). Why buy an off-the-shelf index fund when you can customize a passive portfolio to complement your array of active managers? If you have a small-cap growth bias in your total fund, why not give your "index fund" a large-cap value bias? Make the passive portion of your portfolio do more work than just track an index. Such a customized index fund is a completeness fund.

A true completeness fund (what we sometimes call a custom core portfolio) should be long the style, sectors, or stocks that are under-represented in the managers' aggregate style benchmark. It should also be short the style, sectors, or stocks that are over-represented.

The idea of a completeness fund is not to bet against the active managers, but rather to include areas of the market that the active managers overlook because of their particular styles. The best analogy is to consider a plan sponsor's broad market benchmark as a large lake. Each manager has a favorite fishing hole—the managers' universe or benchmark. Even with many fisherman (managers), there will be large areas of the lake (market) that will not be fished. There may be other areas that are overfished by multiple managers. A completion fund builds a portfolio that is long the overlooked (underfished) areas and short the overlapped (overfished) areas.

Now the complicated part. The conventional way to build a completeness fund is stock by stock. First you construct customized, security-based benchmarks for each of your equity managers. This in itself may take from six months to a year, cost as much as $5,000 to $15,000 for each manager benchmark, and cost the same amount annually to maintain. You would aggregate all the managers' benchmarks and then compare the stocks in the aggregate and their weights to the stocks and weights in the market benchmark. The stocks that are not represented, or are underweighted, are added to the completeness fund, whereas the stocks that are over-represented are sold short. You can shorten this process by using a multifactor model and an optimizer, but even then you may end up with a portfolio with hundreds of stocks, a lot of turnover, and all the commensurate costs. Few plan sponsors can get the authorization to do short sales, and most of the few completion funds that exist today still have a significant tracking error or misfit risk that can't be eliminated because they have no way to eliminate the overlap.[1]

A much simpler way to build completeness funds uses style analysis. Style analysis was developed by Bill Sharpe in 1988.[2] Using only historical returns for indexes and managers, a quadratic optimization program finds the optimum combination of style indexes to track (provide the highest correlation to) a manager or group of managers. As a simple example, we take the following domestic equity managers with the

---

[1] For a more comprehensive and technical explanation of the securities-based completeness fund. see "Defining and Using Dynamic Completeness Funds to Enhance Total Fund Efficiency." David Tierney and Kenneth Winston, *Financial Analysts Journal* (July - August 1990).

[2] See "Determining a Fund's Effective Asset Mix," William F. Sharpe, *Investment Management Review* (November/December 1988) pp. 59-69.

following percentages (as they relate to the total domestic-equity portfolio):

Twentieth Century Mid-Cap Growth 15%
Pilgrim Baxter Small-Cap Growth 10%
Provident Investment Counsel Growth Fund 35%
Wellington Value/Yield 40%

With the above managers, we build a composite and construct a return series to use for our style analysis. We also use the four Russell style indexes. Exhibit 1 shows the optimum percentage of the Russell style indexes needed to give us the highest tracking to this composite. This combination of the Russell style indexes becomes the managers' aggregate benchmark. That composite of style indexes would give us a 96.3% R2 to our fund.

Exhibit 2 shows a style map of that fund. Value to growth is plotted on the horizontal axis, and size is plotted on the vertical axis. Value is on the left, and growth is on the right; large-cap on the top and small-cap on the bottom. The four Russell style indexes (large value, large growth, small value, small growth) are represented by the squares at the four corners. The triangular star represents our fund's style. This fund has a large bias towards small growth when compared to the market (Russell 3000), displayed by the cross.

If we are unwilling to change any of the managers or their respective weights, then we must build a portfolio or completeness fund that will get our current fund's style as close to the market style as possible. The difference in style between our fund, or the managers' aggregate benchmark, and the market benchmark can be seen in Exhibit 3. Here again, it is easy to see how "growthy" our fund is. A completeness fund will offset much of this bias. How much depends partially on how much money we can use to build a completeness fund (i.e., our budget).

Exhibit 4 demonstrates that if our budget for the completeness fund is 20% (of the total fund), then our completeness fund will have to be 100% invested in large value. That will move us from the triangular star to the sun star. Although the correlation of our fund to the market has improved from 87.7% to 93.7%, we still have a significant tracking error and a long way to go.

Exhibit 1 Custom Core Analysis: Asset Allocation Analysis

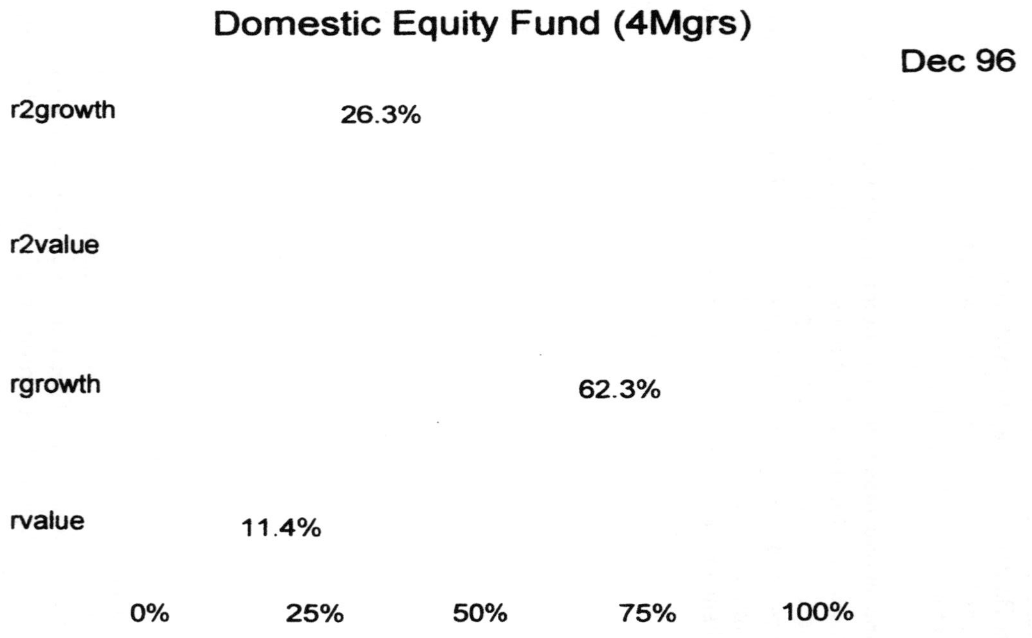

Domestic Equity Fund (4Mgrs)

Dec 96

r2growth   26.3%

r2value

rgrowth   62.3%

rvalue   11.4%

0%   25%   50%   75%   100%

Source: Zephyr Style Advisor: Zephyr Associates, Inc.

Exhibit 2 Custom Core Analysis: Manager Style

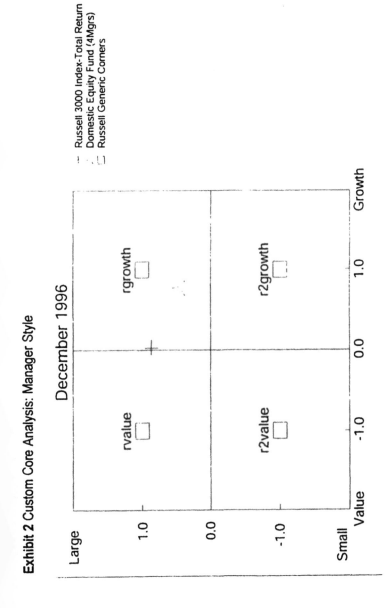

December 1996

Russell 3000 Index-Total Return
Domestic Equity Fund (4Mgrs)
Russell Generic Corners

Source: Zephyr Style Advisor: Zephyr Associates, Inc.

Exhibit 3 Custom Core Analysis: Asset Allocation Analysis

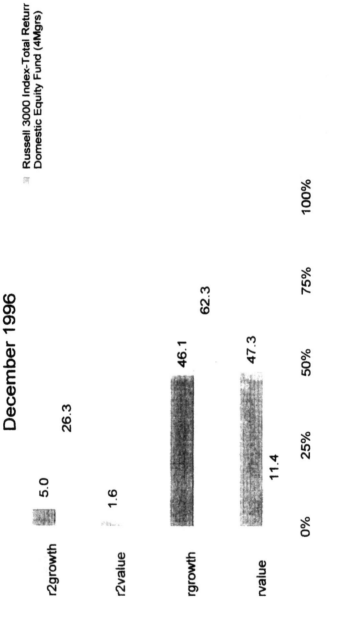

December 1996

Russell 3000 Index-Total Return
Domestic Equity Fund (4Mgrs)

Source: Zephyr Style Advisor: Zephyr Associates, Inc.

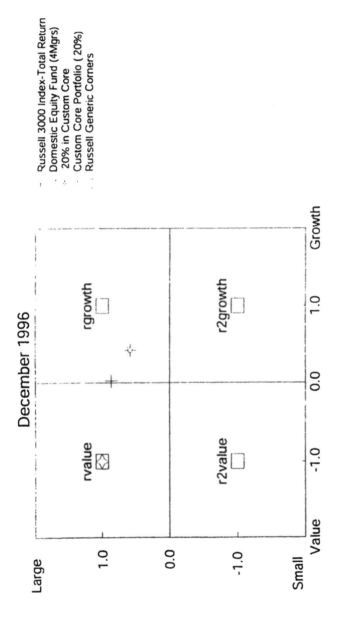

Exhibit 4 Custom Core Analysis: Manager Style

December 1996

Russell 3000 Index-Total Return
Domestic Equity Fund (4Mgrs)
  20% in Custom Core
Custom Core Portfolio (20%)
Russell Generic Corners

Source: Zephyr Style Advisor: Zephyr Associates, Inc.

Earlier, we mentioned that a true completeness fund must short that part of the market that is overexposed in the managers' benchmarks. If we allow the optimizer to go short, we get something that looks like Exhibit 5. With the ability to not only short the style indexes but use the proceeds from the short sell to lever up on the styles we need (in this case large value), we can move our fund up to the market benchmark. Exhibit 6 shows how this was achieved. We shorted small growth and invested the proceeds in large value. Our new fund, which includes the completeness fund, is represented by the third bar in each section. Notice how closely they match the Russell 3000 (cross bar).

Completeness Funds Are Dynamic

Managers' benchmarks change over time because of their changes in style. The aggregate fund's benchmark changes because of the changing weights of the managers. The good-performing managers become a larger portion of the total versus the poor-performing managers, unless the managers are rebalanced often (in the four-manager fund that we created, we assumed an annual rebalancing to the original weights). Another good argument for a completeness fund is that it is a way to rebalance money among your managers without having to actually reshuffle money among them.

Exhibit 7 shows the same example, but in this case it is assumed that every quarter the completeness fund is being dynamically managed. The triangular stars show the drift of the fund if nothing is done. The stars (upper left) show the long/short completeness fund, and the sun stars show the quarterly style points of the fund after the addition of the completeness fund. To see the benefit of the completeness fund, you only have to compare the triangular stars to the suns tars. Notice how the new fund stays consistently close to the Russell 3000.

How practical is building such a completeness fund? I have purposely used an extreme example of a fund with a very large growth bias. If such a fund actually existed, the sponsor or consultant would most likely change the asset allocation among managers, or hire some new managers, in order to get the fund much closer to the market benchmark before even considering a completeness fund. The completeness fund would then require much less money and have much less turnover.

Exhibit 5 Custom Core Analysis: Manager Style

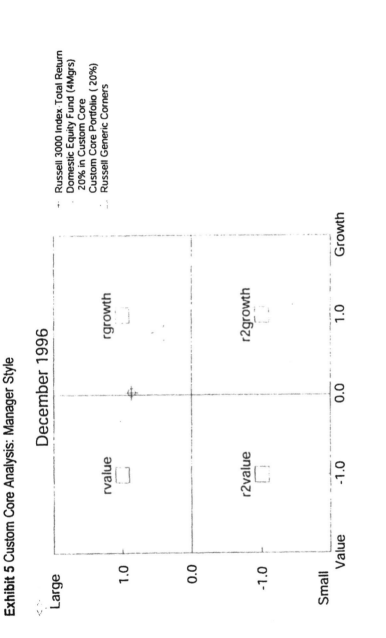

December 1996

+ : Russell 3000 Index: Total Return
    Domestic Equity Fund (4Mgrs)
    20% in Custom Core
    Custom Core Portfolio (20%)
· : Russell Generic Corners

Source: Zephyr Style Advisor: Zephyr Associates, Inc.

Exhibit 6 Custom Core Analysis: Custom Core Asset Analysis

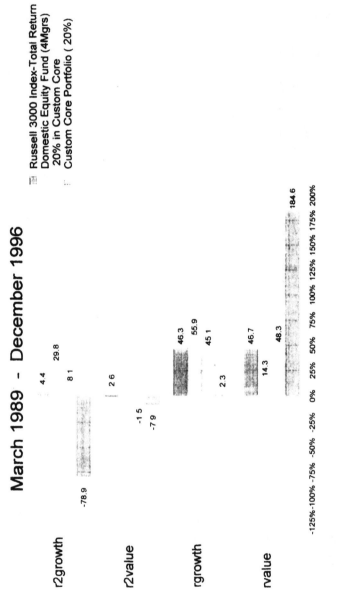

March 1989 – December 1996

Russell 3000 Index-Total Return
Domestic Equity Fund (4Mgrs)
20% in Custom Core
Custom Core Portfolio (20%)

Source: Zephyr Style Advisor: Zephyr Associates, Inc.

Exhibit 7 Custom Core Analysis: Manager Style

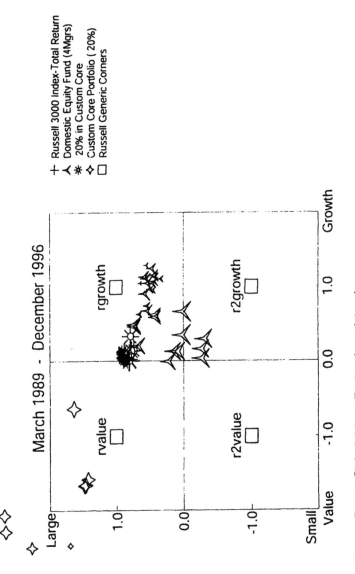

Source: Zephyr Style Advisor: Zephyr Associates, Inc.

I mentioned earlier that the securities-based completeness fund was cumbersome to build because it involved so many different securities. Here you can buy style index funds from a number of managers. You can also buy and sell short large-value and large-growth style index futures. Small-value and small-growth index futures should be available in the relatively near future. The liquidity of these futures as of the end of 1996 is still fairly poor, but would improve dramatically if plan sponsors began to use such indexes as we have suggested.

I believe that it is only a matter of time before this simple but very effective implementation of completeness funds will become popular with large, tax-exempt fund sponsors. It should replace the off-the-shelf index fund and become the passive component of the sponsor's equity fund.

CHAPTER 14

Index Shares

Gary L. Gastineau
Senior Vice President, New Products Development
American Stock Exchange

Clifford J. Weber
Vice President, New Products Development
American Stock Exchange

On January 29, 1993 the American Stock Exchange (AMEX) began trading what has become one of the most successful new financial products in years, Standard & Poor's Depositary Receipts® or SPDRs®, pronounced "spiders", a revolutionary index fund product based on the S&P 500®. In the four plus years since, the SPDR Trust has grown to over $4 billion in assets, and on a typical day approximately 2 million shares worth over $180 million are traded on the Exchange. During 1996, SPDRs were the second most actively traded equity security on the AMEX. The tremendous success of SPDRs has led to the development and listing of a number of similar products. In May, 1995, AMEX began trading MidCap SPDRs™ on the S&P MidCap 400 Index™. Today, the MidCap SPDRs Trust has more than $500 million in assets and was ranked in the top 10 percent of the most actively traded securities on the AMEX in 1996.

In March, 1996, seventeen WEBS℠ (World Equity Benchmark Shares℠) funds, each based on a different single country index of the Morgan Stanley Capital International family of indices, began trading on the AMEX. Shortly thereafter, nine CountryBaskets began trading on the New York Stock Exchange, each based on a different FT-S&P Country Index. Although the CountryBaskets fund was liquidated at the end of 1996, WEBS have grown steadily to a total of nearly $500 million in assets. The AMEX already has plans to continue to develop the product line with a series of "Index Shares," and in June, 1997, AMEX was awarded the license to develop Index Shares based on the Dow Jones Industrial Average. Table 1 lists the currently traded funds.

Table 1 Index Shares as of 6/27/97

Name	Symbol	Launch Date	Index Shares Shares per Creation Unit	Price	Shares Outstanding	Fund Assets
SPDRs						
SPDR	SPY	1/22/93	50,000	88 29/32	32,962,000	$2,930,527,813
MidCap SPDR	MDY	4/27/95	25,000	56 3/16	4,282,000	$240,595,000
WEBS Index Series						
Australia	EWA	3/18/96	200,000	11 9/16	4,000,000	$45,734,754
Austria	EWO	3/18/96	100,000	10 1/2	400,000	$4,150,914
Belgium	EWK	3/18/96	40,000	17 7/16	2,040,000	$35,696,708
Canada	EWC	3/18/96	100,000	13 5/8	1,800,000	$24,218,557
France	EWQ	3/18/96	200,000	15 7/8	1,001,000	$15,992,736
Germany	EWG	3/18/96	300,000	17	1,201,000	$20,227,131
Hong Kong	EWH	3/18/96	75,000	16 11/16	1,201,000	$19,868,299
Italy	EWI	3/18/96	150,000	17	1,800,000	$30,400,867
Japan	EWJ	3/18/96	600,000	14 5/16	12,600,000	$178,116,540
Malaysia	EWM	3/18/96	75,000	13	1,425,000	$18,438,276
Mexico	EWW	3/18/96	100,000	14 3/4	700,000	$10,347,287
Netherlands	EWN	3/18/96	50,000	23 5/16	451,000	$10,504,444
Singapore	EWS	3/18/96	100,000	11 1/8	1,300,000	$14,023,654
Spain	EWP	3/18/96	75,000	21 9/16	450,000	$9,616,955
Sweden	EWD	3/18/96	75,000	19 9/16	375,000	$7,299,484
Switzerland	EWL	3/18/96	125,000	15 11/16	876,000	$13,719,655
United Kingdom	EWU	3/18/96	200,000	16 7/8	1,601,000	$26,679,104
						$485,035,365

Index Shares Mechanics

Index Shares exist at the intersection of traditional open-end mutual funds and closed end funds, incorporating the best features of each structure. Essentially, Index Shares combine the ability to transact intraday in a secondary market like a closed end fund with the mutual fund's ability to create and redeem shares at the fund's net asset value (NAV) at the close on any business day. As we will discuss later, this unique combination of attributes offers significant benefits to investors actively buying and selling the fund as well as to ongoing shareholders of the fund.

Index Shares may be structured as either a Unit Investment Trust (UIT) or an open-ended management investment company under the Investment Company Act of 1940. SPDRs and MidCap SPDRs are structured as UITs; WEBS are structured as management investment companies. There are relative advantages and disadvantages to each of these structures. The structure chosen ultimately depends upon the needs and goals of the fund sponsor and the nature of the index on which the fund is based. The UIT structure may operate at a slightly lower cost than the management investment company structure because it does not employ the services of an investment advisor and therefore does not require a board of directors. However, while the UIT structure is simpler, it allows for significantly less flexibility in managing the fund. For example, unlike the management company structure, the UIT does not allow for any judgment to be exercised on the part of the trustee, precluding the use of futures or other derivatives that allow for more efficient reinvestment of dividends. This lack of flexibility also requires trust policies and procedures to be laid out carefully in advance. The UIT structure typically requires that the trust hold every security included in the underlying index. Management companies, in contrast, utilize an investment advisor who may use judgment in determining whether to hold all of the underlying securities in the index or to invest in an optimized portfolio designed to track the index while minimizing the cost associated with purchasing and holding small positions in illiquid securities. UITs cannot lend out securities held in the trust to earn additional income to offset some of the operating expenses of the fund, so UITs tend to be confined to domestic funds holding large capitalization stocks which tend to offer little opportunity to earn much incremental return through lending. Finally, in contrast to a UIT, a management company may impose a 12b-1 marketing fee. This fee is charged to the fund shareholders and it can help build the assets of the fund, ultimately leading to a lower overall expense ratio for shareholders.

Unlike traditional mutual funds, Index Shares may be bought or sold throughout the trading day in the secondary market on the floor of the American Stock Exchange. And unlike closed end funds, Index Shares may be created and redeemed at NAV on any business day. Table 2 summarizes the major similarities and differences among Index Shares, traditional open-ended mutual funds and closed end funds.

Table 2 A Comparison of Index Shares, Open End and Closed End Funds

	EXTRA Fund	Traditional Open-ended Mutual Fund	Closed-end Fund
1) New shares can be created on any day at NAV	Yes*	Yes	No
2) Old shares can be redeemed on any day at NAV	Yes*	Yes	No
3) Trades in secondary market intraday	Yes	No	Yes

*Creations and redemptions can occur only in Creation Unit size aggregations.

In order to maintain tax benefits similar to those enjoyed by traditional mutual funds and closed end funds, Index Shares must qualify as a regulated investment company (RIC) under the Internal Revenue Code, and thus must adhere to the same diversification requirements, source of return standards and distribution requirements as traditional funds. By meeting these standards, the fund is able to pass through to its shareholders income earned on the assets of the fund without being taxed at the fund level.

Creation/Redemption of Index Shares

One of the most important distinguishing features of Index Shares is the mechanism by which new shares are created and by which existing shares are redeemed. In existing Index Shares, new shares may be created only in multiples of large size aggregations, called Creation Units (or CUs), and only by the physical deposit with the fund of a predetermined basket of stock, plus a cash amount determined at the close on the day of creation, for each Creation Unit aggregation. The cash amount primarily represents accumulated dividends, net of expenses accrued by the fund, on a Creation Unit size aggregation of fund shares. The cash amount also includes a typically much smaller amount called the "balancing cash," which ensures that the total value of the Creation Unit deposit, including cash, exactly equals the NAV of one Creation Unit aggregation of fund shares. Under certain circumstances, such as a restriction on a creator from dealing in a compónent stock in the underlying index, cash also may be paid in lieu of delivering certain securities in the Creation Unit portfolio.

In return for each Creation Unit deposit, an investor receives a fixed number of Index Shares, typically ranging from 25,000 to 600,000, depending on the size of the CU portfolio deposit and the price of the Index Shares. Traditional mutual funds may, and occasionally do, create new fund shares in response to an in-kind deposit of stock or deliver physical shares held by the fund against a redemption of fund shares. However, these transactions are the exception rather than the rule for traditional funds and only occur with very large purchases and redemptions. The great bulk of assets enter a traditional mutual fund by the deposit with the fund company of cash, which the fund uses to purchase securities, and exit the fund by the delivery to the redeeming shareholder of cash, which the fund either draws from available cash kept to facilitate redemption or generates through the sale of portfolio securities in the fund.

Closed end funds do not allow for the creation of new shares or redemption of existing shares each day at NAV, although some of these funds are organized as "interval" funds, which allow for creation and redemption activity to occur only at regular intervals, perhaps quarterly. For the great majority of closed end funds, investors only purchase and sell shares in the secondary market unless a fund issues additional shares through a secondary offering or rights issue.

Secondary Market Trading

The second major innovation of Index Shares is secondary market trading on the AMEX at prices very close to intraday NAV. Unlike traditional mutual funds that only allow purchases and sales directly with the fund once each day at the closing NAV, Index Shares are designed to be traded in an active secondary market on the AMEX floor. A specialist is assigned to each Index Shares as if the fund shares were ordinary common stocks. As with other equity securities, the specialist is responsible for making fair and orderly markets in Index Shares. In addition, market makers on the Exchange floor may add liquidity to the market in Index Shares by making competitive bids and offers for the shares.

Because the shares are basket securities, they tend to be less volatile than individual company stocks and have smaller minimum trade increments. For example, SPDRs and MidCap SPDRs trade in minimum increments of 1/64, while WEBS traded in minimum increments of 1/16 well before this size increment became an industry standard. For domestic Index Shares, the shares have tended to trade at a narrower bid/asked spread than the aggregated individual bid/asked spreads of the underlying basket of shares. The presence of a corresponding futures contract on the same underlying index certainly increases the ability of the specialist to make tight markets. For example, the liquidity of the S&P 500 future at the Chicago Mercantile Exchange improves the liquidity of the SPDR. Table 3 illustrates the distribution of the bid/asked spread of the fund during 1996, both for the SPDR and the MidCap SPDR.

Table 3 Bid/Asked Spread Distribution (1996 Only)*

A. SPDR Trust	Range	% of Total
	1/64 - 1/16	62.61%
	5/64 - 1/8	32.21%
	9/64 - 3/16	2.12%
	13/64 - 1/4	2.76%
	17/64 - 5/16	0.12%
	21/64 - 3/8	0.17%
	> 25/64	0.01%
	Total	100.00%

The price range of shares for 1996 was from 59-31/32 to 76-1/8; consequently, 1/16 was from 0.10% to 0.08% of the share price.

B. MidCap SPDR Trust	Range	% of Total
	1/64 - 1/16	1.71%
	5/64 - 1/8	60.44%
	9/64 - 3/16	32.44%
	13/64 - 1/4	2.28%
	17/64 - 5/16	1.16%
	21/64 - 3/8	0.85%
	> 25/64	1.12%
	Total	100.00%

The price range of shares for 1996 was from 41-13/32 to 51-11/32; consequently, 1/16 was from 0.15% to 0.12% of the share price.

*Excludes period between March 1 and March 15, 1996, for which data was unavailable.

Advantages of Index Shares

Because of their unique structure, Index Shares offer a number of distinct advantages relative to closed end funds and traditional mutual funds. The tendency of closed end funds to trade at a discount to NAV is well documented. Often this discount is attributed to a number of factors that make the funds unattractive to buy, such as poor performance of the fund versus an appropriate benchmark, large unrealized capital gains in the fund or low liquidity and/or high risk assets held by the fund. Infrequently, a closed end fund will trade at a premium due to strong demand resulting from strong performance or limited supply of the fund shares. Certain closed end country funds have sold at premiums because investors cannot invest directly in the country without overcoming significant restrictions. Regardless of the direction, the deviation of the fund share price in the secondary market from NAV is a result of the closed end fund structure. No mechanism exists whereby the shares traded in the secondary market may be exchanged for cash or other securities, the value of which is equal to the NAV of the fund shares. In an attempt to remove this deviation, a fund may structure itself as an interval fund, allowing investors to redeem fund shares at NAV on a periodic basis. However, there are very few of these funds, so it is unclear as to whether discounts or premiums would tend to persist.

Like closed end funds, Index Shares trade in a secondary market on the AMEX. Unlike closed end funds, however, Index Shares are structured so that new shares may be created and existing shares redeemed at closing NAV on any business day. As a result of this daily opening of the fund to creations and redemptions at NAV, Index Shares trade at prices very close to the underlying value of the shares held by the fund. A simple, efficient arbitrage mechanism allows investors to profit from a sufficiently large deviation of the fund share from the underlying value of the securities represented by that share. Consider the case where SPDRs are trading at a premium to their underlying value. If an arbitrageur decided that the premium was significant enough, he could sell the SPDRs and at the same time purchase the appropriate stocks in a SPDR Creation Unit portfolio. Alternatively, he might purchase a futures contract and arrange to take delivery of the 500 underlying stocks in an exchange for physical transaction (EFP). In either case, for each CU portfolio purchased, the arbitrageur would sell 50,000 SPDRs and at the same time notify the fund distributor of his or her intent to create the number of SPDRs corresponding to the number of shares sold and CU's purchased. At the close of trading on the day of a creation, the Trustee determines the NAV per creation unit for the fund and the associated cash component and alerts the National Securities Clearing Corporation (NSCC) of the creation order. The participant is' deemed to have bought the appropriate number of SPDR shares, to have sold the appropriate number of shares of each of the underlying stocks in the CU portfolio and is debited the appropriate cash amount. On settlement date (standard trade date plus three day settlement: T+3) the appropriate number of SPDRs settle into the participant's account to cover the sale of SPDRs on trade date. Similarly, the shares of the 500 stocks bought on trade date settle in his account to cover the delivery of shares to the Trust in exchange for the new SPDR shares. The Trust issues the appropriate number of newly created SPDR shares to DTC prior to settlement. This arbitrage mechanism essentially works in reverse in the case of Index Shares trading at a discount: investors buy fund shares, sell the basket of stocks and redeem fund shares to receive the basket of stocks to deliver. While the extent of deviation from NAV depends in part on market conditions, Table 4 indicates how closely trading in the secondary market historically has tracked underlying NAV as a result of this mechanism for both the SPDR Trust and MidCap SPDR Trust. For international funds, standard practice in the mutual fund industry is to calculate NAV using currency rates as of 11:00 a.m., New York time. Therefore, the relevant deviation for WEBS is of the 4:15 p.m. closing market price on the AMEX versus the closing IOPV, which is described in detail below. The average of this closing deviation over the first five months of 1997, ranged from .01% (1 basis point) in the Italy series, to .83% (83 basis points) in the Singapore series. For all 17 WEBS series, the average deviation from IOPV over this period was .44% (44 basis points).

To help arbitrageurs estimate whether Index Shares are trading at a sufficient premium or discount, and to help investors recognize that Index Shares trade very close to their underlying value, AMEX publishes under a separate symbol the intraday market value of the stocks in the current CU portfolio, together with the estimated cash amount per creation unit based on the previous day's close, on a per fund share basis. The AMEX is enhancing this calculation for SPDRs during 1997 to reflect as closely as possible the stock and cash positions of the overall trust on a per-SPDR share basis. Similarly, AMEX publishes for each WEBS series an intraday Indicative Optimized Portfolio Value (IOPV) that reflects the current market value of the securities in the current CU portfolio. The intraday IOPV is based on the most recently reported trade prices of the underlying securities converted into U.S. dollars using real-time currency conversion rates together with the projected accumulated dividends, net of expenses, through the current day, all on a per-WEBS share basis. By

Table 4 Frenquency Distribution for SPDR Trust and MidCap SPDR Trust: Highs and Lows vś. Net Asset Value*

A. SPDR Trust

Range	Closing Price on AMEX Above Trust NAV		Closing Price on AMEX Below Trust NAV	
	Frequency	% of Total	Frequency	% of Total
0 - .25%	457	95.01%	459	89.82%
.25 - .5%	22	4.57%	44	8.61%
.5 - 1%	2	0.42%	8	1.57%
1 - 1.5%	0	0.00%	0	0.00%
1.5 - 2%	0	0.00%	0	0.00%
2 - 2.5%	0	0.00%	0	0.00%
2.5 - 3%	0	0.00%	0	0.00%
3 - 3.5%	0	0.00%	0	0.00%
> 3.5%	0	0.00%	0	0.00%
Total	481	100.00%	511	100.00%

Close was within 0.25% of NAV better than 92% of the time, and within 0.50% of NAV better than 99% of the time.

B. MidCap SPDR Trust

Range	Closing Price on AMEX Above Trust NAV		Closing Price on AMEX Below Trust NAV	
	Frequency	% of Total	Frequency	% of Total
0 - .25%	114	36.77%	71	57.26%
.25 - .5%	108	34.84%	30	24.19%
.5 - 1%	80	25.81%	20	16.13%
1 - 1.5%	6	1.94%	2	1.61%
1.5 - 2%	1	0.32%	0	0.00%
2 - 2.5%	1	0.32%	1	0.81%
2.5 - 3%	0	0.00%	0	0.00%
3 - 3.5%	0	0.00%	0	0.00%
> 3.5%	0	0.00%	0	0.00%
Total	310	100.00%	124	100.00%

Close was within 0.25% of NAV better than 47% of the time, and within 0.50% of NAV better than 76% of the time.

*From inception of Trust through 12/31/96.

providing a very, very close replication of the net asset value every fifteen seconds during the trading day, AMEX allows the investor to be comfortable that he or she is transacting at a fair price in the secondary market. This confidence should enhance liquidity in the market for Index Shares.

Just as Index Shares afford the investor significant advantages over closed end funds, so too do they offer significant advantages over traditional open-end mutual funds. First and foremost, Index Shares offer a level of flexibility not typically available in traditional mutual funds. Index Shares may be purchased or sold on the AMEX at any time during the trading day until 4:15 p.m., while traditional mutual funds typically allow purchases and sales to occur only at 4:00 p.m. on any trading day. Thus, during a volatile period where the market is moving and an investor does not want to wait until the end of trading to buy or sell, he or she can transact intraday in a continuously quoted market on the Exchange floor just as in the case of a share of stock. Although it is difficult to estimate the value of the ability to trade at a fair price intraday, as Tables 5 and 6 suggest, there may be opportunities in the course of a trading day to buy or sell Index Shares at a more advantageous price than closing NAV, even after reflecting transaction costs such as commissions and the bid/asked spread.

Ongoing shareholders are protected by separating secondary market trading activity on the Exchange from creation and redemption activity. By allowing buyer and seller to interact directly on the Exchange, the fund does not incur any of the costs associated with the purchase of stocks to invest daily net inflows of cash into the fund or with the sale of stocks associated with daily net outflows of cash. The ongoing shareholder is protected from the costs that otherwise would be generated by other holders buying and selling fund shares. From the inception of SPDRs through December 1996, almost ten times as many shares have been traded in the secondary market as have been created by share deposits directly with the SPDR Trust. This turnover had no direct impact on the Trust or ongoing shareholders since the trades occurred in the secondary market outside the fund.

The prospectus of a traditional mutual fund often allows the fund distributor to reject the purchase request of an investor who has been an active trader of the fund shares. In fact, many fund families limit the number of times in a year an investor may buy and sell funds or switch between funds. In all cases, this restriction has been imposed to mitigate the negative impact of trading activity on ongoing shareholders. To protect the ongoing shareholder from the costs associated with creations and redemptions that do occur in Index Shares, the creating or redeeming investor pays a transaction charge to cover the cost to the fund of processing the order. Since creations and redemptions are done in kind, the

Table 5 Daily Percentage Price Ranges: Average and Frequency Distribution for SPDR Trust and S&P 500 Composite Index; Highs and Lows vs. Close*

S&P 500 COMPOSITE INDEX

	Daily % Price Range		Intraday High Value Above Closing Value		Intraday Low Value Below Closing Value	
Range	Frequency	% of Total	Frequency	% of Total	Frequency	% of Total
0 - .25%	6	0.60%	526	53.02%	328	33.06%
.25 - .5%	223	22.48%	231	23.29%	302	30.44%
.5 - 1%	518	52.22%	169	17.04%	269	27.12%
1 - 1.5%	177	17.84%	41	4.13%	67	6.75%
1.5 - 2%	45	4.54%	18	1.81%	20	2.02%
2 - 2.5%	15	1.51%	5	0.50%	5	0.50%
2.5 - 3%	6	0.60%	1	0.10%	0	0.00%
3 - 3.5%	0	0.00%	1	0.10%	0	0.00%
> 3.5%	2	0.20%	0	0.00%	1	0.10%
Total	992	100.00%	992	100.00%	992	100.00%

Average Daily Range: 0.82%

SPDR TRUST

	Daily % Price Range		Intraday High Price Above Closing Price		Intraday Low Price Below Closing Price	
Range	Frequency	% of Total	Frequency	% of Total	Frequency	% of Total
0 - .25%	20	2.02%	481	48.49%	347	34.98%
.25 - .5%	243	24.50%	265	26.71%	318	32.06%
.5 - 1%	459	46.27%	161	16.23%	234	23.59%
1 - 1.5%	192	19.35%	60	6.05%	69	6.96%
1.5 - 2%	49	4.94%	13	1.31%	15	1.51%
2 - 2.5%	18	1.81%	11	1.11%	6	0.60%
2.5 - 3%	8	0.81%	0	0.00%	2	0.20%
3 - 3.5%	1	0.10%	1	0.10%	0	0.00%
> 3.5%	2	0.20%	0	0.00%	1	0.10%
Total	992	100.00%	992	100.00%	992	100.00%

Average Daily Range: 0.83%

*From inception of Trust through 12/31/96. Source: FactSet Research Systems, Inc.

Table 6 Daily Percentage Price Ranges: Average and Frequency Distribution for MidCap Trust and S&P MidCap 400 Index; Highs and Lows vs. Close*

S&P MIDCAP 400 INDEX

	Daily % Price Range		Intraday High Value Above Closing Value		Intraday Low Value Below Closing Value	
Range	Frequency	% of Total	Frequency	% of Total	Frequency	% of Total
0 - .25%	10	2.30%	254	58.53%	162	37.33%
.25 - .5%	98	22.58%	74	17.05%	96	22.12%
.5 - 1%	224	51.61%	67	15.44%	133	30.65%
1 - 1.5%	70	16.13%	27	6.22%	35	8.06%
1.5 - 2%	19	4.38%	7	1.61%	7	1.61%
2 - 2.5%	7	1.61%	3	0.69%	0	0.00%
2.5 - 3%	3	0.69%	2	0.46%	1	0.23%
3 - 3.5%	2	0.46%	0	0.00%	0	0.00%
> 3.5%	1	0.23%	0	0.00%	0	0.00%
Total	434	100.00%	434	100.00%	434	100.00%

Average Daily Range: 0.82%

MIDCAP SPDR TRUST

	Daily % Price Range		Intraday High Price Above Closing Price		Intraday Low Price Below Closing Price	
Range	Frequency	% of Total	Frequency	% of Total	Frequency	% of Total
0 - .25%	21	4.84%	205	47.24%	182	41.94%
.25 - .5%	76	17.51%	85	19.59%	96	22.12%
.5 - 1%	224	51.61%	100	23.04%	119	27.42%
1 - 1.5%	70	16.13%	22	5.07%	30	6.91%
1.5 - 2%	29	6.68%	17	3.92%	2	0.46%
2 - 2.5%	4	0.92%	2	0.46%	2	0.46%
2.5 - 3%	3	0.69%	1	0.23%	1	0.23%
3 - 3.5%	5	1.15%	1	0.23%	1	0.23%
> 3.5%	2	0.46%	1	0.23%	1	0.23%
Total	434	100.00%	434	100.00%	434	100.00%

Average Daily Range: 0.86%

*From inception of Trust through 12/31/96. Source: FactSet Research Systems, Inc.

cost tends to be minimal. For example, the transaction fee charged by both the SPDR and MidCap SPDR to create or redeem 10 Creation Units is just $3,000, or roughly 1 basis point to 2 basis points. For WEBS, the associated fees range from $1,800 to $8,900 for ten CUs, depending on the Series. These charges equate to approximately 1 basis point to 6 basis points of the value of the shares being created.

The physical exchange redemption mechanism will tend to make Index Shares more tax efficient for ongoing shareholders than traditional mutual funds. Under current Internal Revenue Code provisions, the in-kind exchange of shares on Index Shares redemption is not a taxable event to the fund. Therefore, since transactions in the secondary market occur away from the fund and since redemptions are effected by in-kind exchange of shares, neither of these events cause gains to be realized within the fund. In fact, the only event that would require significant sales and purchases within the fund would be a change in the composition of the underlying index. In this case, the fund must transact to rebalance its portfolio to maintain the fund's tracking of the index. However, even this impact may be lessened in the Index Shares structure. When a redemption occurs, the fund may deliver out to the redeeming shareholder the lowest cost-basis stock in the fund, thereby "stepping up" the fund's basis. If there is a fair amount of redemption activity in addition to creation activity, the fund has the opportunity to consistently "step up" its basis, lowering the capital gains which will be generated by trades inside the fund and which must be distributed to shareholders. The likely net impact of this practice is to defer realization of capital gains longer than traditional mutual funds. This may make Index Shares more attractive in terms of estate planning than traditional mutual funds, since the cost basis of shares held at death is stepped up when the shares are passed to heirs.

A much wider range of order types is available to the buyer/seller of Index Shares than to a traditional mutual fund user. As with any publicly traded stock, Index Shares can be bought or sold using market orders, limit orders, at the close or at the open orders, not-held orders, percentage orders, scale orders, sell "plus" or buy "minus" orders, stop orders, stop limit orders, switch orders, or time orders. Traditional mutual funds generally allow the equivalent of a market on close order only. Investors may find the ability to transact during the trading day using a variety of different order types to be very attractive in implementing many investment or trading strategies. Additionally, brokerage firms often accept Index Shares as good cover for some short index options positions.

Index Shares may be sold short, something not commonly possible with conventional mutual funds. Further, because Index Shares represents ownership in a portfolio of securities, it may receive an exemption from the Securities and Exchange Commission (SEC) with regard to the "tick test" of the 1934 Act short sale rule. SPDRs, WEBS and Coun-tryBaskets all received this exemption. Therefore, unlike individual shares of common stock that may be sold short only at a price higher than the last trade at a different price, these Index Shares may be sold short even at a price lower than the previous trade at a different price-a downtick. Of course, as with all securities, arrangements to borrow the shares must be made before they may be sold short. The attractiveness of shorting Index Shares is evident in the SPDR. As Table 7 shows, short open interest in the SPDR frequently has been in the range of 15 percent to 20 percent of the shares outstanding, much higher than the typical listed stock that has short interest of 1 percent to 2 percent of its capitalization. WEBS combined short open interest has ranged from 5 percent to 8 percent over the period.

The Future of Index Shares

In the future, there will be a great variety of Index Shares from which an investor can choose. AMEX already is developing a series of successor funds based on a variety of equity indices. Over time, the Index Shares construct should prove flexible enough to accommodate a variety of products beyond broad market equity index funds. For example, more narrowly based sector index funds would be a natural extension, allowing investors to switch funds freely as many times as they wish without penalty, because secondary market trading takes place outside the fund. Also, there may be substantial interest in fixed income index funds. More fund variety will allow simple allocation or reallocation of assets directly on the Exchange trading floor by buying and selling equity and fixed income funds. There may even be actively managed Index Shares. Of course, the extension of the structure from equities to other asset classes like fixed income and from passively managed to actively managed portfolios will take time and likely will require new product structure innovations.

Finally, there is one additional piece of the puzzle which we believe will be critical to the future evolution and growth of the Index Shares marketplace. Introducing options directly on these funds will help

Table 7 Short Open Interest as Percentage of Total Shares Outstanding

Date	Percentage SPDR	MidCap SPDR	WEBS	Date	Percentage SPDR	MidCap SPDR	WEBS
Feb-93	1%			Apr-95	30%		
Mar-93	3%			May-95	17%	27%	
Apr-93	4%			Jun-95	17%	0%	
May-93	6%			Jul-95	14%	1%	
Jun-93	10%			Aug-95	21%	0%	
Jul-93	8%			Sep-95	19%	14%	
Aug-93	9%			Oct-95	17%	0%	
Sep-93	20%			Nov-95	18%	5%	
Oct-93	15%			Dec-95	17%	0%	
Nov-93	10%			Jan-96	11%	1%	
Dec-93	12%			Feb-96	11%	27%	
Jan-94	9%			Mar-96	18%	4%	
Feb-94	10%			Apr-96	20%	9%	5%
Mar-94	11%			May-96	22%	7%	5%
Apr-94	16%			Jun-96	22%	15%	5%
May-94	18%			Jul-96	19%	25%	5%
Jun-94	12%			Aug-96	20%	22%	6%
Jul-94	14%			Sep-96	24%	24%	6%
Aug-94	18%			Oct-96	21%	11%	7%
Sep-94	21%			Nov-96	22%	17%	7%
Oct-94	23%			Dec-96	21%	12%	7%
Nov-94	20%			Jan-97	20%	10%	6%
Dec-94	20%			Feb-97	22%	10%	6%
Jan-95	17%			Mar-97	23%	11%	6%
Feb-95	18%			Apr-97	23%	9%	7%
Mar-95	25%			May-97	17%	6%	8%

increase overall fund assets and provide the investor with a more powerful tool to customize his or her risk/reward profile. The AMEX has filed with the SEC for approval to trade options on Index Shares. These options will be settled on exercise by the physical delivery of the underlying fund shares, just like a standard stock option traded today. Investors will be able to use the same types of strategies for funds as those currently in place for individual stocks, such as covered call writing, protective put buying, buying a call or writing a put as alternative ways to participate in securities markets.

Endnotes

PDR is a service mark of PDR Services Corporation, a wholly owned subsidiary of the American Stock Exchange, Inc.

"S&P®," "Standard & Poor's 500®," "Standard & Poor's Depositary Receipts®" "SPDRs®," "S&P MidCap 400 Index™," and "MidCap SPDRs™" are trademarks of The McGraw-Hill Companies, Inc., and have been licensed for use by PDR Services Corporation and the American Stock Exchange, Inc. SPDRs and MidCap SPDRs are not sponsored, endorsed, sold or promoted by Standard & Poor's (S&P), a division of The McGraw-Hill Companies, Inc., and S&P makes no representation regarding the advisability of investing in SPDRs.

"World Equity Benchmark Shares" and "WEBS" are service marks of Morgan Stanley Group Inc. used under license by WEBS Index Fund, Inc. "MSCI" and "MSCI Indices" are service marks of Morgan Stanley & Co. Incorporated used under license by WEBS Index Fund, Inc.

"Dow Jones Industrial Average[SM]", "DJIA[SM]," and "Dow Jones[SM]" are trademarks and service marks of Dow Jones & Company, Inc. (Dow Jones) and have been licensed for use for certain purposes by PDR Services Corporation and the American Stock Exchange, Inc., pursuant to a License Agreement with Dow Jones.

References

Angel, James J., Chance, Don M., Francis, Jack Clark and Gastineau, Gary L. "Comparison of Two Low-Cost S&P 500 Index Funds," *Derivatives Quarterly*, 2, 3 (Spring, 1996), pp. 32-38.

Kleiman, Robert T., "Index Stocks: An Introduction to SPDRs: S&P 500 Depositary Receipts," *AAII Journal*, (January, 1997), pp. 23-26.

CHAPTER 15

Fixed-Income Indexing

Roland Lochoff
Senior Investment Manager, Fixed Income
PanAgora Asset Management

Introduction

Given the equity market's move to indexing, it was natural to ask whether similar logic might be applied to other asset classes. Because bonds may represent a large share of the sponsor's portfolio, they came under particular scrutiny. As fund sponsors developed sophisticated evaluations of fixed income investments, bond investment goals went from emphasizing yield to total return, to total return, to active return over a benchmark, and finally to risk-adjusted active return. This caused the parameters of benchmark returns and risks to be carefully calibrated, allowing active management performance to be easily compared to the benchmark.

Clear patterns emerged. Bond and stock markets diverged. The bond market was probably less efficient than the stock market. On the one hand, it was clear that active managers who emphasized interest rate forecasting were dominated by the index. On the other hand, the bond market continues to be a disparate field, a traded frenetically over the phone, with many strange instruments poorly priced and held in portfolios for reasons other than investment performance. This allows informed money managers to exploit inefficiencies and beat the capitalization-weighted index. Furthermore, the close òbservation of benchmark risk and return raised questions about whether in fact standard, capitalization-weighted bond indexes, analogous to equity indexes, were an efficient representation of the market as posited by the Capital Asset Pricing Model (CAPM).

Technology that helps overcome many of the inefficiencies has been developed. Managers have access to data that shows bond details and price moves. They can use models to price embedded options and pre-payment behavior similar to those that Wall Street had developed inter-nally for its own use. But as technology advances, it also spawns new fixed-income structures, creating a renewed spiral of inefficiency and opportunity. Be it collateralized mortgage obligations (CMOs) or struc-tured notes, the stories of "bigger fool" investors failing fill the newspa-pers. Each failure is, of course, matched by a success—a case for active management. The net result is that managers over time have hewed clos-er, but not too close, to the index.

The Piper Universe of active fixed-income managers for the five years ending December 31, 1996, showed the Lehman Aggregate index in the eighth decile of performance and the eighth decile of risk as measured by the standard deviation of returns. While this showed that, at the aggre-gate level at least, there is a correlation between return and risk—a cor-nerstone of efficient market theory—a large range of anomalies did exist.

The information ratios (active return divided by active risk) of bond managers are higher than active equity managers. To those who have spent even a single morning trading bonds, this is not surprising—the archaic nature of bond markets may mean that in the aggregate prices clear, but when disaggregated, blooming, buzzing confusion can lead to exploitable inefficiency.

Where does this leave indexing? Rather than a comment on the futil-ity of indexing, it is a statement of how much there is to gain from the insights and technologies that indexing creates. Indexing will drive fixed-income into a more modern age, an age less controlled by a cartel of bro-kerages, an age where individual investors will be able to invest in bonds without fear of arcana and illiquidity, where they can spread their capital market risk efficiently across several asset classes.

First, this chapter will address the basics of indexing to standard domestic bond indexes. Some of these ideas can be adapted to interna-tional indexes, but additional considerations must be added; these are covered next. Later sections will explore the way to efficiently invest pas-sively in fixed income.

The Dimensionality of the U.S. Bond Market

The first salient fact of bond indexing is that unlike many equity indexation processes, *full replication* is impossible. While it is not difficult to buy all 500 stocks in the S&P 500 in the correct proportions, it is not feasible to buy all the issues in the Lehman Aggregate index; many of the bonds are simply unbuyable. It is not uncommon for a few holders to own 100% of a particular issue and have no interest in selling, particularly at the price at which the bond is carried in the index. The reasons for the illiquidity are many, but include institutional rigidities like companies being forced to hold issues that would be sold at a book loss—a situation that in a time of rising rates is common.

Therefore, once the decision to passively replicate a capitalization-weighted index is made, the details of indexing, by necessity, require a decomposition of sources of potential return and risk in the index. Any deviation of the portfolio from the index on any of these dimensions will result in a portfolio at risk of having performance that deviates from the index. It should be noted that it is quite possible that portfolios with very different characteristics than the index can have performance similar to the index for periods, but only by understanding the *complete* dimensionality of the market can every aspect be replicated.

The universal variables of bond indexing are as follows:

• Changes in the level of interest rates.

• Changes in the shape of the term structure.

• Interest rate volatility.

• Mortgage prepayments.

• Changes in spreads.

• Specific bond risk.

There are two broad approaches to building portfolios that cover all the nuances underlying these universal variables: stratified sampling and risk model matching through optimization. These approaches are often used complementarily.

Stratified Sampling

As the name suggests, this technique simply involves understanding the shape of the index along its dimensions and choosing a selection of bonds that represent a subset of bonds in the index and replicate the market behavior of that subset.'In practice, it is possible to use bonds not contained within the index to construct a representative sample, but this can lead to problems, which we will discuss in the "Pitfalls of Indexing" section below.

As an example of sampling, if we segment the corporate index into categories arrayed by industry and quality, we can construct a matrix that contains within each box salient characteristics for each industry/quality combination, such as percent in index and duration of that segment. Then the problem becomes choosing bonds of a given industry and quality that represent the same proportion as the portfolio and have the same duration. Unfortunately, even within the corporate index there are more than two dimensions. For example, duration may be matched, but the sample may end up having bonds with much more embedded option exposure than the index equivalent. While duration may be matched now, if rates change, this will no longer be the case.

Thus it can be seen that stratified sampling consists of overlaying matrix of several dimensions such that each matrix resembles the subindex and, in combination, the total matches the index (see Figure 1).

Optimization

While stratified sampling, if properly executed, will lead to a portfolio that will mimic the index, it is not necessarily the most efficient way to build a portfolio. Since many of the dimensions of the stratification are not independent, matching each separately leads to portfolios that may be more inflexible than necessary. Because of liquidity and transaction costs, this can lead to return drag relative to the index.

As an example of this inflexibility, consider a portfolio that falls short of the index in two dimensions. First, it needs additional exposure to A-rated Industrials, but it also needs to have its duration extended. Assume too, that the A-rated Industrial subsample already matches the index. Sampling would suggest the necessity of buying an A-rated Industrial at the duration of the subsample and adjusting other subsectors whose durations had drifted below their subsample ideals. Would it be possible to kill two birds with the same stone, simultaneously addressing the corporate sector and duration shortfall by buying a longer A-rated Industrial?

Optimization-based techniques rely on mathematical models that distill the dimensionality of risk and return to its key components. Algorithms are designed to match this dimensionality in the most parsimonious way. Optimizers are established to consider the marginal utili-

Figure 1 Stratified Sampling
Sample Decompositions

- Sector Decomposition

- Quality Decomposition

- Coupon by Sector

- Maturity Decomposition

- Coupon by Mortgage Seasoning

- Present Value of Cash Flows

- Duration, Convexity, Etc.

- Coupon by Collateral to Prepayment

- Coupon by Collateral to Convexity

- Embedded Option Exposure

- Shift, Twist, Butterfly Risk

- Etc.

ties of various bonds relative to index. Thus, a potential trade is evaluated by a single, comparative number.

Optimizers also have the advantage of allowing explicit factors, such as trading-off the advantage of tighter matching of the index versus the costs of trading in order to reach that goal. A risk model also allows for useful statistics that show the amount of tracking for each dimension of risk and also predict the total tracking closeness of the portfolio relative to the index.

In practice, with funds of reasonable size, sampling and optimization are used in combination. Sampling is used to initially structure a portfolio; optimization is used for periodic evaluation and rebalancing.

Tracking Error

Tracking error is a measure of how closely a portfolio tracks (or fails to track) an index. It is calculated as the annual standard deviation of the portfolio's return less the index's return. No convention exists on whether the tracking error should be computed from daily, monthly, quarterly, or returns of any other periodicity, although if active returns are distributed as a normal distribution over every sampling period, tracking error computed from any periodicity will not differ. A passive portfolio's active return should be as close to zero as possible.

In practice, for bond portfolios it is difficult to realize tracking errors of zero. Some of this dispersion is real, some of it an artifact of inadequate pricing. Real tracking error will arise from the inability to fully replicate. Even careful sampling and optimization will still yield some factors beyond control—most particularly, that the index is unmanaged and is not subject to transaction costs. In addition, a portfolio that holds 500 bonds to represent the approximately 6,500 bonds in the index, is subject to greater specific name risk than the index. Nevertheless, over time, errors made by careful indexers should cancel each other out.

Inadequate pricing is a constant bane for both active and passive managers, but more so for passive managers. Active managers often claim that a random positive effect is the result of skill. A negative random effect causes soul searching and a call for performance attribution, but even then active returns are normally larger than the random fluctuations and can, therefore, be accommodated with more aplomb. For passive managers, any random fluctuation stands out like a sore thumb.

The reason for inadequate pricing is simple. As we described in the introduction, fixed-income trading is a somewhat archaic and arcane activity. The net result is that even for the subset of bonds that actually trade, the prices are not widely distributed. For the bonds that do not trade, inferences about a "fair price" must be made. Pricing services offer these inferences, but the root prices are usually derived from a broker's best estimate. Since brokers are paid to trade bonds rather than price those that do not trade, this is usually a hurried and crude process.

Several years ago, the person in charge of the primary index purveyor tried to have a third of the brokers quote prices in dollars, a third to quote prices in spread off reference Treasuries, and a third to quote prices in yield terms. He hoped to be able to triangulate a better price from three estimates. The results were not helpful. Until more transparent and liquid trading mechanisms are in place and commonly used, this problem will be part of bond index fund management. At every pricing date, every index fund manager will partake in a game known generally as "Hunt for the basis point." '

Mechanisms to trade bonds more efficiently and transparently are emerging. As vested interests who benefit from the current structure are forced to retreat in the face of the technology, we expect the situation to improve and that these developments will have side effects on the way bonds' interchangability is viewed. This may enhance liquidity, development of basket trading, index futures, and the like, increasing equity efficiency and the awareness of equity indexing's attractions.

Figure 2 summarizes the methodologies that a particular firm uses to construct bond index funds.

Rebalancing

There is an old joke: What's the difference between a bond and a bond trader? The answer is that bonds mature. This, and coupon flow, are the reasons why bond rebalancing is a different proposition than equity index fund rebalancing. Thus, in rebalancing, price fluctuations matter less, while investing interim cash flows matter more than with stocks. The net of this is that turnover for a bond index fund will be somewhere on the order of ten times greater than for an equity index fund.

Each index purveyor follows different conventions about how to treat cash flows. Some indexes are reconstituted daily; others assume month-end flows. When managing an index fund, it is clearly important to uncover all the details of the process and replicate them as best as one can with the tracking portfolio. Until indexes and portfolios are rebalanced in real-time, concepts like "backward-looking" and "forward-looking" constructions will be part of the business. As an example, most indexes are constituted with bonds that have maturities of one year or greater. Since a bond's maturity is known with certainty, the issue is whether the maturity is measured at the beginning or the end of the index period.

Pitfalls for Indexers

There are several apparently small errors an index fund manager can make that compound into larger-than-acceptable tracking error.

1. Oversimplified sampling. While sampling is straightforward, it is not difficult to overlook a dimension of the bond market. That dimension may pass unnoticed until a particular movement in the

Figure 2 Investment Process

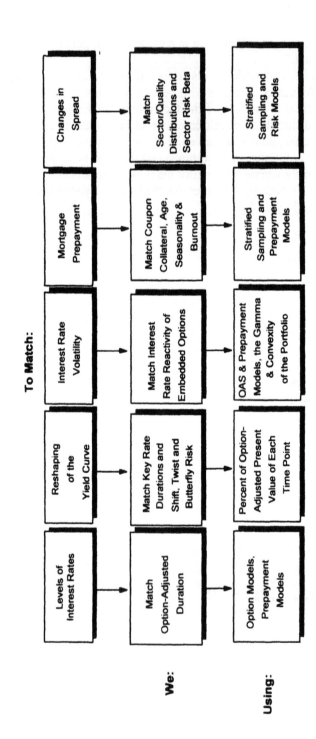

market hits the overlooked dimension, skewing performance. An example would be an equivalent array of seasoning in mortgage-backed securities (MBSs). Mortgages identical in every respect except seasoning can have a very divergent performance.

2. Mortgage prepayment dynamics. The mortgage market represents approximately 30% of the capitalization of broad market indexes and is the most difficult subsector to index. This is because mortgage-backed securities have embedded options whose exercise of which is determined both by financial and behavioral incentives. While corporate bonds often have embedded calls, puts, and option-exposed sinking funds, the exercise of these options is well understood and the behavioral component relatively modest. The mortgage market has developed dramatically, with innovations in instruments and changing conduits for refinancing and reselling. On top of that, housing prices have appreciated to the point that mortgage debt is such a significant portion of the payer's financial profile that "letting things go" is financially very costly. Finally, household formation, marital stability, and relocation have changed the average life of mortgages. Predicting all these activities in combination with shifting financial incentives, means that understanding prepayments is critical. In active management, this leads to tremendous opportunities to add or subtract value. Indexing takes away the guesswork, but the dimensionality of the sampling or the sophistication of the risk model for mortgages must be high enough to address this sector.

3. Transaction costs/excessive turnover/portfolio slippage. As mentioned, indexes are unmanaged. Real portfolios have to be traded. This means that intelligent choices must be made about trading off a degree of portfolio mismatch to the index relative to the costs of creating a match. Many indexers also understand shortcomings in the index and use those shortcomings to their advantage to compensate for the inevitable transactions cost drag. Unfortunately, perfectly anticipating the consequences of these actions is not possible. While it is normally prudent to tolerate a small slippage in the face of constant rebalancing, a particular market event could be dramatic enough to create a performance that does not match the index.

4. Owning securities not in the index or selective reweightings. One of the choices that managers have to make is whether to buy securities outside the index. It is well known that mere membership in

the S&P 500 is enough to alter the price of stocks. While bond indexes are broad enough to minimize this effect, there is a temptation "to lean against" the index. A classic (and not unreasonably exploitable) example is on-the-run Treasuries. The most recently issued Treasuries (the "on-the-runs") trade at higher prices than their "off-the-run" brethren due to better liquidity, occasional "specials," and securities lending. An index fund, with its buy and hold philosophy, does *not* need to pay extra for this liquidity. Thus, indexers typically overweight "off-the-runs" relative to th index.

Another example is mortgage dollar rolls. These are essentially forward contracts on delivery of mortgage pools. Income may be realized by temporarily "loaning" the securities before delivery. This is the inverse of the "off-the-run" effect. Here the portfolio accrues the benefit of providing liquidity. These activities are not riskless relative to the base activity, but the risks are usually so small that they are commonly used.

This philosophy can be extended to other subsectors, including bonds not in the index, the idea being that such bonds are functionally identical, but cheaper. In fact, the indexes have rules for inclusion. A bond is excluded if it has "features" or an issuer that does not conform to the index specifications. Features can make the bond behave differently than its "functionally identical" equivalent. They may be cheaper today, but they may be *even* cheaper tomorrow. The distinction between passive and active management becomes blurred. In our view, sticking with bonds within the index is the only way to adhere to the passive discipline.

Enhanced Indexing

The distinction between indexing and enhanced indexing, and that between enhanced indexing and active management, is vague, determined in large part by the preconceptions of the classifier.

An objective measure would be to make distinctions based on the predicted tracking error of the strategy. For example, an index fund should have less than 10 basis points tracking over the course of a year; enhanced indexing should take the range to perhaps 50 basis points; and active management is anything beyond that. There are problems with this approach, but it is better than alternatives that are added after-the-fact as marketing labels.

The key point about enhanced indexing is that anyone who claims to be an enhanced indexer must be a pure indexer at some point. Only by leveling the playing field to an indexlike framework do anomalies show in stark risk/return terms. Indexing fixed income showed demonstrably how there are opportunities to beat the index. Without indexing, these "opportunities" as often as not were examples of misjudged risk as mispricing.

Indexing to International Fixed-Income Benchmarks

While most of the principles are similar, there are obviously extra dimensions involved in international indexing. Most obviously, the two largest sources of risk are country selection and currency. In addition, some of the summary statistics that are useful for single-country indexing break down when applied internationally.

Sampling works well when applied to country selection, since it is simply a question of matching the country percentage in the index. Below that level things get more complex. Many markets do not have the depth that the United States has, and liquidity becomes a real issue. The trade-off between close matching and transaction costs becomes important, especially since transaction costs in some countries can be high. There are ways around this by using futures contracts to track a country. Futures have very low transaction costs and generally offer good variability. Futures also have the advantage of simplifying the issue of currency hedging which we will cover next. However, using Futures moves into the realm of synthetic indexing, which this chapter does not cover. The issue of liquidity is of sufficient import that one international index purveyor differentiates itself from its competitors by promulgating liquidity-tiered indexes.

If the index to be matched is unhedged, indexing loses a layer of complexity. Many want international bonds hedged, for good reason. This involves selling forward contracts in the exact amount of the value of the bond. Theoretically, as the bond fluctuates in value, the value of the hedge should change. In fact, the indexes make assumptions about the frequency of hedge rebalancing, which means that trading currency forwards should coincide with this exact date (and time!). Rebalancings also involve underlying bond activity which changes hedges. Needless to say, currency hedging gives the indexer numerous opportunities to generate tracking error.

Optimization approaches to international indexing are interesting because the degree of precision achievable with detailed, stratified sampling is lower than with domestic-only indexing. Given that there are many variables at stake, with fewer bonds that can feasibly fill the role, and higher trading costs, the need for parsimonious portfolio construction becomes greater.

Well-worn, useful concepts that apply to the whole index and the portfolio-like duration, which work very well in a domestic context, become meaningless with international indexes. Domestically, duration summarizes the reactivity of a portfolio to a change in interest rates. It assumes that rates across the term structure move in parallel. This is a simplifying assumption, but it describes about 85% of the volatility of returns attributable to interest rates and, thus, is a useful measure. Internationally, the assumption that rates move in parallel across all countries is so poor that duration is not a useful portfolio-wide measure.

Does Indexing to Broad Capitalization Indexes Make Sense?

After all this labor and attention to detail, we ask broader questions. Do the broad indexes represent an efficient bogey that in the long run, particularly after fees, outperform active managers? Furthermore, if we assume that active managers have *no* skill, is the index beatable? In broad terms, does a broad index have economic meaning?

The S&P 500 index is a capitalization-weighted combination of 500 stocks. Indexers mimic this index by buying the stocks in the same proportions as the index. Financial theory says that this makes sense. If markets are efficient, money should flow to companies that are in the best position to invest the money for the highest returns. As their prospects for profits increase, so should their stock price. When the stock price increases the proportion of that particular stock in the index, will increase other stock prices remaining equal. This will have the consequence of attracting more indexing money. Finally, that company will no longer have the best investment opportunities, and its proportion in the index will stabilize. In short, efficient markets funnel money to companies that are the most efficient consumers.[1]

---

[1] Statisticians usually presume that the S&P 500 is the investable universe. Theoreticians clearly understand that there are stocks outside the S&P 500, stocks outside the United States, and other asset classes, and even good investment opportunities that have yet to have successful conduits for financing developed. The latter set is the true "market." The two groups usually agree not to talk about this discrepancy.

By analogy, fixed-income indexes have been constructed as capitalization-weighted combinations of large universes of bonds. These indexes are used as performance benchmarks by almost all institutional investors. This causes large sums of money to be concentrated around the framework of the indexes.

We asked a simple question. Do capitalization-weighted bond indexes make any sense? We certainly cannot make claims about the indexes representing an efficient claim on debt capital. If a firm (or sovereign state) issues lots of debt, is that good or bad? Some may say that large debt is a bad sign. On the other hand, debt issuance may result from efficient choices among the supply and demand for capital among the debt and equity markets.[2]

In fact, there is considerable evidence that choices made for issuing and buying debt are inefficient. For example, the well-known Ibbotson and Sinquefield data show that intermediate bonds have outperformed much riskier long bonds. As another example, the upward-sloping yield curve implies that there are higher yields available for very little incremental interest rate risk. Thus, over any reasonable horizon, portfolios of one-year duration bonds outperform three-month bonds by an amount far in recompense to the incremental risk.

We can surmise why this is so. The polite way is to refer to clienteles. Entities who are significant buyers may be subject to tax profiles that have no natural counterweight. The impolite way suggests that there are significant rigidities built into the system that allow bad habits to persist for long periods of time. If the market were to become more transparent and economic equilibrium forces were less impeded (increased indexing as one force), prices would reflect more of a collective supply/demand equilibrium than they now do.

The rest of this section creates a framework for analyzing whether capitalization-weighted bond indexes are efficient. It looks at the empirical evidence to prove that, at least heretofore, cap-weighted indexes can be systematically beaten. It will show that it is possible to create portfolios with *no active management* that beat the index.

A reasonable starting point is to let market prices steer us toward the sectors of the bond market offering the best combination of return and risk. A standard approach is to calculate the Sharpe Ratio of an asset or asset class. The Sharpe Ratio (SR) is defined as follows:

---

[2] Another approach within the framework of the Capital Asset Pricing Model (CAPM), when all stocks and bonds are held in a "market" portfolio, is that Corporate bonds deliver the stock since the stocks are, in effect, short the bonds, and the net position is in unleveraged stock. Sovereign debt is more of a problem, since "we" issue it. But, we hold the liabilities (future taxes), and the assets which should (given some distributional leapfrog) net out.

Sharpe Ratio

$$SR = \frac{Ret - rf}{\sigma \, (Ret)}$$

SR = Sharpe Ratio

Ret = Return

rf = Risk Free Rate

σ = Annual Standard Deviation

The higher the SR, the higher the excess return available per unit of risk. As long as return per unit of risk is rising, we are better off. If the best SR is available only at levels of risk that are too high or too low, we can adjust to the desired risk habitat by either borrowing or lending at the risk-free rate to be in the exact risk habitat of preference.

Figure 3 illustrates the concept. Point M represents the highest SR of the efficient frontier. Prior to M on the efficient frontier, the SR will decrease. After M, the SR also declines. The straight line RF-B represents different combinations of the optimal portfolio M and the risk-free rate allowing the investor to choose the level of risk appropriate to his or her level of risk tolerance, all with the same (and highest) SR.

Many insights can be gained through this framework. It allows direct comparison of the financial efficiency of two indexes. It also can be used to create an optimally efficient index which is then compared to the standard, capitalization-weighted index. Let's work through an example.

As mentioned above, the Ibbotson and Sinquefield data reveal that intermediate bonds have outperformed long bonds. For the entire period of monthly data dated from January 1926 through June 1996, the mean annualized return to intermediate bonds was 5.18% per year, *versus* 5.02% for long bonds. Moreover, the risk of intermediate bonds was 4.27% per year, *versus* 7.63% for long bonds. This data yields a SR for intermediate bonds that is twice the magnitude of the long bond SR (0.34 *versus* 0.17). This results applies similarly over almost any horizon of the Ibbotson and Sinquefield data.

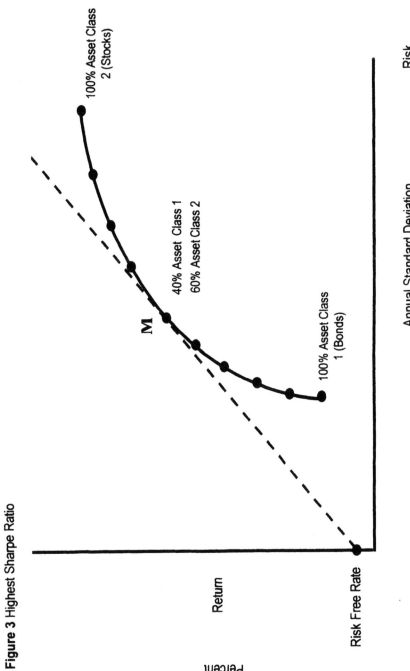

Figure 3 Highest Sharpe Ratio

Clearly, long bonds are less efficient than intermediate bonds. Since long bonds are part of the capitalization-weighted index, this result implies that "better" indexes can be constructed. As one example, we can create a synthetic long bond index with a SR of 0.34, but with an annual standard deviation of 7.63% by combining the intermediate bond index with a short position in the risk-free asset. The return of the "reconstructed long bond index" would be 6.32% per year, in contrast to the actual 5.02%. Over 70 years, the compounded difference means that a $100 investment would total $7,286, *versus* $3,423 *for the same level of realized risk*.

We believe this is an example of a better mousetrap. Others have argued that the overall liability structure should be taken into account. Perversely, rather than this resulting in shorter leveraged portfolios, it results in longer portfolios. This ignores the fact that other asset classes may act to defease liabilities and suggests that maybe all capitalization-weighted indexes, considered independently, inadequately represent the market.

Summary

Many of the lessons of equity indexing can be applied to bond indexing. The economic rationales are also similar; however, there are significant differences.

As regards to pure vanilla indexing—the most salient difference is the inability to create portfolios that fully replicate. This presents the indexer with a host of issues, some interesting, but mostly concerned with the technical arcana that has made the fixed-income market so beloved by its practitioners and so banal to investors.

From a broader, economic equilibrium perspective, fixed income offers fascinating territory both for theoretical speculations and empirical investigation. It brings home the fact that state-of-the-art investing (and not only fixed-income investing) is rapidly evolving, and we still have much to uncover. Perhaps the popularity and consequent economic forces that indexing creates have cast the first light on the quest for rationalizing investments and demystifying the investing priesthood.

CHAPTER 16

The Tax Advantages of Indexing

William G. Zink
Vice President, Global Structured Products Group
State Street Global Advisors

The Impact of Taxes on Investment Returns

Almost every review of investment results, whether in the popular press, investment newsletters or other media, looks at results on a before-tax basis. This is probably not surprising given the breadth of the audience addressed and the variety of potential taxes and rates that may be levied depending upon the type of entity and its location. Looking at returns on an after-tax basis is perceived as too complicated or too dependent on individual circumstances.

An examination of taxation at the individual level confirms our assumption of complexity. One has not only the federal tax rates to consider but also in most circumstances state taxes and, to a lesser extent, local taxes as well. Table 1 presents the familiar federal tax Schedule Y-1 for married filing jointly. This schedule has five different marginal rates depending on income level. In addition to Schedule Y-1, the federal tax code also includes Schedule X, Schedule Y-2 and Schedule Z. These additional schedules have the same marginal tax rates as Schedule Y-1, but they become effective at different income levels. For long-term capital gains, the federal tax rate is the individual's marginal rate or 28%, whichever is lower.

Table 1 Schedule Y-1

If the amount on Form 1040, line 37, is over -	But not over	Enter on Form 1040, line 38	of the amount over -
$0	$40,000	—15.0%	$0
40,000	96,900	$6,015.00 + 28.0%	40,100
96,900	147,700	21,919.00 + 31.0%	96,900
147,700	263,750	37,667.00 + 36.0%	147,700
263,750	—	79,445.00 + 39.6%	263,750

State tax rates range from a low of 0% (there are still a few states that have no income tax) to a high of 11.0%. There are also approximately 20 municipalities levying taxes that range from 0.5% to 4.86%.

When looking at investment returns and the impact that taxes have on returns, we need to consider the composition of returns, how much is capital gains and how much dividends, the level of capital gains that are recognized on an annual basis, and the individual's marginal tax rate and capital gains tax rate. The combinations of federal, state and local taxes, depending on location and income, are large. However, if we assume a federal long-term capital gains rate of 28% and combine this rate with varying ordinary rates in 10% increments between 30% and 50%, we create a series of tax scenarios, one of which should come close to any specific situation.

To move forward with our analysis we must make some assumptions concerning returns. We need to estimate both level of returns and the composition of returns, that is, the mix of capital gains and dividends. For returns we will look at five scenarios: a 10% annual average return made up of 7% price gain and 3% dividend gain, a 10% annual aver-age return made up of 8% price gain and 2% dividend gain, a 10% return consisting of a 6% price return and a 4% dividend return, a 15% average return consisting of a 12% price gain and a 3% dividend gain and a 5% scenario with a 2% price gain and a 3% dividend gain. Again, by choosing some combination of investment returns and tax rates an individual should be able to find a case that comes close to matching his or her own tax situation and returns estimate.

Figures 1, 2, 3, 4 and 5 show ending after-tax value for $1,000 invested at the beginning of the investment horizon for various combinations of tax rates, return scenarios and investment horizons. We also show the effective after-tax rates of return for a 30-year investment horizon. In the figures we compare a no tax situation to a situation where taxes are levied on both capital gains and dividends annually and the situation where dividends are taxed annually and capital gains are taxed at the end of the investment period. It is evident from these diagrams that the longer the investment horizon and the larger the capital gains component of returns, the greater the benefit from delaying capital gains taxes. Delaying the recognition of capital gains can significantly add to after-tax investment returns. Examined from the other direction, paying annual capital gains taxes can seriously erode real investment return.

Let's examine Figure 1 in more detail. This figure shows the value of $1,000 invested for up to 30 years. The assumed average return is 10% per year, the capital gains tax rate is 28%, and the ordinary tax rate is 30%. We show how the investment grows with no taxes, and with a price gain/dividends split of 7%/3%, 8%/2% , and 6%/4% and both capital gains taxes and taxes on dividends paid annually or dividend taxes paid annually and capital gains taxes paid at the end of the investment horizon. Figure 1 shows that with a high turnover investment, one which causes capital gains to be recognized and taxed annually, the after-tax investment return is insensitive to the split in returns between capital gains and dividends. With an ordinary tax rate of 30% the difference in the ordinary rate and the capital gains rate is insufficient to differentiate the various return mix scenarios. However, Figure 1 does demonstrate the advantage of delaying capital gains and the added benefit of choosing an investment with a greater capital gains component. Delaying capital gains can help offset the impact of higher ordinary tax rates when compared to a strategy with high annual capital gains recognition. Incidentally, our graph also shows the huge bite taxes take out of investment returns.

Figures 2 and 3 are similar to Figure 1 except that we increase the ordinary tax rate to 40% and 50% respectively. Increase in the ordinary tax rate, aside from lowering the overall returns, favors a return mix leaning toward a high relative capital gains component for the high turnover strategy as well as the strategy that pays capital gains only at the end of the investment horizon. As the spread between the capital gains rate and the ordinary rate increases, the advantage of an investment strategy with a higher component of capital gains and the delaying of gains increases.

In Figure 4 we show terminal value and 30-year average after-tax returns for an investment with a 5% average return consisting of 2% price return and 3% dividend return. The capital gains tax rate is 28%, results are shown for ordinary tax rates of 30%, 40%, and 50%, with capital gains and dividends taxed annually or dividends taxed annually and capital gains taxed at the end of the investment horizon. Even with the capital gains component of return smaller than the dividend component, it still pays to delay recognition of capital gains. However, the small component of returns attributable to capital gains diminishes the ability of delaying gains recognition to compensate for increasing ordinary rates.

Figure 5 shows the dramatic advantage of delaying capital gains where the gains component is a large percentage of the assumed return. All the scenarios paying capital gains taxes at the end of the investment horizon significantly outperform the scenarios where cap gains taxes are paid annually. An investment strategy with a large capital gains component coupled with the delaying of capital gains recognition can go a long way toward offsetting the impact of high ordinary tax rates.

Investment Activity Determines Tax Liabilities

To reiterate the conclusions of the section above, the larger the component of returns due to capital gains and the longer the investment horizon, the greater the benefit from delaying gain recognition. This creates a very interesting conundrum. Traditionally we hire investment managers to make good investment decisions, to sell one investment holding and to buy another that is expected to do better. The activity we expect an investment manager to engage in is the very activity that leads to capital gains recognition and the payment of capital gains taxes. The more investment manager activity or turnover, the greater the recognized capital gains and the greater the capital gains tax.

All this investment activity and the resulting taxes might still be acceptable if the active investment returns were sufficiently superior to offset the taxes. A look at comparative investment results over the past several years would seem to refute this objective. For example, over the past 20 years (1977 through 1996), the S&P 500 Index has outperformed more than 50% of the general equity funds in 12 of those years. If we compare returns on a three-year or five-year basis, the gap widens. For the 10 years ending on December 31, 1996, the S&P 500 returned +15.3%, compared to a return for the average general equity fund of +13.1%, outperforming 79% of all managed equity funds, and this is on a before-tax basis. The average equity mutual fund has annual turnover in excess of 100%. This means that on average the portfolio holds a security for less than one year. So not only does all that active investment management generate lots of capital gains to be taxed, but it also fails to produce excess returns.

Figure 1 Value of $1,000 Invested in Year 0, 10% Average Return, 28% Capital Gains Tax, 30% Ordinary Tax

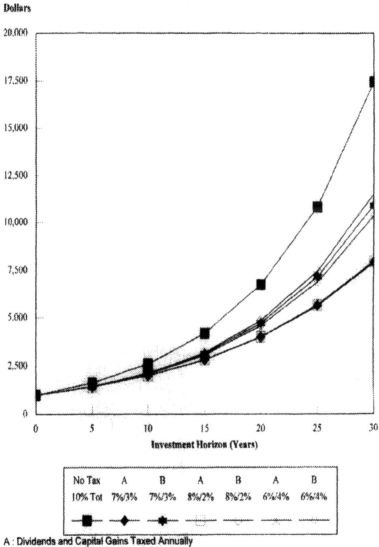

A : Dividends and Capital Gains Taxed Annually

B : Dividends Taxed Annually, Capital Gains Taxed On Redemption

Annual Return Split : X% Price Return/Y% Dividend Return

Figure 2 Value of $1,000 Invested in Year 0, 10% Average Return,
28% Capital Gains Tax, 40% Ordinary Tax

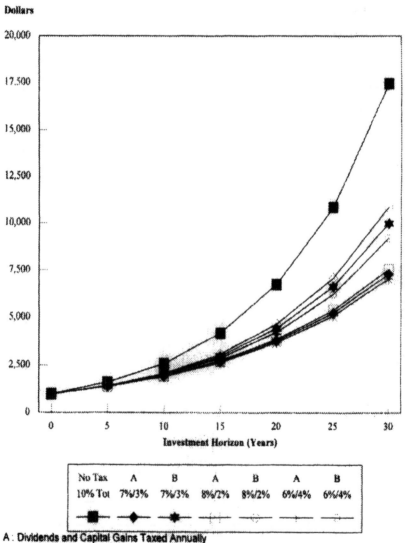

A : Dividends and Capital Gains Taxed Annually
B : Dividends Taxed Annually, Capital Gains Taxed On Redemption
Annual Return Split : X% Price Return/Y% Dividend Return

Figure 3 Value of $1,000 Invested in Year 0, 10% Average Return,
28% Capital Gains Tax, 50% Ordinary Tax

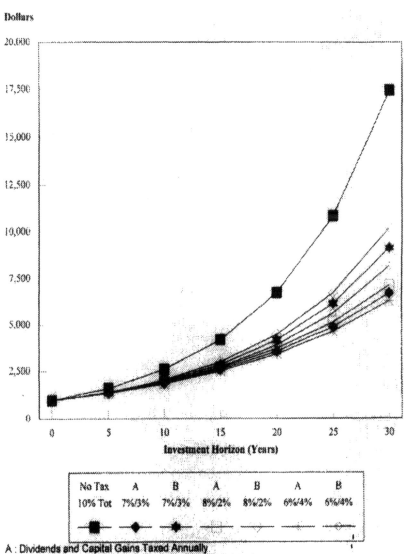

A : Dividends and Capital Gains Taxed Annually

B : Dividends Taxed Annually, Capital Gains Taxed On Redemption

Annual Return Split : X% Price Return/Y% Dividend Return

Figure 4 Value of $1,000 Invested in Year 0, 5% Average Return,
28% Capital Gaihs Tax, 30%, 40% and 50% Ordinary Tax

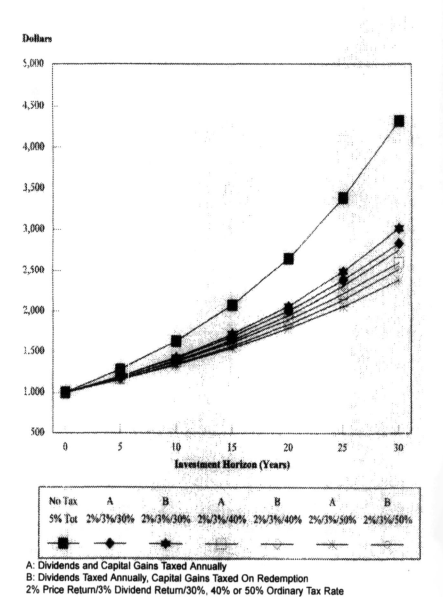

A: Dividends and Capital Gains Taxed Annually
B: Dividends Taxed Annually, Capital Gains Taxed On Redemption
2% Price Return/3% Dividend Return/30%, 40% or 50% Ordinary Tax Rate

Figure 5 Value of $1,000 Invested in Year 0, 15% Average Return, 28% Capital Gains Tax, 30%, 40% and 50% Ordinary Tax

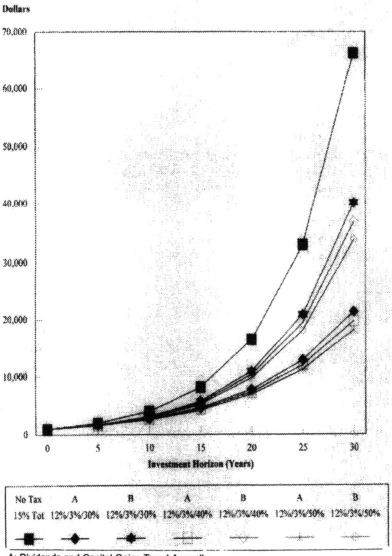

A: Dividends and Capital Gains Taxed Annually
B: Dividends Taxed Annually, Capital Gains Taxed On Redemption
12% Price Return/3% Dividend Return/30%, 40% or 50% Ordinary Tax Rate

Tax Advantages of Popular Index Strategies

Our prior analysis shows delaying the recognition of capital gains and choosing a strategy favoring capital gains as opposed to dividends can significantly add to after-tax investment return. Index strategies, often referred to as passive management, involve no active buying and selling of stocks to "improve" investment returns. At first glance, the "passive" holding of stocks to produce index returns should involve low turnover and hence low capital gains recognition. Additionally, the dividend component of returns will vary for different index strategies and should also be taken into consideration. Table 2 lists several popular index funds with historical returns, turnover, annual dividends and recognized capital gains. The figures are actual numbers taken from the published results for a popular family of index funds. An examination of the table reveals the expected pattern of returns due to dividends. The greatest annual return from dividends is in the S&P Large Cap Value Index while the smallest return is in the Russell 2000 portfolio. The remaining funds line up based upon their average capitalization; the larger the capitalization the greater the component of return due to dividends.

Table 2 Index Funds

Index Fund	Return	Turnover	Dividends	Recognized Capital Gains
S&P 500	19.6%	5.0%	2.6%	0.4%
S&P Large Cap Growth	20.7%	27.0%	1.9%	0.3%
S&P Large Cap Value	18.3%	29.0%	3.1%	1.7%
Wilshire 5000	17.9%	3.0%	2.2%	0.6%
Wilshire 4500	15.6%	19.0%	1.5%	3.6%
Russell 2000	14.8%	27.0%	1.4%	4.3%

Note: Return, Turnover, Dividends and Recognized Capital Gains are Actual Annual Numbers from a Popular Family of Index Funds Averaged Over 1994-1996.

We next need to look at capital gains recognition that should be related to annual fund turnover. While index management involves no active selection of stocks, it does require trading to maintain the portfolio's similarity to the index. Indexes do change and, as we will see, the amount of change can vary significantly. In general the more specialized an index, the greater the potential changes and, hence, turnover. For example, the Wilshire 5000 encompasses the entire U.S. stock market and should therefore have the lowest turnover. A holding in a Wilshire 5000 fund would only be sold as a result of a takeover or a bankruptcy (in which case there isn't likely to be a gain). At the other extreme, we have the Russell 2000 that can have stocks migrate up into the Russell 1000 or drop off the small end. Those dropping off the small end are not likely to generate gains but those moving up will. Again, we would expect annual recognized capital gains to be linked to annual turnover with higher turnover causing higher recognized gains.

The actual results follow this pattern for the Russell 2000, Wilshire 4500 and S&P Large Cap Value funds but then depart the pattern for the S&P Large Cap Growth fund. The Growth fund has a high level of turnover but on average the lowest recognized capital gains of all the funds reviewed. Examining the process used to maintain the index offers an explanation for this apparent anomaly. Twice a year, in December and again in June, Standard & Poors ranks the companies in the S&P 500 based upon their price-to-book ratio and creates two equally weighted universes. The Value Index contains the companies with the lower price-to-book ratios, and the Growth Index contains those with the higher ratios. Stocks sold out of the Large Cap Growth Index will be those names with relatively lower price-to-book ratios when compared to the previous index reconstitution. In other words, the Growth Index will sell stocks whose price in general has declined and therefore are less likely to generate capital gains. There is a second explanation for the low level of gains; hinted at by the pattern of gains (i.e., 0% for two years and 1% in the most recent year). The fund is relatively new and many of the names moving out of the fund may not have been in it long enough to accumulate gains. As the fund ages, this is less likely to be true.

The capital gains recognition of the last two funds on our list are also a surprise with the S&P 500, with slightly higher turnover, having lower recognized capital gains than the Wilshire 5000. The Wilshire 5000's higher recognized capital gains are most likely the result of the methodology used to manage the fund. The Wilshire 5000 Index includes in excess of 7,000 companies, and it is impractical to own all of them. Managing the fund requires owning some subset of the index and overweighting certain issues to compensate for the missing names. If an overweighted stock were taken over, it would most likely be sold out of the fund at a gain and since it was overweighted the gain would exceed its apparent weight in the index.

Figure 6 shows returns for our funds using average data for the last three years to set annual price and dividend returns and recognized annual capital gains. The results are presented assuming a 28% capital gains tax and an ordinary income tax rate of 40%. In general the greater the average return the better the long-term results. In the case of the Wilshire 5000, the after-tax return is equal to the after-tax return for the S&P Large Cap Value Fund in spite of the Value Fund's greater before-tax return. This result is due to the Value Fund's higher dividends and annual recognized capital gains.

Since the last three years may not accurately reflect the long-term expected returns for these various funds, we also show results, in Figure 7, using total annual returns of 10% for each of the funds. In these scenarios we use the same recent data for the funds to project the annual dividends component of returns and the annual component of recognized gains. The differences in after-tax returns are due solely to the tax consequences of the funds' varying dividends and annual recognized gains. The S&P Large Cap Growth Fund with the lowest annual recognized capital gains and relatively low annual dividends produces the best results. At the other extreme, the Russell 2000 Fund with the highest annual recognized capital gains and the lowest annual dividends is the worst performer. Unfortunately, the low level of dividends was not sufficient to overcome the high level of turnover and resulting recognized capital gains.

In general, index strategies that represent large market segments, such as the Wilshire 5000 and the S&P 500 are naturally tax efficient. They have low turnover and therefore low annual recognition of capital gains and their breakdown of returns between price returns and dividend returns favors price returns, minimizing annual ordinary taxes. The S&P Large Cap Growth strategy also appears to be tax friendly. It has a small dividend component of returns and, although the turnover for this strategy is high, it involves selling stocks that have decreased in value and, therefore, are less likely to generate gains.

Figure 6 Value of $1,000 Invested in Various Index Strategies,
28% Capital Gains Tax, 40% Ordinary Tax

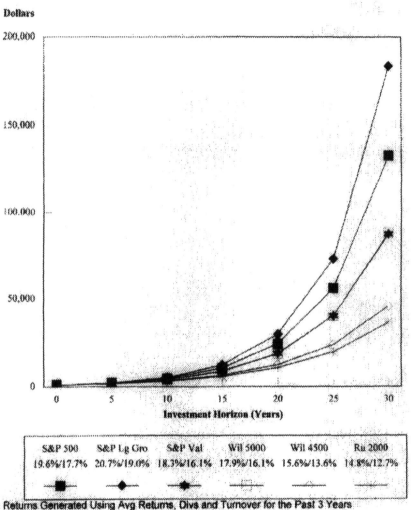

Returns Generated Using Avg Returns, Divs and Turnover for the Past 3 Years
Figures Represent Before And After Tax Returns For 30 Year Horizon

Figure 7 Value of $1,000 Invested in Various Index Strategies, 10% Average Return, 28% Capital Gains Tax, 40% Ordinary Tax

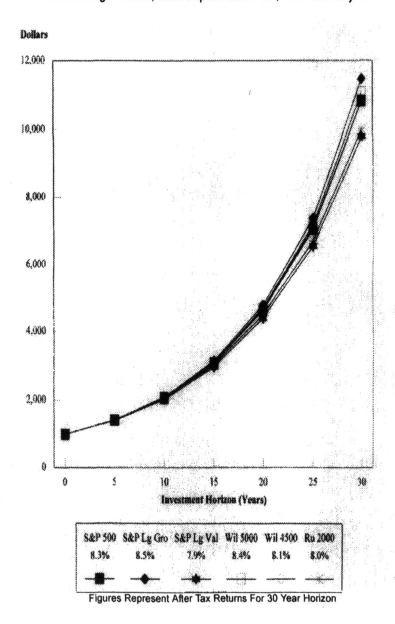

Figures Represent After Tax Returns For 30 Year Horizon

CHAPTER 17

Optimizing Performance

Wai C. Chiang
Managing Director, Portfolio Management
Prudential Investments

This chapter presents a practitioner's approach to running index funds. In particular, I would like to discuss certain insights from my experience that can help maximize the total return of an index fund while still adhering to the investment strategy of indexing.

The strategy of indexing has proven to be a successful one over the years, yet it is not as easy as it seems to replicate the performance of a benchmark index. On a year-by-year basis, even the most established index funds have not been able to consistently *match* their benchmark index's returns.

There is considerable competition in money management, and everyone is vying to achieve the best returns possible within a given strategy. Managing an index fund and doing it well over time requires seasoned experience and knowledge. By sharing some of my experience and the subtleties involved in indexing, I hope to help one avoid the pitfalls and shorten the learning time it takes to produce good index fund returns.

Allow me to relate a story. An acquaintance, in the investment marketing field, once said to me "You can do indexing on the back of an envelope." The proper response to this sentiment should be a definite and emphatic "No! *Successful* index fund management is not a simple scratch- pad exercise." Unfortunately, a lack of respect for indexing

307

represents the uninformed view of many who never tried to manage an index fund. If they had—and when they do—they will find that it is not easy to keep up with a benchmark index and even harder to compete against other indexers in performance.

Consider the following table of numbers:

1996 23.03 23.21 23.02 20.70 23.36 *22.96*
1995 37.57 36.91 37.56 37.49 37.29 *37.58*

Can you guess what these numbers are? They represent a sampling of gross total returns for five major S&P 500 Index funds and the respective Index return (the far right-hand number in each row above). Each column is the *same indexer* over the two years. One might ask, Why is there such a variation in index performance?

The Difficulty of Matching an Index Return

Let's examine why sometimes just trying to do what an index fund is supposed to do—that is, match the performance (i.e., total return, price appreciation plus dividends) of a benchmark index—can be so difficult.

The benchmark index (henceforth called Index) is merely a "paper" calculation that has no actual market impediments to the performance it reports. The Index makes a number of assumptions regarding such factors as transaction costs, the reinvestment of dividends and its timing, corporate actions, and changes in the index. For example, changes in the constituents of Indexes are made instantaneously at the close of the business day. The Indexes assume that there are no problems in making the changes regardless of the liquidity of the stocks. Nor are there any deleterious effects on the price of the changing securities.

Even if the daily market volume of the stock to be added or deleted from the Index is very thin, the benchmark index can change its composition immediately, unlike in a real fund. Furthermore, when there is a change in an Index, a profound ripple effect occurs in a real portfolio as money has to be redistributed across all its constituent members. This would then produce additional transaction costs, a detriment to performance not even considered in an Index's "performance."

There are other factors that make matching an Index's performance difficult, including: how the dividends paid by stocks are treated by the

Index versus by the fund; the amount of uninvested cash in the fund; the volatility of the stock market itself; and the fact that actual funds have client capital flows and Indexes don't. Some of these factors may be specific to a particular benchmark Index.

In brief, transaction costs, existing in a real fund and non-existent in a benchmark or "paper" Index, is one of the keys to why it's so difficult to match an index in performance. This difference in performance, called "tracking error" in the indexing business, becomes the bane of indexers. So, despite the simplicity of the concept of indexing, *exactly matching* the paper benchmark Index's "performance" is an elusive and probably unattainable goal over time.

What is attainable is tracking closely to an Index and maximizing the potential return available to a real index fund. This maximizing of return can enhance a fund's index returns or merely keep the portfolio on track with an index over time. This is the theme not only of this chapter, but of this book.

Maximizing an Index Fund

One can talk about maximizing an index fund's return from two broad perspectives. First, one can talk of ways to optimize performance by *adding to the return* that one can get out of an index fund. This situation is analogous to helping the "revenue" side of the fund. Learning the techniques and methods to do this, start by first, *knowing the Index* one is benchmarked against. Then, while one is actually running the index fund, one can add to its return by the way he or she handles *corporate actions* and *changes in the Index*, and possibly by *lending securities*.

Second, one can alternatively look to reduce the "cost" side of the index fund. It cannot be stressed enough how critical this is to an index fund. Minimizing transaction costs is elemental to operating an index fund. This involves *using stock index futures, structuring the fund to handle the cost of capital flows* and utilizing different *trading techniques*. These items will be discussed in the "Trading and Transactions Cost Management" section of this chapter.

Finally, at the end, we will combine all the "revenue" and "cost-saving" techniques with an overall philosophy and operating strategy for managing an index fund.

Adding to the Fund's Returns

Know Your Index

While there are general practices that one can employ for the fund management of any index, there are also specific nuances that apply only to each specific Index benchmark. One should understand the particularities of the Index one chooses as the fund's benchmark. For example, here is a brief but, certainly not exhaustive discussion of some Index particularities.

The Standard & Poor's Indexes

S&P Indexes in the aggregate, and the S&P 500 Index specifically, are the most widely used index fund benchmarks for the U.S. stock market. As with all Indexes, changes in its composition is cause for resultant changes in actual funds (portfolios) that are benchmarked to them. Due to the number of funds indexed to the S&P 500 Index, any change in composition will have a profound effect on the prices of the securities involved.

In general, Indexes that, for most part, have predictable changes in their composition, as well as a known time for the changes, will tend to be susceptible to a "front-run" in the marketplace. If the composition for an index is determined by a measurable or simple, calculable criterion, then there will be people predicting the changes. If the date for the change is known, there will be trading ahead on those predicted changes to take advantage of the expected price pressure exerted by the multitude of index funds needing to buy or sell those securities.

Unlike some other Indexes, the changes in composition in the S&P Indexes are not determined by a preset group of factors. Rather, there is an investment committee at Standard and Poor's that makes subjective decisions based on a number of factors. However, once a decision is announced, there is no avoiding the impact the change in the Index has on the marketplace. In earlier days, changes in the S&P 500 Index were announced after the market close, effective as of that day's closing prices. Obviously, index funds would have a very difficult time matching the Index's performance because the price of the stock added to the Index would experience an instantaneous jump up upon opening the next morning, and conversely for the stock that was dropped.

Subsequently, Standard and Poor's changed its policy in October of 1989, and currently pre-announces the changes whenever possible. While this makes it easier for index funds to match the S&P Indexes on the price of the changing stocks, it hasn't done away with the price impact the changes have on the stocks added to or deleted from the Index. If any-thing, it has extended its effect over more days and added more opportu-nity for people to try to profit from the anticipated pricing pressures.

In terms of how they treated dividends, in the mid-80's, the S&P cal-culated its 500 Index performance using an assumption that dividends were only reinvested periodically (e.g., quarterly). With such an assump-tion, it was easier for funds to show out-performance relative to the S&P 500 Index during an upward market because the funds' dividends were reinvested sooner than assumed in the benchmark Index. However, today the S&P Indexes assumes that accrued dividends are reinvested the day the stock goes ex-dividend. This assumption makes it difficult for real funds, because in many cases they have to wait a week or more before actually receiving the dividend. Until it's received, the dividend sits as an accrual in the funds.

Primary versus Composite Close Prices

A final point on the S&P Indexes is that the Index securities are valued each day using *primary* market closing prices. These are the 4:00 P.M. Eastern Time closing prices of the securities, as traded on the exchange that is the primary one listing that stock. For example, the primary mar-ket for IBM is the New York Stock Exchange (NYSE), and it's primary closing price is the last traded price for IBM on the NYSE of that day. For other listed stocks, it might be the American Stock Exchange (ASE). For over-the-counter (OTC) stocks, the prices used are those prices printed at approximately 90 seconds after the 4:00 P.M. Eastern Time exchange cut-off.

While the use of primary market close prices is well suited to mutu-al funds that have a daily time requirement to be valued, it is not nearly as compatible with institutional funds. Historically, institutional funds frequently were priced using the *consolidated composite* closing prices rather than the primary market close. The consolidated composite close prices are compiled as of 5:15 P.M. Eastern time. These prices are from other exchanges besides the primary exchange, and from third-market trading networks, like Instinet (a Reuter's company), that trade stocks even past the 4:00 P.M. close. As such, *institutional funds that use the composite prices may show a different return than the benchmark Index using primary market prices over the same time period.*

This effect is most noticeable when there is a distinct pricing dis-crepancy on the last day of a reporting period (i.e., a calendar year, a quar-ter, or a month). Historically-speaking, year-end 1995 was a good exam-ple of the problems resulting when there were differences between the two sets of prices. Exhibit 1 illustrates the monthly, annual, and December month-end daily total returns from 1995, valued using primary market close prices versus the corresponding returns using composite close prices.

Exhibit 1 Comparison Of S&P 500 Index Returns Using Primary Market Close Prices Versus Composite Close Prices

	Jan.	Feb.	Mar.	Apr.	May	June
Primary	2.59	3.90	2.95	2.95	4.00	2.32
Composite	2.60	3.88	2.96	2.93	3.95	2.35

July	Aug.	Sep.	Oct.	Nov.	Dec.
3.32	0.25	4.22	-0.36	4.39	1.93
3.33	0.27	4.20	-0.35	4.40	1.85

	1996 Total Returns	Dec. 1995 Monthly Returns	Jan. 1996 Monthly Returns	Last Trading Day in 1995 Dec. 29, 1995 Daily Return	First Trading Day in 1996 Jan. 2, 1996 Daily Return
Primary	37.58%	1.93%	3.40%	0.297%	0.780%
Composite	37.48%	1.85%	3.44%	0.226%	0.842%
Difference	.10%	.08%	-.04%	0.071%	-0.062%

Source: Primary close price returns from Standard & Poor's Inc.
Composite close price returns from Wilshire Associates

Using the primary market close prices, the S&P 500 reported a December monthly return and annual return of 1.93% and 37.58%, respectively. The same period returns using consolidated composite close prices were 1.85% and 37.48%, respectively. For the year, there was an 0.10% difference in total return between the two sets of prices, of which 0.07% occurred on the last day.

These pricing differences are very short-lived (usually lasting only one day) and reverse quickly. They tend to occur when there is a sharp market move going into the 4:00 P.M. close accompanied by high volume. However, after the market-on-close orders are filled, the after-market (those markets that trade after the 4:00 P.M. close) may show a rebound in prices. This results in the sometimes substantial differences in closing prices and consequent returns.

When these pricing differences occur intra-month, they are reversed out the next business day and are not noticeable. But if they occur at year-end, it may become important because they cause a noticeable (though really temporary) tracking error between the fund and its benchmark.

The differences in the day-ending prices merely reflect the capturing of a rapidly changing state of prices at two distinct points in time. The reversal the next day is then the relaxation of the prices to a more stable period of price movement. Of course, since the two sets of prices ended the prior day at different levels, the return to a more compatible set of prices the next day would result in an reversal of returns.

In our example shown in Exhibit 1, the pricing effects of December 29, 1995 did in fact reverse on the first trading day of 1996. The January 2nd data showed that the daily return from using the primary prices trailed that which used the composite prices by about 0.06%. This negative difference nearly offset the December 29, 1995 difference, where the primary return was 0.07% higher.

On a monthly return basis, December and January, one can also see a reversal, but it is not as precise nor as evident as the daily reversal just discussed. This is because pricing differences are a daily occurring phenomenon. On any given day, the price differences may or may not be significant. Therefore, by the next month's end, there could be another daily discrepancy that mitigates any offset to the prior month's return difference.

When this type of performance difference occurs, the portfolio manager must understand what has happened and be able to explain the effect to his or her clients. Thus, it is important for the portfolio manager to understand the nuances of the benchmark he or she has chosen. This is particularly true for an index fund, because every basis point of performance difference might be questioned given the misconceptions of how "simple" it is to track an Index.

Knowledge of the specifics of one's benchmark is important and can be a factor in how one manages a fund. Sometimes knowing the cause for the variance in return between the fund and the Index can provide some opportunities to capture additional return or prevent an inappropriate alteration to the fund. For example, one might unnecessarily rebalance a portfolio and generate added transaction costs if one mistook a temporary phenomenon for a permanent tracking divergence.

In Appendix A, I have added a discussion on the Index particularities of the Wilshire Indexes.

Handling Corporate Actions

What are Corporate actions? These are the decisions that a portfolio manager of a fund has to make when one of the companies in his or her portfolio has a corporate re-structuring, or buys back stock, or is involved in a merger or acquisition. The shareholder—in this case, usually the portfolio manager—is asked to make a decision on the various alternatives presented to him by the company involved. Some of these situations can be hostile, as in a take-over, or they can be straight-forward, as in a stock buy-back. Nevertheless, corporate actions provide a fertile opportunity to help maximize the possible return to an index fund.

Let's now look at some of the more common corporate actions and the decisions that the fund manager can make to benefit from these situations.

The Dutch Auction

This is a situation where a company is looking to buy back a certain amount of shares outstanding, within a given price range. A price range is generally offered to the shareholders between which the shareholders can tender their stock to the company. For example, XYZ company wants to buy back 10,000,000 shares at a price no higher than $20 and no lower than $10. Currently, the stock of XYZ is trading at $9.

Naturally, shareholders would want to get the highest price possible for their shares, while the company is looking to buy back the shares at the lowest possible price. The rules of this auction state that the shareholders must submit their offer price and the quantity of shares they are willing to sell. Meanwhile, the company will pay one price, and this is the lowest price offered that still allows them to buy all the shares that they desire. This price is then the "clearing price," and all those who tendered their shares at or below this price, will have their stock purchased at the clearing price.

Using our previous example, assuming two million shares each were tendered at the respective price of $10, $11, $12, $13, $14, $15, $16, $17, $18, $19, and $20, then the clearing price for the company to buy back 10 million shares is $14 per share. *Everyone* who tendered their stock at or below $14 per share will get their stock purchased by the XYZ Company at $14 per share. Those who tendered above $14 per share will *not* have any of their stock purchased. Obviously, they priced their shares too high.

Therefore, the price at which one selects to tender at is key because one can provide added returns to the portfolio by selling his stock above the prevailing market price. But if one is too greedy, one prices oneself out of the market. This was a simplified example, of course, because there are other mitigating considerations, such as: how many shares to tender; and what happens if, after one tenders, the market price moves above the eventual clearing price; or if, after the stock is tendered, the company is dropped from the Index, and one must wait for the completion of the tender to have the cash to rebalance the fund?

Generally the rule of thumb is that one can add value to a fund by tendering to a Dutch auction if part of the available price range for the auction is higher than the current market price. The strategy is to get one's shares taken as part of the auction and at a price above the market price. One way to increase the probability of this occurring is to offer one's shares at a price *only slightly* above the market price. One can tender at a price allowing some margin for normal price volatility, but not too high above the prevailing market price, expecting to get a windfall. In this manner, the odds are that one's stock will get taken by the auction and possibly, at an even higher price than it was tendered at.

The amount of shares to be tendered must also be considered. Stock that is purchased by the company will reduce the shares outstanding of the stock in the Index. If one doesn't participate in the Dutch auction and the shares outstanding of the stock are reduced, one will eventually have to sell out a proportionate amount of shares, as well as rebalance the portfolio. This action generates transaction costs, which in turn reduces performance.

On the other hand, if one tenders more shares from the fund than are required to be market-weight proportionate, then different risks arise. Assuming that all the tendered shares are taken at an above-market price, an index manager can presumably buy back the shares he needs to have proper portfolio weight of the stock and make a profit. However, this tender strategy will fail, if in the interim period of time when the tendered shares are taken by the company but before the fund is paid, the stock's market price rises above the auction clearing price. The index manager must then pay out more than he receives to buy back the necessary shares.

While there is no absolute infallible strategy, the recommended solution is the one that gives the least downside risk. One conservative strategy that will allow for some value-added return without exposing the portfolio to a lot of risk, is to tender an amount of shares equal to (or only slightly greater than) the percentage of shares outstanding being bought back by the company. That is, if a company is reducing its shares outstanding by 5%, one would tender approximately 5% of the portfolio's holdings in that company.

Tender Offers From Mergers and Acquisitions

Tender offers resulting from mergers and take-overs are other corporate actions that a portfolio manager has to decide on. Generally speaking, when two companies are in the Index and are engaging in a friendly merger, one normally accepts the terms of the deal if there are no third parties bidding or other extenuating circumstances. One of the companies will probably be absorbed in a stock transaction by the other. Accepting the tender offer and getting shares of the new or remaining company is a frictionless way to acquire the proper number of shares of the new company without engaging in costly market transactions.

However, as was said about indexing in general, things are not always as easy as they seem. If the company being acquired is in the Index, but the acquiring company is not, or if a company in the Index is being taken private, then there are additional decisions to be made. While the tender offer might be attractive (i.e., above the prevailing market price for the stock), the company may be replaced in the Index prior to the completion of the tender and the receipt of payment for the stock. The question to be answered then is: is it better to, *not* tender the stock, wait for the announcement of the change in the Index and then sell out the stock in the open market; or to tender the stock (to get the value-added in the price) and assume the risk of the Index and /or it's new member stock possibly moving up in price while one waits to receive the proceeds of the tender?

A classic example of this situation occurred in February 1989, when RJR Nabisco was to be taken private and dropped out of the S&P 500 Index. At the time, RJR was one of the largest holdings in the Index, and the tender offer gave the shareholders an appreciable value-added above the prevailing market price. However, for Index fund portfolio managers, tendering the stock to the buy-out meant, in essence, that approximately 1.1% of an S&P 500 fund would be in a cash receivable for an unknown number of days. In general, it often takes several weeks after a tender before exact pro-ration rates are determined and cash is paid out for tender offers.

What actually occurred was that during the tender period, the S&P 500 Index announced that it was dropping the $22 billion RJR from its Index and adding another company, First Union, with a smaller, $2.3

billion market value. This replacement meant a major rebalance in S&P 500 Index funds. The quandary to index managers was whether to tender and get the premium relative to market price or sell in the open market and have the cash immediately to rebalance the portfolio.

Corporate mergers and acquisitions can provide significant opportunities for index funds to outperform their respective benchmarks. This was particularly true for S&P 500 Index funds in the mid-1980's, due to the large number of leveraged buyouts and takeovers.

In cases of hostile takeovers, the question is whether or not to tender to the hostile offer. To complicate matters even more, there may be competing offers for a company. These situations must be researched to determine the better offer. While there is no perfect formula, what appears to work is patience; tendering and re-tendering, if necessary, to the better offer, and not abstaining from the tendering process. Eventually, the successful bidder will become obvious. At times, it may appear that if you tender to one bidder and the second bidder has the same deadline, you would be left out if you chose the losing bid. This is usually not the case, though. What normally happens is that the winning bidder will then extend their deadline to allow all other stockholders to change their tender selection. So the best word of advice is to be patient and keep abreast of the changes in development. The custodial banks should alert the fund manager when a change in tender offers occurs or when a new decision is required.

Spin-Offs, Rights and Warrants

For the most part, spin-offs, rights and warrants are extra- corporate actions that affect portfolios when companies restructure. Normally, the portfolio can benefit from these issues by selling them. Spin-offs that are not in the Index must be sold off anyway, and exercising rights and warrants is of dubious value, requiring research into the companies and resulting in holding more shares of the companies than optimal. Thus, if one can generate additional revenue to the portfolio by selling these items, one should do so. As a reflection of the value of these rights and warrants, there are often no market bids for these issues.

Changes in the Index

Opportunities to add some value to an index fund can often arise when compositional changes are made to the Index. As was mentioned earlier, there is an impact on the market price of a stock when it is added to (or dropped from) a widely tracked index. This impact is caused by not only the index funds trading in the respective stock but also by others in the marketplace who trade 'ahead (i.e. "front-run") in anticipation of the increased activity in the stock. An index manager must recognize this fact and then determine if his fund can take advantage of this phenomenon.

In the case where index changes are made at a set time of the year and primarily under a measurable parameter, such as market capitalization, some market participants have tried to forecast what those changes will be. The purpose of this forecasting is to be able to position themselves early to take advantage of the expected pricing pressures that the multitudes of index funds will exert on the relevant stocks in order to effect the compositional changes.

In the case of the S&P Indexes, it is well known that there is a positive return effect on a stock's price when it is added to the S&P 500 because of the billions of dollars that are invested in S&P 500 Index funds. Similarly, there is a negative return impact for deletions from the S&P 500 index. A number of studies have been made on this phenomenon, which I like to refer to here as the "S&P inclusion effect." Studies have shown that for both additions and deletions, there is a significant effect on the stock price on the announcement date. Subsequently, there is also significant post-announcement price movement into the effective date of the change in the Index (i.e. the "inclusion date," the day of inclusion and deletion). Finally, there is also a significant price-reversal, in general, following the inclusion date.

Exhibit 2 illustrates an example of the relative return patterns for the S&P 500 inclusion effect for additions over the entire period spanning announcement to inclusion to post-inclusion. This graph clearly illustrates both the return increase after announcement, the peak in prices on inclusion date, and the drop-off in price after inclusion.

Several comments must be made. One is that the relative price pattern for deletions is very similar to that for additions, but only inverted. So going forward, we can speak in terms of additions only for simplicity's sake. A second observation is that the positive price return measured on announcement day is practically unattainable to fund managers. The prices tend to gap up at the open after announcement. Third, since the mid-1980's the S&P inclusion effect appears to have increased appreciably. There are probably several reasons for this including the increase in the amount of money invested in the S&P Indexes, the advent of the pre-announcement policy allowing for more speculation, and a greater awareness of the indexing substitution methodology.

Exhibit 2 S&P 500 Inclusion Effect (includes only additions with 5-day
pre-announcement period

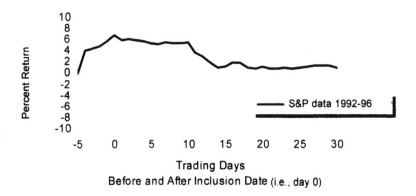

Trading Days
Before and After Inclusion Date (i.e., day 0)

Source: Goldman Sachs and Prudential Investments

The important issue is that the prices *are* affected, and what can an
indexer do? In general, an indexer is not a speculator, and he or she
should not try to forecast what the price of the stock will be when it does
go into the relevant index. Speculators make their living trying to buy the
stock as soon as they hear the news of its inclusion in an Index or once
they forecast that it'll be included. Likewise, market makers, if they
already own the stock, immediately mark-up its price. They are only
interested in getting the maximum profit out of a short-term demand for
a stock because of its inclusion in an index.

Indexers, on the other hand, are looking to buy the stock because they
need to own it in their fund to maintain performance with the relevant
index. However, because of the speculators and market makers, what they
now find is that the stocks that they want to buy have jumped in price.
The prevailing market price then effectively has some speculative premium built in, and the dilemma is, how long will this premium last? For
stocks added to an Index, like the S&P 500, part of the premium gained
after announcement will persist over time, but the speculative portion will
dissipate. Typically, when the market opens after an announcement of a
stock's inclusion in the S&P 500 Index, a premium is already put in place.

Generally, the premium will increase into the close on the day of the stocks' inclusion in the index, *but* (and herein lies the pitfall) sometimes it collapses just before the close.

The question is, when should an indexer buy? The most conservative answer is to merely buy at the inclusion day's close because that is the price at which the underlying Index is calculated. Yet, the close is *not* always the best time for an index fund, and particularly if one is interested in optimizing performance. First of all, if the stock is an over-the counter (OTC) stock, there is not really an official close price that a buyer (or seller) will be guaranteed to get. One would place an order with a market maker, and would have to pay the bid-ask spread on the stock. That is, a buyer will have to pay the offer price, and a seller will get the bid price. At best, the closing stock price might be the same as the price the indexer got for his or her order, but at worst, it will be unfavorable by the amount of the bid-ask spread. The latter situation can easily occur if the close was marked on an opposite order (bid or ask) after the indexer's trade.

This means that the index fund might have to pay an additional spread difference for all the OTC shares it bought at the close in order to maintain the same composition as the underlying Index. Thus, while the Index's performance was calculated at the "closing prices," the index fund buying at the close would have its performance reduced by having to pay commissions (on at least the listed issues) as well as, possibly, an additional spread on OTC issues. This is one explanation why it is difficult over time to even keep up with an Index's performance.

The second reason why simply buying at the close is not always the best decision is that there are often better alternatives with no additional risk. One such avenue is that brokers may offer to sell the stock for the Index inclusion to an index fund at a slight discount to the closing price and at slightly lower-than-normal commission. For example, if XYZ stock is going into the Index on day T, some brokers may offer to guarantee you the Index closing price (even if it's an OTC stock) minus an additional eighth or a quarter, at a penny per share commission for listed stocks. This is certainly more attractive than one having to do an agency trade market-on-close and paying a higher commission plus the possibility of the spread for an OTC stock.

There are a number of reasons why brokers can sometimes make such an offer. The reasons are the same ones that may lead an indexer to decide he or she should not always trade at the close for stock changes in the Index: i.e., there may be a speculative premium built into the price; the liquidity is inordinately thin for the stock; and that a large order could muscle the stock price going into close. If these factors exist for a particular stock, then a broker can provide the price guarantee because he already has a profit on hand and is sure he can control the closing price. Furthermore, the more orders that a broker can attract to be traded through his brokerage by this guarantee, the greater the profit the broker will make.

Knowing that some these conditions exists, an indexer can add value to his fund by deciding to trade non-conventionally. In a sense, an indexer can try to do the same analysis the aforementioned broker has done. Generally speaking, the key is the liquidity of the stock to be bought (or sold). Less liquid stocks tend to maintain their premium going into the close on the day of inclusion. If a stock has already increased in price quite a bit going into the day of inclusion, then there is less to be gained by trading in advance of the close. As a very rough rule of thumb, recent announcements of a stock's inclusion in the S&P 500 Index seem to add about a 4% immediate premium in price. There might then be a tradable additional premium of 3% to be gained. For example, one may consider trading ahead for some portion of the stock in question if it is very illiquid and a large quantity of stock must to be bought by index funds and the speculative premium resulting from the announcement of its inclusion is still relatively small.

Another alternative strategy one can undertake is to consider trading after the stock's inclusion in the Index, rather than only in advance of its inclusion or at the close on that day. The rational for this action is that the speculators will have left the stock after making their gains, and the speculative premium will be gone. One may be able to buy the new stock in the Index at a relatively lower prices by merely having the patience to wait a number of days. Obviously, there is an element of risk involved in terms of the funds' performance, because one is assuming stable or relatively higher stock prices of the other issues in the Index in order for this strategy to be successful.

Finally, it is clear that there is no one method that will always work. Rather, one has to examine the various circumstances for each inclusion in the Index; consider the alternatives and perhaps taking a multi-prong approach (e.g. spreading out the trading over time). While we have talked mainly about inclusion in the index, a similar analysis can be made for divesting those stocks leaving the index.

The inclusion effect is most acute for the S&P 500 and is not really an issue yet in the much smaller capitalization S&P 600 Index, despite the latter's overall lower individual stock liquidity. *The key factor then is the liquidity relative to the number of shares needed to be transacted.* In other words, the inclusion effect is a function of the dollar demand from the index funds required to purchase the security and the supply represented by that respective stock's liquidity.

Shares Outstanding Changes

Speaking of the S&P Indexes, aside from outright changes in their composition, there are also changes made, at times, to the constituent stocks' shares outstanding. When the change in the shares outstanding of a company alters the market value of that company, it affects the market value of the entire Index and the relative weighting of all the companies in the Index.

For example, corporate actions such as share issuance or share repurchase (i.e. "stock buy-back") would, respectively, increase or decrease a company's market value. On the other hand, shares outstanding changes resulting from stock splits and dividends would not affect the market value of a company.

Consequently, when an Index adjusts the shares outstanding of a company such that it affects its market value, there is a need to buy or sell stocks in order for a fund to remain replicated to the Index. These changes in shares outstanding then produce similar opportunities (though generally of lesser magnitude) to that of a company being added or dropped from the Index. Therefore, one can apply a similar analysis, as previously discussed, in determining how to maximize the fund's return relative to the Index when buying or selling the additional shares.

Securities Lending

Securities lending is an activity an equity fund may undertake to try to add some value to their returns. The fund can lend out its long position in equity securities to someone wanting to borrow the securities. In return, the borrower posts a certain amount of collateral, which generally exceeds the value of the borrowed securities (e.g., 102% of the market value of the lent security). In addition, the collateral is marked-to-market daily to maintain the slight premium. While the borrowers gets a certain rate of return on his or her collateral, it will be less than what the lender can earn on the collateral through his or her short-term interest fund (or STIF).

Securities lending has an appeal to clients—because who would refuse added revenue, at seemingly at "no risk?" However, as with other aspects of indexing, things are not as easy as they seem, and there are tradeoffs to be made in running a securities lending program.

First, the fund would have to have a securities lending program and operation in place. Depending on the nature of the investment management firm, one might have to set up such a program, and provide for human and material resources. Such an operation is expensive and therefore reduces the net proceeds from any securities lent.

Secondly, from my experience, the securities that are in demand to be borrowed generally tend to be targets of takeovers or tend to be in smaller capitalized issues. While securities of large-capitalization index funds, like those pegged to the S&P 500 Index, may at times be requested in securities lending, the demand is generally not high relative to the size of their float. For any given S&P 500 fund, the added return from having a securities lending program will probably be small to negligible, e.g., in the order of a magnitude of maybe one or two basis points of performance per annum.

The types of funds that have greater demand for its constituent stocks are the broad-based and extended funds, such as those based on the Wilshire 5000 Index, and the Russell 2000 and 3000 Indexes. Since in general the float of smaller capitalized stocks is less than its larger cap brethren, managers of such broad-based funds may be asked to have their entire position of a stock lent out. Hence, the added return to the portfolio may greater than in the aforementioned large-cap situation. This, however, may turn out to be a two-edged sword

The problem that securities lending may cause, particularly in smaller capitalization funds, is interference in terms of portfolio management. Securities that are borrowed for longer time periods tend to be for stocks that were sold short. These stocks could be on loan for an extended amount of time (I have seen cases of over a year). When an index portfolio manager re-balances a fund and decides to sell the lent securities, he or she may run into some difficulties. Sometimes the lent securities are very difficult to get back. It may take a month or more. The securities in question may have been, in turn, lent out again by the borrower. In the meantime, the index portfolio manager has a fund that is out-of-balance.

Other times, for some reason, the borrower would rather forego the collateral than return the stock. In this case, the securities lending people will have to go through time-consuming procedures to exercise a "buy-in," which means, purchasing the required security in the open market and then charging the borrower for the purchase.

Trading and Transaction Costs Management

It is in the implementation, particularly trading, where one can make or break an index fund. The frictional cost of trading is the main determinant on whether one can operate a successful index fund or not.

Obviously, there are numerous avenues of trading for an index fund in today's market. For example, one could trade in the underlying stocks, or in derivatives like stock index futures, options, and options on futures. One could trade in combinations of the two, such as in index arbitrage, or in swaps, or in exchange-for-physicals (EFPs). One can also ask a broker to do a "basis trade," where the client gets the stocks and the broker hedges himself with the derivatives.

Within stocks, one could do agency trades, principal trades, or some variations of the two on a negotiated, profit-sharing basis. Stocks can be worked individually, name by name, in small quantities, or as blocks. One can also trade programs or packages of stocks electronically via a broker or through a broker's DOT ("Designated Order Turnaround") box. These basket trades can be done in slices or "waves," or all at once. Program baskets can also be traded within the third market (i.e., direct with other institutions clearing through a broker) on various available crossing networks.

Obviously, the subject of trading and transaction costs is an extensive one, and a short chapter like this one cannot do justice to it. In general, to even try to match an underlying Index, one must minimize the level of transaction costs in all aspects of trading, starting with commissions, and, more importantly, with the market impact cost of buying and selling. I will next try to highlight some methods that can be used to reduce the transaction costs impact on a fund.

Stock Index Futures

Using Futures versus Cash Market

In managing an index fund, the more alternatives there are in executing one's strategy, the greater the opportunities there are to improve the results. This is especially true when an index fund has the capability to use stock index futures. In this context, I am talking about its use as just an adjunct to trading in stocks; and not to create a synthetic index fund using all futures (that is a topic for another time.)

Trading in stock index futures can provide a number of advantages. One of the main advantages is the relatively low transaction costs. In measuring transaction costs, one could take into account the commission cost and the market impact of trading a stock or a future. Exhibit 3 shows the estimated, one-way transaction costs for various size stock baskets. These numbers may even be aggressive (i.e., low) because they assume that one only has to pay one-half the bid/ask spread. Alternatively, if one were to execute in futures, the rule of thumb is that it would only cost approximately one-tenth the transaction costs of trading in stocks.

Exhibit 3 Estimated One-Way Transaction Costs For Various Stock Baskets (all costs shown in basis points)

	Comm.*	50% of B/A Spread	Price Concess.**	Total
S&P 500				
$5 MM	5.7	15.0	0.0	20.7
$25 MM	5.7	15.0	0.0	20.7
$50 MM	5.7	15.0	4.5	25.1
$100 MM	5.7	15.0	9.0	29.6
$250 MM	5.7	15.0	20.9	41.6
S&P MidCap				
$5 MM	9.9	30.0	0.0	39.9
$25 MM	9.9	30.0	0.0	39.9
$50 MM	9.9	30.0	12.0	51.8
$100 MM	9.9	30.0	24.0	63.8
$250 MM	9.9	30.0	47.9	87.8
Russell 1000				
$5 MM	6.2	16.3	0.0	22.5
$25 MM	6.2	16.3	0.0	22.5
$50 MM	6.2	16.3	5.4	27.8
$100 MM	6.2	16.3	10.7	33.2
$250 MM	6.2	16.3	25.0	47.5
Russell 2000				
$5 MM	15.0	65.5	0.0	80.5
$25 MM	15.0	65.5	0.0	80.5
$50 MM	15.0	65.6	32.7	113.2
$100 MM	15.0	65.5	58.9	139.4
$250 MM	15.0	65.5	111.3	191.7

* assumes $0.03/share commission cost
**assumes the basket is traded over a maximum of 1 day
Source: PaineWebber, Inc.

For example, using pre-November 1997 contract data, the institutional commission cost of futures trading is about $20 per contract, round trip.[1] This would be half a basis point on a market value of $400,000 for the S&P 500 Index future contract (i.e., using a futures price of 800). Add to this a 10-cent spread as the market impact to execute the futures contract. So, in total, we are looking at 1.75 basis points to transact $5 to $10 million in futures compared to the 20.7 basis points to transact in stocks. Of course, as with the stock example, the greater the dollar value of futures to transact, the greater the potential market impact portion of the transactions costs. But in general, the point is that the expected transaction costs are less using futures.

Another advantage of using futures is the perfect replication of the Index that one can buy with just one contract. The assumption here is that there exists an index futures contract based on the benchmark index (e.g., S&P 500 Index futures for an S&P 500 fund). For example, if the S&P 500 Index future is currently at a value of 800, then for $400,000 (i.e., 800 x the $500 multiplier per contract), one can get coverage for the entire S&P 500 Index. This would not be possible if one had to transact in stocks for the same amount of money. One certainly could not buy exact proportions of 500 different stocks with $400,000, even using *odd lot* trades. One would need approximately $25 million to fully replicate the S&P 500 Index if one wanted to transact in stocks using round lots (i.e., 100 shares minimum).

The Futures Roll

In addition to the benefits of having futures positions in one's fund, one can also think about maximizing return when it comes to the Index futures' quarterly expiration. The straightforward approach is to let the futures position expire upon the expiration date and buy the requisite amount of stock. This approach is especially favorable if the futures contracts were previously purchased during the quarter at a discount below fair value. Hence, one can lock in the added-value gain.

However, another alternative would be to "roll" the futures position forward to the next expiration period or beyond. The advantage of doing so would be that one retains the flexibility of the use of the futures for such matters as fund withdrawals. In addition, the opportunity to roll

---

[1] In November of 1997, the S&P 500 Index futures contract split its multiplier in half, from 500 to 250. Consequently, the institutional commission cost of futures trading may also change. The specific numbers of these examples may change, but not the advantages of using futures.

futures might provide some additional pick-up in return if the calendar spread (i.e., the price difference between contracts of different expirations) is trading cheaper than fair value. It is important then that the portfolio manager knows what the fair value criterion is for his or her futures contracts.

Opportunities to roll the futures cheaply may depend on a number of factors, including: the quarter of expiration (e.g., March or December), the number of days to expiration, the direction of interest rates and the stock market, and the level of open interest in the expiring contract.

I have found that most Indexers tend not to roll their futures position forward beyond the December expiration, thus putting less pressure on buying the calendar spread during this time (i.e., to "buy the spread" in this case would mean buying the forward quarterly contract while selling the nearby contract). The reason is probably twofold: 1) year-end window dressing and 2) avoidance of the possibility of futures closing cheap to fair value at the year-end mark-to-market (and thus, the fund incurring a negative tracking divergence due to the negative margin variance).

Waiting until the last few days, and particularly the last day before expiration, to try to roll your futures forward using the spread market can be extremely treacherous. I would recommend finishing your futures "roll" trading before this time period to avoid being squeezed. The spread can be very illiquid on the last day.

Normally, one can find good guidance about whether the futures spread will trade cheap or rich leading into expiration from a number of brokers. This is especially true of those brokers who have extensive contacts with derivative players such as hedge funds, asset allocators, and index funds.

Structuring the Fund to Capture Cost

Capital Inflows and Outflows

Funds would normally welcome additional capital inflows while discouraging outflows from the fund. Index funds, though, are slightly different in that any capital flows (in or out) can be a source of consternation. The reason for this is that index funds are judged by their ability to produce Index-matching returns. However, capital flows require trading, and trading produces transaction costs, and transaction costs reduce returns. The less an index fund has to trade, the better its chances of at least matching the underlying Index.

There are a number of *structural approaches* taken by index funds to deal with the cost impact of capital flows. These approaches include:

charging a fixed-dollar fee for each capital flow; limiting the number of flows allowed over a given period; not allowing telephone transfer and requiring only mail requested transfers; and charging a transactions fee based on the cost incurred by the fund to invest or divest the capital flow. Naturally, the method used could also entail a combination of the above-mentioned approaches, as well as others, including waiving any fees except in the most extreme cases.

The main purpose of these different approaches is to help an index fund perform the way it is advertised to perform.

If a transactions charge is imposed by the fund, these fees are put back into the fund as income to bolster performance and make up for any loss due to transacting for the capital flows. By limiting the number of openings to a fund, the fund reduces the number of times it has to trade, while aggregating and netting inflow with outflows, thereby reducing trading costs.

While a fixed- dollar fee is most common in mutual funds where the capital flows tend to be relatively small, a very interesting structural technique called a "buffer account" is used principally in commingled (i.e., involving multiple participants sharing) institutional index funds. A buffer account can be a physically distinct account or it can be an accounting artifice serving the same purpose.

To Buffer or Not to Buffer

Accounting-wise, *the purpose of the buffer-account is to isolate and identify the transaction costs associated with trading a particular capital flow.* Once these costs are identified, they can be charged back directly to the parties initiating the capital flow.

If a physically distinct buffer account is used to trade and settle the stocks, then the cost of the trades will be embedded in the market value of that account. Illustrating an example of a capital inflow: a client's money goes into the buffer, stocks are purchased in the buffer and are then transferred in-kind into the index fund at the closing prices of the day. Whether the transaction costs are, high or low, they are incorporated in the market value of the buffer: if the transaction costs were high, then the client buys less "units" (i.e., shares) of the index fund; and if the costs were low, they would buy relatively more "units."

If the accounting buffer artifice is used rather than a physically distinct account, then one must keep track of the execution prices and calculate the transaction costs relative to the closing price. In this case, the stocks are traded and settled in the index account itself. So one must do a little more work by assiduously accounting for the costs generated by trading the capital flow as well as determining what the Index fund's unit price is without these trades. Once that is determined, one can calculate the number of units bought by the client's capital flow. In this manner, the transaction costs generated by the trades are borne solely by the client whose capital flow initiated the trade.

Thus, in both methods of "buffering" the capital flows, the actual transaction costs are captured and only those clients whose flow initiated the trades, pay for the trades. The other participants in the commingled account are shielded from these costs. This is the essence of the argument for using a buffer, and it is a strong one because it appeals to the clients' sense of self-interest or "fairness," particularly if they are not the clients initiating the capital flows. From an index fund's' perspective, the advantage of this methodology is that the performance is not burdened by any of these transaction costs generated. So these funds can show performance figures that eliminate much of the normal costs of trading because these costs are passed on to the clients.

Why would any index fund not use a buffer? The answers are more subtle, but basically the use of a buffer can limit the flexibility of the index fund to possibly do better for the client. Most definitely, the lack of not having a buffer system puts more of an onus on the skill of the index manager to provide value to the portfolio in order to make up for the transaction costs absorbed directly by the fund.

The debate is not as simple or straight-forward as it may seem. One could spend a lot of time evaluating the question, so let's just examine some of the possible drawbacks of using a buffer.

When the transaction costs are passed on to the client through a buffer mechanism, one assumes that the client will examine those costs. Hence, the least-risk trading alternative for an index manager operating under this system is to trade at or very near the market close. The reason is because the client is receiving that day's units of the fund, and the fund and its benchmark Index are valued at the closing prices. Closing prices are an easily identified standard of comparison, and the index manager probably does not want to be faulted for not getting the prices at which the Index's securities are marked.

Unfortunately, for very large amounts of capital flows, effectuating the trade at one point in time (like the market close), can materially influence stock prices. Forcing all the trades at the close will adversely affect the resultant market value of the stocks traded. This in turn may reduce the number of units the client can buy into the fund or the dollar amount he or she can receive if it's a requested withdrawal. So, while the flows were invested at or near the market close prices for the Index, the client may have done better if the trades were worked over a period of time so as not to influence the market closing prices.

Let's consider an example. Assume a client wishes to withdraw a large amount of money. If a buffer is used, then in order to capture the transaction costs of the trades generated, the trades will most likely be done on the close, for reasons previously noted. However, the large amount of stocks sold at the close to raise cash for the withdrawal may cause the prices of those stocks to fall substantially, depending on the stocks' liquidity. Thus, the market value of the index fund falls for that day due to the lower market close prices. The client will get the cash value of his or her units, which is based on the fund's closing market value, which has fallen. In fact, the client will get less dollars for the liquidated shares of the fund than probably would have been the case if the trades didn't force down prices at the close.

This is just a basic example; and there are many varying factors that could affect the result, such as whether one is buying a fully replicated basket or a subset of the fund and whether the stocks are listed or OTC. Nevertheless, one can see that from a client's point of view there may be times the client would benefit if the fund didn't buffer its transaction costs. If there were no transaction charge-back to the client for capital movement, then the client wouldn't have to pay a cost to invest or divest and thus retains more of his or her assets. The client's costs are shared in the commingled fund, which may or may not be advantageous, depending on who is initiating the flows. However, if an index manager can produced good index performance without the benefit of a buffer, then a client has the best of both worlds—good index performance and no additional charges for capital flows. However, this is easier said than done.

In general, having the ability to pass on the transactions costs will help the index by reducing a source of drag on performance. So to buffer is a good thing; however, the caveat is that the buffering or transaction costs capturing mechanism should allow for trading flexibility. Trading flexibility (e.g., as to choice of using stocks or derivatives, and ability to work the trade) can be used to help the client and increase the value of the index fund. The real question may not be to buffer or not, but rather, can the structural mechanism of buffering trades be made flexible enough to suit the best interests of the fund and the client?

Remember: The greater the trading flexibility one has, the greater the opportunities there are to reduce market impact and lower transaction costs.

Trading Style

Trading Intra-day or At-the-Close

Earlier, I had discussed some of the possible disadvantages of trading market-on-close. While from a job risk perspective, it may seem that trading at the close is a lower risk strategy, I believe that capable index portfolio managers should do what is best for their clients and for fund performance. Therefore, depending on the size of the trade, the liquidity of the stock, and the availability of matching the other side of the trade, one must consider trading intra-day. Simply trading at market-on-close prices will *always* leave one behind the benchmark Index because of commissions and the OTC stock spreads.

Using Limit Prices

By trading intra-day, there is the possibility of avoiding the cost of the bid-ask spread on stocks. This is done by using limit prices when trading. An index fund can try to get paid for providing liquidity by offering the stocks it has to sell at the prevailing "ask" price. Similarly, the fund can passively try to buy its stock at the prevailing "bid" prices. The cost of the bid-ask spread is much more significant than the commission cost associated with the trade.

Obviously, though, by trading intra-day, one is opening the fund up to some market risk if the market moves too much in one direction. One can hedge against this, in part, by continually monitoring the trades and the stock market, and adjusting the fund using futures or the volume of the stocks traded to maintain a fully invested position. The trader should try to capture small, incremental gains whenever possible. One must strive to help the fund's' performance by adding gains (or reducing cost) a little bit at a time. There is no easy way to do it.

Crossing Trades

Another trading alternative that should be considered by index funds involve the various "crossing networks.". These are facilities, generally set up by brokers, to match trades between parties (i.e., institutions) outside of the listed exchanges and OTC market-makers. Technically speaking, these crossing networks are considered the "third market." The brokers provide the clearing of the trades. For this service, the trades are charged a commission, but usually much less (e.g., a penny per share for 2,000 shares or more) than that charged by regular "street" brokers.

In these "crossing network" trades, the essential concept is similar to the one that was mentioned before in trading passively using limit prices: to avoid paying at least part of the bid-ask spread and to do so without influencing the prices (i.e., to reduce market impact). Generally, the clearing price of the intra-day trades between the two participants is the midpoint between the bid-ask spread. For the after-hours trades, the market close price is used.

In trading through these networks, there are issues that the index manager still must make decisions on. One of these is, what does one do with the stocks that weren't matched on the networks (these are often referred to as the "residual shares")? Another decision to be made is, when is the best time to execute trades using the various "crossing" networks? One will find that there are certain special opportunistic times to trade with a particular crossing system. The attractiveness of each crossing network depends on the overall participation on that network and whether the inventory available on that network matches yours.

These crossing facilities have became popular in the latter half of the 1980's. Currently, there are a handful of them in the business.

Time Is an Ally

One final point to make in the area of trading is a very general one and, as a result, there are always exceptions and possible differing views. My opinion is that in index trading, one should view time as an ally to accomplish one's trading needs. Of course, no single factor is always to be used unwavering, but in general the ability to "work" a trade over time can be beneficial in minimizing the market impact.

In theory this is so because for an index fund, the stocks that one buys or sells are primarily determined by the results of a quantitative re-balancing rather than on some fundamentals analysis or news information that will supposedly move the stock. Thus, one is not necessarily incurring an opportunity loss by prolonging the trading window. In fact, one may save transactions costs for the fund and/or client by not forcing the trades into the market place.

Corroborating evidence to support the opinion that time in general can help save costs can be seen in Exhibit 4, which shows how one broker/dealer calculated the trading cost estimates for a basket of stocks as a function of the number of days-to-trade. As is noticeable, the less the urgency to transact, the lower the effective cost. This is especially true for the less liquid, smaller capitalization stocks for which these numbers were calculated. Of course, there are simplifying assumptions made here and there may be some opportunity costs if the market moves against the direction of the trade. Nevertheless, the main point is that the *greater the immediacy of the trade, the greater the cost.*

Exhibit 4 Trading Cost Estimates As A Function Of Number Of
Days-To-Trade

Buying Stock Transaction's Cost Per Shares($)*		Selling Stock Transaction's Cost Per Shares ($)*	
1 day	0.279	1 day	0.390
2 days	0.211	2 days	0.292
3 days	0.187	3 days	0.254
4 days	0.165	4 days	0.223
5 days	0.159	5 days	0.214
6 days	0.150	6 days	0.201
7 days	0.131	7 days	0.172
8 days	0.123	8 days	0.160
9 days	0.109	9 days	0.141
10 days	0.102	10 days	0.130

*Transaction cost per share stated as an equivalent commission cost.
Source: Goldman Sachs

Putting It All Together to Maximize Return

Finally, let's see if one can bring everything discussed together into a strategy for managing index funds in order to maximize total return. I have reviewed many of the possible tools that an index manager may use in the quest to optimize return, but utilizing all these disparate tools can be confusing unless there is an overall philosophy of and operating strategy for the management of an index fund.

Philosophy

Maximizing index fund returns is not a passive exercise. This should be the overall philosophy of index management if one wants to achieve excellent index returns. Clearly, an index manager must make many decisions. The greater the flexibility he or she has to make those decisions, the greater the opportunity the fund has to perform better. While the objective of an index fund to replicate returns may sound simple, I believe that it is impossible to structure (i.e., automate) any fund to per-form optimally in all circumstances. Thus, how an index manager exer-cises his role is vital to the fund's performance.

It is ironic, then, that while an index manager's role may be relative-ly invisible to those outside the fund, his or her impact on a fund is very obvious because the fund's relative performance is so easily gauged.

Operating Strategy

The operating strategy that I have used to accomplish the goal of maxi-mizing the index fund's return is to: *minimize negative tracking variance but allow for positive tracking variance when it occurs.* Positive tracking variance is out-performance, which benefits the fund's clients. Negative tracking variance, on the other hand, is under-performance. To achieve the best possible return to the fund using an index strategy, try to focus on reducing only negative tracking error.

Using the tools and techniques previously discussed, one can imple-ment this operating strategy. An index fund over time will have tracking variance (or error). Some of this tracking error is unbiased in direction, but some is biased, like that due to transaction costs, which produce only negative tracking error.

When a fund has positive tracking variance, from whatever source, I would recommend that the portfolio manager not be too quick to reduce it. For example, for a broad-based index fund holding only a subset of the benchmark universe of stocks, it is not unexpected that there will be peri-od of material over-performance. This is due to holding less than 100% of the benchmark's holdings (i.e., sampling is used). Likewise, even for an Index that one can perfectly replicate, like the S&P 500 Index, there will be times, due to additions and deletions, or shares outstanding changes, or spin-offs, that an imperfect replication arises. If this results in positive tracking error, I would suggest that one try to capture that posi-tive gain before it reverses.

To operate in such a manner, one must be diligent in continually mon-itoring the fund's relative performance. Through solid decision making in areas that were elaborated on, such as corporate actions, the portfolio manager can also provide some positive value-added to the fund's return.

The portfolio manager should endeavor to reduce the level of the neg-ative tracking error, biased or unbiased, with the help of the aforemen-tioned tools. Negative tracking error will undoubtedly occur in any real portfolio. Yet by using a strategy that allows for *positive variance to be accepted* over time, this will provide a cushion against future under-performance and permit one' to maximize fund returns while using an index strategy.

Appendix

The Wilshire Indexes

These are the indexes that are created by Wilshire Associates Incorporated. The two major Indexes created by Wilshire Associates Incorporated are the Wilshire 5000 and Wilshire 4500 Equity Index. These index names are really misnomers, since there are more than 5,000 securities in the Wilshire 5000 and more than 4,500 securities in the Wilshire 4500. Currently, there are over 7,000 securities represented in the Wilshire 5000, and more than 6,500 equity securities in the Wilshire 4500 Index. By definition, the Wilshire 4500 Equity Index is the Wilshire 5000 Index with the 500 securities of the S&P 500 Index securities excluded.

The Wilshire 5000 was christened back in the 1974, when Wilshire Associates first started its Index and when there were, in fact, approximately 5,000 securities in their definition of the U.S. stock market. Officially, the Wilshire 5000 Equity Index is defined as an index that measures the performance of all U.S. headquartered equity securities with readily available price data. Thus, it excludes companies like Royal Dutch, which although traded in the U.S., is not a U.S. headquartered company.

The Wilshire 5000 Index is valued daily, and there are certain details to its valuation that are not widely known. The Wilshire 5000 is a dynamic universe that on any given day will increase or decrease in size depending on certain guidelines. Over time, there have been changes to some of their valuation rules. The following guidelines were implemented on July 1, 1996:

- Additions to the Index will be implemented once a month after the month-end close. Wilshire Associates plan to release a list of the planned additions two business days before month-end.

- Issues spun-off from Index members will be added to the Index as soon as prudently possible.

- A security will be excluded from the Index on the day it does not price but, may reenter when it resumes pricing.

- Bulletin board issues are excluded on by the assumption that they do not have consistently readily available prices.

- Initial public offerings (IPOs) will generally be added at the end of the month (provided they have a "good" shares outstanding value).

Related to the issue of valuation and returns reported for the Wilshire Indexes, there is another interesting fact. As with the S&P 500 Index, the Wilshire 5000 Index value is reported daily in newspapers and wire services. However, whereas the S&P 500 uses primary market close prices to value itself on a timely manner for inclusion in the next day's news publications, the Wilshire 5000 Index uses a different methodology. In order to have a value and a price change for the Wilshire 5000 Index to be included in next day's papers, the Index calculates its daily price change by using a weighted average of the change of certain Index subgroups. For example, the Wilshire 5000 Index's capitalization was composed of approximately 81% NYSE, 2% AMEX, and 17% OTC stocks. The daily price change for the Wilshire 5000 Index is then calculated using a formula of taking 81% of the NYSE Composite price change plus 2% of the AMEX Composite price change and 17% of the NASDAQ Composite price change. Thus, unlike the S&P 500 Index, the daily Wilshire 5000 Index price change is not calculated using the aggregate of the individual underlying securities' closing prices.

However, the Wilshire 5000 Index does subsequently use the individual securities' *consolidated composite closing prices* to value their index for total return purposes. Wilshire also factors in dividend income on an ex-dividend basis. So, although the daily price return reported is of a less precise nature, the total return is precise using individual security prices.

The Licensing of Financial Indexes: Implications for the Development of New Index-Linked Investment Products

James A. Overdahl
Risk Analysis Division
Office of the Comptroller of the Currency

The author acknowledges helpful discussions with Albert Neubert, Gary Myers, Tom Gira, and George Wilder. The views expressed herein are those of the author only and do not necessarily reflect the views of the Office of the Comptroller of the Currency.

Introduction

The ever-increasing popularity of index investing has made the business of creating and maintaining financial indexes a valuable enterprise for index producers like the Standard & Poor's Corporation (S&P). Ultimately, the underlying source of value for index producers resides in their claim that financial indexes possess certain property attributes afforded protection under various state and federal laws. As a result, index producers have the power to authorize the terms by which other parties may use their indexes and to collect licensing fees from these parties. For example, S&P has negotiated a license with the Chicago Mercantile Exchange (CME) granting it exclusive rights to trade a futures contract based on the S&P 500 index.

At the same time, index producers have vigorously protected their indexes from unauthorized use. For example, in 1982 S&P sued to prevent the Commodity Exchange, Inc. (Comex) from trading a futures contract based on an index essentially identical to the S&P 500 index.[1] In this case, S&P's claim that its property rights to the S&P 500 index had been misappropriated by Comex was recognized. In a similar case, Dow Jones & Company (Dow Jones) sued to prevent the Chicago Board of Trade (CBT) from trading a futures contract based on an index identical to the Dow Jones Industrial Average.[2]

The primary purpose of this chapter is to describe the types of licensing and property issues existing between producers and users of financial indexes. Such a description is essential to a book on index investing because of the way these issues affect the development of new, index-linked financial products by investment companies, insurance companies, financial exchanges, commercial banks, issuers of structured notes, and dealers of privately negotiated derivatives.

This chapter is addressed to four audiences. The first audience consists of investment industry practitioners who must cope with licensing and property issues in developing new, index-linked products and in obtaining index-related information. The second audience consists of attorneys, who will find that the legal cases involving financial indexes pose particularly challenging questions about intellectual property law. The third audience consists of economists, who will find that the particular property rights questions raised in the context of financial-index licensing disputes pose more general economic questions about the function of markets, the discovery of prices, and the nature of competition. Finally, the fourth audience consists of financial market regulators who, it is hoped, through a more explicit awareness of the property characteristics of financial indexes, can more carefully consider regulatory actions that may trigger licensing disputes between index producers and regulated entities who are developing new, index-linked investment products.

The remainder of this chapter is arranged as follows. The general terms of licensing arrangements used by index producers to authorize the use of their indexes by other parties are described first. The next section

---

[1] *Standard & Poor's Corporation vs. Commodity Exchange, Inc.,* 538 F. Supp. 1063 (S.D.N.Y. 1982); *Standard & Poor's Corporation, Inc. vs. Commodity Exchange, Inc.,* 683 F.2d 704 (2d Cir. 1982).

[2] *Dow Jones & Company, Inc. vs. Board of Trade of the City of Chicago,* 546 F.Supp. 113 (1982); *Board of Trade of the City of Chicago vs. Dow Jones & Company, Inc.,* 439 N.E. 2d 526 (Ill. App. 1982); *Board of Trade of the City of Chicago vs. Dow Jones & Company, Inc.,* 456 N.E. 2d 84 (Ill. 1983).

describes the evolution of state and federal law concerning intellectual property claims to financial indexes and related financial information. Then, the current scope of property protection afforded to index producers by state and federal courts is examined. This section includes a discussion of how recent developments in the law concerning copyright and the application of misappropriation theory may impact the property rights of index producers.[3] Conclusions complete the chapter.

Licensing Agreements Between Index Producers and Developers of Index-Linked Products

The ability of index producers to restrict the use of their indexes through licensing arrangements is rooted in their claim that financial indexes possess certain property attributes afforded protection under various state and federal laws. By enforcing property restrictions on the use of their indexes, index producers seek to protect two valuable things: their effort and their reputation. In the first instance, the effort expended on creating and maintaining financial indexes includes such things as the research conducted to select index components, along with their relative weights, and other so-called "sweat-of-the-brow" investments. For example, S&P employs a staff of analysts to determine the best candidate components for inclusion in its various indexes. In the second instance, the reputation of the index producer is a valuable asset that can potentially be harmed by the actions of other parties using the index name. For example, in the early 1980s, because Dow Jones feared that its association with a futures contract based on the Dow Jones Industrial Average would harm its reputation in its news gathering business, it refused to authorize the use of the average for futures trading even though a considerable sum of money was offered.[4]

To protect their effort and reputation, index producers restrict the use of their indexes to those who have authorization. The terms of authorized use is contained in the licensing agreement between the index producer and index users. Licensing agreements include a variety of terms about contract length, scope of exclusivity, frequency of updates, reputational

---

[3] See *Feist Publications, Inc. vs. Rural Telephone Service Co.*, 111 S. Ct. 1282 (1991), on the limits of copyright protection to information works and the American Law Institute's Restatement *(Third) on Unfair Competition* (1993) for its recommendations on limiting the applicability of misappropriation theory as a means of protecting intellectual property.

[4] 546F. Supp., *supra* note 2 at 121, fn 8.

effects, errors and omissions, and conditions of termination. Many of the details of these licensing agreements are considered proprietary but the general terms are known from public sources.

In general, index producers exercise control over the use of their indexes through a permission review system; i.e., requests for the use of the index are screened by the index producer to determine whether such use is permissible and, if permissible, the amount of the licensing fee. The primary criterion for deciding whether or not to allow such use is how the use will affect the index producer's reputation.

Typical terms in licensing agreements include clauses giving either party the right to terminate the agreement if material damage or harm is occurring or likely to occur to the reputation or goodwill of either party. Typically, the index producer will reserve the right to review and approve all prospectuses, registration statements, advertisements, brochures, and other promotional materials related to the licensee's product that in any way refer to the indexes of the index producer. Also specified are the conditions under which the index producer may cease the compilation and publication of the index.

These terms include an acknowledgment by the licensee that the index trademarks are the exclusive property of the index producer and that the index producer owns the rights in and to the index and the proprietary data contained within the index (e.g., the weights and selection of index components). The licensee also agrees to print a proprietary notice in all informational materials acknowledging the index producer's proprietary rights and disclosing that their use was obtained by license.

A typical agreement includes specifics about the frequency at which the index will be calculated and disseminated to the licensee. The frequency specified in S&P contracts, for example, is at least once every 15 seconds. The license also contains an exculpatory clause specifying that the index producer does not guarantee the accuracy or completeness of the index or the data therein. The license also specifies the jurisdiction where disputes will be settled. Finally, the license specifies the amount of the licensing fees to be paid to the index producer.

Index producers will not require licenses for all uses of their indexes. For example, using a stock market index for performance comparison in a company's annual report would not require a license. Generally, the rule of thumb is that any time the index user receives value from using the index producer's name in a commercial application, it will be necessary for the user to obtain a license authorizing the index's intended use.

Licenses Between Index Producers and Index Funds

Index funds license for the right to use the index as the basis of their port-folio and to use the index name in promotional material. For example, the Vanguard Group, Inc., licenses with S&P for the right to market its Index Trust 500 mutual fund based on the S&P 500 index. Another example includes Nomura Corporation Asset Management, Inc., which licenses with the National Association of Securities Dealers (NASD) for the right to market a mutual fund based upon the NASDAQ 100.

Licensing terms for mutual funds are generally not exclusive. A typical licensing fee for a mutual fund specifies a minimum amount plus a variable amount based on a percentage of the average daily net assets of the fund, computed periodically. The fee schedule may also specify a maximum annual amount.

Index funds held in unit trusts will also require a license from the index producer if the fund is used for commercial purposes. For example, S&P licenses the American Stock Exchange (AMEX) to create a long-term unit, equity-basket investment trust which accumulates and holds a portfolio of common stocks intended to track the price performance and dividend yield of the S&P 500 index. Shares from this trust, called the SPDR Trust (for Standard & Poor's Depository Receipts), are then trad-ed like shares of stock. AMEX also licenses for the use of other indexes which serve as the basis for long-term unit investment trusts, including a portfolio of stocks designed to track the S&P MidCap 400 index and another designed to track the Dow Jones Industrial Average.

Licenses Between Index Producers and Insurance Companies

Insurance companies offer a variety of index-linked annuity products that are marketed as investment products for qualified defined benefit pension plans and defined contribution pension plans. Examples of such products include the Enhanced Bond Index Fund offered by Pacific Mutual Life Insurance Company; the Index 500 Plus product offered by CNA; the KeyIndex and KeySelect products offered by Keyport Life Insurance Company; the ELI Deferred Annuity, the ELI 500 Index Option, and the ELI 500 Immediate Annuity products offered by Jackson National Life Insurance Company; and the Vista 500 Market Index Annuity offered by Physicians Life Insurance Company. All of these products have returns linked to the S&P 500. In addition, CNA offers a group annuity product, the Commodity Index Annuity Contract, whose return is linked to the Goldman Sachs Commodity Index. The promotional literature for each of these insurance products indicates that a licensing agreement exists between the insurance company and the index producer for the use of the index producer's trademarks and service marks.

Licenses Between Index Producers and Financial Exchanges

Financial exchanges have developed a number of index-linked products requiring licensed authorization from index producers. In general, licenses with financial exchanges are exclusive, because both index producers and futures exchanges perceive advantages to avoiding market fragmentation. Financial exchanges compete with each other for the exclusive right to trade index-linked products for a set period of time, normally 5 to 10 years. The meaning of the term "exclusivity" can vary across licensing agreements: It may refer to worldwide exclusivity, or it may refer to more limited exclusivity, such as across a set of time zones or across a continent. Typically, licensing fees are based on trading volume, e.g., $.10 per contract traded.

Bloomberg L.P. reports more than 150 exchange-traded index-linked futures, futures options, and spot options contracts traded worldwide as of March 1997. The volume leader in index-linked futures and futures options trading is the CME, which trades contracts written on the S&P 500, the S&P MidCap 400, the S&P 500/BARRA Growth Index, the S&P 500/BARRA Value Index, the Nikkei Stock Index, the Goldman Sachs Commodity Index, the FT-SE 100 Share Index, the NASDAQ 100, the Dow Jones Taiwan Index, the Russell 2000, the Índice de Precios y Cotizaciones, and the Major Market Index. The CME licenses for the rights to use each of these indexes as the basis for its futures and futures options contracts.

Financial exchanges are also producers of indexes. For example, the AMEX, the New York Stock Exchange (NYSE), and the CME have each constructed their own indexes. The AMEX trades instruments based on its own indexes as well instruments based on indexes of others it is licensed to use. For example, AMEX has developed sector indexes, such as the Tobacco Index, the Pharmaceutical Index, the Internet Index (the @Net Index, developed jointly by the AMEX and Inter@tive Week Enterprises), and the de Jager Year 2000 Index (developed jointly by the AMEX and de Jager & Company, Ltd.). The exchange also has a proprietary interest in many other indexes, including international indexes like the AMEX Hong Kong 30 Index. At the same time AMEX licenses with S&P for the rights to trade the previously mentioned SPDRs and MidCap SPDRs. AMEX also licenses with the European Options Exchange for the rights to use the name "Eurotop 100 Index" and with Morgan Stanley for the Morgan Stanley Consumer Index and the Morgan Stanley Cyclical Index. A complete listing of AMEX index-linked products can be found at http://www.amex.com/options/intro.htm#hong.

Futures exchanges like the CME and CBT have become increasingly interested in commodity indexes as a means to facilitate cash settlement of commodity futures and futures options contracts. In 1997 the CME switched from physical delivery to cash settlement (based on an index) for several of its livestock contracts. This switch occurred in response to concerns of government regulators and commercial users of commodity futures about the process of physical delivery. The new interest in cash settlement of commodity futures contracts has provided new opportunities to the futures exchanges to create and license commodity indexes.[5]

Index warrants are exchange-traded products which also require a licensing agreement between the index producer and the exchange. Some index warrants approved for trading in the United States include the Nikkei 225 Stock Average (a trademark and service mark of Nihon Kezai Shimbun, a major Japanese newspaper), the FT-SE 100 (a trademark and service mark of The Financial Times Limited and the London Stock Exchange), the CAC-40 (a registered trademark of the Société des Bourses Francaises SA), the Eurotop 100 Index (a registered trademark of the European Options Exchange), and the Japan Index (a service mark of the AMEX).

In the late 1980s, the AMEX, the Philadelphia Stock Exchange, and the Chicago Board Options Exchange (CBOE) each attempted to trade an index product called an Index Participation, or IP. An index participation is a generic name for a perpetual, zero net supply contract entitling the buyer (the long) to receive quarterly from the seller (the short) dividends equal in amount to those paid to an underlying index portfolio. In addition, once per quarter, long-holders would have the right to cash-out based on a price equal to the value of the underlying portfolio. In 1989 the Chicago futures exchanges and the Investment Company Institute sued the Securities and Exchange Commission (SEC), claiming that IPs were merely poorly disguised stock index futures contracts and should not have been approved by the SEC.[6] Although the primary issue in this case was the allocation of regulatory jurisdiction between the SEC and the Commodity Futures Trading Commission (CFTC), a licensing issue

---

5 See "More Contracts Are Settled Through Cash," *The Wall Street Journal,* April 7. 1997 p. C7.

6 *Chicago Mercantile Exchange. Board of Trade of the City of Chicago, and Investment Company Institute vs. Securities and Exchange Commission.* 883 F.2d 537 (7th Cir. 1989).

did arise because of the CME's exclusive license with S&P to trade S&P 500 futures. A logical inference from the claims in the Chicago exchanges' lawsuit was that the trading of IPs based on the S&P 500 undermined the exclusive rights for which the CME had previously contracted.

Licenses Between Index Producers and Commercial Banks

Commercial banks offer a variety of index-linked products that may require a license from the index producer. One product is the index-linked certificate of deposit (CD), where the interest payable on a CD depends on the return on a specified index over some period of time. Also, bank mutual funds may be marketed as index-linked. Equity-index-linked CDs have been offered by Citicorp, Chase, Bankers Trust, Charter One, Shawmut, NationsBank, Republic Bank of New York, Bank of America, and other banking institutions.[7]

Bank CDs may be linked to indexes other than stock indexes. For example, College Savings Bank in Princeton, New Jersey offers the College CD, whose interest rate is based on a copyrighted formula used to compute a tuition index for the nation's 500 largest private colleges.

Licenses Between Index Producers and Issuers of Structured Notes

Issuers of index-linked structured notes must license for the use of the index. Structured notes based on proprietary indexes fall into four categories. The first group includes contracts written on commodity indexes. Commodity indexes potentially available for license include the Knight-Ridder/Commodity Research Bureau Index, the Goldman Sachs Commodity Index, the Merrill Lynch Energy and Metals Index, the Bankers Trust Commodity Index, and the JP Morgan Commodity Index.

The second group includes equity-linked notes, or ELNs. Peng and Dattatreya (1995) summarize the types of equity indexes that are

---

[7] See Charles Baubonis, Gary Gastineu, and David Purcell, "The Banker's Guide to Equity-Linked Certificates of Deposit," *Journal of Derivatives,* Vol.1, No. 2 (Winter 1993).

available for constructing ELNs.[8] An example of an index-linked note is the Stock Index Grown Note (SIGN) issued by the Republic of Austria. As with exchange-traded derivatives, an ELN written on the Dow Jones Industrial Average does not currently exist. Dow Jones has only recently displayed an interest in possibly licensing their indexes for use in products like structured notes.

The third group includes bond-indexed notes, also called Total Return Index Notes (TRINs). For example, Shearson Lehman Brothers Holdings has issued a structured note whose value is linked to the Lehman Brothers BAA Bond Index. Candidate indexes for bond-indexed notes include The Bond Buyer Municipal Bond Index, the Bloomberg/EFFAS indexes, the Goldman Sachs Bond Indexes, the JP Morgan Bond Indexes, the Merrill Lynch Bond Indexes, and the Salomon Brothers Bond Indexes.

A fourth group includes currency indexes, such as the Major Market Currency Index published by Paine Webber Incorporated and the Big Mac Index published by the Economist Newspaper.

Structured notes can be written on more than one index as part of the same contract, meaning that more than one license may be required to trade the instrument.

Licenses Between Index Producers and Dealers of Privately Negotiated Derivatives

Financial index prices are used as "official" references in the coupon-setting algorithms of privately negotiated, index-linked derivatives. For example, NASD estimates that they license 10 to15 privately negotiated products each year linked to the NASDAQ 100. S&P also licenses the use of their indexes to most major dealers in privately negotiated derivatives.

The indexes used as the basis of privately negotiated derivatives transactions are largely the same as those used for structured notes. The reader is referred to that section for the types of indexes used.

It is important for the reader to recognize that privately negotiated derivatives transactions may present certain legal issues due the nature of

---

[8] Scott Y. Peng and Ravi E. Dattatreya, *The Structured Note Market: The Definitive Guide for Investors, Traders & Issuers.* Chicago: Probus Publishing Company, 1995. For additional details on equity-linked structured notes see Christopher L. Culp and Robert J. Mackay, "Structured Notes: Mechanics, Benefits, and Risks," in *Derivatives Risks and Responsibilities,* eds. Robert A. Klein and Jess Lederman (Chicago: Irwin Professional Publishing. 1995).

such transactions. Privately negotiated index-linked transactions completed without an enforceable licensing agreement between the index producer and the derivatives dealer may give rise to the losing counterparties
claiming that the derivatives contract is voidable or otherwise legally
unenforceable.

Exculpability Clauses Covering Errors in Calculating the Index

One issue arising in the licensing of indexes is the extent to which the
index producer is liable for mistakes in calculating the index. Errors in
calculating indexes happen infrequently, but with regularity. A scan of
The Wall Street Journal Index reveals at least 15 instances between 1982
and 1996 where errors in calculating a financial index occurred and where
the errors were newsworthy enough to report. The issue of liability for
errors has landed in court on at least two occasions. In one case, seven
Vanguard Group Inc. mutual funds sued Thomson Publishing Company
and six municipal brokers for allegedly mispricing the 40-bond municipal-bond index used as the basis for trading a municipal-bond futures
contract traded at the CBT. The six brokers supplied bond prices to
Thomson, the publisher of The Bond Buyer Municipal Bond Index.[9]
This dispute had not been resolved as this chapter goes to press.

In a second case, a class-action suit was filed in Chicago charging
that S&P used an erroneous price to calculate the closing index value on
options expiration day in December 1989.[10] As a result, options traders
in the stock-index options pits at the CBOE allegedly lost a total of more
than $1 million. The suit charged S&P with "negligent miscalculation" of
its stock market indexes. The error occurred on Friday, December 15,
1989, during a so-called "triple witching hour," when stock options,
stock-index options, and futures all expired on the same day. Shortly after
the stock market closed that day, the NYSE reported erroneously that
Ford stock had settled at $44.75 a share. A few minutes later, the
exchange corrected its error, reporting that Ford actually closed at $43.75.
But according to the suit, the data-processing service that S&P used to
calculate its index values didn't catch the mistake, and the error was
incorporated into the S&P 100 and S&P 500 indexes.

---

[9] "Vanguard Funds Sue Thomson, Six Brokers Over Index Pricing," *The Wall Street Journal.* May
20, 1997. p. A4.

[10] *Rosenstein v. Standard & Poor's Corp..* 636 N.E. 2d 665 (Ill. App. 1 Dist. 1993).

The plaintiff argued that his cause of action was a breach of S&P's duty to use due care in calculating and disseminating index values which it knew were going to be used by the Options Clearing Corporation (OCC) for automatic settlement of options contracts. S&P responded by denying that the obligation to provide information creates a duty to the plaintiff or other traders; that it is a publisher protected by the first amendment; and that S&P Indexes are merely the products of its editorial judgment rather than misrepresented facts.

In the end, the Appeals Court held that the relationship between the plaintiff and the S&P was voluntarily entered into via each party's contract with the CBOE. Therefore, the court gave effect to the exculpatory clause contained in the license agreement between CBOE and S&P.

The Appeals Court said that "S&P's liability has been expressly exculpated by the terms of the license agreement between S&P and CBOE, and incorporated into the rules of the CBOE, which regulate the plaintiff's transactions."[11]

Financial Indexes as Intellectual Property: Past and Present

This section describes some of the battles that have been fought by index producers to establish and enforce their property claims to financial indexes and related financial information. These property battles from the past, while not necessarily applicable to contemporary battles, form the "big picture" for understanding the evolution of the law concerning financial indexes that continues to the present day.

International News Service v. Associated Press

The modern-day legal battles over property rights to financial indexes have their roots in the shoot-to-kill battles of the First World War. It was during the First World War that a legal dispute arose between the Associated Press (AP) and the International News Service (INS) over property rights to the news from the front-line battles in Europe.[12] Although the facts in the case were not specifically about financial indexes, the case remains significant insofar as it demonstrates one method of

---

[11] Id. At 666.

[12] International News Services vs. Associated Press. 248 U.S. 215 (1918).

providing intellectual property protection to financial indexes through the common law tort of misappropriation. The case is also relevant because of its role in two 1982 cases concerning financial indexes.

In this particular case, AP's European correspondents sent news bulletins from the war's front lines to AP's bureaus in the eastern United States. AP then published the bulletins on bulletin boards and in early-edition member newspapers without notice of copyright, in effect making the bulletins part of the public domain. AP's rival, INS, lawfully obtained AP's published East Coast bulletins and relayed copies to INS's Midwest and West Coast papers, which competed with AP's newspapers. Although AP could claim no copyright in its bulletins, the U.S. Supreme Court held that the commercial value of AP's bulletins could still be protected as a form of "quasi property" against commercial misappropriation by competitors.[13]

The key to the Court's holding was that AP had suffered a competitive injury as a result of INS's actions. The scope of AP's property right was limited: It was effective against AP's direct competitor, INS, but not against the public at large, and the duration of the right lasted only as long as the information contained in AP's wire service reports had commercial value. The Court held that AP's investment of "enterprise, organization, skill, labor, and money" warranted recognition of this property right.[14] By copying the news bulletins, the Court held that INS had engaged in a form of "unfair competition" by "endeavoring to reap where it has not sown" and "appropriating to itself the harvest of those who have sown."[15]

The misappropriation theory, as enunciated in *International News Service,* became significant in two 1982 cases concerning property rights to financial indexes. These modern-day legal battles appear to have been sparked, in part, by a December 1981 requirement of the CFTC permitting trading in stock index futures contracts only if the contracts were based on widely known and well-established stock indexes. As a result of the CFTC's requirement, futures exchanges abandoned their efforts at creating their own independent indexes and focused on constructing

---

[13] *Id.* at 236.

[14] *Id.* at 236.

[15] *Id.* at 239-240.

futures contracts based on the most widely known and well-established stock indexes of the day—the S&P 500 and the Dow Jones Industrial Average.[16]

The dispute over property rights to financial indexes arose when S&P and Dow Jones objected to the unauthorized use of their indexes by the futures exchanges. These cases are described below.

Standard & Poor's vs. Comex

The first case involved a dispute between S&P and Comex.[17] Comex had unsuccessfully sought to obtain a license from S&P to use the S&P 500 index as the basis for futures contracts to be traded at the Comex. However, S&P was unwilling to license its index because it had previously entered into an exclusive licensing agreement with the CME. Having failed to obtain a license, Comex constructed a "Comex 500 Index" and linked it with the S&P 500 index without S&P's authorization. In its complaint, S&P charged trade name and trademark infringement, likelihood of confusion, misappropriation of property rights, and copyright and Lanham Act violations.

A U.S. district court ruled in favor of S&P.[18] In making its decision, the court noted that the S&P and Comex were competitors in the sense that S&P derived licensing revenue from the trading volume of CME's futures contracts.[19] The court noted that the S&P price index was developed and marketed by S&P at considerable expense and effort. Moreover, computation of minute-by-minute and daily changes in the index depended on certain inputs developed solely and exclusively by S&P. In supporting S&P's claim of misappropriation by Comex, the district court stated, "Comex is misappropriating the S&P 500 Index and the skills, expenditures, labor and reputation of S&P in generating and producing the S&P 500 Index, for Comex's own advantage and profit by creating a futures contract based on the S&P 500 Index."[20] In essence, the district

---

[16] See, for example, 456 N.E. 2d *supra* note 2 at 89: "The record shows that the plaintiff sought to develop its own index prior to the CFTC's requirement that the contracts be based on well-known, well-established indexes."

[17] 538 F. Supp.; 683 F.2d *supra* note 1.

[18] 538 F. Supp., *supra* note 1.

[19] *Id.* at 1068.

[20] *Id.* at 1071.

court ruled that Comex intended "to link S&P with Comex as a commercial prop for futures contracts based on a 500 stock index."[21] Using a similar argument, the court of appeals later affirmed the order of the district court.[22]

Dow Jones vs. Chicago Board of Trade

A related case involved Dow Jones and the Chicago Board of Trade.[23] In February 1982, the CBT applied to the CFTC to trade stock index futures based on the Dow Jones averages. The CBT Indexes were identical to the Dow Jones averages, and when Dow Jones changed a component stock or revised the devisor, the CBT would make the same change so that the CBT indexes would remain identical to the Dow Jones averages.[24]

Dow Jones claimed that the CBT's futures contracts constituted commercial misappropriation of the Dow Jones averages. Dow Jones sought to stop the CBT from trading their futures contracts, both by suing and by threatening to suspend publication of its stock averages.[25] The court supported the claim of Dow Jones, noting that "[t]he selection of stocks used to compute the average is arrived at through the use of considerable financial expertise and experience and is based on Dow Jones's determination of which stocks are likely to reflect the overall activity of the stock market in their individual fluctuations in price."[26] The Supreme Court of Illinois affirmed that the CBT could not use the Dow Jones averages without the permission of Dow Jones.[27]

In this case the court recognized that Dow Jones had a "proprietary interest in its indexes and averages which vests it with the exclusive right to license their use for trading stock index futures contracts."[28] What makes this case different from the S&P case is that Dow Jones did not claim that the CBT was a competitor. Competitive harm, it will be

---

[21] *Id.* at 1065.

[22] 683 F.2d, *supra* note 1.

[23] 546 F.Supp.; 439 N.E. 2d; 456 N.E. 2d, *supra* note 2 .

[24] 456 N.E. 2d, *supra* note 2, at 86.

[25] *The Wall Street Journal,* "Dow Jones Threatens to Suspend Averages Over Futures Dispute." May, 14 1982, p. C36. S&P also reserved the right to discontinue the dissemination of its index (see 538 F. Supp., *supra* note 1, at 1068).

[26] 439 N.E. 2d, *supra* note 2, at 528-29.

[27] 456 N.E. 2d, *supra* note 2.

[28] 456 N.E. 2d, *supra* note 2, at 90.

recalled, was a prerequisite for misappropriation claims as enunciated in *International News Service*. Instead, Dow Jones argued that the tort of misappropriation needed a broader interpretation so that "enterprising pirates" could not avoid the application of the doctrine.[29] The court held that despite the fact that the CBT's use of the Dow Jones index was not in competition with Dow Jones's primary use of the index, Dow Jones was entitled to protection against misappropriation of the index.

The court also addressed the issue of whether the CBT's use of the Dow Jones index would cause injury to Dow Jones. Dow Jones claimed that the CBT's futures contract would exploit the reputation of Dow Jones "without compensating it for its good will."[30] Dow Jones claimed that its involuntary association with the CBT's trading activities would impair its news-gathering abilities if the public lost faith in Dow Jones's integrity.[31] Dow Jones argued that the CBT's futures contract could possibly generate a negative reputation effect that could reduce the value of the Dow Jones index in its traditional market. The fact that Dow Jones refused CBT's offer of 10 cents per contract for a license to use the name[32] is evidence consistent with the argument that Dow Jones valued its exclusive use highly and feared a negative reputation effect.

Implications of Dow Jones Case for New Product Development

The apparent expansion of misappropriation theory to noncompeting firms (at least in Illinois) as enunciated in the Dow Jones case presents several issues concerning new product development. At issue is the balance between the rights of creators of intellectual property and the rights of society to obtain the widest productive use of intellectual property. Commenting on this balance, Richard Epstein has observed, "it would be a giant mistake to assume that the only objective of the law in the area of property rights is to prevent free riding by others," and "[O]ne of the essential conditions of living in a free and prosperous society is the freedom to use information (if not grain) sown by others."[33] Epstein adds, "[e]veryone knows that unanticipated benefits are worth having at least to

---

[29] *Id.* at 88.

[30] *Id.* at 88.

[31] 546 F. Supp., *supra* note 2 at 121, fn 8.

[32] 456 N.E. 2d. *supra* note 2 at 89-90.

[33] Richard A. Epstein, *"International News Service vs. Associated Press*: Custom and Law As Sources Of Property Rights in News," *Virginia Law Review*, Vol. 78, pp. 85-128, 1992.

some degree. Dow Jones, which had sufficient incentive to produce the average before, still has that incentive because there is no direct competition; there is, therefore, nothing about the creation of this novel futures contract that diminishes the gains that Dow Jones gets from producing its index."[34]

Expanding the misappropriation theory to noncompeting firms threatens to block the follow-up commercial use of valuable information in ways unforeseen by the index producer. This fear was expressed in Justice Simon's dissent to the Dow Jones decision: "The [CBT] proposed to use information that Dow Jones had freely allowed the public to acquire in a business that Dow Jones has not shown the slightest interest in pursuing. If "unjust enrichment" has become the only element for the tort of misappropriation . . . there will be few commercial ideas and little information left in the public domain."[35] Justice Simon argued, with an eye on the development of new, index-linked financial products, that "unless society can demand that owners of intellectual property allow it to be appropriated by people who have developed novel and productive uses for it, the pace of innovation will slow."[36] Justice Simon added that "to the extent that intellectual property rights are to be expanded beyond their common law limits, it would be better to leave the matter to Congress. . . and to the State legislature."[37]

Epilog: The CBT, after abandoning its efforts at developing a futures contract based on the Dow Jones index, entered into a licensing agreement with the AMEX to use the rights to the Major Market Index. AMEX declined to renew this agreement in 1993 and licensed the index instead to the CME. In 1996, Dow Jones for the first time agreed to license one of its indexes for futures trading. This license gave to the CME the rights to trade futures and options on the Dow Jones Taiwan Stock Index.[38] In June 1997 Dow Jones announced that it had signed licensing agreements with the CBT, the CBOE, and the AMEX authorizing the trading of investment products linked to the Dow Jones Industrial Average.

---

[34] *Id.* at 123.

[35] 456 N.E. 2d, *supra* note 2 at 93.

[36] *Id.* at 91.

[37] *Id.* at 91.

[38] *The Wall Street Journal.* "Dow Jones Taiwan Index Is Licensed for Trading." September 13. 1996, p. C17.

An Aside on Individual Stocks Versus Stock Indexes.

In contrast to the cases involving stock indexes, the courts have also considered whether an issuing company has property rights to the shares of stock it issues.[39] In 1987, the AMEX commenced trading put and call options on Golden Nugget common stock without the firm's consent. Golden Nugget sued the AMEX for misappropriation of Golden Nugget property. The court recognized that the claims in the case were novel and stated, "To succeed on any of its claims, Golden Nugget must persuade us that it has a property or other protectable interest in Golden Nugget common stock owned by its shareholders."[40] The court, however, found it "impossible to conceptualize a property right of the plaintiff that has been misappropriated."[41] The court held that Golden Nugget had no right to stop options trading.

The Current Scope of Intellectual Property Legal Protections

In the United States there are four general sources of intellectual property protection that must be considered in connection with the development of new financial indexes or index-linked products. These include the law of: 1) trade secrets, 2) copyrights, 3) patents, and 4) trademarks and service marks. In addition, financial indexes left unprotected by these intellectual property theories may be residually protected through the common law tort of misappropriation, as witnessed in the cases described in the previous section.

Trade Secrets

Although trade secret law has not been used as the basis for protecting financial indexes to date, it could potentially be used to protect certain forms of information created by index producers. Trade secrets are governed by state as opposed to federal law. In recent years, however, trade secrets law has been codified in the Uniform Trade Secrets Act (UTSA), thereby providing a measure of uniformity across states in the application and development of this area of law.

---

[39] *Golden Nugget, Inc. v. American Stock Exchange, Inc.*, 828 F.2d 586 (9th Cir.1987).

[40] *Id.* at 590.

[41] *Id.*

In order for a claim to succeed under trade secret law, there must be a confidential relationship between the index producer and the user. The breach of this confidential relationship gives rise to a trade secret claim. With financial indexes, trade secret protection could potentially be feasible for the dissemination of real-time index weights and values from an index producer (e.g., S&P) to an index user (e.g., the CME). A contract could be structured where retransmission of real-time information could only occur by extending the confidential relationship to the subscribers of the services of information vendors like Quotron or Bloomberg. The duration of this property right would be limited to real-time information and would not apply to widely disseminated hourly or end-of-day quotations. Further discussion of property rights to real-time financial information can be found in Mulherin, Netter, and Overdahl (1991a, 1991b).[42]

Applying trade secret protection to financial indexes could be modeled after the property protection afforded to the real-time financial information produced on the floor of organized financial exchanges like the CME. As a result of this protection, financial exchanges license use of this information to information vendors and their subscribers. Bronfman and Overdahl (1992) discuss these licensing arrangements and show that licensing fees for real-time financial information are the second largest source of revenue for financial exchanges like the CME.[43] Such a model could potentially be used as the basis for protecting a property interest in real-time information associated with financial indexes.

Copyright Law

Although copyright protection has been claimed by index producers, the scope of protection is unclear, especially given the Supreme Court's holding in *Feist Publications, Inc. v. Rural Telephone Service Co.*,[44] which

---

[42] J. Harold Mulherin, Jeffry Netter, and James A. Overdahl, "Prices Are Property: The Organization of Financial Exchanges From a Transaction Cost Perspective," *Journal of Law and Economics*, October, 1991; and "Who Owns the Quotes? A Case Study into the Definition and Enforcement of Property Rights at The Chicago Board of Trade," *The Review of Futures Markets*, 1991.

[43] Bronfman, Corinne, and James A. Overdahl, "Would the Invisible Hand Produce Transparent Markets?" Working Paper No. 92-10, Division of Economic Analysis, Commodity Futures Trading Commission, Washington, D.C., June 1992.

[44] 111 S. CT. 1282, *supra* note 3.

sharply reduced the copyright protection afforded to certain types of "fact-based" information products. The Court declared that originality, and not the investment of resources or "sweat of the brow," was a minimum, constitutionally mandated prerequisite for copyright protection.

The Court held that for a work containing no written expression, only facts, to meet the constitutional minimum for copyright protection it must feature original selection or arrangement.[45] It could be argued that lists and compilations of index components are entitled to copyright protection because the index producer's selection and arrangement result from thoughtful evaluation and choice in determining which members of a given population merit inclusion in the list.

In addition to lists and compilations, a computer program used to compute the index is copyrightable. Also, formulas and algorithms used to compute the index, like the "College CD" previously referred to, are copyrightable.

Copyrightable subject matter can be protected only under federal law. This is important because it means that federal preemptions would seem to apply to state misappropriation protections covering copyrightable subject matter. However, the 1976 Copyright Act contains broad language that does not explicitly explain when misappropriation protections should be exempted from federal preemption.

Generally, copyright protection under the 1976 Copyright Act lasts for the life of the author plus 50 years, although other terms of protection for varying amounts of years also exist. For more information on copyright protections in the financial industry see Trzyna (1992) and Kaye (1991).[46]

Patent Law

Patent law protection is available for "any new and useful process, machine, manufacture, or composition of matter." A financial index is not patentable subject matter by itself. However, a patent can indirectly protect an index by protecting some computerized aspects of the index. For example, a computer system used to compute an index is patentable. Such

---

[45] 111 S. CT. 1282, *supra* note 3 at 1283.

[46] See Trzyna, Peter K., "Legal Protections For Innovative Financial Products and Services," in *Financial Engineering*, Second Edition, John F. Marshall and Vipul K. Bansal, editors (Miami: Kolb Publishing, 1992); and Laurence Kaye, "A Question of Copyright," *Futures and Options World*, September 1991.

a patent can protect the index producer for the 17-year life of the patent. As with copyright, patentable subject matter can be protected only under federal law. Misappropriation protections covering patentable subject matter is subject to federal preemption.[47]

For a more complete treatment of the subject of the scope of patent protection for financial products, see Trzyna (1992).[48]

Trademarks and Service Marks

Trademarks and service marks (together, "marks") are the most common form of intellectual property protection for financial index producers. Trademarks and service marks protect against another's use of a mark that is likely to cause confusion, mistake, or deceit.[49] For an index producer, a mark can be used to limit the extent to which index users can be associated with the producer's index. Index producers commonly register trade names, trademarks, and service marks to identify their products. For example, S&P owns the designations "Standard and Poor's," "S&P," "Standard & Poor's 500," "S&P 500," and "500." Trademarks rights may be transferred or licensed to others for use.

For more information on the use of marks in the financial industry, see Trzyna (1992).[50]

The Weakening of Misappropriation Protections

State misappropriation protections for producers of financial indexes may be limited in the future because of preemption by federal copyright and patent laws. To the extent that misappropriation protection survives it will likely be as a residual protection for intellectual property attributes that are not copyrightable or patentable subject matter. Misappropriation protections are further threatened by recent efforts to dispense with the misappropriation tort altogether.[51]

---

[47] *Bonito Boats. Inc. v. Thunder Craft Boats. Inc.*, 109 S. Ct. 971 (1989).

[48] Trzyna, *supra* note 46.

[49] *Id.* at 704.

[50] *Id.* at 703.

[51] See, for example, the American Law Institute's Restatement (Third) on Unfair Competition (1993).

To the extent that misappropriation theory prevails, however, it potentially affords the index producer a strong form of protection. The scope of this protection is similar to a patent, except that patents expire, whereas the rights extended under misappropriation theory are presumably perpetual. With misappropriation protection, index producers can prevent others from using their indexes without showing that it is a trade secret, without showing that it was obtained unlawfully, and without showing "palming off" or customer confusion. Nor is a copyright or patent required for this protection. And, as Myers (1996) has noted, this right does not appear to be leavened by a "fair use" defense.[52]

Conclusion

Index producers and developers of new, index-linked products have been striving to create a balance between their conflicting interests. On the one hand, index producers claim that strong intellectual property protection is necessary to give them the incentive to invest in the creation and maintenance of their indexes. On the other hand, developers of these products claim that there is nothing about the development of new, index-linked products that diminishes the gains that index producers receive. This struggle between competing interests has evolved along with the evolution of the law concerning intellectual property. The result of this struggle has been that index producers hold recognized intellectual property claims to their indexes under certain circumstances. Index producers exercise their property rights by authorizing the terms by which other parties may use their indexes and by collecting licensing fees from these parties.

An understanding of the licensing and property issues related to financial indexes is critical to the successful development and marketing of index-linked products. Since the law related to financial indexes continues to evolve, index producers and developers of index-linked investment products should seek careful legal counseling from experienced and reputable practitioners in intellectual property law before consummating a licensing agreement.

---

[52] Myers, Gary, "The Restatement's Rejection of the Misappropriation Tort: A Victory for the Public Domain," *University of South Carolina Law Review*, Vol. 47, pp. 673-706. 1996.

Index